GOOD KING HENRY
Leaves and flowering spikes

GOOSEFOOT
Leaves and tips

GORSE
Flowers

GROUND ELDER
Leaves

HEATHER
Flowers / leafy stems
(late summer)

HERB BENNET
Roots

HOP
Flowers (late summer)

HORSE-RADISH
Roots

HYSSOP
Flowers and leafy stems

JUNIPER
Berries

LAVER
Whole seaweed

LIME
Flowers and leaves

MALLOW
Leaves

MARSHMALLOW
Flowers

MEADOWSWEET
Flowers and leaves

MINTS
Leaves

MUSHROOMS, FIELD
Caps and stems

OAK
Leaves

PARASOL MUSHROOM
Caps

PIGNUT
Roots

PUFFBALLS
Whole plant above ground

RASPBERRY
Berries

ROCK SAMPHIRE
Leaves

ROSES
Flowers and leaves

ROSEMARY
Leafy stems

ROWAN
Berries

SAGE
Leaves and tips

SALAD BURNET
Leafy stems

SAVORY,
WINTER AND SUMMER
Leaves

SEA BEET
Leaves

SEA LETTUCE
Whole seaweed

SEA PURSLANE
Leaves and tips

SHAGGY CAP
Caps

SOAPWORT
Whole plant, including root

SORREL
Leaves

SOUTHERNWOOD
Leafy stems

SOW-THISTLE,
SMOOTH AND PRICKLY
Leaves

TANSY
Leaves

THYME
Leafy stems

WALL PENNYWORT
Leaves

WHITE DEAD NETTLE
Leaves

WILD BASIL
Leaves

WILD MAJORAM
Leaves, flowers and tips

WILD STRAWBERRY
Berries

YARROW
Leaves

AUTUMN

BEECH
Nuts

BILBERRY
Berries

BORAGE
Leaves, flowers and tips

BLACKTHORN
Fruits (sloes)

BRAMBLE
Blackberries

CHANTERELLE
Caps and stems

CHESTNUT
Nuts

CHICKWEED
Whole plant, except root

CLEAVERS
Seeds

CRAB APPLE
Fruits

DANDELION
Roots

ELDER
Berries

FENNEL
Leaves and seeds

HAWTHORN
Berries

HEATHER
Flowers and leafy stems

HOP
Flowers

HORSE-RADISH
Roots

JUNIPER
Berries

MUSHROOMS, FIELD
Caps and stems

OAK
Acorns

PARASOL MUSHROOM
Caps

PUFFBALLS
Whole plant above ground

ROSES
Hips

ROSEMARY
Leafy stems

SAGE
Leaves

SAVORY, WINTER
Leaves

SHAGGY CAP
Caps

SORREL
Leaves

SOUTHERNWOOD
Leafy stems

WHITE DEAD NETTLE
Whole plant, except root

YARROW
Leaves

EDIBLE WILD PLANTS & HERBS

A COMPENDIUM OF RECIPES AND REMEDIES

PAMELA MICHAEL

PAINTINGS BY CHRISTABEL KING

GRUB STREET · LONDON

TO MY DAUGHTER, JANE, AND GRANDSON ERIC, WHOSE PASSION FOR WILD FOOD IS A CONSTANT INSPIRATION.

ACKNOWLEDGEMENTS

To my husband, Maurice, who ate and drank all the experiments, submitted to the lotions and potions, and encouraged me all the time. His flair for research, and knowledge of languages supplied the information I would otherwise have missed. A lifetime of books spent with him was a good grounding for this happy task. And to our son, Ian, my unending thanks for all his typing, help and advice involved with producing the extra material for this new edition.

Published in 2007 by
Grub Street, 4 Rainham Close, London SW11 6SS
Email: food@grubstreet.co.uk
Web: www.grubstreet.co.uk

Reprinted 2007, 2008, 2009

First published in 1980 by Ernest Benn Limited as *All Good Things Around Us*

A CIP block for this title is available from the British Library

10 digit ISBN 1-904943-73-X
13 digit ISBN 978-1-904943-73-0

Printed and bound in India

AUTHOR'S NOTE
All the illustrations show the plants at the best time for picking and have the edible parts illustrated.
For everyone's convenience, throughout the recipes, we have indicated Metric, American and English equivalent measures in that order. Use one set of measures only.

CONTENTS

INTRODUCTION 8

AGRIMONY *Agrimonia eupatoria* 10

Fresh Agrimony Tea 11
Dried Agrimony Tea 11
To Dry Agrimony 11
Gargle for a Relaxed Throat 11

ALEXANDERS *Smyrnium olusatrum* 13

Alexanders Stems as a Vegetable 13
Alexanders Buds as Salads 14
Alexanders Sauce 14

ASH *Fraxinus excelsior* 14

Pickled Ash Keys 16
Ash Walking Stick 16

BALM *Melissa officinalis* 16

Balm Butter with Fish 18
Balm and Borage Wine Cup 18
A Refreshing Drink in Fever 18
Balm Wine 18

BEECH *Fagus syluatica* 19

Beech Leaf Gin 20
Beechnuts, Roasted 20
Beechnut Nibbles 21
To Preserve Beech Leaves for Winter
    Decorations 21

BERGAMOT *Monarda didyma* 21

To Dry Bergamot 23
Bergamot in Salad 23
Bergamot Sauce 23
Fresh Bergamot Tea 23
Dried Bergamot Tea 23

BILBERRY *Vaccinium myrtillus* 24

Compôte of Bilberries 25
Bilberry Stirabout 25
Bilberry Muffins 25
Bilberry Jam 26
Bilberry and Apple Jelly 26
Bilberry Juice with Muesli 26
Fresh Bilberry Leaf Tea 26
Bilberry Liqueur 26
Bilberry Wine 27

BLACKTHORN *Prunus spinosa* 28

Wild Kissel with Sloes 29
Sloe Jelly 29
Sloe Syrup 29
Sieved Sloe and Apple Jam 29
Sloe Cheese 29
Sloe Gin 31
Sloe Wine 31
Crystallised Blackthorn Blossom 31
Blackthorn Walking Stick 31
Slow Marking Ink 31

BOG MYRTLE *Myrica gale* 32

Bog Myrtle and Lamb Stew 33
Bog Myrtle Ale 33

BORAGE *Borago officinalis* 34

Borage with Cottage Cheese 36
Borage Flower Syrup 36
Dried Borage Tea 36
To Dry Borage Flowers 36
Sugared Borage Flowers 36
Borage Flowers in Ice Cubes 36

BRAMBLE *Rubus fruticosus* 37

Blackberry Sorbet 39
Blackberry Ice Cream 39
Blackberry Mousse 39
Spiced Blackberry Crumble 39
Wild Blackberry Cobbler 40
Blackberry and Elderberry Jam 40
Sieved Blackberry and Apple Jam 40
Blackberry and Sloe Jelly 40
Bramble Jelly 41
Spiced Bramble Jelly 41
Spiced Blackberry Pickle 41
Blackberry Chutney 42
Blackberry Syrup 42
Blackberry Cordial 42
Blackberry Vinegar 42
Blackberry Liqueur 43
Blackberry Wine 43

BROOKLIME *Veronica beccabunga* 43

To Prepare Brooklime for Salads 44
Brooklime Sandwiches 44

BROOM *Cystisus scoparius* 45

Pickled Broom Buds 45

BURDOCK *Arctium lappa, A. minus* 45

Burdock Stems 46
Stirfry with Burdock Stems 46

CARRAGHEEN *Chondrus crispus* 48

To Dry Carragheen 49
Carragheen Honeycomb Mould 50
Carragheen Pudding 50
Carragheen or Irish Moss Bath Gel 50

CONTENTS

CHANTERELLES 51
Cantharellus cibarius
To Prepare Chanterelles 52

SWEET CHESTNUT *Castanea sativa* 52
To Store and Prepare Sweet Chestnuts 54
Chestnut Soup 54
Chestnuts with Brussels Sprouts 55
Chestnuts and Red Cabbage 55
Chestnut and Sausage Stuffing 55
Marrons Glacés 56

CHAMOMILE *Chamaemelum nobile* 56
Chamomile Tea 58
Chamomile Hair Rinse 58

CHICKWEED *Stellaria media* 59
Chickweed Soup 59
Chickweed as a Vegetable 60

CLEAVERS *Galium aparine* 61
Cleavers Coffee 62
Cleavers Deodorant 62

CLOVER, RED AND WHITE 63
Trifolium pratense, T. repens
White Clover Sandwiches 63
Clover Syrup 63
Fresh Clover Flower Tea 64
Dried Clover Flower Tea 64
To Dry Clover Flowers 64

COLTSFOOT *Tussilago farfara* 65
Coltsfoot Syrup 66
Fresh Coltsfoot Tea 66
To Dry Coltsfoot 66
Dried Coltsfoot Tea 66
Coltsfoot Wine 66
Coltsfoot Wine, old method 66

CORN SALAD *Valerianella locusta* 68
In Salads 68

CRAB APPLE *Malus sylvestris* 70
Crab Apple Syrup 71
Crab Apple and Mint Jelly 71

Crab Apple Butter 71
Spiced Crab Apples 71
Crab Apple Wine 73
Verjuice 73
Wassail Bowl 73
Crystallised Crab Apple Blossom 74

DANDELION *Taraxacum officinale* 74
Dandelion Soup 75
Dandelion and Ham Mould 75
Pissenlit au Lard 76
Dandelion as a Vegetable 76
Dandelion and Beetroot Salad 76
Dandelion Coffee 76
Dandelion Fizz 78
Dandelion Wine 78
Dandelion Wine, old method 78

DULSE *Palmaria palmata* 79
To Dry Dulse 79

ELDER *Sambucus nigra* 81
Pickled Elder Shoots 82
To Pickle Elder Buds 83
Elderflower Fritters, plain 83
Elderflower Fritters, alcoholic 84
Elderflower Water Ice 84
Elderflower and Gooseberry 85
   Ice Cream
Elderflower Syrup 85
Ice Cream with Elderflower Syrup 85
Elderflower and Rhubarb Jam 85
Elderflower Drink 86
Elderflower Fizz 86
To Dry Elderflowers 86
Elderflower Tea 86
Elder Vinegar 86
Elderflower Liqueur 88
Elderflower Wine 88
Elderflower Water 88
Elderflower Face Cream 88
Elderflower Hand Lotion I 89
Elderflower Hand Lotion II 89
Elderflower Face Lotion 89
Elderflower Lotion for Sunburn 89
   and Chapped Hands

Elderflower Jelly for Hands 89
Elderflower Lotion for the Eyes 89
Elderberry Soup 90
Elderberry Sorbet 90
Wild Summer Pudding 90
Elderberry and Blackberry Jelly 90
Elderberry and Crab Apple Jelly 91
Elder Rob 91
Fresh Elderberry Drink 91
Elderberry Chutney 91
Spiced Elderberry Sauce 92
Elderberry Wine 92
Elder Pith Fishing Float 92

FENNEL *Foeniculum vulgare* 93
Fish with Fennel Sauce 95
Fennel and Gooseberry 95
   Sauce with Mackerel
Creamy Fennel Sauce 96

GARLIC MUSTARD 96
Alliaria petiolata
As a Vegetable 98
Garlic Mustard Sauce for Fish 98

GLASSWORT *Salicornia europaea* 99
Samphire in Salad and as a Vegetable 100
Samphire Pickle 100
Sweet Pickle for Samphire 100

GOOSEFOOT *Chenopodium* 101
Goosefoot Soup 104
Goosefoot Flan 104
As a Vegetable 104

GORSE *Ulex europaeus* 104
Pickled Gorse Buds 106
Gorse Flower Syrup 106
Gorse Buds Tea 106
Gorse Flower Liqueur 106
Gorse Wine 107

GROUND ELDER 107
Aegopodium podagraria
Ground Elder Soup 108
Ground Elder Salad 108

Ground Elder Rice Cakes 108
Ground Elder as a Vegetable 110

GROUND IVY *Glechoma hederacea* 110
Ground Ivy Tisane 112
Ground Ivy Tea, Dried 112
To Dry Ground Ivy 112

HAWTHORN *Crataegus monogyna* 112
Hawthorn Leaf Tea 113
To Dry Hawthorn Leaves 113
Flowrys of Hawthorn 113
Hawthorn Flower Syrup 115
Hawthorn Flower Ice Cream 115
Hawthorn Flower Wine Cup 115
Hawthorn Flowers in Ice Cubes 116
Hawthorn Flower Liqueur 116
Hawthorn Flower Wine 116
Hawthorn Berry Jelly 116
Hawthorn Berry Chutney 116
Hawthorn Berry Wine 117

HAZEL *Corylus avellana* 117
Brown Rice with Hazelnuts 119
Wild Pesto 119
Chocolate Hazelnut Gateau 119
Greek Nut Cake 120
Hazelnut and Fruit Loaf 120
Hazel Walking Stick 120

HEATHER *Calluna vulgaris* 121
To Dry Heather Flowers 122
Dried Heather Flower Tea 122
Heather Pillows 122

HERB BENNET *Geum urbanum* 123
Herb Bennet with Apple Pie 124
Bread Sauce Flavoured
    with Herb Bennet 124

HOP *Humulus lupulus* 127
Hop Shoots 128
Hop Pillow 128

HORSE-RADISH 129
Armoracia rusticana

Horse-Radish Sauce 131

Hans Andersen Sandwich 131
Tartar Sandwich 131

HYSSOP *Hyssopus officinalis* 131
Meatballs with Hyssop 133
Hyssop Syrup 133
Fresh Apricot Flan with Hyssop 133
Hyssop Dessert 134
Hyssop Tea 134
To Dry Hyssop 134

JUNIPER *Juniperus communis* 134
Pork Spare Rib with Juniper
    Berry Stuffing 136
Braised Pheasant with Juniper 136
Beef Casserole with Prunes
    and Juniper 137

LADY'S SMOCK 137
Cardamine pratensis

LAVER *Porphyra umbilicalis* 139
Laverbread 139
Welsh Breakfast Cakes 140
Slokeen 140
Laver Sauce with Lamb 140
Sloke Jelly 140

COMMON LIME *Tilia vulgaris* 141
Lime Flower Tea, fresh 143
To Dry Lime Flowers 143
Dried Lime Flower Tea 143
Lime Flower Wine 143
Lime Leaf Sandwiches 144

COMMON MALLOW 144
Malva sylvestris

Mallow Soup 147
Mallow as a Vegetable 147

WILD MARJORAM 147
Origanum vulgare

Dumplings with Wild Marjoram 149

MEADOWSWEET 149
Filipendula ulmaria

Stewed Apple with Meadowsweet 150

Meadowsweet with Rhubarb 150
Meadowsweet Syrup 150
Fresh Meadowsweet Tea 150
Dried Meadowsweet Flower Tea 150
Dried Meadowsweet Leaf Tea 152
How to Dry Meadowsweet 152
Meadowsweet Wine Cup 152
Meadowsweet Liqueur 152
Meadowsweet Wine 152

MINTS *Mentha* 153
Mint Jelly 156
Peppermint Tea 156
Sparkling Peppermint Tea 156
Mint Leaves in Ice Cubes 156
Dried Peppermint Tea 156
To Dry Peppermint 156
Crystallised Peppermint Leaves 157
Eau-de-Cologne Mint Bath Essence 157

MIXED HERBS 157
Spring Tart 158
Gardener's Revenge or Nettle and
    Ground Elder Pizza 158
Rice with a Wild Flavour 159
Wild Salsa 159
Sauce au Vert with Fish 159
Spring Sauce with Lamb 160
Wild Herb Sauce 160
Wild Spring Salad 160
Wild Sandwiches 160
Herby Scones with Cheese 161
Wild Fruit Crumble 161
Bath Bags 161
Herbal Surgical Spirit 161

FIELD MUSHROOM 162
Agaricus campestris

To Prepare Field Mushrooms 163
Pickled Mushrooms 163
Mushroom Ketchup 164

OAK *Quercus robur* 164
Acorn Coffee 166
Oak Leaf Wine 166

PARASOL MUSHROOM   167
Lepiota procera

To Prepare Parasol Mushrooms   168

PIGNUT   *Conopodium majus*   169
Vegetable Broth with Pignuts   169
Pignuts with Salad   170

PRIMROSE   *Primula vulgaris*   171
Primerolle or Primrose Potage   172
Pickled Primroses   172
Crystallised Primroses   172

PUFF BALLS   *Lycoperdon perlatum*   173
To Prepare Puff Balls   175
Giant Puff Balls, Stuffed   175

RAMSONS   *Allium ursinum*   175
Green Garlic Butter   177
Ramsons Sauce, Cold   177
Ramsons Sauce, Hot   177
Casserole of Beef with Ramsons   177
Ramsoms Bulbs in Salad   177

WILD RASPBERRY   *Rubus idaeus*   178
Wild Raspberry Sweet Omelette   179
Wild Raspberry Cranachan   179
Wild Raspberry Jam   179
Wild Raspberry and Orange Jam   179
Wild Raspberry Liqueur   180
Wild Raspberry Wine   180

ROSES   *Rosa*   181
Wild Rose Petal Jam   183
Wild Rose Petal Conserve   183
Balmoral Flan   183
Syllabub with Wild Rose Petal
   Conserve   184
Wild Rose Petal Ice Cream   184
Baked Soufflé with Wild Rose
   Petal Conserve   184
Wild Rose Petal Syrup   184
Wild Rose Petal Sandwiches   184
Crystallised Rose Petals   185
Wild Rose Petals in Ice Cubes   185
Wild White Rose Petal Water   185

Rose Petal Astringent   185
Rose Petal Moisturising Lotion   185
Wild Rose Petal Moisturising Cream   185
Fresh Rose Leaf Tea   185
Dried Rose Leaf Tea   185
To Dry Wild Rose Leaves   185
Rose Hip Soup   186
Thick Rose Hip Soup   186
A Tarte of Hips   186
A Persian Sweet
   made with Rose Hips   188
Sauce Eglantine   188
Rose Hip Syrup   188
Rose Hip Jam   189
Rose Hip and Crab Apple Jelly   190
Rose Hip Wine   190

ROSEMARY   *Rosmarinus officinalis*   190
Chicken with Rosemary   192
Oranges with Rosemary   192
Rosemary Conserve   192
Rosemary Fruit Cup   192
Rosemary Flowers in Ice Cubes   193
Crystallised Rosemary Flowers   193
Rosemary Water   193
Rosemary Astringent Lotion   193
Rosemary Moisturising Cream   194
Rosemary Hair Tonic   194

ROWAN   *Sorbus aucuparia*   194
Rowan Jelly   195
Rowanberry Bitters   195
Rowanberry Liqueur   195
Rowanberry Wine   196

SAGE   *Salvia officinalis*   197
Bacon and Onion Tart
   with Fresh Sage   198
Roast or Fried Dumplings
   with Fresh Sage   198
Fresh Sage Tea   198
Dried Sage Tea   199
To Dry Sage   199
Sage Tea for Sore Throat   199
Old-fashioned Medicinal Sage Tea   200
Sage Hair Rinse   200

SALAD BURNET   200
Sanguisorba minor

Salad Burnet with Cottage Cheese   201
Salad Burnet with Drinks   201
Salad Burnet Vinegar   201

ROCK SAMPHIRE   202
Crithmum maritimum

Rock Samphire as a Vegetable   204
Rock Samphire Pickle I   204
Rock Samphire Pickle II   204

WINTER SAVORY   205
Satureja montana

Rice Stuffing for Chicken
   with Savory   206
Savory with Beans   206
Butter Beans in a Garlicky Sauce   206
   with Savory
Broad Bean and Mushroom Salad   208
   with Savory

SCURVY GRASSES   *Cochlearia*   208
Scurvy Grass for Salads   210
Scurvy Grass Sandwiches   210

SEA BEET   210
Beta vulgaris ssp. maritima

Sea Beet Soup   210
Sea Beet as a Vegetable   212
Sea Beet Flan   212

SEA LETTUCE   *Ulva lactuca*   212
Sea Lettuce Soup   213

SEA PURSLANE   214
Halimione portulacoides

Dressing for Sea Purslane Salad   215

SHAGGY CAP   *Coprinus comatus*   215
Baked Shaggy Caps   217

SOAPWORT   *Saponaria officinalis*   217
Soapwort Shampoo with Herbs   219
To Clean Upholstery   219
   with Soapwort

COMMON SORREL *Rumex acetosa* 219

Sorrel Soup 220
Anguille au Vert à la Flamande 220
Sorrel Sauce 221

SOUTHERNWOOD 222
Artemisia abrotanum

Southernwood Cake 223
Southernwood Tea 223
Southernwood to Repel Moths 224

SOW-THISTLES 224
Sonchus asper, S. oleraceus

Sow-Thistle Soup 226
Sow-Thistle as a Vegetable 226

STINGING NETTLE *Urtica dioica* 227

Stchi or Green Borscht 228
Cream of Nettle Soup 228
Nettle and Oatmeal Stuffing 230
  for Chicken
Spiced Nettles with Oatmeal 230
Nettle Pudding 230
Baked Nettles and Potatoes 231
Nettles as a Vegetable 231
To Dry Nettles 231
Dried Nettle Tea 231
Nettle Wine 231
Nettle Rinse and Hair Tonic 232

WILD STRAWBERRY 232
Fragaria vesca

Wild Strawberries 234
  with Cream Cheese
Wild Strawberry Leaf Tisane 234

TANSY *Tanacetum vulgare* 235

Tansy Omelette 236
Soused Mackerel with Tansy 236
Mackerel with Tansy Stuffing 236
Savoury Chicken Pancakes 237
  with Tansy
Roast Lamb with Tansy 237
Cold Belly Pork with Tansy Sauce 238
Lamb Chops with Tansy Stuffing 238
Tansy with Cabbage 238

Tansy Mayonnaise 240
Tansy Pudding 240
Tansy Cake 240

THYME 241
Thymus vulgaris

Thyme in Cooking 242

WALL PENNYWORT 242
Umbilicus rupestris

Wall Pennywort in Salads 244
  and Sandwiches

WHITE DEAD NETTLE 244
Lamium album

White Dead Nettle and 245
  Sorrel Omelette
White Dead Nettle Shampoo 246
  for Greasy Hair

WILD CABBAGE *Brassica oleracea* 246

To Cook Wild Cabbage 246

WOODRUFF *Galium odoratum* 248

Woodruff Tea 249
To Dry Woodruff 249
Woodruff Sweet Bags 249
Maibowle 249

YARROW *Achillea millefolium* 250

Yarrow Soup 252
Yarrow as a Vegetable 252
Yarrow Leaves and White Sauce 252

OTHER EDIBLE PLANTS 253

WINE MAKING 254

BIBLIOGRAPHY 256

INTRODUCTION

Since this book was first published, nearly twenty-five years ago, a lot has changed and yet nothing has changed. Fads and fashions in food are always adapting to modern lifestyles and eating habits. New dishes are invented, cooking methods altered and simplified, and some ingredients, like fats and sugar, much reduced or dropped altogether.

But the plants, the wild plants, are the same as ever. There is something immensely reassuring about foraging for rock samphire in May, and finding it still abundant and in just the same spray-swept places. Providing the bulldozers have not been active, the same stretch of hedgerow will sprout a crop of wild sorrel each spring, and as long as the roadman and his flail haven't ripped off their branches, the hawthorn and the elder will still yield their abundance of fragrant blossoms, to re-awaken one's enthusiasm for the annual drinks and dishes they inspire.

The fun and interest of foraging for wild food is never-ending. The miniature beauty of herbs and wild plants an amazing revelation, and the satisfaction of making new and unusual dishes from an excursion into the country, will bring you rewards far beyond a trip to the supermarket.

This book is not meant to be about survival or how to live off the land; it is rather intended as a guide for using herbs and wild plants in much the same way as our ancestors did, before we lost the old knowledge and came to rely entirely on shops for our food and drink and beauty preparations. Even the vegetables from our gardens, grown for size and the heaviest crop, have a limited range of flavours, though it would be as wrong to belittle the gardening skills which have developed them from strains of wild plants, as it is to belittle the skills of our ancestors who used herbs and plants in so many ways that we have forgotten. Beautiful things like primroses, violets and cowslips grew in real abundance and although they were picked in lavish quantities, there were fewer people to reap the natural harvest: the world abounded with wild life, plants as well as birds and animals, fish and insects, and Nature's delicate balance was not disturbed. Today we must be scrupulously careful of the wild things that remain, using only those which have a robust foothold in our environment. Do not uproot carelessly or pick greedily and be aware that certain plants these days are protected by The Countryside Act before you pick them.

Happily, most of the plants in this book can be classed as 'persistent weeds', and are robust enough to harvest without damage, but even primroses, mallows and other less abundant wild flowers can easily be grown from seed, or little plants, if you have a garden or allotment or even some pots on a balcony. The following list of firms supply wild seed and plug plants for nearly all the edible plants in this book.

British Wild Flower Plants Burlingham Gardens, 31 Main Road, North Burlingham, Norfolk NR13 4TA
Tel: 01603 716615, Email: office@wildflowers.co.uk **www.wildflowers.co.uk**

Devon Wildflower Seeds Brambles, Laburnum Terrace, Abbotskerswell, Newton Abbot, Devon TQ12 5PT
Tel: 01626 364652, Email: johanna_westgate@hotmail.com

Ecoseeds Old Sawmill Workshop, The Farmyard, Castel Ward Estate, Strangford, Co Down BT30 7LS
Tel: 028 4488 1227, Email:info@ecoseeds.co.uk **www.ecoseeds.co.uk**

Flower Farms Carvers Hill Farm, Shalbourne, Marlborough, Wilts SN8 3PS
Tel: 01672 870782, Email: effable@btinternet.com **www.wildflowerfarms.com**

Forestart Church Farm, Hadnall, Shrewsbury, Shropshire SY4 4AQ
Tel: 01939 210638, Email: sales@forestart.co.uk **www.forestart.co.uk**

Hurrell & McLean Seeds Ltd Beverley Road, Cranswick, Driffield, East Yorkshire YO25 9PF
Tel: 01377 271400, Email: nick@hurrells.fsbusiness.co.uk **www.hmseeds.co.uk**

Kings Seeds (and Suffolk Herbs) Monks Farm, Coggeshall Road, Kelvedon, Colchester, Essex CO5 9PG
Tel: 01376 570000 (01376 572456), Email: sales@kingsseeds.com; sales@suffolkherbs.com **www.kingsseeds.com;
www.suffolkherbs.com**

Landlife National Wildflower Centre, Court Hey Park, Liverpool L16 3NA
Tel: 0151 737 1819, Email: info@landlife.org.uk **www.landlife.org.uk**

Mike Mullis Wild Flower Plants 1 Chantry Cottages, Warbleton, Heathfield, East Sussex TN21 9PT
Tel: 01435 830578, Email: mm.wfp@tesco.net

Mires Beck Nursery Low Mill Lane, North Cave, Brough, East Riding, Yorks HU15 2NR
Tel: 01430 421543, Email: admin@miresbeck.co.uk **www.miresbeck.co.uk**

Natural Surroundings Bayfield Estate, Holt, Norfolk, NR25 7JN.
Tel: 01263 711091, Email: loosely@farmersweekly.net **www.naturalsurroundings.org.uk**

Northumberland Wild Flowers Hunter's Hollow, Todstead, Longframlington NE65 8AU
Tel: 01665 570207, Email: info@northumberlandwildflowers.co.uk **www.northumberlandwildflowers.co.uk**

Poyntzfield Herb Nursery Black Isle, By Dingwall, Ross-shire, Scotland IV7 8LX

Tel: 01381 610352, Email: info@poyntzfieldherbs.co.uk **www.poyntzfieldherbs.co.uk**

Really Wild Flowers Spring Mead, Bedchester, Shaftesbury, Dorset SP7 0JU
Tel: 01747 811778, Email: rwflowers@aol.com **www.ReallyWildFlowers.co.uk**

Scotia Seeds Wildflowers of Scotland, Mavisbank, Farnell, Brechin, Angus DD9 6TR
Tel: 01356 626425, Email: scotiaseeds@btconnect.com **www.scotiaseeds.co.uk**

Scott's Wildflowers Swallow Hill barn, 31 Common Side, Distington, Workington, Cumbria CA14 4PU
Tel: 01946830486, Email: wildflowers@btinternet.com **www.scottswildflowers.co.uk**

Shipton Bulbs Y Felin, Henllan Amgoed, Whitland Carmarthenshire SA34 0SL
Tel: 01994 240125, Email bluebell@zoo.co.uk **www.bluebellbulbs.co.uk**

Weald Meadows Initiative Hastings Road, Flimwell, East Sussex TN5 7PR
Tel: 01580 879500, Email: meadows@highwelad.org **www.highweald.org**

Yellow Flag Wildflowers 8 Plock Court, Longford, Glos GL2 9DW
Tel: 01452 311525, **www.wildflowersuk.com**

COMMON AGRIMONY
Agrimonia eupatoria

Agrimony grows in many grassy places throughout Britain, Europe and Scandinavia. It is found by roadsides, hedge banks and the edges of fields, but does not occur far north or on high ground. The plant is perennial, 30-60 cm/1-2 ft tall, slender and with toothed, pinnate leaves consisting of six or eight lateral leaflets which increase in size towards the largest, terminal leaflet, and are interspersed with several tiny leaflets of irregular sizes. Both leaves and stems have a slightly rough texture. Agrimony flowers throughout the summer, and the tapering yellow spikes often stand above the surrounding growth. Each flower is tiny, with five yellow petals, there are usually unopened buds, open flowers and small hooked burrs on the flowering spike at the same time. The burrs are deeply furrowed and hang downwards like little bristly, brown bells, which cling to everything, and ensure the plants' distribution.

There are two tall species of agrimony in North America, which the Indians used for treating fevers. John Josselyn mentions 'Egrimony' among the plants he found growing wild in New England in the 17th century, and William Coles, the English herbalist of that time, says 'it is called in English Agrimony or Egrimony', he adds 'it is also called Agrimonia which is the name whereby it is best known in Shops'. This gives one an intriguing glimpse of the sort of thing stocked by shops in the 17th century, and suggests that agrimony was widely used, and maybe more effective than we give it credit for.

Eupatoria, the plant's second scientific name, refers to King Mithradates Eupator, who is believed to have first discovered the virtues of agrimony. King Eupator experimented with poisonous plants and their antidotes, which he tried out on criminals, and is himself supposed to have taken a small amount of poison and its antidote every day of his life, in his search for an all-purpose antidote that would act on every poison.

Almost all the early physicians and herbalists agreed that 'there is no plant so generally applicable for all diseases that proceed from the Liver'. The Slav peasants used agrimony for treating liver disorders and Sir John Hill, the 18th century physician, gave a prescription for agrimony root with honey, that was to be taken thrice daily for jaundice, a disease that affects the liver. Even modern herbalists recommend agrimony tea as an aid to digestion and for correcting disorders of the liver; and prescribe an infusion of agrimony, which is astringent and contains tannin, as a gargle for a relaxed throat, and to apply to skin rashes and abrasions as a healing compress. So the early physicians were not always so wide of the mark.

Endearingly, in medieval times, people would lay agrimony under their pillows to ensure a sound night's sleep.

FRESH AGRIMONY TEA SUMMER

I have read that the leaves and flowers of agrimony have a fresh scent, like apricots, which retain their fragrance when dried, with a delicate aroma that is a good substitute for tea. Agrimony may be one of the plants that has lost much of its former scent, however, country people in France still enjoy a tisane made with agrimony and, if flavoured with lemon juice and a little honey, the tea has a clean, refreshing taste.

6-8 agrimony stems, leaves and flowers
250 ml/1 cup/½ pint boiling water

Put the agrimony in a jug, bruise with a wooden spoon and pour on the boiling water. Cover with a clean cloth and leave until cold. Strain, and drink with a squeeze of lemon juice.

DRIED AGRIMONY TEA

1 heaped teaspoon dried agrimony
250 ml/1 cup/½ pint boiling water

Put the agrimony in a small jug, pour on the boiling water and leave to infuse for 7-10 minutes. Strain into a cup and sweeten with honey.

TO DRY AGRIMONY SUMMER

Pick the whole plant above ground, and tie in bunches of five or six stems. Hang head downwards from the slats or pipes in an airing cupboard, or in any warm dry room. When the flowers and leaves are dry and crisp, chop finely or put them through a parsley mill and store in screw-topped jars away from the light.

GARGLE FOR RELAXED THROAT

Agrimony contains tannin and a volatile oil which is astringent and justifies its old use as a country medicine.

Modern herbalists claim it has valuable properties and the infusion may be used as a gargle for a relaxed throat or a cupful sipped slowly 3 or 4 times a day will help control diarrhoea in adults and children.

1 litre/5 cups/2 pints boiling water
2 large handfuls agrimony (stems, leaves and flowers)

Put the agrimony into a jug and bruise slightly with a wooden spoon. Pour on the boiling water, cover and infuse for 10 minutes. Use the liquid cold as a gargle or to drink and make a fresh supply each day.

COMMON AGRIMONY – *AGRIMONIA EUPATORIA*

ALEXANDERS – *SMYRNIUM OLUSATRUM*

ALEXANDERS

Smyrnium olusatrum

A lexanders is an odd name for a plant. It was known as *Petroselinum Alexandrinum* (parsley of Alexandria) in medieval Latin and is one of the many Mediterranean plants introduced into Britain by the Romans. It grows in Western Europe and in Britain, particularly near the sea. It is unusual for Alexanders to grow inland and, where it does, it is usually on chalk. The plant was introduced and cultivated in America, but is not found growing wild.

The strong, bushy-looking umbellifer is biennial and grows up to 11/4 metres/4 ft high. The leaves appear at the end of winter and are a bright shining green, consisting of three broad, toothed leaflets with a veined, membraneous bract enclosing the base of the leaf stalks. The flowers grow in fat, round umbels which are tightly massed and a vivid lime green, although most field guides describe Alexanders as yellow. The plant flowers in the spring, and the buds are at their best for eating while still unopened.

Alexanders was planted as a vegetable in the early monastery gardens, and it is often found growing prolifically by the ruins of old abbeys and castles in Ireland and the west of England, but it was also used medicinally, and William Coles claimed that Alexanders seed, powdered and taken in wine 'is very powerful for expelling the after-Birth . . . and availeth against the bitings of Serpents, and breaketh wind, and is therefore good for the Collick'. The roots stewed, or eaten raw with vinegar, would 'in the time of Lent, to help to digest the crudities and viscous humours that are gathered in the Stomach by the much use of Fish at that time . . .'

Culpeper said 'it is usually sown in all the gardens in Europe' and John Evelyn recommended Alexanders as a plant for the kitchen garden, and included the buds as an ingredient for salads. In *The Accomplished Cook, or the Art and Mystery of Cookery*, 1675, Robert May gave a detailed recipe for 'A Grand Sallet of Alexander Buds', in which the buds were lightly cooked and mixed with capers, currants and slices of lemon. The recipe told one to 'scrape on sugar', (sugar, in those days, was made into a cone, or block, and had to be grated or scraped off) 'and serve it with good oyl and wine vinegar', all ingredients that will make a delicious salad today.

ALEXANDERS STEMS AS A VEGETABLE

EARLY SPRING

The stems are very succulent and the strange aniseed smell disappears during cooking, leaving a vegetable with a mild, but subtle flavour. The best part of the stem is at the bottom, so ferret about in the surrounding growth and cut the stems as low to the ground as you can.

SERVES 4

2 handfuls Alexanders stems
butter

Trim away the leaves and green part of the stems, and reserve the lower parts which are white and pale. Wash the stems thoroughly and cook in boiling salted water for 5-10 minutes, until a fork easily pierces one of the thickest stems. Drain, and serve with melted butter.

ALEXANDERS BUDS AS SALAD SPRING

These delicate lime-green flower buds are very good in mixed salads, or served on their own with a French dressing.

SERVES 4
500 ml/2 cups/1 pint Alexanders buds
3 parts olive oil to 1 part white vinegar
salt and freshly milled black pepper

Wash the buds if necessary and trim away any stalks. Cook in a little boiling salted water for 2-3 minutes until tender. Drain, and allow to cool. Toss the buds in the dressing and turn into a shallow dish, or serve on top of a mixed salad.

ALEXANDERS SAUCE LATE WINTER

At the end of winter, when young Alexanders leaves are only 5-8 cm/2-3 ins high and their bright green shows up vividly among the sere grasses of the previous year, they have a fresh taste of parsley and make a good substitute for parsley sauce when the herb is often limp with frost. The sauce is delicious with fish or chicken, and the chopped leaves can be added to fish cakes, or a fish pie, or scattered over salads.

1 tablespoon butter
1 tablespoon plain flour
250 ml/1 cup/½ pint milk
salt and freshly milled black pepper
2-3 tablespoons finely chopped Alexanders leaves
  (pick about two handfuls)

Melt the butter in a small saucepan and stir in the flour. Gradually add the milk, stirring continuously until the sauce has thickened and is smooth. Finally add the seasoning and the chopped Alexanders leaves and serve at once.

ASH

Fraxinus excelsior

The ash belongs to the same family as the olive tree, it is widespread and common throughout Britain and is found all over Europe and Scandinavia. Related species, *Fraxinus americana*, *F. pennsylvanica* and *F. oregona* grow wild in the United States. When mature, the ash grows to a lofty tree, with smooth grey bark which becomes scaly when the tree is old. The triangular black flower buds are very characteristic and conspicuous when the tree is bare, in the spring they open into dense clusters of purplish stamens and greenish white styles, and since the flowers are wind pollinated, they have no need of petals to attract insects. The leaves are graceful, consisting of lanceolate, sharply-toothed leaflets in opposite pairs ending in a terminal leaflet. The winged fruits, or ash keys, which hang in drooping bunches, are small and green in the late spring and finally ripen into dry, dark brown fruits which hang on the trees until the following spring.

Ash timber is stronger and more elastic than any other; it was 'much used in Coaches, Carts, ploughs, and other instruments of husbandry, but especially to make Pikes for souldiers', according to William Coles. Hop poles, ladders and railway wagons were also made from ash timber.

In early medicine the bitter bark was used for its tonic and astringent properties to treat rheumatism and diseases of the liver, the fruits were recommended for flatulence, and an infusion of the leaves was believed to reduce obesity and

ASH – *FRAXINUS EXCELSIOR*

relieve dropsy. Coles claimed that three or four leaves taken in wine each morning 'doth make those leane that are fat', and said the ashes of the bark (lye) cured 'leprous, scabby or scal'd heads'. Under a mysterious disorder, 'the whyte Morphewe . . . which doth come by defaut of nutrytyve virtue', the Tudor physician, Andrew Borde, advised that the face should be washed with powdered gentian root and vinegar, and rubbed with a skarlet cloth . . .and to bedwarde anoynt the face with oyle of the ashe kayes'. Culpeper took exception to the idea which 'had its rise from Gerard or Pliny . . .' 'that if an adder be encompassed around with ash-tree leaves, she would sooner run through fire than through the leaves; the contrary to which is the truth, as both my eyes are witness.' Modern herbalists recommend an infusion of ash leaves—25 g/^{1}/$_2$ cup/1 oz to 500 ml/2 cups of boiling water taken over 24 hours—as an effective laxative that is gentler than senna.

PICKLED ASH KEYS SPRING

I have come across several old recipes for pickled ash keys, or 'ashen keys', some of them recommend prolonged soaking, and some prolonged boiling, but as well as losing flavour, I have found that ash keys tend to toughen the longer they are cooked, but they should be boiled up twice in fresh water to avoid bitterness. The essential thing is to pick the ash keys when they are very small and young. The immature keys should be handing in little green bunches, and if you bite one raw, it should be crisp, but in no way fibrous or stringy. They make a good and very unusual pickle.

500 ml/2 cups/1 pint measure green ash keys,
  without stalks
water—see recipe
1 level teaspoon ground cloves
1 level teaspoon ground cinnamon
3 or 4 blades mace
2 bay leaves
6 peppercorns
1 level teaspoon allspice
1/2 level teaspoon ground ginger
1 level teaspoon salt
2-3 tablespoons brown sugar, or 1 tablespoon honey
450 ml/scant 2 cups/3/4 pint cider vinegar

Pick away the little stalks from the ash keys and wash them thoroughly, put them in a pan with enough cold water to cover, bring to the boil and simmer for 5 minutes. Drain, and return to the pan, cover with fresh cold water and bring to the boil for a second time, cover the pan and simmer for another 5 minutes, drain thoroughly and pack the ash keys into warm dry jars to within 1/2 cm/1 in of the top.

Put the spices, salt and sugar, or honey, into a bowl, stir in the vinegar and stand the bowl in a pan of water—cover it with a plate. Bring the water slowly to the boil and keep boiling for 5 minutes. Remove the bowl from the hot water and allow to stand for 2-3 hours, until quite cold. Strain the liquid into a jug and pour over the ash keys, filling the jars to the brim. Screw on plastic lined lids, or, if using metal lids, line with vinegar-proof paper or two thicknesses of greaseproof paper. Store for 3-4 months to allow the pickle to mellow.

ASH WALKING STICK WINTER

Treat exactly the same as hazel, see page 120. When polished, an ash walking stick acquires a lovely silvery-grey sheen.

BALM
Melissa officinalis

Also known as bee balm and lemon balm, the former from its irresistible attraction for bees, the latter because, when crushed, the leaves give off a refreshing scent of lemon. It was introduced into Britain from the Mediterranean where it grows almost too vigorously in gardens, and is occasionally found growing wild in the south of England as a garden escape. In America, the plant grows wild by roadsides, woods and waste places, and is found from Maine to Kansas and southwards to Florida and Arkansas. It also grows on the Pacific coast.

The plant is perennial, reaching 30-60 cm/1-2 ft in height. The leaves are toothed, pointed oval in shape and very wrinkled, with the lowest leaves heart-shaped and growing on longer stalks. The white flowers are tiny and throughout the summer grow in clusters at the base of the upper leaves. It is very easy to propagate balm from bits of the root in spring or autumn, and there are generally a mass of self-sown seedlings round the plant, which will all grow if transplanted.

Balm was probably at its peak of popularity in Elizabethan days, and was not only used in salads, as tea and to flavour wine, but was considered a wonderful remedy for depression and a poor memory. John Evelyn is often quoted as saying 'Balm is sovereign for the brain, strengthening the memory and powerfully chasing away melancholy'; and in Thomas Cogan's *Haven of Health*, 1584, a drink made with balm was recommended for the Oxford students who, even in those days, suffered from depression: 'It is an hearbe greatly to be esteemed of students, for by a special property it driveth away heaviness of mind, sharpeneth the understanding, and encreaseth memory'.

Indeed, balm was used as a herbal medicine in Roman times, and the leaves steeped in wine were believed to cure scorpion stings and the bites of 'venomous beasts'. Balm leaves were used to heal wounds, and Gerard wrote, 'the juice of Balme glueth together greene wounds', he also recommended it for toothache and 'for those that cannot take breath unlesse they hold their neckes upright'. Even modern herbalists claim that the balsamic oils of balm have an anti-putrescent effect and can be used as a dressing for wounds, and in modern pharmacy are used in a number of aromatic spirits and waters. A compound aromatic spirit, *Agua carmelitana*, prepared from a mixture of fresh balm, lemon peel, cinnamon, nutmeg, coriander and other aromatics is still used as a digestive stimulant and as a fragrant, stimulating application to the skin.

The passion that bees have for balm led the early botanists to believe that Dioscorides' *melissophyllon*, or bee leaf, and Pliny's *apiastrum* which he recommended planting near hives for the bees' delight, was balm. John Gerard wrote 'the hives of bees being rubbed with the leaves of bawme, causeth the bees to keep together, and causeth others to come with them', and Dr. Losch advised rubbing the inside of bee hives with balm to stop the bees from 'vagabonding', and one wonders if any modern bee-keepers have tried this old method of preserving their colonies.

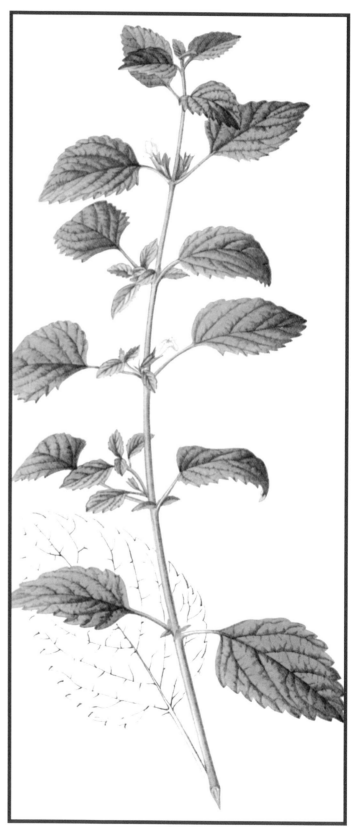

BALM – *MELISSA OFFICINALIS*

BALM BUTTER, WITH FISH SUMMER AND AUTUMN

The lemon tang of balm is very good with fish. If you shape the butter into a roll before putting it to chill, you can slice off rounds for individual portions of grilled or fried fish.

1 small handful lemon balm—the top sprigs
100 g/½ cup/4 oz butter
salt and black pepper

Wash the balm leaves, remove the stalks and chop the leaves finely. Put the butter in a bowl and cream with a wooden spoon until soft. Mix the chopped balm into the butter with a fork, and add a seasoning of salt and black pepper. Shape into a roll, and leave in the refrigerator to firm up. Drain off any brown juice that will have run from the leaves, slice in 1 cm/half-inch rounds and serve.

BALM AND BORAGE WINE CUP SUMMER

The lemon fragrance of balm, and cucumber freshness of borage combine to make this one of the most cooling drinks for a summer party.

1 bottle white wine (ideally a Chardonnay)
6 sprigs balm tips
6 flowering sprigs borage
1 tablespoon sugar, or ½ tablespoon honey
6 slices lemon
soda water—see recipe

Put the balm and borage in a glass jug with the sugar, or honey, the lemon and wine. Cover and stand in the refrigerator to chill thoroughly.

Before serving, add soda or sparkling mineral water—about one-third to two-thirds of the wine.

A REFRESHING DRINK IN FEVER

(FROM AN OLD RECIPE)

'Put two sprigs of balm and a little wood sorrel into a stone jug, having first washed and dried them; peel thin a small lemon, and clear from the white; slice it and put a bit of peel in; then pour in 3 pints (1½ litres/7½ cups) of boiling water, sweeten and cover it close.'

BALM WINE SUMMER

The slight lemon fragrance of balm gives a clean tang to this medium dry white wine.

activated yeast (p. 255)
2 litres/10 cups/4 pints measures young balm leaves and tips
1 kilo/5 cups/2 lbs sugar
200 g/1½ cups/½ lb chopped raisins
2 lemons
5 litres/9 quarts U.S./1 gallon water
2 tablespoons cold tea or 1 teaspoon grape tannin

Wash the balm leaves, put them in the plastic bucket with the sugar, raisins and thinly pared rind (not pith) and juice of the lemons, bruise the leaves with a wooden spoon, pour on the boiling water and stir until the sugar dissolves, cover the bucket with a clean cloth and leave until cool, (about 70°F, 20°C) then stir in the cold tea, or grape tannin, and activated yeast. Cover the bucket with its lid and leave in a warm place for one week. Strain the liquid into the fermentation jar and follow the method given on page 254.

BEECH – *FAGUS SYLVATICA*

BEECH
Fagus sylvatica

Many of the steep slopes of England's South Downs are clothed with natural beech woods, descriptively known as beech hangers. Beech trees prefer chalk and sandy soils and are only indigenous to Britain south of Yorkshire, but have been widely planted in woods and parks all over the British Isles and are a common forest tree throughout the temperate zones of Europe and Asia Minor. In America, *fagus sylvatica* is planted as an ornamental tree, and their native tree, *fagus grandiflora*, grows wild all over the eastern states.

The beech is one of the most beautiful trees, tall and lofty with a smooth, grayish trunk and gracefully symmetrical branches and twigs. In April and May the leaves are of so pure a green they embody the colour of spring itself, and when seen from below the undersides shine with silky white hairs and appear almost transparent against the sunlight. The beech has a second burst of glory in the autumn, when the leaves glow like copper and remain a bright tawny brown after all other colours have drained from the woods. In spring, the tree has male flowers like small greenish tassels, and inconspicuous female flowers in upright pairs. In early autumn the ground beneath the trees may be covered with the fallen nuts, or beech-mast, which in some years is very abundant. Inside each bristly brown husk lie two or three shiny, three-cornered nuts, and from them an oil can be extracted which was used in the old days as fuel for lamps and in cooking, and, in America to make beechnut butter. In times of famine people ate the nuts and, in fact, they are delicious when roasted, although rather slow and finicky to prepare. Deer and many other animals and birds will eat beechmast, and in France it was fed to pheasants and poultry. It was a common practice throughout most of Europe to turn pigs out in the woods in the autumn to eat the fallen beechmast and acorns. What a wholesome, pleasant life compared with that of their wretched descendants, reared on concrete floors, forced into iron cages and crammed with antibiotics in our modern intensive pig units.

There were three words for beech in Anglo-Saxon, *boc, bece* and *beoce*. The second, *bece*, has given us the name for the tree, the first *boc*, has become book in English. In modern German *Buche* is beech and *Buch* without an *e*, is book, and in Swedish the word *bok* means both book and beech. Runic tablets, which were the first form of book, were thin boards made of beech wood. William Coles described a strange use for the water found in hollow beech trees, saying: 'it will cure both Man and Beast of any Scurf, scab or running Tetters, if they be washed therewith'; in modern medicine, beech tar it used for eczema, psoriasis and chronic skin diseases. The tar is an ingredient of a syrup—still used as an expectorant in the treatment of bronchitis.

BEECH LEAF GIN SPRING

Richard Mabey describes this liqueur in his wonderfully informative book *Food for Free*. He calls it beech leaf *noyau*, and suggests it originated in the Chilterns, where there are large areas of beech woods. The original has a dash of brandy added, but I was so enchanted by the miraculous lime green gin that I was afraid to alter the ethereal colour and substituted white rum for the brandy. It seems to achieve the requisite kick. The flavour is distinctive, but difficult to describe, as elusive and delicate as the colour.

FILLS 1 GIN BOTTLE AND 1 SMALL EXTRA BOTTLE
1 bottle gin
225 g/1 cup/^{1}/2 lb sugar
125 ml/^{2}/3 cup/^{1}/4 pint water
1 miniature bottle white rum

Pick a large quantity of beech leaves on a dry day. Pick off the woody stalks and bud scales. Pack the leaves loosely into glass jars, pour over some of the gin and press the leaves under with a wooden spoon. Add more leaves until they reach within 2^1/2 cm/1 in of the top of the jars, then fill up with gin to the brim. Screw on the lids, and leave in a dark cupboard for a fortnight. Strain the liquid into a measuring jug through a nylon strainer and squeeze out the leaves. There should be about ^{3}/4 litre (1^1/4 pints, or 3^1/2 cups) of green liquid.

Heat the sugar and water in a small pan, stirring until the sugar has dissolved, then boil up for 2-3 minutes, and set aside to cool. Add the white rum and cooled syrup to the jug of green gin, and pour carefully into clean bottles, cork with new corks or screw on caps.

BEECHNUTS, ROASTED

LATE SUMMER AND EARLY AUTUMN

Roasted beechnuts are just as delicious as any nuts you can buy; but as they are one of the fiddly and time-consuming wild things to prepare, although quick to pick, one can never keep pace with all one would like to eat. They should be gathered in early autumn when they start to fall, and may be picked off the ground or from the trees. Take plenty, as some may not contain any kernels. You can use the empty outer cases for dried flower arrangements; after a day or two indoors the cases open into four 'petals', with bristly, russet-brown backs and a lining the texture of velvet, they have a short stalk which can be wired onto fine twigs or stiff grass stems, to support the dried cases. Any of the three-cornered nuts that are empty make attractive chunky necklaces if you thread a darning needle with strong thread and stab it through the middle of each nut, sliding one on top of another until you have a long, light chain of shiny, leathery nuts. Either tie the ends of the thread together, or finish by sewing on two lengths of narrow, russet-coloured velvet ribbon to tie behind the neck.

BEECHNUT NIBBLES

Keep the beechnuts indoors for 12-24 hours until the cases open, and the three beautifully packaged little nuts will drop or shake out.

Any quantity of beechnuts
Fine sea salt

With a small sharp knife take off the leathery brown outer skins and spread the kernels in a single layer on a shallow baking tin. Roast in a hot oven for 5-10 minutes, seeing they don't scorch. When cool enough to handle, scrape or rub off the inner brown skin and roll the nuts in salt.

Store in a tin.

TO PRESERVE BEECH LEAVES FOR WINTER DECORATIONS SUMMER

Beech leaves are easy to preserve in glycerine and water and acquire beautiful colours ranging from a bright, light tan to deep olive brown. Leaves picked early in the summer will be a lighter brown than those gathered later, but the sprays must be cut before the leaves start to change to autumn colours, while the sap is in the twigs and they can 'drink' the preserving brew.

about 12 sprays beech leaves
450 ml/scant 2 cups/3/4 pint bottle glycerine
3/4 litre/33/4 cups/11/2 pints boiling water

Have ready a couple of deep jugs or jars that will hold about six sprays each. Cut away the lowest small twigs and leaves from the sprays so you have a length of stem to stand in the containers, and crush or split the lower 2 ins/5 cm.

Pour half the bottle of glycerine into each of the jars and then pour half the boiling water into each. While it is still hot, stand the sprays in this mixture and leave them in a cool place for about a fortnight. When the undersides of the leaves look oily they are ready, and the sprays should be laid on newspaper on a flat surface for two or three days, and then stored in empty vases until needed for dried flower arrangements.

BERGAMOT
Monarda didyma

Bergamot is a perennial garden herb with such showy scarlet flowers that it is worthy of the herbaceous border. The plant grows 60-120 cm/2-4 ft high on stiff stems which are square and grooved. The large, toothed, pointed oval leaves are rough on both sides and grow in pairs, they are dark green and often tinged with red. From mid-summer onwards the large pompons of scarlet flowers grow in whorls at the top of the stem. There are white and pink varieties, but the red, or Cambridge Scarlet, is the one most usually grown. Bergamot is a member of the mint family and, like all the mints, prefers a deep, moist soil and can be propagated by its creeping roots or from cuttings. It can also be grown from seed sown in the spring, and should be kept well watered in dry weather.

The whole plant is deliciously aromatic and bees go mad about it. Like lemon balm, it is sometimes called bee balm. Bergamot's scientific name comes from the 16th century Spanish physician Nicholas Monardes, who discovered it.

BERGAMOT – *MONARDA DIDYMA*

The plant is a native of North America and grows in woods and thickets from New York to Michigan and southwards to Georgia and Tennessee. It was widely cultivated and has escaped into the wild from Quebec to New Jersey. The leaves make a famous tisane known as Oswego Tea, which is mildly sedative and is good for colds and sore throats, as it contains the antiseptic, thymol. Bergamot was introduced into this country in the 18th century by John Bartram of Philadelphia, who founded a flourishing business exporting plants and seeds from the New World, and importing plants from Europe. Bartram was a wonderful man, Linnaeus referred to him as 'the greatest natural botanist in the world'. He started life as a farmer, built his house with his own hands, yet, self-taught and unqualified, he became botanist to the King for the American Colonies, under George III, and in 1729 he started the famous Botanic Gardens in Philadelphia, where he built up the finest collection of native plants in America.

TO DRY BERGAMOT SUMMER

The leaves and flowers of bergamot are considered by modern herbalists to have a mildly sedative effect, and the sweetly-scented leaves are used in perfumery and pot pourri.

Pick the leaves and flowers on a dry day and spread them on wire racks or cardboard lids and put them in the airing cupboard for a few days until dry and crisp. Alternatively, you can cut the stems and hang them upside down in bunches in an airing cupboard, until they are dry and crisp. Strip off the dried flowers and leaves and crumble them. Store in screw-topped jars away from the light.

BERGAMOT IN SALAD SUMMER

Add a few finely chopped bergamot leaves to a green salad and scatter a few of the brilliant scarlet flowers over the top.

BERGAMOT SAUCE SUMMER

Bergamot is very good with hot bacon, poultry or game, you may use the leaves fresh or dried, but fresh leaves have the better flavour.

1 tablespoon finely chopped fresh bergamot leaves,
    or 2 teaspoons dried bergamot leaves
1 tablespoon butter
1 small onion
1 tablespoon flour
250 ml/1 cup/1/2 pint milk,
    or chicken stock if serving with poultry
salt and freshly milled black pepper
lemon juice, optional

Wash the leaves, if fresh, and pat dry before chopping finely. Melt the butter in a small saucepan, peel and finely chop the onion, and fry gently in butter until soft and yellow. Shake in the flour and stir to blend, draw the pan off the heat and add half the milk, or chicken stock, stirring all the time, then return the pan to the heat and stir briskly while adding the remaining liquid. When the sauce is smooth and thick, add the chopped bergamot leaves, season with salt and pepper, and finish with a squeeze of lemon juice.

FRESH BERGAMOT TEA SUMMER

Bergamot leaves have strongly spicy scent rather like a mixture of rosemary and sage, and make a good herbal tea.

about 10 fresh bergamot leaves
250 ml/1 cup/1/2 pint water

Wash the leaves and put them in a small jug, bruise lightly with a wooden spoon, pour on the boiling water, cover and infuse for 7 minutes. Strain into a cup and drink hot; or allow to cool and chill in the refrigerator and drink iced, with a slice of lemon.

DRIED BERGAMOT TEA

When tea was boycotted in America after the Boston Tea Party, bergamot was used as a substitute.

2 teaspoons dried bergamot
250 ml/1 cup/1/2 pint water

Put the bergamot into a small jug, pour on boiling water, cover and infuse for 7 minutes. Strain into a cup and drink hot with sugar and lemon.

BILBERRY

Vaccinium myrtillus

BLAEBERRY, WHORTLEBERRY *V. myrtillus* BLUEBERRY, HUCKLEBERRY *V. augustifolia*

The bilberry grows on moors and heaths, and in open woods, throughout Scotland and the north and west of England. It thrives on high ground and is rare in south-east England except where the soil is acid, as in the Surrey hills. In the low-lying counties of Cambridgeshire and Suffolk it is entirely absent. Bilberries are found throughout northern Europe and Scandinavia, and a larger member of the family grows wild in the United States, which is their famous blueberry. There are many species in America and they are distributed widely from California to Canada and Alaska, the Washington coast and Oregon, and from Montana to Colorado and the southern Sierra Nevada.

The bushy, deciduous plant is 30-60 cm/1-2 ft tall and often grows in large patches. The wiry, green twigs are angled, and the pointed oval, slightly-toothed leaves are bright green in summer, turning to red in the autumn before they fall, leaving the plant bare in winter. The drooping, pink or pinkish-green flowers are inconspicuous, and appear in spring and early summer. They are globular and hang singly, or in pairs, like little inverted goldfish bowls. In the autumn the fruits ripen into purplish-black berries with a characteristic blue bloom, each berry is globular with a hard, flattened top.

The indelible juice of the berries produces a dark blue or purple dye. Before World War I the berries were imported from Germany for dyeing woollen cloth, and during the war bilberries were gathered as a dye stuff in Britain, rather than as food. William Coles in 1657, referred to the juice which 'giveth a Purplish colour to the hands and lips of them that handle and eat them' and he described how 'Painters, to colour Paper and Cards, do make a kind of Purple blew colour, putting there to some Allome and Galls, (oak galls) whereby they can make it lighter or sadder (darker) as they please'.

Bilberry leaves contain tannin and quinic acid and have been used as an additive and substitute for tea, and a decoction of the leaves and stems as a mouthwash and gargle. The dried fruits have diuretic and astringent properties, and an extract is still used in herbal medicine to treat diarrhoea and dysentery.

COMPOTE OF BILBERRIES

LATE SUMMER, EARLY AUTUMN

Bilberries make a wonderful dark purple compote which stains everything it touches, but is worth it. We discovered masses of them one year in Norway when staying far from the village shop. We never grew tired of them for dessert, nor wholly rid ourselves of the stains.

SERVES 3 OR 4
500 g/2 cups/1 lb bilberries
4-5 tablespoons water
4-5 tablespoons sugar, or 3 tablespoons honey

Wash the bilberries and remove any stems and leaves. Put the water and sugar, or honey in a saucepan, bring to the boil stirring all the while. Boil fast for 3 minutes, then tip in the bilberries, lower the heat and cook gently for 5-10 minutes until the berries are tender. Pour into a dish and serve cold with cream, which makes lovely swirls in the purple juice.

BILBERRY STIRABOUT LATE SUMMER, EARLY AUTUMN

This is an old recipe for fruit cooked in batter which is made rather like a sweet Yorkshire pudding in the oven. You can use any soft fruit, or rhubarb, but bilberries are particularly nice. Preheat the oven to (400°F, 200°C or Gas 6) before you start, as you need to have the butter bubbling in the dish to receive the batter.

225 g/1 cup/8 oz bilberries
100 g/1 cup/4 oz plain flour
pinch salt
2 eggs
250 ml/1 cup/1/2 pint milk
2-3 tablespoons sugar, or 1 tablespoon honey
25 g/2 tablespoons/1 oz butter

Wash the bilberries and remove any stalks or leaves. Sift the flour and salt into a large bowl. Separate the eggs, putting the whites in one bowl and the yolks and milk in another, whisk the yolks and milk lightly together and tip half the amount into the centre of the flour, mix with a wooden spoon, then beat until smooth. Slowly add the rest of the milk mixture and beat well again, stir in the sugar, or melted honey, and the prepared bilberries and set aside. Thickly smear a medium-sized ovenproof dish with butter, and put it in the hot oven until the butter is bubbling.

Whisk the egg whites stiffly and fold into the bilberry batter.

Pour into the dish of sizzling butter and bake in the hot oven for 30-35 minutes until well risen and golden. Sprinkle with plenty of sugar as soon as you take the pudding from the oven, and serve hot with cream.

BILBERRY MUFFINS LATE SUMMER

The recipe for these American-style muffins is taken from the classic American cookbook *Joy of Cooking*, known simply to its American followers as 'The Joy'. The original is for blueberry muffins, but our little British bilberries—whortleberries—blaeberries—what you will—are just as good for baking.

The instructions for the American muffins are slightly unnerving, urging one 'not to bother about the lumps' and for the final mixing to be very swift 'not more than 10–20 seconds'. Have faith, the swift mixing seems to work, and the lumps do disappear.

For baking, you will need the proper narrow, deep muffin tins, or waxed paper cases of the same shape, which you can stand in a baking tray made for individual Yorkshire puddings.

The recipe makes 12 muffins.

225 g/2 cups/8 oz plain flour
2 teaspoons baking powder
1/2 teaspoon salt
75 g/1/3 cup/3 oz granulated sugar
3 tablespoons melted butter
2 free range eggs
200 ml/3/4 cup/7 fl oz milk
100-150 g/1/2 cup/4–5 oz bilberries, picked over

Well grease 12 muffin tins and pre-heat the oven to 200°C / 400°F / Gas 6.

Sift the flour, baking powder and salt into a large bowl and add the sugar.

Melt some butter in a small saucepan over a low heat. Break the eggs into a smaller bowl, whisk lightly and add the milk. Measure 3 tablespoons of melted butter into the egg and milk mixture and stir together.

Add this mixture to the dry ingredients and stir together as swiftly as you can, for not more than 10–20 seconds, any remaining lumps will disappear in the baking. Finally, quickly stir in the bilberries.

Fill the muffin tins two-thirds full and bake in the pre-heated oven for 25 minutes.

Allow to stand for a few seconds before turning out onto a wire rack.

BILBERRY JAM LATE SUMMER, EARLY AUTUMN

As well as tasting good with scones, oat cakes or crumpets, bilberry jam makes a homely rice pudding something of a treat, unless you cannot bear rice pudding under any guise.

1 kilo/2 lbs bilberries
strained juice of 2 large lemons
3-4 tablespoons water
1 kilo/4 cups/2 lbs sugar

Wash the berries gently, and remove any stalks and leaves or bits of grass and moss, drain and put the bilberries in a large pan with the lemon juice and water. Bring to the boil, cover and cook gently until the berries are soft, about 10 minutes. Add the sugar and heat gently, stirring continuously until the sugar has dissolved, then boil fairly rapidly in the open pan for 7-10 minutes, stirring frequently to stop the jam sticking. When thick, and showing signs of setting when dripped on a cold saucer, pour into warm dry jars, cover with waxed circles while hot, and seal with cellophane covers when cold.

BILBERRY AND APPLE JELLY

LATE SUMMER, EARLY AUTUMN

The bilberries should be fresh and not over-ripe, and the apples as green as possible. This jelly has a deep, rich colour, and a sharp sweetness that is delicious with English muffins or hot buttered toast.

MAKES ABOUT 2 KILOS (4 LBS) JELLY
1 kilo/2 lbs bilberries
1 kilo/2 lbs cooking apples
sugar—see method

Wash the bilberries and put them in a saucepan with just enough water to cover, slice the apples but do not peel or remove the cores, and put the slices in a separate saucepan with just enough water to cover. Bring both pans to the boil and cook each fruit separately until soft and pulpy. Tip the contents of both saucepans into a scalded jelly bag or double thickness of muslin, and allow to drip for 1 hour. Measure the juice into a saucepan and add 300 g/1½ cups/¾ lb sugar to each 500 ml/2½ cups/1 pint juice. Heat slowly and stir to dissolve the sugar, then boil rapidly for about 10 minutes until a little of the liquid jells when dripped on to a cold saucer. Skim, and pour into warm dry jars. Cover with waxed circles while hot and seal with cellophane covers when cold.

BILBERRY JUICE WITH MUESLI

LATE SUMMER, EARLY AUTUMN

When needing fresh fruit with your breakfast muesli, add some juiced blueberries for a wake-up flavour.

For each helping of oatmeal:

150 g/½ cup/5 oz fresh bilberries,
    put through a liquidiser with a squeeze of lemon juice
1 tablespoon runny honey
2 tablespoons plain yoghurt

Stir all together with the oatmeal.

FRESH BILBERRY LEAF TEA

LATE SUMMER, EARLY AUTUMN

Bilberry leaves are mildly astringent, and make a refreshing tea.

a small handful fresh bilberry leaves
500 ml/2 cups/1 pint boiling water
honey and lemon to taste

Put the bilberry leaves into a jug. Pour over the boiling water, stir and cover with a saucer, and leave to infuse for 10 minutes. Strain into cups, and drink warm with honey to sweeten, and a slice of lemon.

BILBERRY LIQUEUR

The wild berries are small and not always easy to find in large quantities, but you should find enough to half fill an empty whisky bottle.

You can use cultivated blueberries which are a larger, juicier version of our native bilberries and, if you are using them, follow the quantities of fruit and spirit as for Sloe Gin on page 31 but reduce the amount of sugar by half.

About 450 g/2 cups/1 lb bilberries
1 bottle whisky
115 g/½ cup/4 oz granulated sugar

Pick away any small stalks or leaves from the bilberries and put them in a large jug with the whisky and sugar and stir thoroughly to dissolve some of the sugar. Pour all the contents of the jug into glass jars, or wide-necked bottles, cork or screw on the lids, and leave in a cool room for 3 months. Every other day invert the jars to shake up the liquid.

Strain the liqueur through a double thickness of muslin until perfectly clear. You may need to do this several times, and be careful not to squeeze out the bilberries left in the muslin.

Pour into an empty whisky bottle and cork or screw on the cap firmly. The liqueur is now ready to enjoy, but does improve with age.

BILBERRY WINE LATE SUMMER, EARLY AUTUMN

Bilberry wine is the most wonderful colour, a dark, glowing burgundy red. This recipe makes a medium sweet dessert wine which, if left to mature thoroughly, is good enough to drink after dinner.

activated yeast (p. 255)
1.5 kilos/3 lbs bilberries
5 litres/9 U.S. quarts/1 gallon water
1.5 kilos/6 cups/3 lbs sugar
2 lemons
2-3 tablespoons cold tea
  or 1 teaspoon grape tannin (sold for wine-making)

Wash the bilberries and remove any stalks. Put the berries in a plastic bucket and crush them with a wooden spoon, pour on the boiling water, then add the sugar and the thinly pared rind (no pith) and strained juice of the lemons, stir until the sugar has dissolved, cover the bucket with a clean cloth and allow to stand until cool, (about 70°F, 20°C). Stir in the cold tea, or grape tannin, and the activated yeast, cover the bucket with its lid and stand in a warm place for four days. Strain the liquid into the fermentation jar (dark glass for red wine) and follow the method given on page 254.

BLACKTHORN
Prunus spinosa

Blackthorn is common in hedgerows, woods, and thickets throughout Britain, except in the north of Scotland. It is found in south-east Europe and the temperate regions of Asia, and was introduced into, and is now naturalised in, most parts of North America. Blackthorn grows as a branching, often crooked little tree or tall shrub, 1-4 metres/4-12 ft high, with dark, blackish-brown bark, and small, neat, matt green oval leaves. The tree blossoms in early spring before the leaves appear, the open flowers are starry, with five white petals and a ring of tiny gold or coral anthers, and they grow in massed clusters with buds like little tight white balls. The fruits, which are known as sloes, are like diminutive black plums and are, in fact, one of the wild ancestors of our many varieties of cultivated plums. Sloes start to ripen at the end of summer and at first are covered with a dense blue bloom, later turning purple to glossy black; they can be picked right through the autumn. The twigs have long sharp thorns which give a painful stab or scratch that often swells and turns septic, so one should be careful when picking sloes, or cutting blackthorn for walking sticks.

The tree often flowers during a bout of cold, windy weather, following a mild spell which started the buds swelling, and country people refer to this as 'the blackthorn winter'. The hedgerows are such a wonderful sight of foaming, fragile whiteness when the blackthorn blossoms, that a coinciding wintry spell is tolerable with the promise of better things ahead.

The old herbalist, William Coles, claimed that the astringency of the fruit and bark of the 'Black-thorn or Sloe-Bush' was good for bleeding, diarrhoea, infected wounds and swellings and all sorts of 'gripings and gnawings in the stomach'. Robert Thornton wrote 'the inspissated(!) juice of the unripe fruit is very astringent and is called *Acacia Germanica*'. So this thick brew of unripe sloes must have been like a proprietary medicine in the 17th and 18th centuries.

The French physician, Dr. Losch, prescribed a tisane of blackthorn flowers as a mild laxative which acts gently 'but purges to the depths'. He also advised it as a blood purifier for children with skin eruptions. Losch said that sloes were used to give colour to inferior wines and that a brandy 'of exquisite taste' could be made by macerating sloe stones in the spirit. Sloe stones have been found in prehistoric Swiss lake dwellings; one can hardly imagine prehistoric man eating raw sloes, when not even the birds will touch them, and one wonders in what ways, medicinal or magical, the fruits may have been used so long ago.

WILD KISSEL WITH SLOES EARLY AUTUMN

Kissel is made with any red, or dark red summer fruits: raspberries, cherries or blackcurrants, either mixed together or by themselves. The juice was always thickened with arrowroot and should be sweet and well-flavoured. The dark, strongly flavoured little hedgerow fruits make a very good version of this traditional Austrian dish. You can omit the red wine, but it does improve the flavour.

SERVES 6
250 ml/1 cup/1/2 pint sloes
250 ml/1 cup/1/2 pint blackberries
500 ml/2 cups/1 pint elderberries
500 ml/2 cups/1 pint water
300 g/11/2 cups/3/4 lb sugar, or 6 tablespoons honey
1 orange
1 level tablespoon cornflour or arrowroot
3-4 tablespoons red wine
a little extra sugar

Wash the fruit and strip away all the stalks, put the mixed fruits into a large saucepan with water and sugar, or honey. Bring slowly to the boil and stir until the sugar or honey has melted, then cover and simmer gently for 10-15 minutes. Pour into a basin and stand until cold.

Pare the rind from the orange and squeeze out the juice. Mix the cornflour and strained orange juice together in a cup. Strain the juice from the stewed fruits into a saucepan, add the orange rind and wine and bring slowly to the boil. Add the slaked cornflour and stir constantly while the juice thickens and clears, then draw off the heat. Add the stewed fruits and pour into a bowl. Serve cool, but not chilled.

SLOE JELLY LATE AUTUMN

Wait until the sloes are really ripe towards the end of autumn. They make a lovely jelly the rich colour of port.

1.5 kilos/6 cups/3 lbs sloes
3/4 litre/33/4 cups/11/2 pints water
700 g/3 cups/11/2 lbs sugar to 600 ml/21/2 cups/1 pint juice

Wash the sloes and put them in a large saucepan with the water which should barely cover the sloes. Boil gently for about 20 minutes until the fruit is soft, mash occasionally with a wooden spoon to help the juice to run. Drip through a double thickness of muslin, or a jelly bag, overnight. Measure the juice into a saucepan, add the sugar and bring slowly to the boil, stirring

continuously until the sugar has dissolved, then boil fast for about 10-12 minutes until the liquid gels when dripped on to a saucer. Skim and pour into warm, dry jars. Cover with circles of waxed paper while hot, seal with cellophane circles when cold.

SLOE SYRUP LATE AUTUMN

Make sloe syrup in exactly the same way as sloe jelly, but boil the juice and sugar for 5 minutes only, skim, and bottle while still hot, cork or screw on the caps when cold. The syrup will keep in the refrigerator for months. Serve with ice cream or rice pudding. It makes a refreshing drink, 2 tablespoons to a tumbler of water, or soda water.

SIEVED SLOE AND APPLE JAM AUTUMN

By sieving the fruit you get rid of the numerous little sloe stones and the resulting jam has a nice smooth texture. It is easier to press the jam through a sieve, than to use a food mill, because the stones jam the mechanism.

MAKES 2 KILOS (4 LBS) JAM
500 g/2 cups/1 lb sloes
1 kilo/2 lbs cooking apples
water—see recipe
1.5 kilos/6 cups/3 lbs sugar

Wash the fruits and remove any stalks from the sloes. Cut up the apples roughly, it is not necessary to peel or remove the cores. Put the fruits together in a large pan with just enough water to stop them burning, bring slowly to the boil, cover and cook gently for 20 minutes. Rub the mixture through a coarse sieve and discard the sloe stones. Return the pulp to the pan, add the sugar, heat slowly and stir well until the sugar has dissolved, then boil fast in the open pan for 4-5 minutes, stirring frequently to prevent the jam sticking. Pour into warm dry jars, cover with waxed circles while hot, seal with cellophane covers when cold.

SLOE CHEESE AUTUMN

Old-fashioned fruit cheeses are rarely seen nowadays, but they are delicious and well worth making. A long, slow cook is necessary to achieve the thick consistency. Cheeses are set in small moulds or jars from which they can be turned out and sliced, for serving with cold ham and boiled bacon or with cheese, or for spreading on bread and butter. Damson cheese is a well known old-fashioned preserve, and sloes make an almost identical version.

BLACKTHORN – *PRUNUS SPINOSA*

750 g/3 cups/1¹⁄₂ lbs sloes
water—see recipe
sugar—see recipe
¹⁄₂ teaspoon cinnamon
¹⁄₄ teaspoon ground cloves

Wash the sloes and remove any twigs and leaves, a few little stalks don't matter. Put the sloes in a saucepan, cover with water, bring to the boil and cook slowly in the covered pan until very soft. Rub the fruit through a large nylon strainer or sieve.

Measure the pulp, it should be about 500 ml/2 cups/1 pint into a saucepan, stir in the cinnamon and cloves and add the sugar—450 g/2 cups/1 lb to each measure of pulp, bring slowly to the boil, stirring until the sugar has dissolved, then lower the heat to the slowest simmer, and if possible stand the pan on a wire gauze mat. Stir fairly often to stop the mixture sticking and keep simmering for 50 minutes-1 hour, until a clean line is momentarily left on the bottom of the pan when the spoon is drawn across, and the pulp is thick and creamy with no free liquid on the surface.

Smear the inside of some small pots or jars with glycerine, so that the cheese can be turned out when set, fill the jars with hot cheese and cover with a circle of waxed paper. Cover with cling film when cold.

SLOE GIN AUTUMN

This is a delicious old recipe which warms one to the marrow on a cold day. The original used sugar candy, hardly seen nowadays, it was sold in rough lumps of tawny-coloured unrefined sugar strung on a string, and was quite incredibly hard. We used to crunch it as children, amazingly without breaking every tooth in our heads. Demerara sugar can be used in its place.

1 kilo/4 cups/2 lbs sloes
1 litre/32 fl. oz U.S./1 quart gin
300 g/2¹⁄₄ cups/³⁄₄ lb demerara sugar
100 g/¹⁄₂ cup/¹⁄₂ lb white sugar

Pick the sloes when dry, remove the stalks and prick each sloe with a sharp silver fork, or a darning needle. Put the sloes in a large jug with the gin and all the sugar, and stir thoroughly with a wooden spoon, not all the sugar will dissolve in this process. Pour all the contents of the jug into a clean glass jar, or demi-john, cork with a new clean cork and leave in a cool room for 3 months, remembering to invert the jar to shake up the liquid every other day.

Then strain the sloe gin through a double thickness of muslin

until perfectly clear, it may be necessary to do this several times until it is really clear, and on no account squeeze out the sloes left behind in the muslin.

Pour into clean dry bottles and cork securely with new corks. Be patient, and wait a year before drinking this excellent liqueur.

SLOE WINE AUTUMN

This deep, ruby-red wine becomes quite full-bodied and mellow if left to mature, so try to wait a year at least, before opening the first bottle.

activated yeast (p. 255)
1.5 kilos/6 cups/3 lbs sloes
5 litres/9 quarts U.S./1 gallon water
1.5 kilos/6 cups/3 lbs sugar
250 g/1¹⁄₂ cups/8 oz chopped raisins

Wash the sloes and remove any large stalks, put them in a plastic bucket and pour on the boiling water, stir and mash with a wooden spoon, then add the sugar and chopped raisins, stirring until the sugar has dissolved. Cover the bucket with a clean cloth and leave until cool, (about 20°C, 70°F) then stir in the activated yeast. Cover the bucket with its lid and stand in a warm place for 10 days, stirring daily, Strain into the fermentation jar (dark glass for a red wine) and follow the method given on page 254.

CRYSTALLISED BLACKTHORN BLOSSOM

EARLY SPRING

Blackthorn blossom is edible, and the open flowers may be crystallised or sugared to preserve them by the same methods given for borage flowers on page 36. They become frosty-white, and any indomitable do-it-yourself Mum could use them to make enchanting wedding cake decorations for an early spring bride.

BLACKTHORN WALKING STICK WINTER

Treat exactly the same as hazel, see page 120. Blackthorn makes a particularly good thumb stick. It is very strong and, when polished, has a fine dark, rich shine.

SLOE MARKING INK AUTUMN

As well as providing drinks and preserves, sloe juice makes good marking ink. If you stab a pen nib into a raw sloe and write with the juice on handkerchiefs or linen, the red letters are indelible.

BOG MYRTLE
Myrica gale

SWEET GALE

og myrtle grows as a low bush, or shrub, from 15 cm or a few inches to 1½ metres /4 ft in height. It is found in bogs, fens and on damp moors, and is rare in England, except round the north-west coasts and in a few places in the New Forest, but in the west of Scotland and Ireland it is common and in places grows in great profusion. Bog myrtle used to be common in the Fen district, but drainage has reduced its habitat. The plant is found in similar places throughout Western Europe and Scandinavia, and in America from Labrador to Alaska and southwards to North Carolina.

The shrub is deciduous, with shiny, red-brown twigs and small, narrow-oval toothed leaves, darker green above, paler and grayish-green beneath and speckled with tiny, gummy spots, which are the resinous glands. Bog myrtle flowers in the spring, before the leaves appear, and has male and female flowers on separate plants; the long, orange-coloured, male catkins are stalkless and grow in crowded clusters, the female catkins are red, thicker and shorter than the male, and very closely set. When the plant is in flower, the air is scented with its lovely resinous smell.

Bog myrtle leaves were used for flavouring ale long before hops were brought to England, and were mentioned by Gerard and Turner in their herbals, Gerard saying Gale Beer was 'fit to make a man quickly drunk'! The dried leaves were used for scenting linen and to keep away fleas, one of the plant's country names is flea-wood, and in Sweden it was used as a flea-repellent. Another local name, candle-berries, comes from the old practice of boiling the catkin-bearing stems in water, and then skimming off the waxy substance which floated to the surface and was used as candle wax.

Bog myrtle has been put to many uses: the bark gave a yellow dye and was used for tanning leather, and the Swedes made a decoction of the leaves and used it to treat the itch and other skin irritations. In parts of France the peasants believed that decoctions of the leaves would bring on menstruation and even procure abortion, and in China an infusion of the leaves was drunk as a herbal remedy for stomach upsets. In many places the berries were dried and used as a spicy flavouring for soups and stews, a custom that is worth following today.

BOG MYRTLE AND LAMB STEW

SPRING, SUMMER, EARLY AUTUMN

Bog myrtle has a strong, aromatic taste, but is definitely bitter and should be used with discretion. It is complementary to lamb in the same way as rosemary, and when roasting a leg or shoulder of lamb you can insert small sprigs of bog myrtle into slits made in the meat with a sharp knife. Use about five or six sprigs for a 1.5 kilo/3 lb joint.

This stew is for summer time, but in the winter you can use the same recipe, substituting carrots and swedes/yellow turnips (U.S.) for the peas and white turnips.

750 g/1½ lbs boned shoulder of lamb,
   OR 1 kilo/2 lbs middle neck
2 tablespoons dripping
2 medium onions
2 or 3 small white turnips
¾ litre/3¾ cups/1½ pints stock
1 tablespoon dried bog myrtle leaves
1 kilo/4 cups/2 lbs fresh peas
2 teaspoons sugar, or 1 teaspoon honey
salt and pepper

Trim the fat and skin from the lamb and cut into neat pieces. Heat the dripping in a heavy-bottomed pan and brown the meat on each side. Peel and chop the onions and turnips and fry gently with the meat, add the stock, dried bog myrtle, and sugar or honey. Season with salt and pepper. Bring to the boil, cover the pan with a close-fitting lid and simmer gently for about 1 hour. Add the shelled peas and continue to cook for about 15 minutes, until the peas are tender.

BOG MYRTLE – *MYRICA GALE*

BORAGE

Borago officinalis

Borage is probably only truly native in the western Mediterranean, but can sometimes be found growing wild near houses or on waste ground in Britain, and is grown in gardens all over Europe, and North America, where it sometimes grows wild west of the Cascade Mountains in Oregon and Washington, and in Idaho, Montana, Utah, Wyoming, Colorado and North and South Dakota. It also occurs in scattered places in Nebraska and Kansas.

Borage is an annual, and if left alone will seed itself and come up every year in the same place. It is a stout and hairy plant, growing 1-1¼ metres/3-4 ft tall with hollow, juicy stems. The alternate leaves are large, wrinkled and pointed-oval in shape, the lower leaves are stalked. All the leaves have hairy upper surfaces and prominent veins on the undersides, which are covered with little prickly hairs. The flowering season is long, from early summer until well into the autumn, and the flowers, which grow in loose spikes, are the plant's real beauty. They are star-shaped and a vivid blue, occasionally mauve or pink, but usually a true azure, shading to white in the centre from which a cone of dark stamens stands out prominently; alternating with the five blue petals are the almost black calyx teeth. The whole design and colour scheme is so extraordinarily elegant that one realises why John Parkinson wrote in his 17th century herbal, 'they have alwaies been enterposed among the flowers of womens' needle-work.'

Most of the old herbalists agreed with Pliny's claim that borage makes one happy. Gerard wrote 'it maketh a man merry and joyful', adding that it would exhilarate the mind and drive away sorrow, sadness and dullness. Coles said the leaves, flowers and seeds of borage were 'very cordiall, and helpe to expell sadnesse and melancholy', and he launched into a long inventory of diseases to be treated with borage from fevers, jaundice, itch, ring-worm, scabs, sores, consumption, swooning, inflamed eyes, ulcers in the mouth and throat, the falling sickness and passions of the heart, to which, if it were not enough, he added that it would help 'to resist and expell the poyson, or the venome of other Creatures'.

John Evelyn, the famous 17th century diarist, recommended borage sprigs in wine 'to receive the hypochondriac and cheer the hard student'. However, Sir John Hill disagrees with all the other authorities and sounds the one disparaging note, 'borage has the credit of being a great cordial; but if it possesses any such virtues, they are to be obtained only by a light cold infusion; so that the way of throwing it into cold wine is better than all the medicinal preparations, *for in them it is nauseous*'.

Being spared the medicines, we can still follow the delicious practice of 'throwing it into cold wine' or rather into a jug of chilled Pimm's.

BORAGE – *BORAGO OFFICINALIS*

BORAGE WITH COTTAGE CHEESE

EARLY SUMMER—AUTUMN

The tips and leaves of borage are succulent and cucumbery and make a nice slimming lunch with cottage cheese and crispbread. The garnish of heavenly blue flowers takes some of the anguish out of dieting—the old herbalists assure us that borage 'doth cure melancholy'!

6-8 young borage leaves
a few blue borage flowers
1 small carton cottage cheese
freshly milled black pepper

Wash the leaves, dry them, then slice or chop finely. Lift the blue flowers from the hairy calyx. Turn the cottage cheese into a small bowl and mix with a good grinding of black pepper. Stir in the chopped leaves and arrange the flowers on top in a circle, with one in the centre.

BORAGE FLOWER SYRUP EARLY SUMMER—AUTUMN

This is a pleasantly flavoured light syrup which you can add to fruit salads or compotes. It is also a refreshing pick-me-up when you are tired, a tablespoonful at a time.

1ST DAY
1 cup borage flowers
boiling water to cover

2ND DAY
1 cup fresh borage flowers
sugar—see recipe

Put the flowers, including the hairy green calyx, into a small bowl. Pour over enough boiling water to cover the flowers, cover the bowl with a cloth and leave to steep overnight.

Next day pick fresh flowers—borage produces a new batch every day—strain the liquid from the first lot of flowers into a small pan, bring to the boil and pour into a bowl containing the freshly picked flowers. Cover and leave to steep for 8-10 hours.

Strain, pressing out all the juices from the flowers with a wooden spoon, and measure the liquid into a saucepan. Add an equal quantity of sugar (200 g to 250 ml/1 cup to 1 1/4 cups/ 1/2 lb to 1/2 pint). Heat slowly and stir until the sugar has dissolved, then boil fast for 5 minutes. Skim, and when cold pour into a bottle with a screw-on cap. Store in a cool place.

DRIED BORAGE TEA

When dried, the flowers retain much of their glorious blue and make a greeny blue infusion which has a fresh tea-like flavour.

1 teaspoon dried borage flowers
250 ml/1 cup/1/2 pint boiling water

Put the flowers in a warmed jug. Pour on the boiling water, cover and infuse for 10 minutes. Strain into a cup and drink hot, or iced with a dash of lemon juice.

Fresh borage does not make good tea.

TO DRY BORAGE FLOWERS

EARLY SUMMER—AUTUMN

Pick the flowers in dry weather and leave them on the calyx. Spread the flowers on a sieve and dry in an airing cupboard or boiler room for two or three days, or in a cool oven for two or three hours until they are brittle. Store in an airtight jar away from the light.

SUGARED BORAGE FLOWERS

EARLY SUMMER—AUTUMN

The glorious blue of borage flowers preserves well. They make beautiful decorations for cakes and desserts. An easy way of preserving flowers is to paint them with a white-of-egg wash and sprinkle with sugar before drying.

borage flowers
1 egg white
1 tablespoon water
granulated (U.S.)/caster sugar
a fine water colour paint brush

Put the egg white and water in a cup and stir with a fork to mix lightly. Paint each side of the flower very thinly with the egg and water wash, it is important not to use too much. Sprinkle each flower lightly with sugar, and dry them on a sieve. Store in a tin or jar between layers of waxed or greaseproof paper to protect them.

BORAGE FLOWERS IN ICE CUBES

EARLY SUMMER—AUTUMN

Bright blue borage flowers look enchantingly pretty frozen into ice cubes for summer drinks.

BRAMBLE

Rubus fruticosus

BLACKBERRY

The bramble flourishes in most parts of the Old World and the New, and is so tough and adaptable that, as every gardener knows, it will grow from a crack between stones. In America, the bramble is also known as brombeere and fingerberry.

There are many species and sub-species, the flowers all have five petals, varying from deep mauve-pink to white; they first appear in early summer, followed by hard green berries which ripen at the end of summer, turning first red, then shining black when they are sweet and juicy. Often there are green, red and ripe blackberries on the same stem at the same time, the largest and sweetest is the one at the tip, which ripens first. The fruit of some plants is large and luscious, that of others is hard and has more pips than flesh, but by mid-autumn all the berries have turned watery and tasteless.

The leaves consist of three or five large leaflets, broad at the base and tapering to a point, with toothed edges and small prickles on the undersides. They are grayish underneath, and when a summer wind ruffles the leaves, a hedgerow of brambles is like rippling silver. In the autumn, the leaves turn wonderful shades of crimson and wine-red, and remain until the next year's leaves appear.

The plant grows fast, throwing out strong, thorn-clad stems which bend over as their length quickly increases; where these stems touch the ground they put out little roots from which fresh stems grow; which is why a bramble thicket turns to something like Sleeping Beauty's forest in next to no time.

In many parts of England country folk believed in the curative and magic powers of the prickly, arching stems. In Cornwall, a person suffering from boils, would crawl, or be dragged through the bramble hoops, a remedy that would seem to be nearly as painful as the affliction; in Gloucestershire they believed that a ruptured baby would be healed if passed beneath the arching stems, and in many places it was thought that rheumatism would be cured by crawling beneath the brambles. One cannot help thinking that if you had the suppleness and agility to follow that treatment, you were not much in need of the cure.

Brambles were used in ancient Greece as a remedy for gout, and in the sixteenth century Gerard recommended decoctions of the leaves, roots and stems for loose teeth, piles, sore throats, sore mouths, diarrhoea and 'eies that hang out'. Many of the early herbalists recommended the leaves as a dressing for swellings, burns and scalds, and the buds of the bramble leaves boiled in spring water and sweetened with honey for a sore throat, which was cooling and astringent.

Evidence that blackberries were eaten in England in Neolithic times came to light when the well-preserved body of a Stone Age man was dug out of the clay on the Essex coast, and blackberry pips were found in the contents of the stomach. As one reaches through the thorns to gather blackberries, it gives one a strange feeling to think that four thousand years ago our ancestors were risking the same scratches for the same reward.

BRAMBLE – *RUBUS FRUTICOSUS*

BLACKBERRY SORBET LATE SUMMER, EARLY AUTUMN

Both these blackberry ices are best if you transfer them from the freezer to the main part of the refrigerator about half an hour before you are ready to serve them. The sorbet is deeper in colour than the ice cream, but both are so utterly delicious that one wouldn't know which to choose. For a party you could serve both, and everyone will unfailingly want both.

500 ml/2 cups/1 pint purée of ripe, sieved blackberries
juice of 1/2 lemon
225 g/1 cup/1/2 lb granulated sugar, or honey
1/8 litre/2/3 cup/1/4 pint water
1/8 litre/2/3 cup/1/4 pint thick cream

Press the blackberries through a fine sieve or food mill, add the strained lemon juice and set aside. Put the sugar and water into a saucepan, bring to the boil and stir until the sugar or honey dissolves, then boil fast for 3 minutes; when cool add the syrup to the blackberries. Lightly whip the cream, stirring a little milk into the carton if it is very thick, and fold this into the blackberry mixture. Pour into plastic containers and cover with a lid or kitchen foil. Freeze until slushy, turn out into a bowl and beat up with a wooden spoon, then return mixture to the containers and freeze until firm. A food processor beats out the ice crystals in a minute.

BLACKBERRY ICE CREAM

LATE SUMMER, EARLY AUTUMN

750 g/41/2 cups/11/2 lbs ripe blackberries
250 g/11/2 cups/8 oz icing sugar/(U.S. confectioners' sugar)
juice of 1/2 lemon
250 ml/1 cup/1/2 pint thick cream

Press the blackberries through a fine sieve or food mill, you can liquidise them but a sieve will remove the pips. Add the sugar and strained lemon juice to the blackberry purée. Lightly whip the cream, and fold into the blackberry mixture. Pour into plastic containers and cover with a lid or kitchen foil. Freeze until slushy and then turn out into a bowl and beat up with a wooden spoon until smooth and creamy. Return to the containers and freeze until firm. Use a food processor to beat out the ice crystals.

BLACKBERRY MOUSSE LATE SUMMER, EARLY AUTUMN

When blackberries are plentiful one should use them in every possible way, from homely preserves and pies to more sophisticated desserts, like this mousse.

500 g/3 cups/1 lb blackberries
125 g/1/2 cup/4 oz sugar
juice of 1 lemon
3 tablespoons/4 tablespoons/3 tablespoons water
15 g/3 teaspoons/1/2 oz powdered gelatine
150 ml/1/3 cup/1/4 pint thick cream
2 egg whites

Wash the blackberries if dusty, drain and cook gently with the sugar and strained lemon juice for about 5 minutes, until the berries are quite soft. Measure the water into a small bowl, sprinkle in the gelatine and set aside to soak for 5 minutes.

Draw the pan of blackberries off the heat, add the soaked gelatine and stir until dissolved. Rub the fruit and juice through a fine sieve or food mill and discard the pips. Leave the purée until it is cold and just starting to set.

Lightly whip the cream and fold into the blackberry purée. Then whisk the egg whites stiffly and fold them into the mixture with a metal spoon. Turn into a glass dish and chill until firm.

SPICED BLACKBERRY CRUMBLE

LATE SUMMER, EARLY AUTUMN

Served hot or cold with plenty of lightly whipped cream, blackberries with a dash of cinnamon, make a good and unusual crumble.

SERVES 4

1 kilo/6 cups/2 lbs blackberries
50 g/3 tablespoons/2 oz sugar
1/2 teaspoon ground cinnamon
CRUMBLE
150 g/21/2 cups/6 oz plain flour
100 g/1/2 cup/4 oz butter
4-5 tablespoons demerara sugar

Pick over the blackberries, wash them if necessary and put them in a buttered ovenproof dish. Mix the sugar and cinnamon together and sprinkle over the berries.

Sift the flour into a bowl, cut the butter into pieces and rub into the flour, then rub the sugar into the mixture until it resembles breadcrumbs. Sprinkle over the blackberries and spread level. Bake in the centre of a hot oven (400°F, 200°C, or Gas 6) for 30-35 minutes until the top is firm and golden.

WILD BLACKBERRY COBBLER EARLY AUTUMN

This is an early American recipe which makes a lovely pudding when the evening air has an autumnal nip. The bubbling hot berries with a sweet batter crust are a luscious combination.

500 g/3 cups/1 lb blackberries
200 g/1 cup/8 oz sugar
1 tablespoon lemon juice
butter—see recipe
100 g/1 cup/4 oz plain flour
2 level teaspoons baking powder
1/2 level teaspoon salt
1 medium egg
4-5 tablespoons milk
50 g/4 tablespoons/2 oz melted butter

Mix the blackberries with 150 g/3/4 cup/6 oz of the sugar and the lemon juice and put the mixture into a pie dish with a few flakes of butter dotted over the top. Set aside.

Make the batter by sifting the flour, baking powder and salt on to a piece of greaseproof paper. Break the egg into a bowl, stir in the remaining sugar and beat thoroughly with a wooden spoon. Then add the milk and melted butter and stir together. Tip in a little of the sifted ingredients and beat well, then add the rest and continue to beat until the batter is smooth. Pour the batter over the blackberries and bake in a moderate oven (350°F/180°C/Gas 4) for 30-35 minutes, until the top is golden brown. Serve piping hot with plenty of chilled whipped cream.

BLACKBERRY AND ELDERBERRY JAM

LATE SUMMER

The combined berries make a jam that is full of flavour, with a hint of smoky sweetness from the elderberries. It is particularly good as a filling for little jam tarts or spread on hot brown toast when the weather is cold, and reminds you of the late days of summer when you went foraging and returned with stains, scratches, and a full basket. The elderberries should be really ripe. They turn almost black, the branches droop downwards, and even the little stalks on which the berries grow have turned from green to dark red or purple.

1.5 kilos/9 cups/3 lbs blackberries
1.5 kilos/9 cups/3 lbs elderberries, stripped from their stalks
sugar—see method

Wash the fruit and strip the elderberries from their stalks through the prongs of a fork. Weigh your saucepan while empty, then tip the berries into the pan and cook slowly for 20 minutes, mashing occasionally with a wooden spoon to help the juice to run. Weigh the pan of fruit, subtracting the weight of the empty pan, and to each 450 g/3 cups/1 lb of fruit add 350 g/11/2 cups/3/4 lb of sugar, bring slowly to the boil, stirring until the sugar has dissolved. Cook steadily for about 10-15 minutes until the jam has thickened. Keep well stirred to prevent scorching during cooking. Pour into warm dry jars, cover with circles of waxed paper while hot, seal with cellophane covers when cold.

SIEVED BLACKBERRY AND APPLE JAM

EARLY AUTUMN

You can make this jam with blackberries alone if, in place of the apples, you add the juice of 1 lemon when you start to boil the pulp and sugar together. Sieving the fruit gives a nice smooth texture for people who dislike blackberry pips. Choose sound berries that are not over-ripe, and green apples, for a good set.

750 g/41/2 cups/11/2 lbs blackberries
3-4 tablespoons water
2 medium cooking apples
sugar—see method

Remove any stalks and wash the blackberries if necessary. Put them in a large saucepan with the water and start to cook slowly. Meanwhile cut the apples into quarters and remove the cores, but do not peel, then slice the quarters into the pan of blackberries, cover and cook gently until all the fruit is soft, mashing well together with a wooden spoon. Rub through a sieve or food mill and weigh the pulp. Return the pulp to the pan with an equal quantity of sugar, bring slowly to the boil, stirring until all the sugar has melted, then boil fast in the uncovered pan for about 5 minutes until the mixture sets softly when dripped on to a cold saucer. Pour into warm dry jars, cover with waxed circles while hot, seal with cellophane covers when cold.

BLACKBERRY AND SLOE JELLY EARLY AUTUMN

You can vary the proportions of sloes and blackberries according to which fruit is most plentiful that season, but use rather less sloes then blackberries, as the former have a stronger taste and tend to overpower the blackberry flavour. The jelly is good with scones.

1.5 kilos/12 cups/4 lbs blackberries
750 g/3 cups/11/2 lbs sloes

1 litre/5 cups/2 pints water
sugar—see method

Remove any stalks from the fruit and wash if dusty. Put the sloes and blackberries into a large pan with the water. Bring to the boil and cook gently for 20 minutes until the fruit is soft, mash with a wooden spoon occasionally to help the juice to run. Remove from the heat and drip through a double thickness of muslin, or a jelly bag for 3-4 hours, or overnight if more convenient. Measure the juice into a large pan and to each 500 ml/2 cups/1 pint add 400 g/2 cups/1 lb sugar. Bring slowly to the boil stirring continuously to dissolve the sugar, then boil fast for about ten minutes until the liquid gels when dripped on to a cold saucer. Skim, and pour into warm, dry jars, cover with circles of waxed paper while still hot, and seal with cellophane covers when cold.

BRAMBLE JELLY LATE SUMMER

Choose sound, rather under-ripe fruit, as blackberries that are soft and over-ripe make a jelly that lacks flavour and tends not to set well. For the best flavour and colour the cooked fruit should only take an hour to drip and the final boiling should only take 5-7 minutes. You will find this makes an exceptionally fresh tasting jelly.

2 kilos/8 cups/4 lbs blackberries
375 ml/scant 2 cups/3/4 pint water
juice of 2 lemons
sugar—see method

Wash the berries and put them in a large saucepan with the water. Cover the pan and cook gently until the berries are soft, about 15 minutes, mashing once or twice with a wooden spoon. Tip the cooked berries into a scalded jelly bag or double thickness of muslin, and hang up to drip for 1 hour.

Measure the juice into a large saucepan and add 400 g/2 cups/1 lb sugar for each 500 ml/2 cups/1 pint, add the strained lemon juice and heat slowly stirring continuously until all the sugar has dissolved, then boil hard for 5-7 minutes until the liquid gels when dripped on to a cold saucer. Skim and pour into warm, dry jars, cover with waxed circles while hot, and seal with cellophane covers when cold.

SPICED BRAMBLE JELLY LATE SUMMER, EARLY AUTUMN

The vinegar and spices in this recipe liven up the mellow flavour of blackberries and make a sweet-sharp jelly to eat with all cold meat and poultry.

1 kilo/6 cups/2 lbs blackberries
1 teaspoon ground ginger
1/2 teaspoon cinnamon
sugar—see method
1/2 teaspoon ground cloves
8 tablespoons/10 tablespoons/8 tablespoons cider vinegar

Wash the blackberries and put them in a large saucepan with the spices and vinegar. Heat slowly and cook for about 10 minutes until the berries are soft, mashing with a wooden spoon occasionally to help the juice to run. Drip through a jelly bag or double thickness of muslin for a few hours, or overnight if more convenient. Measure the juice and to each 500 ml/2 cups/1 pint add 400 g/2 cups/1 lb sugar. Heat together in a large pan, stirring continuously until the sugar has dissolved, then boil fast in the open pan for 3-4 minutes, until the liquid gels when dripped on to a cold saucer, skim and pour into warm dry jars, cover with waxed circles while hot, seal with cellophane covers when cold.

SPICED BLACKBERRY PICKLE

LATE SUMMER, EARLY AUTUMN

This pickle is especially good with cold chicken, cold turkey or any game.

500 ml/2 cups/1 pint blackberries
250 ml/1 cup/1/2 pint white vinegar
1 teaspoon ground ginger
1/2 teaspoon ground cinnamon
1/4 teaspoon ground cloves
1/4 teaspoon allspice
1 bay leaf
1 blade mace (or small pinch ground mace)
250 g/1 cup/8 oz sugar

Soak the blackberries in the vinegar overnight with all the spices, but keep back the sugar. Next day strain the spiced vinegar into a saucepan, reserve the fruit, but take out the bay leaf and the mace, if using whole mace. Boil up the vinegar for 5 minutes, then add the sugar, stirring until it dissolves, and then boil steadily for a further 5 minutes. Add the blackberries, lower the heat and simmer gently for 5 minutes more.

Lift the blackberries out with a slotted spoon and put them into clean jars. Boil up the liquid in the pan until it is syrupy and reduced a little, then skim and pour over the blackberries. Cover with waxed circles while hot, seal with cellophane covers when cold.

BLACKBERRY CHUTNEY LATE SUMMER, EARLY AUTUMN

This chutney particularly enlivens cold chicken or ham, it also improves a ham sandwich if spread thinly over one slice of the bread.

1.5 kilos/9 cups/3 lbs blackberries
500 g/1 lb cooking apples
500 g/1lb onions
1 litre/5 cups/2 pints malt vinegar
15 g/1 teaspoon/$1/2$ oz salt
15 g/1 teaspoon/$1/2$ oz dry mustard powder
15 g/1 teaspoon/$1/2$ oz ground ginger
1 teaspoon ground mace
$1/4$ teaspoon cayenne
500 g/$2^{1}/4$ cups/1 lb brown sugar

Wash the blackberries and remove any stalks, peel and chop the apples and onions and put them in a large saucepan with the vinegar, salt and spices. Bring to the boil, stir with a wooden spoon, cover the pan and cook gently for 1 hour. Rub the mixture through a fine sieve or food mill, return to the pan, add the sugar and heat slowly, stirring until all the sugar has dissolved. Bring to the boil and cook uncovered in the pan for about 15 minutes until the chutney is thick. Pour into warm dry jars, cover with waxed circles while hot, seal with cellophane covers when cold.

BLACKBERRY SYRUP LATE SUMMER, EARLY AUTUMN

The syrup will store for several months in the refrigerator. As a hot weather drink it is delicious diluted with water, with ice cubes and a squeeze of lemon juice added. For chilly nights, or if you have a cold, drink plenty of the syrup with a slice of lemon and boiling water. As with most wild fruit syrups, it greatly enlivens vanilla ice cream and any pudding with a bland taste that requires the sweet tang of fruit.

500 g/3 cups/1 lb blackberries
500 g/2 cups/1 lb sugar
2-3 tablespoons water

Put the blackberries and water into a jar with a loose lid, or a jug with a saucer to cover it. Pour half the quantity of sugar on to the fruit. Stand the jar or jug in a saucepan of hot water, bring to the boil, and simmer for $1^{1}/2$ hours. Strain the contents into a saucepan, pressing out all the juice with the back of a wooden spoon. Add the rest of the sugar to the pan, bring to the boil, and stir until the sugar has dissolved, then boil steadily for 5-6 minutes. Skim carefully and allow to cool a little, then pour into clean bottles. Cork, or screw on the tops when cold.

BLACKBERRY CORDIAL LATE SUMMER, EARLY AUTUMN

This thick sweet syrup is spiced with cinnamon and cloves and fortified with brandy. It makes a marvellous warming bed-time drink which is soothing and sleep-inducing. Put 2 or 3 tablespoons of cordial in a mug and top up with boiling water.

The cordial is also delicious with plain or apple yoghurt, and a steamed apple pudding is made special by putting 2 tablespoons of the cordial into the bottom of the bowl before lining it with a dough made with flour and finely chopped suet. Pour a little more cordial over the top of the pudding after it has steamed, and has been turned out of its bowl for a wonderful mingling of flavours, apple and blackberry, cinnamon, cloves and brandy.

500 ml/2 cups/1 pint blackberry juice
500 g/2 cups/1 lb sugar or 6 tablespoons honey
8 cloves
1 teaspoon cinnamon
6-8 tablespoons brandy

Rub raw ripe blackberries through a fine sieve or food mill. Measure the juice into a saucepan with the sugar, or honey, and the spices. Bring slowly to the boil, stirring until the sugar or honey has melted, then boil gently for 5 minutes and remove the cloves. When cool stir in the brandy. Bottle when cold.

BLACKBERRY VINEGAR LATE SUMMER, EARLY AUTUMN

Fruit vinegars were once an important item of the still room, they were taken as refreshing drinks during fever and as unfailing thirst quenchers. Two teaspoons diluted in a tumbler of water make a refreshing drink when you feel the prickly throat symptoms at the onslaught of a cold, or on a hot day the same drink, with a few ice cubes, is wonderfully bracing and thirst-quenching and children love it. Wild raspberries and redcurrants can be made into vinegars in exactly the same ways as, of course, can the garden varieties.

MAKES 250 ML, $2^{1}/2$ CUPS, 1 PINT

500 g/3 cups/1 lb blackberries
cider vinegar—see recipe
sugar—see recipe

Remove the stalks from the blackberries and put them in a china or earthenware dish so they lie only 2¹/₂-5 cm/1-2 ins deep. Pour on enough cider vinegar to cover the berries, then cover the dish with a plate and leave to stand for three days.

Drip the berries through a strainer for 12 hours, then measure the juice into a saucepan and add 200 g/1 cup/¹/₂ lb sugar to 250 ml/1¹/₄ cups/¹/₂ pint juice. Bring to the boil, stirring until the sugar has dissolved, simmer gently for 5 minutes, then skim and bottle when cold.

BLACKBERRY LIQUEUR

Rich and fruity, this warming liqueur, made when blackberries are plentiful will keep for years, but it is lovely to drink at all stages.

1 kilo/6 cups/2 lbs blackberries
1 litre/5 cups/2 pints vodka
250 g/1 cup/8 oz granulated sugar

Pick the blackberries on a dry day and remove any stalks, then follow the method given for Sloe Gin on page 31 but without pricking the berries.

BLACKBERRY WINE LATE SUMMER, EARLY AUTUMN

Blackberries make one of the best country wines, with a full, fruity flavour, and a marvellously rich, deep red colour.

activated yeast (p. 255)
2 kilos/12 cups/4 lbs blackberries
5 litres/18 U.S. pints/1 gallon water
pectic enzyme—sold for wine making
1.5 kilos/6 cups/3 lbs sugar

Blackberries need pectic enzyme which is sold in shops that stock wine-making equipment, and has instructions on the packet for using with 5 litres (18 U.S. pints, 1 gallon) wine.

Wash the blackberries and remove any stalks, put them into the plastic bucket and crush with a wooden spoon. Pour on the boiling water, stir well, cover with a clean cloth and allow to cool, (about 70°F, 20°C) then add the pectic enzyme. Cover the bucket with its lid and stand for 24 hours, then stir in the activated yeast, cover again with the lid and allow to stand in a warm place for four days, stirring daily. Strain the liquid through a double thickness of muslin into a large bowl, or divide between two bowls, add the sugar, stirring until the sugar has dissolved. Pour into the fermentation jar (dark glass for a red wine) and follow the method given on page 254.

BROOKLIME
Veronica beccabunga

Brooklime is found growing in wet places all over Britain and Scandinavia and throughout Europe. The European species is occasionally found in the United States, but the very similar American brooklime, *Veronica americana*, is their true native, and is widely distributed from Newfoundland to Alaska, and southwards to North Carolina, Tennessee, Missouri, Nebraska, Mexico and California. It flourishes in all wet and swampy places, in streams and ditches and by the margins of ponds. Probably the first thing to draw your attention to the plant will be its small but intensely blue flowers, which appear throughout the summer and grow in opposite pairs from the angles of the leaves; occasionally a form with pink flowers can be found. The oval, toothed leaves are shiny and rather fleshy and thick, they grow in opposite pairs up the smooth fat stems. The plant spreads quickly from these succulent stems, which creep through water and damp undergrowth, throwing out little clumps of roots at intervals.

In the Middle Ages brooklime was used for treating gout, and for a long time it was valued as a diuretic and anti-scorbutic. A 'spring drink' was made from infusions of brooklime and scurvy grass with the juice of Seville oranges, and taken to prevent scurvy and to tone and purify the blood. In the 18th century, Sir John Hill wrote 'brook lime has great virtues, but must be used fresh gathered, for they are lost in drying, the juice in Spring is very good against the scurvy', and in his *Family Herbal*, Thornton observed 'the juice is said neither to turn sour or putrid by keeping and can only be esteemed as a mild refrigerant' (reducing fever through perspiration). The fresh leaves were applied to cuts and burns, probably their cool dampness was found to be soothing.

BROOKLIME FOR SALADS SUMMER

Brooklime makes good sandwiches and is an excellent addition to salads. Pick several stems of brooklime and soak in three or four changes of fresh water. Shake dry, and pick the leaves from the stems. Use them whole in a mixed salad with a good vinaigrette dressing.

BROOKLIME SANDWICHES SUMMER

Pick and prepare as in the previous recipe, then slice the leaves into shreds and fill slices of buttered wholemeal bread, add a few snipped chives and a little salt and pepper, before closing as a sandwich.

BROOKLIME – *VERONICA BECCABUNGA*

BROOM
Cytisus scoparius

B room buds may be pickled in exactly the same way as gorse buds, see page 106, but amateur botanists take care to pick our native broom, *Cytisus scoparius*, which also grows throughout Europe and Scandinavia and flowers in late spring, and not the poisonous Spanish broom, *Spartium junceum*, which flowers much later in the summer, and has differences of leaf, twig and flower described in all good field guides. There is an American *Cytisus*, the Turpentine Broom, which grows on desert slopes from New Mexico and California, southwards to Mexico and northwards to Utah. As the name suggests, it smells of turpentine, and was used medicinally by the Indians.

BURDOCK

GREATER BURDOCK *Arctium lappa* LESSER BURDOCK *A. minus*

T he burdocks are widespread throughout Europe and are common in England, though less so in Scotland. The plants were introduced into America from the old world, and have become established on waste ground throughout the United States, where the lesser burdock is more common there than the greater; but both are widespread throughout America.

Burdocks are well known for the large prickly burrs which, in autumn, catch on to clothes and animals' fur. In summer the tall, stiff plant has showy, oval, thistle-like purple flower heads growing at the end of the branching stems and from the angles of the large leaves; but it is in the spring, when the stems are tender and good to eat, that you should look for the big, heart-shaped flannelly leaves that are very distinctive. Young burdock grows from the ground rather like rhubarb, but its leaves and stems are smaller, grey-green above, and mealy white beneath and covered with soft, flannelly down. They appear at the same time and often in the same place as the leaves of the Wild Arum, or Lords and Ladies, which is a poisonous plant; but the latter's leaves are vivid green and shiny, sometimes spotted, and although not unlike the shape of young burdock leaves, you cannot confuse them if you look for the grey-green colour and flannelly texture of burdock's large leaves, each growing from the root on a separate stem. Foxglove, another poisonous plant, is grey-green and downy, but the leaves grow from the main stem, not on separate stalks.

A decoction of the dried root is diuretic and promotes perspiration in fevers, and in World War II, the County Herb Committees organised the collection of many plants, including burdock. The roots, leaves and seeds of burdock all played a part in early medicine. In the Middle Ages leprosy was treated with burdock; later, decoctions of the roots and leaves were used for such varied ailments as eczema, boils, indigestion, scurvy, rheumatism and hysteria; the leaves were applied as cooling dressings to ulcers, bruises and tumours, and Culpeper produced a long list of complaints which would be eased by burdock. None of them, however, were more spectacular than his claim that 'by its leaf or seed you may draw the womb which way you please, either upward by applying it to the crown of the head in case it falls out; or downward in fits of the mother, by applying it to the soles of the feet: or if you would stay it in its place apply it to the navel, and that is one good way to stay the child in it'! Culpeper believed that every plant was under the influence of one, or more, of the planets, and for burdock he claimed that 'Venus Challengeth this herb for her own. See more of it in my Guide for Women.'

BURDOCK STEMS SPRING

The stems have a very mild flavour, with perhaps a trace of celery. They are an attractive, vivid green and should be cooked briefly, otherwise this colour is lost and they become yellowish. Pick the stems when they are still young, and tender enough to cook quickly.

They do stain your hands when raw, so wear rubber gloves when preparing them.

SERVES 4

a bundle of stems you can hold in two hands
salt and pepper
butter

Cut the stems close to the ground, and cut off and throw away the large, flannelly leaves.

Peel, or scrape with a knife the grayish skin which covers the juicy, bright green stems, they will be about the thickness of a pencil; drop the stems into cold water, and change the water 2 or 3 times as it becomes discoloured. Cook the stems in a large pan of boiling, salted water for 5-6 minutes, until tender. Drain well, and serve on a hot dish with some melted butter and plenty of freshly milled black pepper.

Burdock stems are good served cold in a vinaigrette dressing or as an addition to any mixed green salad.

STIR-FRY WITH BURDOCK STEMS SPRING

A grandson, who shares my passion for wild food, gave me this recipe. It is as easy as it is good. The quantities are for two people. If you double the recipe it is best to cook it in two batches, unless you are using a wok, or a very large frying pan.

175 g /1½ cups /6 oz prawns—fresh or frozen
1 large green pepper
6 spring onions
handful of mange tout, or sugar snap peas
1 small red chilli
8 young burdock stems
1 clove garlic
3 tablespoons sesame oil
salt

Prepare all the ingredients before starting to cook. If using frozen prawns, defrost according to the packet. Halve and de-seed the pepper and cut into thin strips. Trim the spring onions, leaving on some of the green, and slice finely. Top and tail the mange tout. De-seed the chilli and cut into fine pieces. Scrape the skin from the burdock stems with a sharp knife and cut them into 2 ½ cm / 1 inch lengths. Peel and crush the garlic.

Heat the oil in a large frying pan, or wok, and when just starting to smoke, lower the heat very slightly and add the prawns and all the prepared vegetables. Stir together for 2 or 3 minutes until the vegetables are just starting to 'give', but are still very crisp. Add a good pinch of salt and serve straight from the pan.

BURDOCK – *ARCTIUM LAPPA, A. MINUS*

CARRAGHEEN

Chondrus crispus

IRISH MOSS

Carragheen is found growing abundantly in pools and rocks uncovered at low tide on the Atlantic coasts of Europe and North America and occurs on the English Channel and North Sea coasts of Britain and Europe, but is rare in the Baltic. It grows profusely in clusters of short, flat fronds, 5-15 cm/2-6 ins long that branch out into fan shapes from the flat central stem which is attached to the rocks by a disc-shaped holdfast. The colour varies from purplish- to yellowish-brown, and in pools the fronds often have an opalescent purplish sheen. The seaweed is full of mucilage and can be used either fresh or dried for making blancmanges and jellies and for thickening soups and making face creams. It was used in many ways by the fisher folk of the western coasts and islands of Scotland.

Carragheen jelly was taken as a demulcent medicine for coughs and peptic ulcers, and still has many uses in modern medicine, as a basis for medicated jellies and as an emulsifying agent for cod liver and other oils, and as a substitute for gelatine in invalids' jellies. When penicillin was newly discovered it was grown as a culture on agar-agar jelly which had to be imported from Japan and, for obvious reasons, this source dried up in the last war, when penicillin was still very much the new wonder drug. It was discovered that *Chondrus crispus* and *Gigartina stellata*, a closely related seaweed which grows at the lowest tide levels, provided a jelly which was suitable for producing penicillin; so the County Herb Committees organised parties of volunteers to gather the seaweeds, and I was lucky enough to be working where some of the collections were made. I have read since that the seaweed was collected under considerable difficulties from the rocky, storm-swept Atlantic coasts, but I must confess that it was one of the greatest larks of the war. It invariably occurred during a weekend of idyllic summer weather, one's fellow gatherers were a marvellous gang of friends, school children and servicemen on leave. One waded and splashed across the rocks that were revealed at low tide, and had a huge picnic when the tide came in. After two or three hours of grubbing in seaweed and salt water, even my farm-grimed hands were freshly laundered and free of stains. At the end of the day the Navy produced a couple of open boats and our heavy, bulging sacks were taken off the beaches by grinning sailors who enjoyed the whole thing as much as we did. In the summer of 1944 many tons of seaweed were collected, it was before people were as conservation-minded, and we were picking for penicillin, and ruthlessly dragged up the seaweed by the handful. Now that we have learned to have more respect for plants we should always cut seaweeds above the root, which is not a true root but a holdfast, and leave a section of the stem from which the plants can regenerate.

CARRAGHEEN – *CHONDRUS CRISPUS*

TO DRY CARRAGHEEN SPRING AND SUMMER

Pick a fairly large quantity of carragheen, as it shrinks when dried and, being very light, 25 g/1 oz of weed is quite a lot in bulk. About two normal-sized carrier bags full is a rough guide, and they are useful things to cart about over rocks and boulders. When you take the carragheen home, wash it thoroughly in fresh water to remove any pebbles or sand and then put the weed to bleach outdoors on a large piece of muslin or old sheet, spread on the grass.

All the information I had was from books which said to spread the weed on grass or on a wind-free surface out of doors. The latter is impossible to arrange since the weed takes 7-14 days to bleach, and as it grows lighter even a breeze will scatter it. Grass is a suitable surface as the seaweed clings to it, but after one day I found the earthworms were pulling it

under to conduct their invaluable business of converting humus into soil, hence the need for a piece of muslin or sheet to foil the worms.

Having spread your carragheen on a piece of material laid on the grass, you must sprinkle it with fresh water from a watering-can daily, unless it rains. It sounds a nuisance, but it only takes a few moments, and the result is fascinating, each day the weed is shrivelled and dry, and each time you water it, it relaxes, unfolds and hisses gently and daily lightens in colour from brown, to purple, to crimson, to pink, to cream. When all the carragheen is cream coloured with, perhaps, a few pink edges, take it indoors, spread it thinly on trays and stand the trays by a sunny window for an hour or two until the weed is perfectly dry. Snip off any tough bits of stalk and store in paper bags or jars until needed.

CARRAGHEEN HONEYCOMB MOULD

Dried carragheen has almost no taste and can be used as a pure vegetable substitute for gelatine in most recipes. The dried weed does not give as firm a set as gelatine, and I have not been able to coax the fresh weed to set at all, even using quite large quantities. However, when you add an egg to the mixture it immediately thickens and starts to settle into a bubbly, honeycomb consistency.

You can vary the flavour of this dessert by substituting an orange for the lemon; or make a spiced pudding with a teaspoon of ground cinnamon or ginger and grate a little nutmeg on top after it has set.

SERVES 4
15 g/1/4 cup/1/2 oz dried carragheen
scant 3/4 litre/33/4 cups/11/2 pints milk
pinch salt
1 lemon
1 tablespoon brown sugar, or honey
1 egg

Put the weed into a bowl and pour on the cold milk, stir with a wooden spoon and leave to steep for 30 minutes. Pour the mixture into a saucepan, add the salt and finely grated lemon rind, bring slowly to the boil, then turn the heat down to the slowest possible simmer and cook gently for 20 minutes, stirring occasionally, until the mixture is thick and smooth. Stir in the sugar or honey and strained lemon juice and allow to cool for 10 minutes. Whisk up the egg in a bowl and strain the carragheen mixture over the egg, stirring briskly as the mixture thickens and turns spongy. Pour into a glass serving dish, or a wetted mould, and turn out the pudding from the mould when set.

CARRAGHEEN PUDDING

This is a Scottish recipe from the west coast and the Western Isles. It was traditionally served with cream, or sour cream, the latter being considered the better. Some melted heather honey or a sprinkling of dark brown sugar mixed with a little cinnamon is also good.

SERVES 4
50 g/1 cup/2 oz dried carragheen
1 egg
500 ml/2 cups/1 pint milk

Put the carragheen in a bowl, pour on the boiling milk, stirring briskly to dissolve the weed, then stand in a warm place for 2 hours. Whisk up an egg and stir it into the carragheen mixture, which at once will thicken into a spongy consistency.

CARRAGHEEN OR IRISH MOSS BATH GEL

SPRING AND SUMMER

The natural jelly in seaweed makes a wonderfully invigorating shower or bath gel. To test it, my daughter and I used nothing else for a fortnight and found that it was every bit as cleansing as soap and had a softening effect on the skin. Just rub handfuls of the gel all over the body and sluice off in the bath or shower. It also works as a shampoo.

Instead of lavender water, you could use 2 tablespoons of orange flower water to scent the gel, or boil a few sprigs of rosemary in 250 ml/1 cup/1/2 pint of water for a few minutes and add the strained liquid to give a herbal fragrance.

MAKES ABOUT 1 LITRE (5 CUPS OR 2 PINTS)
11/2 litres/71/2 cups/3 pints fresh carragheen, or Irish moss
11/4 litres/61/4 cups/21/2 pints water
2 tablespoons lavender water
2 or 3 drops edible green colouring, optional

Soak the carragheen in fresh water and wash it thoroughly, removing any stones or debris in the process. Put the seaweed and water into a large saucepan, bring to the boil, cover and simmer for 30 minutes.

Rub the seaweed mixture through a sieve or strainer, stir the lavender water into the gel and add green colouring. Pour into jars or bottles when cold.

CHANTERELLES

Cantharellus cibarius

Chanterelles are found in deciduous and conifer woods throughout Britain, Europe and Scandinavia, and are widely distributed throughout the United States. They may appear from early summer and, according to the season, continue to grow right through to the autumn. They are bright golden yellow and funnel-shaped when developed; the tiny, young specimens, often growing beside the older ones, are domed and have an unevenly wavy in-rolled edge. As the fungus grows larger it becomes flatter with a depression in the centre, until it finally looks like a little yellow umbrella that has blown inside out. The wide-set, shallow gills fork and re-unite as they run down the stem, which is thick, and tapers towards the base. Chanterelles reach about 9 cm/3¹/₂ ins in height and the caps vary from 2¹/₂-7¹/₂ cm/1-3 ins across.

The chanterelle is one of the most popular and best known fungi on the continent and throughout Scandinavia, where it is served in restaurants and sold in shops and markets, and has a truly delicious flavour and firm texture.

CHANTERELLES – *CANTHARELLUS CIBARIUS*

Similar to the chanterelle is *Hygrophoropsis aurantica* which has gills that fork, but do not re-unite, and is usually more orange than yellow, but it is quite harmless, though lacking the wonderful flavour of the chanterelle. *Cantharellus infundibuliformi* and *Craterellus cornucopioides*, the Horn of Plenty fungus, are also funnel shaped, but dark brown in colour. They are edible and may be cooked as chanterelles, though I have not eaten them myself.

TO PREPARE CHANTERELLES SUMMER AND AUTUMN

The earthy base of the stem should be trimmed away and the fungus well washed under the tap. As chanterelles are tough, they must always be simmered for 15 minutes in water or milk, then drained and sliced, before frying in butter over a medium-low heat for 10-15 minutes. Or they can be sliced and added to soups and stews in which they may simmer for a few minutes. They are superb with fried or scrambled eggs and bacon, with steak, or chops, or a mixed grill.

SWEET CHESTNUT
Castanea sativa

The sweet, or Spanish chestnut was introduced into Britain and is widely naturalised in the south of England. It is found throughout southern Europe, Asia Minor, and in the countries of the Mediterranean where it may grow to a great size; there are some fine specimens of old chestnuts in Windsor Great Park, where they were planted in the 18th century.

When mature, the sweet chestnut is a massive, lofty tree with a columnar trunk covered in deeply-furrowed, dark grayish bark. As the tree ages, the trunk twists, so that the furrows turn spirally like the strands of a huge rope. The large, narrow, pointed leaves are shiny and sharply toothed, with conspicuous, regularly-spaced veins, which remain on the trees until late in the autumn, and turn to lovely shades of pale gold. In summer, the tree bears long, yellowish catkins with an almost sickly fragrance. Some catkins are composed entirely of the male, pollen-bearing flowers, others have mostly male, and some female flowers in clusters of two or three near the twig. These develop into the glossy brown, edible nuts which are flattened on one side and drawn up into a point at the top. Two or three nuts are enclosed within a spiny green case, described by William Coles as 'prickly like an urchin' (hedgehog), and when they ripen and fall from the trees, the ground beneath does look as if it was covered with little green hedgehogs. Small unripe chestnuts may drop, or be blown off the trees at the end of the summer, but in England they are not fully ripe and fit to eat until autumn, and then only after a warm, sunny summer.

Chestnut leaves have been prescribed by modern herbalists to treat whooping-cough and other violent coughs and respiratory illnesses, and the old herbalists, Culpeper and Coles both recommended the dried nuts pounded and made into an 'electuary' with honey, as 'a first rate remedy for cough and spitting of blood'. Coles, like most of the sixteenth

SWEET CHESTNUT – *CASTANEA SATIVA*

and seventeenth century herbalists, accepted the Doctrine of Signatures and applied it when selecting the plants he prescribed. The theory was that the appearance or colour of a disease was linked to the appearance or colour of the plant that would cure it. Thus a yellow flower would cure yellow jaundice, and the white-spotted leaves of lungwort were used against 'the infirmities and ulcers of the lungs', and many of the plants growing from rocks were believed to 'break the stone'. The greatest exponent of this theory was an Italian, Giambattista Porta, but it is usually associated with the German, Phillippus Bombast von Hohenheim, who lived in the fifteenth century and became internationally known as 'Paracelsus'. Through him, the Doctrine of Signatures became the latest fashion in medicine and was accepted by herbalists and occultists throughout Europe.

When faced with the need to apply the Doctrine of Signatures to the chestnut's appearance, Coles approached the matter with some modesty. 'Everyone will be apt enough to discover the Signatures that this Nut beares. . . So that a small hint will be sufficient. It is not ordinarily delivered, that this Nut should stir up Venery . . . if the much nourishment they afford, and the windinesse going along with them (both which qualities are very conducible hereunto) be considered'. Coles adds a note of caution 'yet if they be eaten immoderately, they cause the Headach, and are hard of digestion and bind the body'.

The Spanish and Italian peasants appear to escape these side effects, for they eat a lot of chestnuts as a vegetable, as we would eat potatoes, and use the pounded nuts in cooking as a purée or meal for thickening, like flour. John Evelyn gave sweet chestnuts a good reputation as 'delicacies for princes and a lusty and masculine food for rusticks, and able to make women well-complexioned'. In *New England's Rariities Discovered* 1672, John Josselyn described the chestnuts which the Indians sold to the English for '12 pence the bushel' as 'very sweet in taste'. Early in the 1900s a fungus disease of the inner bark attacked and decimated the American trees, much like our Dutch elm disease. Many old stumps produced healthy shoots which, when they attained a moderate size, again were attacked by the killer blight.

Because chestnut timber has the advantages of not rotting easily in the ground, it was used for stakes, fences, pit-props and hop poles and, because of its pliancy, for making wine barrels.

TO STORE AND PREPARE SWEET CHESTNUTS MID-LATE AUTUMN

Wait until the ripe nuts drop from the trees, then take off the prickly green husks, wipe the nuts with a dry cloth and store them in hessian sacks, or cardboard boxes, in a cool dry place; turn them over occasionally to discourage mildew.

There are many well known recipes for using sweet chestnuts, apart from roasting them in the fire, and most recommend boiling the chestnuts for a few minutes before removing the skins; the tough outer skin peels off, but the thin inner skin usually needs to be scraped off and this can be a very tedious performance. A quicker way is to cut off the pointed ends, spread the chestnuts on a baking tray and bake in a hot oven (400°F, 200°C or Gas 6) for about 10 minutes. Keep an eye on the nuts and take out a few at a time; as soon as you can handle them remove the skins with a sharp knife, this way the outer and inner skins come off together.

CHESTNUT SOUP MID-LATE AUTUMN

This is a perfect soup for a dinner party.

SERVES 4–6
500 g/4 cups/1 lb chestnuts
1 onion
1 carrot
25 g/2 tablespoons/1 oz butter
1 litre/5 cups/1¾ pints chicken stock
salt and freshly milled black pepper
1 tablespoon finely chopped parsley
4 tablespoons cream

Remove the skins from the chestnuts as described above. Peel and finely slice the onion and scrape and slice the carrot into thin rings. Melt the butter in a large saucepan, add the onion, carrot and chestnuts, stir and cover with a tight lid and sweat the vegetables gently for 5 minutes. Add the stock, season with salt and pepper, bring to the boil, cover and simmer for 30 minutes. Liquidize the soup, return to the pan and stir in the cream. Re-heat and serve with a sprinkling of chopped parsley.

CHESTNUTS WITH BRUSSELS SPROUTS

MID-LATE AUTUMN

Choose the largest chestnuts and smallest sprouts, the sweet, mealy nuts and crisp sprouts are a great combination.

SERVES 4

1 kilo/2 lbs small sprouts
250 g/2 cups/8 oz chestnuts
25 g/2 tablespoons/1 oz butter

Remove the skins from the chestnuts as described before, then drop them into lightly salted, boiling water and cook gently for 10-15 minutes until tender, but still whole, drain through a colander. Cut a thin slice from the stalk end of the sprouts, (never cut an X in them as this ruins their shape) drop them into lightly salted, boiling water and cook briskly for 4-5 minutes or until tender, but still crisp. Drain well. Melt the butter in a saucepan then tip in the sprouts and chestnuts and shake them in the pan until glistening.

CHESTNUTS AND RED CABBAGE

MID-LATE AUTUMN

Chestnuts also combine well with red cabbage. Prepare and cook the chestnuts as in the preceding recipe, but start cooking the red cabbage first, as it takes longer.

SERVES 4

500 g/1 lb red cabbage
1 teaspoon salt
1 small onion
250 g/2 cups/8 oz chestnuts
1 medium cooking apple
3 tablespoons water
25 g/2 tablespoons/1 oz butter
1 tablespoon vinegar

Remove any blemished outer leaves and tough core and shred the cabbage finely, leave to soak in cold water for 1 hour.

Peel and slice the onion, and peel and quarter the apple. Melt the butter in a large saucepan and add the cabbage, onion and apple, season with salt and add the water and vinegar, cover with a well fitting lid and cook for 45 minutes-1 hour until the cabbage is tender. While the cabbage is cooking, prepare and cook the chestnuts. Drain the cabbage through a colander, and return to the pan with a generous knob of butter, tip in the chestnuts and stir together lightly, finish with a good grinding of black pepper. Serve very hot.

CHESTNUT AND SAUSAGE STUFFING FOR TURKEY

It is rewarding to use chestnuts stored from your autumn foraging at Christmas-time.

If your harvest was meagre, use half the weight of chestnuts to sausage meat. If you gleaned a bumper crop, reverse the quantities to use twice that of chestnuts to the sausage.

225 g/½ lb (or 450 g/1 lb) chestnuts
600 ml/ 3 cups/1 pt turkey stock, made from the neck & giblets
2 sticks celery
2 onions
50 g/4 tablespoons/2 oz butter
450 g/1 lb (or 225 g/½ lb) sausage meat
1 tablespoon chopped parsley
Fresh breadcrumbs – about a teacupful – see recipe

Remove the skins from the chestnuts as before. You can do this ahead of time and keep them in a bowl of cold water until you are ready. Drain and dry the chestnuts on kitchen paper. Put them in a saucepan with just enough stock to cover, add the chopped celery and cook gently until the chestnuts are soft, 30-40 minutes. Drain and allow to cool.

Peel and finely chop the onions, and cook them slowly in the butter until soft and yellow, allow to cool a little, then stir in the broken up sausage meat with a fork. Add the chestnuts whole, or in pieces, and enough stock to mix and moisten. Stir in the parsley. Fork in enough breadcrumbs to bind the mixture, adding a little extra stock to make the mixture moist and pasty.

Fill the turkey cavity with the stuffing, and secure the skin with cocktail sticks, or a skewer.

Weigh the turkey after stuffing to calculate the cooking time.

MARRONS GLACÉS AUTUMN

Marrons glacés are such an expensive luxury that it is rather fun to make your own. Our English wild chestnuts make a delicious mouthful, easier to eat than the huge French marrons.

1 kilo/8 cups/2 lbs chestnuts
500 g/2 cups/1 lb granulated sugar
500 g/3¹/₃ cups/1 lb powdered glucose
2 or 3 drops vanilla extract
500 g/2 cups/1 lb extra sugar, see recipe

Skin the chestnuts as described on page 54. Put them into a saucepan of cold water, bring slowly to the boil and simmer very gently for 20 minutes until the chestnuts are tender, but whole. Drain. Meanwhile make a syrup by heating the sugar and glucose in a generous 425 ml/or scant 2 cups/³/₄ pint, stir until the sugar dissolves, then bring to the boil and drop in the chestnuts, bring again to the boil, then draw the pan off the heat. Leave the chestnuts soaking in the syrup for 24 hours.

2nd Day. Bring the chestnuts and syrup to the boil in the uncovered pan, then draw off the heat, cover the pan and leave again for 24 hours.

3rd Day. Add the vanilla extract, bring the chestnuts and syrup to the boil in the uncovered pan, then draw off the heat and lift the chestnuts out of the syrup with a slotted spoon and stand them on a wire cake rack to drain, with a sheet of greaseproof paper under the rack.

Put the extra 500 g/2 cups/1 lb sugar into a pan with ¹/₈ litre/²/₃ cup/¹/₄ pint water, heat slowly stirring until the sugar dissolves, then bring to the boil and stand the covered pan on a wire gauze mat on the very lowest heat to keep hot while you are glazing the chestnuts. Have ready another saucepan of boiling water and into this drop a few chestnuts at a time, after a few seconds lift them out to drain before dropping in a second batch. Repeat until all the chestnuts are drained.

Pour a little of the hot syrup into a warmed cup and with a thin skewer or knitting needle impale each chestnut and dip it into the hot syrup, then slide them on to the wire rack to drain; when the syrup starts to turn cloudy, pour fresh hot syrup into a clean cup and dip as many chestnuts as you can before the syrup turns cloudy. Repeat with fresh hot syrup until all the chestnuts are dipped. Stand the wire rack of chestnuts in a very cool oven (250°F, 130°C or Gas ¹/₂) with the oven door ajar, and after an hour turn them over carefully so they dry evenly. Cut neat 5 cm/2 ins squares of kitchen foil and line them with exactly matching squares of waxed paper; after 2-3 hours when the chestnuts are quite dry, and no longer sticky, allow them to cool, and wrap each one separately and store in a box or tin.

Any broken pieces of chestnut that remain can be puréed and added to a pudding or cake mixture, and the syrup can be used for stewing fruit or making a caramel custard.

CHAMOMILE
Chamaemelum nobile = Anthemis nobilis

Chamomile grows wild in dry grass and heathland in parts of Europe and in southern England, but it is rather uncommon in Britain. It is cultivated, but does not grow wild in the United States. The plant is perennial and is sometimes known as Lawn Chamomile because of its spreading, turf-forming habit and ability to stand up to being trodden on. The slender, trailing pale green stems are hairy, and the leaves feathery and finely cut. The flowers appear in late summer, they are daisy-like and consist of a conical yellow centre surrounded by white ray-florets which are strap-shaped and end in three pointed teeth. The botanical differences between *C. nobile* and the other chamomiles and related mayweeds are complicated, all have daisy-like flowers and finely cut leaves, and the easiest way to tell them apart is from the delicious apple scent of common chamomile. In Spain the plant is known as *manzanilla*, from *manzana* (apple), and is used to flavour Manzanilla sherry, as well as in herbal tea.

Chamomile has had a long history as a herbal remedy, extending from ancient Egypt and Greece to the present day. Andrew Borde, physician to Henry VIII, included chamomile in a prescription for 'wheltes or pushes the whyche be reed (red) and they be in the rotes of the heer (hair)'. The people in Tudor times must have been afflicted with many unpleasant scalp conditions; no doubt they seldom washed their hair, they habitually wore hats, indoors and out, which were usually made of fur or thick materials, so it is not surprising if the dirt and vermin produced some fairly disgusting disorders. Andrew Borde's treatment at least necessitated washing the head, so it might have helped. 'Take of camomyll an handful, of Fenugreke an once, of Rose leves an handful, sethe (boil) this in white wyne and washe the heed V. (five) tymes at nyghte.'

In his 19th century *Family Herbal*, Robert Thornton recommended chamomile for such varied illnesses as hysteria, flatulence, colic, gout, typhus and 'the vomiting of puerperal women, in the after pains'. He sounded a warning about the use of chamomile tea: 'Although this be a fine remedy, and merits all our praise, still it must be remembered, that

as the cord too tightly strung, relaxes its tone, so as never to recover again, thus the stomach, too much braced by a long-continued use of chamomile tea, loses irrecoverably its tone, and becomes a truly afflicting evil arising from imprudent use of this tonic'.

In herbal medicine the dried flower heads of the cultivated double-flowered plant are used in preference to the single-flowered wild form, which contains a powerful alkali; if taken in large doses, this can act as an emetic and stomach irritant, although it used to be considered the more effective plant in the days when 'purgings and purgations' were the answer to everything.

Chamomile tea is recommended for indigestion and as a mild sedative; and a poultice made from the flowers helps to reduce inflammation. A modern proprietary ointment for nappy rash contains chamomile extract, and the flowers are still used in many shampoos and other preparations for the hair.

Since common chamomile is not common in the wild, it is better to grow the cultivated double-flowered form approved by modern medicine. It produces more flowers than the wild variety, and can be grown from seed.

The delicious medieval custom of making seats turfed with 'chamomile, penny-royall, daisies and violets', could be copied today if you make a low wall of flat stones, fill the cavity with earth and plant the top and sides with chamomile seedlings or runners. Choose a sunny corner in the garden and as the plants grow and clothe the sides and top of the wall, you will have a soft outdoor bench that is permanently fragrant.

CHAMOMILE TEA LATE SUMMER

Gather the flowers when the petals are starting to turn down. They may be used fresh or dried.

25 g/1/2 cup/1 oz fresh chamomile flowers,
   or 15 g/1/4 cup/1/2 oz dried chamomile flowers
250 ml/1 cup/1/2 pint boiling water

Put the flowers in a small jug, pour on boiling water, cover with a saucer and allow to stand for 10 minutes. Strain, and drink warm. The tea has a wonderfully soothing and slightly sedative effect.

CHAMOMILE HAIR RINSE

Culpeper wrote 'the flowers boiled in lee are good to wash the head and comforteth both it and the brain'. A chamomile rinse is a good conditioner and brings out the highlights in blonde hair; if not the brain.

1 cupful fresh or dried chamomile flowers
850 ml/33/4 cups/11/2 pints boiling water

Put the flowers in a large jug and pour on the boiling water. Cover with a plate, and leave until cool. Wash and rinse your hair in the usual way, then strain the chamomile infusion and use as a final rinse.

CHICKWEED

Stellaria media

This is a common weed in fields, hedgerows, waysides and gardens, and most people will be familiar with the low, pale green, trailing plant, with tiny white star-like flowers. It occurs throughout Britain, Europe and in North America, where it grows all the year round. The flowers have five petals notched so deeply that they appear to be ten. The pointed oval leaves grow opposite each other on alternate sides of the round, juicy stem, with side stems branching from the angles of the leaves. If you look at chickweed under a magnifying glass, you can see a line of fine hairs that run up the stem on one side only, this changes to the other side at the next pair of leaves, and so on alternately up the stem; this characteristic distinguishes chickweed from other plants of the same family. The mouse-ear chickweed and common mouse-ear resemble chickweed, but they have stiffer and more hairy stems and thicker, felty leaves often with a white margin, and they look less edible than the obviously tender, juicy *stellaria media*.

The weed was used medicinally in early times as a poultice for boils and carbuncles and for making a green ointment to reduce swellings. It was one of Culpeper's panaceas 'To temperate the heat of the liver . . . for all redness in the face, wheals, pushes, itch, scabs. . . It heleth the sinews when they are shrunk by cramp or otherwise and to extend and make them pliable again by this medicine', which he describes as a brew of chickweed, red rose leaves and the oil of trotters or sheep's feet, 'with God's blessing it will help in three times dressing'.

Throughout the summer, chickweed tends to be favoured by insects, possibly butterflies, as a food plant for their larvae, and at that time is usually full of little hard, brown eggs, therefore pick chickweed before early summer, and again in early autumn when a fresh crop of leaves appears.

CHICKWEED SOUP

SPRING AND AUTUMN, OMITTING SUMMER

Nobody would guess that this was anything but a good spinach soup. The colour and flavour are identical. If you have some cream, it always adds the perfect finishing touch to this type of soup, and a tablespoonful should be stirred in just before serving.

SERVES 4

2 colanders chickweed (after picking over)
25 g/2 tablespoons/1 oz butter
1 medium onion
1 rounded tablespoon flour
3/4 litre/33/4 cups/11/2 pints milk
salt and white pepper

Pick away any roots from the chickweed, and discard any bits of dead leaf or grass, or other foreign bodies. Soak the chickweed in strongly salted water for at least half an hour, then wash very thoroughly in several changes of water. Leave to drain.

Melt the butter in a large pan, peel and slice the onion and sauté gently for a few minutes, then add the chickweed, cover the pan and simmer slowly for 5 minutes. Draw the pan off the heat and shake in the flour, and stir with a wooden spoon. Bring the milk to the boil and pour on to the pan of chickweed, stirring briskly over the heat. Season with salt and pepper, then cover the pan and simmer gently for 15 minutes.

Liquidise the soup. Check the seasoning and reheat. Serve with croutons, or fresh rolls.

CHICKWEED – *STELLARIA MEDIA*

CHICKWEED AS A VEGETABLE

SPRING AND AUTUMN, OMITTING SUMMER

Some books recommend serving the leaves of chickweed raw in salads, but as it tastes exactly like grass I see no merit in this unless you are hard up for bulk, or like grass!

However, chickweed is delicious cooked as a vegetable, and of all the wild plants I have eaten, is the only one that can truthfully be described as 'exactly like spinach'. The flavour is identical to spinach, only the texture is different. The tiny leaves are much softer, but the little stems have a tender crunch.

When you have picked the chickweed, which is reasonably quick, as it grows plentifully and you can drag up handfuls, I suggest you sit while you pick away any roots you may have gathered, as well as the odd bits of grass and twig, as this is the slowest part of the process. The tiny, star-like, white flowers together with the stems and leaves, should all be cooked and eaten.

SERVES 4

2 rounded colanders full of chickweed
25 g/2 tablespoons/1 oz butter
salt and freshly milled black pepper

Pick over the chickweed as described above, then soak in salted water for about an hour. Drain, then wash again in fresh cold water and drain again. Tip the chickweed into a large saucepan with no extra water. Cook gently for 7 or 8 minutes. Drain through a colander, pressing and chopping with a wooden spoon to get rid of as much liquid as possible. Melt the butter in the saucepan, tip in the chickweed and add a little salt and a good grinding of black pepper. Turn the chickweed over in the butter and serve hot. It is good with poached eggs on toast.

Alternatively, you may add a small finely chopped onion, or shallot, to the butter in the pan, sauté until soft, and then stir in the cooked chickweed and seasoning.

CLEAVERS

Galium aparine

GOOSEGRASS, CLIVERS

Cleavers is a straggling annual weed which is widespread and common all over Europe and the British Isles, where it grows abundantly in hedge banks, woods, farmyards and most waste places, and is found throughout North America. John Josselyn noted 'goose-grass, or clivers', among the plants he discovered growing wild in New England in the 17th century. The trailing stems may be 1 1/4 metres/4ft long and climb up and through other plants by means of the hooked bristles which cover them and the leaves, which are narrow and grow in star-like whorls of six or eight. The tiny, white, four-petalled flowers are inconspicuous, growing in small, stalked clusters from the axils of the leaves; they appear throughout the summer, and develop into fruits like little round pill-balls, which are dispersed by the hooked bristles that catch on to animals and clothing.

The scientific name *aparine* comes from the Greek *aparo*, to seize, and the reason for the English name is equally obvious. The plant is a member of the bed-straw family and belongs to the same family, *Rubiaceae*, as coffee, ipecacuanha and cinchona, from which quinine is derived; the dye-plant madder also belongs to the same order, and the roots of cleavers will provide a red dye.

Dioscorides mentioned the stems of cleavers being used as a milk-strainer by the shepherds of ancient Greece, a custom that was still practised in Sweden in Linnaeus's day. In his 16th century herbal, William Coles refers to the Greek shepherds who used cleavers stems 'to take haires out of milk', adding 'and so may our milk-maides, if they want a strainer'. Coles advised cleavers to be eaten as a spring vegetable 'for cleansing the blood, strengthening the liver' and 'fitting the Body for the season that follows, by purging away those *excrementitious dregs* (his italics, no wonder!) which the Winter has bred in them'. He recommended the plant as a dressing for wounds, scabs, sores and ulcers, and said 'the herb stamped (pounded) with Swines-grease . . . helpeth those that have their Paps swollen through curdled-Milke'. In his *Family Herbal*, Thornton endorses this remedy and said Dioscorides 'mentioned an ointment of great efficacy made from the expressed juice of this plant mixed with hog's lard, for discussing tumours in the breast'. This treatment, that survived the span of years between Dioscorides and Thornton, must have had some measure of success.

Modern herbalists and homeopaths recognize cleavers' medicinal properties, and Mrs. Grieves in *A Modern Herbal* writes that an infusion of goosegrass 'has a most soothing effect in cases of insomnia, and induces quiet, restful sleep'.

In the old days, lacemakers stuck the green seed of goosegrass on to pins to make a larger head. Anyone who has known the frustrations of pinning lace or net, with the pins slipping through, might still find this a useful aid to sewing.

CLEAVERS, OR GOOSEGRASS, SEED COFFEE AUTUMN INTO WINTER

The horrible little clinging burrs of cleavers, or goosegrass, make a very good ersatz coffee; in fact I have drunk worse coffee in other people's houses made with real, or instant coffee! It is a tedious process, but if one is desperate for coffee, and has plenty of time, a pleasant, strong, black coffee-flavoured beverage can be made.

2-3 tablespoons (heaped) roasted and ground
  goosegrass seeds
500 ml/2 cups/1 pint boiling water

Pick the plant when it has dried and withered. Strip away as much dry stem as possible. Put the seeds in a large bowl and wash them in cold water. Swish them about and change the water frequently and skim off all the debris that rises to the surface of the water. When you are left with mostly bare, black seeds, looking rather like mock caviar, drain through a strainer and spread the seeds thinly in a shallow roasting tin. Roast in a hot oven (400°F, 200°C or Gas 6) for 20 minutes. Cool, then grind the seeds. Put two or three tablespoons of grounds in a warmed jug and pour on the boiling water. Leave to stand for 10 minutes, then strain into cups and drink hot, either black or white.

CLEAVERS DEODORANT

EARLY SPRING TO LATE SUMMER

A decoction of cleavers makes a perfectly effective underarm deodorant. It keeps for about a week, so fresh batches can be made from early spring, when the plant is newly green, until the end of the summer when it begins to wither.

When you wash after using a deodorant you will generally notice the skin has a slight resistance to soap until a good lather is obtained, cleavers has exactly the same effect on the skin, which is entirely harmless.

1 large handful cleavers, stalks and leaves
1 litre/5 cups/2 pints water

Put the cleavers and water in a saucepan, bring to the boil and simmer for 15 minutes. Leave to get cold, then strain and bottle. Apply to the armpits with cotton wool.

CLOVER

Trifolium

RED CLOVER *T. pratense* WHITE CLOVER *T. repens*

Red and white clovers are abundant and common throughout Britain and most of Europe and Scandinavia, they are found in many grassy and waste places, particularly on farmland, where they have been sown for pasture and remain for years. In America, the clovers are immigrants from the Old World, and grow by roadsides and on lawns and waste ground throughout the United States and Canada. Red clover is the larger of the two and may grow as tall as 46 cm/18 ins high, the plant is perennial, with trefoil leaves which usually have a whitish, crescent-shaped mark half way up each oval leaflet, and triangular, bristle-pointed stipules where they join the stem. The flowers grow in globular, or egg-shaped pinkish-purple heads, the whole plant, particularly the calyx, is downy. Red clover flowers form late spring through to autumn.

White clover, also known as Wild White, Dutch or Kentish clover, is common in all grassy places and is frequently found in lawns, where it spreads rapidly from the rooting junctions between stem and leaves. The trefoil leaves are toothed, with rounder leaflets than those of the red clover, but with a similar, whitish crescent mark near the base. The globular flower heads are smaller than red clover flowers, and are creamy white, the tiny pea-flowers are often tipped with green and, as they start to fade, those at the base nearest the stem wither and turn brown. White clover comes into flower a little later, from early summer onwards.

An infusion of red clover was used by herbalists as a remedy for whooping cough and bronchitis, and the plant, made into poultices, was applied to tumours. Bees seem to prefer white clover to red, and the honey they make from it has a beautiful flavour.

WHITE CLOVER SANDWICHES SUMMER

When grandchildren moan, 'what shall we do?' clover sandwiches may be the answer. The flowers take a while to find and pick, and picking the tiny florets from each flower head takes ages. Somehow, the time involved is not resented, and the sweet, crunchy sandwiches are eaten with delight. Try it!

clover flowers
fresh white bread
butter
caster sugar / U.S. granulated

Pick the florets from the clover heads. Lightly butter thin slices of white bread and sprinkle one slice with sugar and spread the other with clover flowers. Close as a sandwich, and trim off the crusts.

CLOVER SYRUP SUMMER

This is a delicious syrup to add to a fresh fruit salad or any compote of fruit; stored in a refrigerator, it will keep for months. Fruit stewed gently in the syrup is much nicer than when cooked in water with sugar—use 1/8 litre/2/3 cup/1/4 pint syrup to each 500 g/3 cups/1 lb of fruit.

You can make the syrup with red or white clover blossoms, or a mixture of both, the result is the colour of lime juice.

1 tea-cupful clover blossoms
3 tea-cups sugar
1½ tea-cups water

Put the clover blossoms in a bowl. Heat the sugar and water in a small saucepan, stir until the sugar dissolves, then boil fast for 3 minutes. Pour the hot syrup over the clover flowers and leave to stand for 15 minutes, stirring occasionally. Strain into a jug, and when cold pour into bottles and cork, or screw on the caps.

FRESH CLOVER FLOWER TEA SUMMER

Clover tea has a good refreshing taste and is a very pretty pale green colour.

2 teaspoons white clover flowers
250 ml/1 cup/½ pint boiling water

Put the flowers in a jug, pour on the boiling water, cover and infuse for 7 minutes. Drink hot or cool.

TO DRY CLOVER FLOWERS SUMMER

Pick away the stalks and spread the flower heads thinly on trays, cardboard lids or sheets of white paper. Put them in a well-ventilated boiler room, or any warm dry room until the flowers are perfectly dry, which takes three to five days. Store in screw-topped jars away from the light.

DRIED CLOVER FLOWER TEA

Dried clover flowers make a lime green tea, which retains much of its summer freshness.

3 heaped teaspoons dried clover flowers
250 ml/1 cup/½ pint boiling water

Put the dried flowers in a jug, pour on the boiling water and infuse for 5 minutes. Strain into a cup and drink hot.

RED CLOVER – *T. PRATENSE*, WHITE CLOVER – *T. REPENS*

COLTSFOOT

Tussilago farfara

Coltsfoot is widespread and common on damp waste ground throughout Britain and most of Europe and Scandinavia. It was introduced into America from the Old World, and is now widespread all over the northeastern United States, and grows in damp soil from Newfoundland to Minnesota, and southwards to New Jersey and West Virginia. The flowers, which appear at the end of winter, are yellow and not unlike small dandelion heads, but grow on very thick fleshy stems covered with overlapping reddish scales. The fresh flowers are upright, then droop as they fade, but rise up again when the seeds form a round fluffy head. The flowers close in dull weather and at night. At first there may be only a few small leaves while the plant is in flower, sometimes none at all, which led Pliny to believe that coltsfoot had no leaves; however, in late spring and summer the plant produces a crop of very large hoof-shaped leaves—hence the plant's common name of coltsfoot — the undersides of which are covered with a thick, white felt, which clearly distinguishes them from the young leaves of the butterbur, which are similar in shape.

Coltsfoot has several country names which must have been suggested by the shape of its leaves and its history, as a cure for coughs. Coughwort, horsehoof, ass's foot, foalswort and bull's foot. In France it is known as *pas d'âne*.

Coltsfoot leaves have been dried and used in herbal tobacco as a remedy for asthma and bronchitis for centuries. Dioscorides and Galen recommended coltsfoot tobacco for chest disorders, and it was smoked as a herbal remedy in Sweden in Linnaeus's time. Sir John Hill recommended coltsfoot tea for coughs and wrote 'the patient should also have some of the leaves dried and cut small and smoke them as tobacco'. In the 20th century, coltsfoot was the chief ingredient of British herbal tobacco, and a syrup or liquid extract of the dried leaves and flowering shoots is used as a demulcent in cough medicines today. The old apothecaries' signs in Paris were paintings of coltsfoot flowers.

The thick white down on the underside of the leaves was made into tinder by a process of boiling and drying and mixing with saltpetre, which was continued for a long time in the Highlands where, also, the down from the seed heads was used to stuff pillows. It must have been unbelievably time-consuming to collect enough down to fill even one pillow, but families were large in those days and, no doubt, all the children helped. A child today could have fun collecting enough coltsfoot down to stuff a doll's pillow, or maybe a doll's eiderdown made of postage stamp-sized patchwork squares. Let her leave some down for the goldfinches, because they line their nests with it!

COLTSFOOT SYRUP SUMMER

Coltsfoot syrup is easy to make at home and has a very nice taste, it keeps for months in the refrigerator if you store the syrup in small bottles, and will see you through any winter colds and coughs. A tablespoon taken three or four times a day is soothing if you have a hard, dry cough and will help to loosen it. The leaves should be gathered in late spring and summer.

50 g/1 cup/2 oz fresh coltsfoot leaves
1 litre/5 cups/1 quart water
6-8 tablespoons honey

Wash the leaves and pick away the stalks and any part that are withered or attacked by insects, drain and put the leaves and water in a saucepan, bring to the boil, cover and simmer for 30 minutes. Cool a little, then strain the liquid into a clean saucepan and add the honey, heat up and stir until the honey has melted, then boil steadily for 10 minutes in the open pan. Skim very thoroughly, and pour through a fine strainer into a jug. leave until cool. Pour the syrup carefully into the bottles, leaving any sediment behind in the jug. Screw on the bottle caps and store in the refrigerator.

FRESH COLTSFOOT TEA LATE SPRING AND SUMMER

A cupful of coltsfoot tea sipped hot when you go to bed will soothe a dry or tickling cough.

1 small handful fresh coltsfoot leaves
250 ml/1 cup/½ pint boiling water

Wash the leaves thoroughly and remove the stalks and any brown or withered parts, put them in a small jug, pour on the boiling water and bruise the leaves with a wooden spoon. Cover and infuse for 5 minutes. Strain into a cup and drink hot.

TO DRY COLTSFOOT LEAVES

LATE SPRING AND SUMMER

Pick the leaves on a dry day with enough stalk to hang them up by, avoiding any that are discoloured or attacked by insects. Tie five or six leaves together in a bunch and hang them by their stalks from the pipes or slats in an airing cupboard, or in a warm, well-ventilated room. Being thick and felty the leaves take some time to dry, about seven to ten days in the airing cupboard, and longer in a room. When the leaves are really dry and crisp, put them through a parsley mill or crumble them finely, and store in screw-topped jars away from the light.

DRIED COLTSFOOT TEA

Coltsfoot leaves may be dried and stored in jars until needed for winter colds and coughs.

2 teaspoons dried coltsfoot leaves
250 ml/1 cup/½ pint boiling water

Put the coltsfoot in a small jug and pour on the boiling water, cover and infuse for 5 minutes. Strain into a cup and drink hot, with lemon and honey.

COLTSFOOT WINE EARLY SPRING

Coltsfoot flowers make a delicious country wine which has been popular for centuries.

activated yeast (p. 254)
5 litres/9 quarts/1 gallon coltsfoot flowers
2 oranges
2 lemons
5 litres/9 U.S. quarts/1 gallon water
1.5 kilos/7 cups/3 lbs sugar
2-3 tablespoons cold tea
  or 1 teaspoon grape tannin (sold for wine-making)

Pick the coltsfoot flowers when dry, remove the stems and put the flower heads into the plastic bucket with the thinly pared rind (no pith) and the strained juice of the oranges and lemons. Pour on the boiling water, then stir in the sugar until it has dissolved. Cover the bucket with a clean cloth and leave until cool, (about 70°F, 20°C) then stir in the cold tea, or grape tannin and the activated yeast. Cover the bucket with its lid and leave in a warm place for five or six days, stirring daily, then strain the liquid into the fermentation jar and follow the method given on page 254.

COLTSFOOT WINE, OLD METHOD LATE SPRING

This is another old recipe for wine made with baker's yeast spread on toast and fermented in an earthen crock. See page 254 for information about lead- and salt-glazed vessels. You will also need a small wooden cask which holds at least 15 litres/27 U.S. quarts/3 gallons. A new cask should first be filled with cold water and left to soak for 2 or 3 days, then washed out with 10 litres/18 U.S. quarts/2 gallons boiling water in which you have dissolved 250 g/1¼ cups/8 oz washing soda. Rinse out the cask with a metabisulphate solution (see Wine Making Instructions) then rinse thoroughly with cold water. If you buy

COLTSFOOT – *TUSSILAGO FARFARA*

a secondhand cask, make sure it smells clean and sweet, and wash it out with the same solution of soda dissolved in boiling water, followed by fresh water, as above.

7½ litres/13½ U.S. quarts/12 pints coltsfoot flowers
15 litres/27 U.S. quarts/3 gallons water
3 kilos/18 cups/9 lbs sugar
750 g/4½ cups/1½ lb raisins
9 lemons
6 oranges
75 g/3 teaspoons/3 oz baker's yeast
3 slices toast

Use the flower heads only, and spread them in the sun to dry before making the wine. When the flowers are dry, put them in a large crock, pour on the boiling water, cover with a thick, clean cloth and stand for three days, stirring morning and evening. Strain the liquid into a large pan, add the sugar and boil for half an hour, stirring while the sugar dissolves. Pour into the crock and allow to cool. Spread both sides of the toast with fresh yeast and float it on the surface of the liquid, cover with the cloth and stand in a warm place for 24 hours. Remove the toast and pour the liquid into a cask, add the raisins and the pared rind and strained juice of the oranges and lemons. Close the cask and leave for three months, then siphon into clean bottles and cork securely.

CORN SALAD

Valerianella locusta var. oleracea

LAMB'S LETTUCE

This is a pretty little plant which grows from 5-25 cm/2-10 ins high, with smooth, branching stems, and oblong light green leaves that are unstalked and opposite; the tiny flowers are a soft lilac blue, and grow in a small round head at the top of the stem, with smaller clusters springing from the angles of the stem and leaves.

Corn salad grows throughout Britain and Europe and was once common in cornfields, hence the name, but because of crop spraying is no longer so, and like many useful and beautiful wild plants it has practically vanished from arable land. However, in some places, particularly in south-west England, it can be found growing in great profusion on walls and hedge banks, beside footpaths and on waste ground. It is naturalised in the northern states of America.

Corn salad, or lamb's lettuce, is an annual and can be grown in the garden, the seed should be sown in late summer, and will produce plants for winter salads, right through to the spring. The wild plants flower in the spring and summer.

In France it is known as Salade Prêtre, Salade de Chanoine and Doucette, and it is much better known as a salad plant than it is in Britain.

CORN SALAD, OR LAMB'S LETTUCE, IN SALADS

The leaves and flower heads taste faintly of parsley. Pick the plants carefully and wash in fresh water, discard the main stems, but eat the leaves and flowers whole. They are a delicate addition to any green salad, but best of all with sliced beetroot (U.S. beets).

CORN SALAD – *VALERIANELLA LOCUSTA VAR. OLERACEA*

CRAB APPLE

Malus sylvestris

The crab apple grows wild throughout Britain and the temperate zones of Europe, it is rare in the north of Scotland and will not tolerate the heat of southern Europe. A number of related species and hybrids exist in many parts of North America, some of them escape from cultivation. It is not easy to identify the truly wild crab from the infinite variety of cultivated escapes that have hybridised and are naturalised in woods and hedgerows, but the true wild species is a small deciduous tree which has some spines on the twigs and branches. The bark is reddish brown and the toothed leaves are pointed oval in shape and downy. The flowers open in the spring and look just like the blossom of orchard trees, deep pink in the bud, fading to pale pink as they open, with five petals and a ring of stamens with yellow anthers. A crab apple tree in full blossom is a glorious sight, the fragrant, fragile flowers usually crowded with enthusiastic bees.

William Coles described crab apple blossom as 'white with some Red many times mixed with it'. When I first read the early herbals I was often puzzled by a pink flower being described as 'whitish' or 'white meddled, or stained, with red'. Coles described bramble flowers as 'whitish, dasht with a little carnation' and Parkinson referred to the raspberry as having 'whitish round leaves (petals) with a dash as it were of blush cast over them'. In fact pink was not used as an adjective to describe colour until 1720, before which it was only used for the name of garden pinks, (dianthus).

The small fruits of the wild crab are yellowish green and hang in bunches. But different trees produce fruit that ranges from sprays of yellow apples no bigger than a cherry, to quite sizeable small apples with a red or russet flush. The flavour is equally variable, some fruits being unbelievably sour while others are not much sharper than a rather tart cooking apple. Bartholomew Anglicus noted this fact in his 15th century encyclopaedia, 'some beryth sourysh fruyt and harde, and some ryght soure and some ryght swete, with a good savoure and mery'. The apples ripen in early autumn and the ground beneath the trees may be littered with them. One should wait until they fall, as they are difficult to pick from the tree, and not fully ripe until they drop.

Cultivated varieties of apple are usually grafted on to wild crab stock, and apples of all sorts have been eaten by man since the dawn of time. The charred remains of small apples were found in the prehistoric Swiss lake dwellings, and there are references to apples in all the early books on food and medicine. Coles described how 'the inner yellow barke, either of Apple-Tree, or Crab-Tree, boyled with Allom, causeth those things that are put there into to be of a yellow colour', and said 'the juice of Crabs, which we commonly call Verjuice, applyed with wet cloathes to such places as are burned and scalded, cooleth, healeth, and draweth the fire out of them'.

Medieval cooks used verjuice in many dishes as we would use lemon juice. It was a fermented brew made from crab apples, or sour grapes, which keeps in the bottle, like wine. I have included a recipe for verjuice, as it is an asset in the kitchen.

CRAB APPLE SYRUP AUTUMN

This simple syrup will keep for months in the refrigerator and tastes just like expensive commercial apple juice when diluted; put two or three tablespoons of syrup in a glass and top up with soda water. Children love it and the pure ingredients make it a healthy drink. Get them to pick the crab apples, too. One word of warning, as wild crab apples are so full of pectin, you should not let the syrup boil for longer than 3-4 minutes, otherwise you will quickly get crab apple jelly! This is not a disaster, for the same recipe boiled for 5-7 minutes will make a delicious jelly to spread on scones or bread.

2 kilos/4 lbs crab apples
water—see recipe
500 g/2 cups/1 lb sugar
500 ml/2 cups/1 pint juice

Wash the crab apples and cut them in half, nick out any worm-eaten or badly bruised bits. Drop the pieces into cold water as you cut them. Drain and put the crab apples in a large saucepan with just enough water to cover them. Bring to the boil, cover and simmer for 20 minutes until the fruit is soft and pulpy. Strain through a double thickness of muslin overnight.

Measure the juice into a saucepan, and to each 500 ml/ 2 cups/1 pint juice add 400 g/2 cups/1 lb sugar. Bring to the boil, stirring continuously, then boil steadily for 3 minutes. Skim thoroughly, pour into a jug then into clean, dry bottles. Allow to cool before corking or screwing on caps.

CRAB APPLE AND MINT JELLY AUTUMN

Serve this tasty jelly with lamb or pork, the sweet-sharp flavour is very good. It looks attractive in a glass dish so that the green flecks of mint show in the apricot-pink jelly.

3/4 litre/33/4 cups/11/2 pints juice,
    made as in preceding recipe and dripped through muslin
600 g/3 cups/11/2 lbs sugar
3 rounded tablespoons chopped mint
3 tablespoons lemon juice

Measure the crab apple juice into a saucepan and add sugar. Bring slowly to the boil, stirring continuously until the sugar has dissolved, then boil fast for 5 minutes. Stir in the finely-chopped mint and lemon juice, and boil for a few more minutes until the liquid jells when dripped on to a saucer. Skim, pour into warm dry jars and cover with circles of waxed paper while hot, seal with cellophane circles when cold.

CRAB APPLE BUTTER AUTUMN

Spicy fruit butters and cheeses were very popular in Victorian days, they are so good that it is a pity not to revive them. This crab apple butter should be set firmly, but just soft enough to spread with a knife, it is wonderful with hot toast and delicious with grilled bacon or roast pork instead of apple sauce.

MAKES ABOUT 1.5 KILOS (3 LBS)
1 kilo/2 lbs crab apples
250 ml/1 cup/1/2 pint water
250 ml/1 cup/1/2 pint cider
1/2 teaspoon ground cinnamon
1/4 teaspoon ground cloves
sugar—see recipe

Wash the crab apples thoroughly, cut away any bad bits and put them in a large saucepan with the water, cider, cinnamon and cloves. Cook gently until the apples are soft, mashing them well with a wooden spoon. Liquidize the mixture, and measure the pulp back into the pan. To 400 g/11/4 cups/1 lb pulp add 300 g/11/2 cups/3/4 lb sugar, bring slowly to the boil, stirring continuously until the sugar has dissolved, then lower the heat to the slowest possible simmer, and cook in the open pan until the mixture is thick, and when stirred, the spoon leaves a clean line momentarily on the bottom of the pan. Pour into warm dry jars, cover with waxed circles, while hot, seal with cellophane covers when cold.

SPICED CRAB APPLES AUTUMN

In spite of the apples being so small this is not a fiddly recipe, since you leave the skins on and the cores in; keep the jars for 2-3 months before using, when the skins and cores will have mellowed into a soft candy, and nearly all the spicy syrup will have been absorbed into the apples. Serve with lamb, ham or pork.

MAKES ABOUT 1.5 KILOS (3 LBS)
750 g/11/2 lbs crab apples
250 ml/1 cup/1/2 pint cider vinegar
750 g/3 cups/11/2 lbs sugar
1/2 level teaspoon ground ginger
1/4 level teaspoon whole cloves
4 cm/2 ins cinnamon stick

Wash and halve the crab apples and nick out any bad bits. Heat the vinegar and sugar together in a pan, stirring until the sugar has dissolved, then add the spices and crab apples.

CRAB APPLE – *MALUS SYLVESTRIS*

Simmer gently together until the apples are tender but unbroken, then lift them into warm dry jars with a slotted spoon. Remove the cloves and cinnamon stick. Boil up the syrup until reduced to about half, pour immediately over the crab apples, cover with waxed circles while hot, seal with cellophane covers when cold.

CRAB APPLE WINE AUTUMN

Crab apples give a clean, fruity flavour to this medium-dry white wine.

activated yeast (p. 255)
5 litres/9 U.S. quarts/1 gallon crab apples
5 litres/9 U.S. quarts/1 gallon water
1.5 kilos/6 cups/3 lbs sugar
250 g/1½ cups/½ lb chopped raisins

Wash the crab apples and cut them in half, nick out any bad bits, put them into a plastic bucket and pour on the cold (not boiling) water, cover the bucket with its lid and allow to stand for 3 days, stirring daily. Strain the liquid into a large basin, or divide between two basins, pressing out as much juice as possible, and wash out the bucket. Return the juice to the bucket, add the sugar and chopped raisins and stir until the sugar has dissolved. Stir in the activated yeast. Cover the bucket with its lid and leave in a warm place for 24 hours. Strain into the fermentation jar and follow the method given on page 254.

VERJUICE AUTUMN

This recipe for crab apple verjuice is a good substitute for lemon juice in cooking. Sterilize all your containers by washing them in 1 teaspoon sodium metabisulphate dissolved in 500 ml/2 cups/1 pint water, then rinse in clear water twice, this kills any bacteria or wild yeasts that could spoil the brew.

Two or three days before you pick the crab apples start the yeast working as follows:

125 ml/⅔ cup/¼ pint water
1 teaspoon malt
1 teaspoon sugar
½ teaspoon citric acid
1 teaspoon yeast nutrient— sold for winemaking
white wine yeast—quantity given on packet for
    5 litres/18 U.S. pints/1 gallon

Bring the water to the boil in a small pan, add the malt, sugar and citric acid and stir to dissolve. Cover and allow to cool to less than 80°F (25°C), when the outside of the pan feels cool, not warm, then stir in the yeast nutrient and wine yeast, pour into a sterilized bottle and plug with cotton wool. After two or three days, when the top becomes creamy, the yeast will be ready to use.

1 kilo/2 lbs crab apples
3 litres/7½ cups/6 pints water
1 teaspoon citric acid
500 g/2 cups/1 lb sugar

Wash the crab apples and cut them up roughly, place in a large saucepan with 500 ml/2 cups/1 pint water and the citric acid, bring to the boil and simmer for 10-15 minutes, then add the sugar and stir to dissolve, strain the liquid through a nylon strainer into a jug, then pour the liquid into a glass demi-john, top up with the remaining 2½ litres/12½ cups/5 pints cold water. When the liquid has cooled to less than 80°F (25°C) (cool to the touch, not warm), add the activated yeast brew and plug the demi-john with cotton wool. After 24 hours fit a fermentation lock to the demi-john and leave for about a week, the fermentation may be vigorous to start with and may overflow a little. After a week, siphon the liquid into a second demi-john, fit the fermentation lock again and allow the fermenting process to continue for about a fortnight.

Syphon through a length of plastic tubing into sterilized bottles and screw the caps down tightly. The verjuice is ready to use immediately for cooking.

WASSAIL BOWL CHRISTMAS

In the old custom of 'wassailing' on Christmas Eve, roast apples, or crab apples, were an important ingredient of the wassail bowl. Puck's speech in *A Midsummer Night's Dream* refers to this:

Sometimes lurk I in a gossip's
*   bowl*
In very likeness of a roasted crab.

So that you have some crab apples for a wassail bowl at Christmas time, gather a dozen or so of the biggest and soundest you can find late in the autumn. Wrap each apple individually in a small square of newspaper and store them in an outdoor shed or garage. Not even cultivated apples should be stored indoors, however cold the room.

For an authentic touch, the drink should be made with Old Ale, which is darker and stronger than ordinary beer, and is only sold by pubs which supply real ale. Some breweries make a bottled version of Old Ale, but, failing this, a bottled dark brown ale would do. For a children's Christmas party, a delicious and innocuous Wassail Bowl can be made with medium sweet cider. The hot, spiced liquor provides instant inebriation which is speedily over, but creates a glow. Each glass contains a little bobbing apple which loosens shy tongues and gets the giggles going.

MAKES 8 GLASSES

8 crab apples

1 litre/5 cups/2 pints Old Ale, or brown ale,
  or medium sweet cider, for children's version

3 tablespoons brown sugar, or 2 tablespoons honey

2 cm/1 in cinnamon stick

1/2 teaspoon ground ginger

3 or 4 cloves

Wash the crab apples and make a shallow cut in the skin round the equator line of each. Arrange the apples on a buttered roasting tin and set in a moderately hot oven (190°C, 375°F or Gas 5) for 20 minutes. The little apples will puff and split round the middle revealing their soft baked interiors.

Pour the ale or cider into a large saucepan, add the sugar, or honey and the spices, stir, and heat until nearly boiling. Draw off the heat, remove the whole spices and ladle the drink into warmed tumblers, allowing one crab apple for each glass.

For adults in need of restoration, a really full-bodied wassail bowl can be made by adding a generous half teacupful of whisky and an egg beaten up in half a teacupful of thin cream to the pan of hot spiced ale.

CRYSTALLISED CRAB APPLE BLOSSOMS

SPRING

Individual open flowers of the crab apple may be crystallised or sugared to preserve them by the same methods given for Borage Flowers on page 36. Their varying shades of pink look lovely when used to decorate strawberry ice cream or a fresh strawberry mousse.

DANDELION
Taraxacum officinale

Dandelions are found throughout Europe and Scandinavia, and in America are a naturalised weed from the Old World which grows everywhere in lawns, grasslands and open places. Dandelions are so common and well-known that everyone can identify them, their vivid yellow flowers make a blazing show in the spring, and for most of the year can be seen in flower. They do vary greatly in size from little down-trodden specimens in lawns, where they never get a chance to grow more than 2 cm/1 inch or so high, to fine plants 30 cm/ 1 ft tall where the surrounding growth is high and forces them upwards. The leaves vary too; some plants produce leaves with many, very jagged pointed lobes; others have fewer, more rounded lobes, and these are the best as a vegetable and for salads. You can blanch dandelions by earthing up the plants when very young, or by covering them with a flower pot, but the leaves are delicious as a salad and a vegetable without bothering to blanch them, as long as you pick them young, either in the spring, or where they have been cut and fresh leaves have grown up. Dandelions are versatile, for as well as their edible leaves, the flowers can be made into wines, beers and a shrub, like lemonade, and the roots make a very drinkable substitute for coffee.

Dandelion has been known as a diuretic for centuries, the old herbalists valued it for its power to purify the blood and stimulate the bowels and kidneys. Culpeper, who usually disliked his rivals among the English physicians, ends his description of the medical properties of dandelion thus: 'You see here what virtues this common herb hath, and that is the reason the French and Dutch so often eat them in the spring; and now if you look a little farther, you may see plainly without a pair of spectacles, that foreign physicians are not so selfish as ours are, but more communicative of the virtues of plants to people'.

Martindale's *Pharmacopiea* describes a liquid extract made from the dried roots as a bitter and mild laxative. Certainly this property is suggested in many of the old country names, the French *pissenlit*, and English versions of piss-a-bed, wet-a-bed or mess-a-bed. However, I can't help thinking that to produce such spectacular results dandelions would need to be consumed in enormous quantities, and one need not fear the effects of any recipes that follow!

DANDELION SOUP SPRING AND SUMMER

For a wholesome broth, don't bother to sieve the soup, but leave the pieces of leaf whole, they are tender, and a good, deep green, and the flavour is wonderful. For a smoother cream soup, liquidise and stir in a tablespoon of cream before serving.

SERVES 4
two-thirds colander dandelion leaves
25 g/2 tablespoons/1 oz butter
1 small onion
1 medium potato
3/4 litre/33/4 cups/11/2 pints chicken stock (which can be
  made with a bouillon cube)
salt
white pepper

Pick the leaves from the bitter mid-rib, wash well and drain. Melt the butter in a saucepan, finely slice the onion and fry gently in the butter. Peel and dice the potato and add it to the pan of onion, cover with a lid and sweat the vegetables over a low heat for 5 minutes.

Add the dandelion leaves, sweat for a further 5 minutes, then stir in the stock, season with salt and pepper, and cook gently for 15 minutes. Serve hot, with crusty French bread, or croutons.

DANDELION AND HAM MOULD

SPRING AND SUMMER

A galantine of ham with dandelion leaves and hard-boiled eggs is set in a mould with a little gelatine, and can be turned out and served on a mixed bed of lettuce and dandelion leaves; or surrounded with cold cooked peas and garnished with dandelion petals.

SERVES 4
1 good handful dandelion leaves
200 g/1 cup/1/2 lb cooked ham, or gammon
2 hard-boiled eggs
15 g/3 teaspoons/1/2 oz gelatine
150 ml/2/3 cup/1/4 pint water
juice of 1/2 lemon
1cm/1/2 in fresh ginger root, grated
1/2 teaspoon ground cinnamon
freshly milled black pepper
scant tablespoon sugar, or honey
2-3 tablespoons cider vinegar

Strip the dandelion leaves from the mid-rib and wash them in lightly salted water. Dice the ham and cut away any fat, and peel and coarsely chop the eggs. Soak the gelatine in a small pan with the water and strained lemon juice for 5 minutes, then set the pan over a low heat until the gelatine dissolves and the liquid is clear. Put the pieces of ham and egg into a bowl, add the ginger, cinnamon, a good grinding of pepper, and the sugar, or melted honey.

Add the dandelion leaves to the ingredients in the bowl. Stir in the vinegar and mix gently. Pack the mixture into a mould or pudding bowl, previously rinsed out in cold water, pour over the soaked gelatine and chill until set. Un-mould by dipping the bowl into hot water for a few moments, then turn out.

PISSENLIT AU LARD SPRING AND SUMMER

This French country dish is very much nicer than its rather off-putting name suggests! The raw dandelion leaves are served in a dressing of vinegar with bacon fat in place of olive oil, and a seasoning of pepper. The hot bacon fat straight from the pan is a good contrast to the astringent leaves and vinegar. It is wonderful with roast chicken, or, for a light meal, with scrambled eggs or an omelette.

MAKES 2 LARGE HELPINGS

2 handfuls dandelion leaves
6 dry cured streaky bacon rashers
white wine or cider vinegar: 1 part vinegar to 2 parts bacon fat
pepper

Wash the dandelion leaves thoroughly, and strip them from the mid-rib, shred the leaves coarsely and arrange in a shallow dish. Remove the rind and chop the bacon into small squares. Fry the bacon until crisp, but remove from the heat while the fat is still pale in colour—to allow the fat to brown will spoil the dish. Dress the dandelion leaves with vinegar and the hot fat from the pan, add a good grinding of freshly milled black pepper. Top with pieces of bacon and all the scrapings from the pan.

DANDELION AS A VEGETABLE

SPRING AND SUMMER

Dandelion leaves are good cooked as a vegetable. Many of the old cooks described how you should blanch dandelions under a flat stone, or by earthing up, not always easy for people with small gardens lacking wild areas of weed, and not necessary.

SERVES 4

1 colander full dandelion leaves
butter
salt and pepper
a few chives

Strip the leaves from the mid-rib and wash well, then drain and plunge them into a pan of lightly salted boiling water. Cook for 4-5 minutes, and drain, pressing out the surplus liquid with a wooden spoon. Melt a good knob of butter in the pan and toss the dandelion greens in this. Add a grinding of black pepper and a few snipped chives, and serve hot.

DANDELION AND BEETROOT SALAD

SPRING AND SUMMER

The famous French chef Marcel Boulestin described this as a very good winter salad 'though not much thought of in England'. His version used dandelion hearts which had previously been blanched white under a flat stone, but if, as in the previous recipes, you use only the leaf part and discard the bitter mid-ribs, you will find the dandelion greens are mild-flavoured and good.

SERVES 4

4 small beetroot/beets (U.S), sliced
2 handfuls prepared dandelion leaves
salt and pepper
white wine vinegar

Mix the beetroot and dandelions in a shallow dish, season with a little salt and plenty of white pepper, and add enough vinegar to barely cover the salad.

DANDELION COFFEE AUTUMN

In my view this is the best plant for making ersatz coffee. I suggest roasting the dandelion roots twice; once in their original state and again after grinding, as this way you achieve a semblance of that double roast Continental flavour which makes good strong coffee.

It is not necessary to find extra thick roots as they only take longer to bake hard and need to be cut into small pieces. Dig up the roots, trim off the leaves and stems and any small rootlets. Wash off the earth and scrub the roots well, leave them in a warm place to drain and dry. Cut any larger roots in half and into short lengths, spread the pieces on a shallow roasting tin and bake in a hot oven (400°F, 200°C or Gas 6) for 30 minutes until the roots are brown and dry all through—if some are still like baked parsnips in the middle, take out the roots that are hard-baked, and return any soft ones to the oven until they are completely dry. Allow to cool, then grind. Spread the grounds on the roasting tin and roast them for 7 minutes in a moderate oven (350°F, 180°C or Gas 4).

Put 5–6 tablespoons grounds in a warm jug, pour on 500 ml, 2 cups/1 pint boiling water, stir and stand for 30 minutes. Strain into a pan and re-heat.

DANDELION – *TARAXACUM OFFICINALE*

DANDELION FIZZ SPRING AND SUMMER

Gather the dandelion flowers in the sun, when they are fully open. The drink is very mildly alcoholic and though sweet, is quenching, with a hint of the lightest larger flavour. Serve in tall glasses half filled with ice and garnished with a sprig of mint or lemon balm.

1 litre/5 cups/1 quart measure prepared dandelion flowers
2½ litres/4½ U.S. quarts/½ gallon water
1 kilo/4 cups/2 lbs sugar
2 lemons

Trim the stalks from the flowers, but leave the green sepals on and discard any overblown flowers or unopened buds. The prepared dandelions should fill a 1 litre/5 cups/1 quart measure when gently pressed down.

Wash the flowers in a colander and tip them into an earthenware, enamel or plastic container preferably with a well fitting lid. Pour the boiling water on to the dandelions, cover the vessel with a lid, or heavy board or weighted plate, and leave to stand for 12 hours.

Strain the liquid through a double thickness of muslin into a large saucepan. Add the sugar and the pared rind and juice of the lemons. Heat gently and stir until the sugar has dissolved, but do not allow to boil. Strain the liquid into jugs and leave to cool. Pour into clean, dry bottles with strong screw caps. Store in a cool dark place.

The brew is ready to drink in three or four weeks.

DANDELION WINE SPRING AND SUMMER

This is a medium-dry white wine with a fresh, light flavour.

activated yeast (p. 255)
3 litres/13 U.S. pints/3 quarts dandelion flowers
5 litres/9 U.S. quarts/1 gallon water
250 g/1½ cups/8 oz chopped raisins
2 oranges
1 lemon
1.5 kilos/6 cups/3 lbs sugar
2 tablespoons cold tea or 1 teaspoon grape tannin,
    sold for wine-making

Pick the dandelions when fully open on a dry day. Remove the stalks, but leave the green sepals on, put the flower heads into a large bowl and pour on 2½ litres/9 U.S. pints/½ gallon of boiling water. Cover the bowl with a clean cloth and leave the flowers to steep for 2 days, stirring once each day. On the third day tip the contents of the bowl into a large saucepan, add the thinly pared rind (no pith) of the oranges and lemon, and the sugar, bring to the boil, stirring until the sugar dissolves, and boil gently for 30 minutes. Put the raisins and strained orange and lemon juice into the plastic bucket, pour on the boiling contents of the saucepan, then add the remaining 2½ litres/ 9 U.S. pints/½ gallon of water, cold. Cover the bucket with a clean cloth and leave until cool, (about 70°F, 20°C) then stir in the cold tea, or grape tannin, and the activated yeast. Cover the bucket with its lid and leave in a warm place for 3 days. Strain the liquid into the fermentation jar, and follow the method given on page 254.

DANDELION WINE, OLD METHOD

SPRING AND SUMMER

Here is a recipe for wine made in the time-honoured way in a 'stone vessel' and a cask, with baker's yeast spread on a slice of toast floating on the liquid. The 'stone vessel' should be a large earthenware crock and there is a warning in *First Steps in Winemaking* about lead-glazed vessels which are dangerous to use, though seldom found. A very old crock, and some pottery from the Middle East may have a lead glaze which, apparently, is soft enough to dent with a thumbnail. Salt-glazed crocks are safe, and too hard to be dented.

5 litres/9 U.S. quarts/4 quarts dandelion flowers
5 litres/9 U.S. quarts/4 quarts water
small piece root ginger
10 cloves
1.5 kilos/6 cups/3 lbs sugar
1 lemon
small nut fresh baker's yeast
1 slice toast

Use the flower heads only and put them in a large saucepan with the water, crushed ginger root and whole cloves, boil together for half an hour. Stir in the sugar and add the pared rind and strained juice of the lemon, stir to dissolve the sugar and boil up the liquid for half an hour more, strain into an earthenware vessel and, when cool, spread the fresh yeast on both sides of the toast and float it on the surface of the liquid. Cover the vessel with a thick, clean cloth and leave to ferment for two weeks. Strain the wine into clean bottles and cork securely. Store for six months at least.

DULSE
Palmaria palmata

Dulse is a seaweed which grows at the middle- and low-tide levels and is found all round the Atlantic, English Channel and North Sea coasts of Britain, Europe and Scandinavia. It also occurs on the Atlantic and Pacific coasts of North America. Dulse grows on rocks, and sometimes on the big tough stems of several varieties of kelp, which are the largest seaweeds found in British waters.

Dulse is usually a rusty, reddish-brown in colour, the fronds vary from 3-12 ins/8-30 cm in length, and fan out from a wide disc-shaped hold-fast into flattened, irregularly lobed branches. The seaweed becomes tough and dark with age and the younger, delicate specimens are the best to pick.

Dorothy Hartley writes in her 1954 classic work, *Food in England* 'This red seaweed is only eaten in a few places today, usually on the west coast. I think its use must be very old, and dates probably from Eskimo and Icelandic settlements, probably supplying a deficiency in diet for seafaring people. It is interesting I found it most popular in places near the sites of old whaling stations, whereas some other weeds and sea vegetable products are more easily traced to monastic influences.' She then goes on to give a recipe for it stewed saying it takes hours to cook but that maybe because she was using very old, tough fronds. It just needs rinsing and boiling to use fresh but most recipes use dried dulse which goes well with potatoes, fish and seafood.

TO DRY DULSE SPRING AND SUMMER

The seaweed should be washed in fresh water to remove any sand or small stones, and laid outdoors on a piece of muslin to dry. When quite dry and crisp, the bits of dulse should be stored in jars or paper bags.

A few pieces nibbled like potato crisps have a good salty taste and crunchy texture, this is the way dulse is eaten in Ireland. It is also good crumbled over a fish pie.

DULSE SOUP

This is an old Scottish recipe. Use a large cup with a capacity of about 250 ml (1/2 pint).

SERVES 6
6 cups of milk
1 cup cooked dulse
2 cups mashed potatoes
pepper to taste
1 tablespoon melted butter
juice of 1 lemon

Simmer the milk, cooked dulse and mashed potatoes together for about 20 minutes, then either beat well or liquidize in a blender. Season to taste, add the melted butter and the lemon juice and beat again. Heat up and serve immediately.

DULSE – *PALMARIA PALMATA*

ELDER

Sambucus nigra

The elder is a small, deciduous tree or shrub which is common all over the British Isles and Europe. John Josselyn found elder growing in New England in the mid-17th century, which was the North American native *Sambucus canadensis*, and differs very little from the European *S. nigra*. Elder grows in woods, hedgerows, downlands and waste places, and will even sprout defiantly from the walls of old buildings. The trunk is often crooked, branching low down, and the bark, as described by Gerard, 'rugged and full of chinks'. The dark green pinnate leaves consist of five broad, toothed leaflets which have a fetid smell. The flowers are very sweetly fragrant and appear in early summer, growing in large, flat-topped, creamy umbels, each tiny flower with five white petals and five pale yellow anthers. Everything about the elder seems to be made up of fives: each umbel consists of five little flowering heads, four with longer stalks like four fingers, the fifth like a thumb, with a small head on a short stalk. The flowers turn to berries which are hard and green at first, then ripen to a shining purplish-black in early autumn, they hang in heavy, drooping clusters and are very popular with birds.

The elder has been surrounded by mystery and magic; some of it good, some bad: because of the legends that the Cross was made of elder wood and that Judas Iscariot was hanged from an elder tree, people were afraid to cut elders from the hedges, and gypsies avoided burning the wood in their fires. In Denmark, country folk believed that the tree was inhabited by the Elder Mother, *Hylde-Moer*, a guardian spirit who haunted anyone who cut down the tree, and who would persecute a baby laid in a cradle of elder wood. But they also believed that you would see the king of the fairies and his entourage, if you stood beneath an elder tree at midnight on Midsummer's Eve – if you had the courage!

In England, elders were frequently planted near cottages to protect the inmates from lightning and from witches; elder branches were nailed over barns and stables, often in the form of a cross, to ward off evil influences; and the drivers of hearses carried whips of elder wood as a protection against spirits and death, while branches of elder were buried in graves to protect the dead themselves from evil spirits.

In Russia, the peasant believed that the elder was proof against bad spirits, and the Serbs carried a piece of elder at weddings for good luck. In this country, among other sinister beliefs, it was thought that a child beaten with an elder twig would be dwarfed, and that the tree was narcotic and dangerous to sleep under. A more cheerful belief, which I like to encourage, was that an elder tree would only flourish near a house in which happy people lived.

All parts of the elder were used medicinally by the Romans, and in pre-Roman times by the ancient Britons and Celts. In Pliny's day the country people used elderberry juice as a hair dye, and Culpeper described how 'the hair of the head washed with the berries boiled in wine is made black'. John Evelyn claimed that it greatly assisted longevity and that the juice of the berries was effective 'against all infirmities whatever'.

William Coles put forward a theory from the fashionable Doctrine of Signatures, 'the Pith of the Elder being pressed with ones finger doth Pit, and receive the Print of them therein, as the Legs and Feet of Hydropick persons doe;

therefore . . . the juice of Elder, and the Distilled-water of Jews-Ears (a fungus which grows on elder trees) are profitable in the Dropsy. There is hardly a Disease from the Head to the Foot but it cures; for besides the Vertues I have already mentioned, it is profitable for the Head-ach, for Ravings and Wakings, Hypochondriack Mellancholy, the Falling-sickness, the Apoplexy and Palsy, Catarrhes, Tooth-ach, Deafnesse, want of smelling, Blemishes of the Face and Head, Diseases of the Mouth and Throat, the infirmities of the Lungs, Hoarseness, the Pleurisy and Ptisick, Womens breasts being sore, Swooning and Faintness, in Feavours, the Plague, Pox, Measles, Diseases of the Stomack, the Wormes and other diseases of the Gutts, the Hemmorrhoids, the Stone, Diseases of the Matrix etc'; and, as if such all-pervading power over illness was not enough, 'it is said also that if a branch hereof be put into the trench, where a Mole is, it will either drive him forth, or kill him there'.

Thornton's 19th century *Family Herbal* gives a prescription for a dose of elderberry juice, or an infusion of the green bark in wine, which would have the dramatic effect of 'promoting all the fluid secretions'! While Pastor Kneipp, the 19th century Bavarian nature healer, recommended a preserve of elderberries 'for winter use by those who take little exercise, and are condemned to a tranquil, sedentary life'.

Elderberry wine has always had a good reputation, and was once so popular that whole orchards of elders were planted in Kent and the berries sold for wine-making. Cheap port was doctored with elderberry juice to give it a better flavour and colour, in which it was obviously successful for in the middle of the 18th century, the cultivation of elder trees was forbidden in Portugal.

The hard, close-grained wood of old trees was used for shoemakers' pegs, combs, skewers, mathematical instruments and toys. Whistles and popguns were made from the peeled branches, and good fishing floats can be made from the pith of the young twigs. The country people in Pliny's day made musical pipes of elder twigs, and Italian peasants still have a pipe known as *sampogna*, which is made from elder.

In recent medicine an ointment that included elder leaves, *Unguentum Sambuci Viride*, was used for bruises, sprains and chilblains, and *Aqua Sambuci*, elderflower water, is still an ingredient of most skin and eye lotions. A tisane of dried flowers and peppermint is claimed by modern herbalists to be an effective remedy for colds and influenza, which promotes sweating and refreshing sleep.

The bark, root, leaves and berries have been used for making dyes, and the leaves were used as an insecticide when deterrents for fleas and lice were a real necessity. The leaves, in fact, are useful for keeping off flies and midges. If you rub your arms and legs with a handful of leaves, the effects last for about half an hour, and then need to be renewed.

A tree with such a variety of history and folklore, and with so many uses today, deserves to be more widely planted in gardens instead of only gaining a stubborn foothold in hedgerows and railway embankments. Elders are easily grown from cuttings, a young twig broken off and pushed into the ground will strike, and a quick growing wind-break for exposed gardens is soon made from a line of elder shoots. The tree is truly beautiful in early summer with its load of creamy, saucer-shaped blossoms dipping to the ground, their languorous scent is the very essence of drowsy hedgerows and country lanes.

PICKLED ELDER SHOOTS LATE SPRING, EARLY SUMMER

There is a recipe for 'English Bamboo' in Mrs. Martha Bradley's *The British Housewife*, 1750, which uses elder shoots for pickling. I followed the original closely, as her instructions are unusually clear, and found it excellent.

You can gather the shoots in spring and early summer, they tend to sprout from wood that has been lopped or broken off, and also from branches and from the base of trees. Break off the shoots and strip away the leaves. You will need a fair-sized bundle, it is hard to say how many, as you can't tell how much of the shoots are tender until you start cutting them up, but you won't be hurting such vigorous trees by picking the shoots. When prepared, the shoots should pack firmly into two 500 g/ 1 lb jars.

Mrs. Bradley used 1 quart white wine vinegar, 1 quart beer vinegar, 2 oz white pepper, 2 oz black pepper, 3 oz sliced ginger, 1/2 oz mace, 1/2 oz allspice.

Below are the reduced quantities to fill two 500 g/1 lb jars.

a bundle of elder shoots
250 ml/1 cup/1/2 pint white wine vinegar
250 ml/1 cup/1/2 pint cider vinegar
1/2 level teaspoon white pepper
1 level teaspoon black pepper
3 or 4 blades mace
1/2 level teaspoon ground allspice
about 21/2 cm/1 in fresh ginger root finely sliced
    or 1 teaspoon ground ginger

Have ready a large bowl of strongly salted water. With a sharp knife cut the shoots from the base, discarding anything that may be hard or woody—the knife should go easily through the soft, juicy green tops that you will use. Peel the lengths of shoot carefully and immediately drop them into the bowl of salted water. Leave them soaking overnight.

Drain the shoots and rinse them under the cold tap, pat dry in a clean cloth, then cut into lengths of about 21/2 cm/1 in. Gently boil all the pickling ingredients together for 10 minutes. Pack the shoots into warm dry jam jars, strain over the hot pickle, and screw on the lids loosely. To sterilise the pickle, put some folded newspaper in the bottom of a saucepan and stand the jars on it. Fill the pan with cold water to within 21/2 cm/1 in of the neck of the jars. Bring slowly to a simmer, then turn down the heat and keep at the slowest simmer possible for 1 hour. Remove the jars with a cloth and tighten the lids. Stand the jars on newspaper while hot to avoid cracking.

TO PICKLE ELDER BUDS SPRING

'Put the buds in vinegar, season'd with salt, whole pepper, large mace, lemon-peel cut small, let them have 2 or 3 walms over the Fire; then take them out and let the Buds and Pickle both cool, then put the buds into your Pot and cover them with the Pickle', so wrote John Nott, cook to the Duke of Bolton in 1723. The only addition I have made to his recipe is some sugar, as the original was very sharp and vinegary. Picked in the spring, the little sage-green, granular buds make an excellent pickle, with a soft texture and a sharp, refreshing tang that goes well with all cold meats. None of your friends will guess what the pickle is made with, but I guarantee they will enjoy it.

500 ml/2 cups/1 pint measure unopened elderflower buds,
    picked when green
12 peppercorns
1 level teaspoon salt
5-6 blades mace, or 1/4 teaspoon ground mace
6-8 shreds lemon peel
500 ml/2 cups/1 pint distilled vinegar
4-6 tablespoons sugar

Snip off the little flower stalks with scissors, wash the buds and leave them to drain in a strainer until dry. Put the buds in a saucepan with all the other ingredients, bring to the boil, stir, and simmer in the uncovered pan for 10 minutes. Pour into a large bowl to cool and remove the mace and lemon peel. Spoon the elder buds into clean, dry jars to within 1 cm/1/2 in of the top and fill with the pickling liquid to the brim. Screw on plastic-lined lids, or if using metals lids, line them with 2 thicknesses of greaseproof paper. Keep the pickle for three or four months to mellow.

ELDERFLOWER FRITTERS, PLAIN EARLY SUMMER

There are lots of old recipes for elderflower fritters, and modern ones from Germany, where they eat them still. The flat heads of blossom should be dipped once in the batter, it is better not to coat them thickly, or they end up in the pan as a rather stodgy pancake, instead of being lacy, crisp and light.

SERVES 4
12-15 heads of elderflowers
75 g/1/4 cup/3 oz plain flour
pinch salt
1 egg
4 tablespoons/6 U.S. tablespoons milk

3 or 4 tablespoons water
oil for frying

Remove any insects from the elderflowers and trim off the stems leaving a short length to hold them by. Sift the flour and salt into a bowl. Separate the egg, put the yolk in a cup with the milk and water, and mix together lightly with a fork. Tip this mixture into the flour and beat with a wooden spoon until smooth. Whisk the egg white stiffly and fold into the batter with a metal spoon.

Pour some oil into the frying pan to a depth of 1 cm/^{1}/$_2$ in and heat up until a drop of batter sizzles and turns brown when dropped in. Dip each elderflower into the batter and shake off any surplus, lay the flowers flat side downwards in the hot oil. While this side cooks, snip off the stalks with scissors, then turn the fritters over to brown on the other side—it takes 2-3 minutes to cook. Drain the fritters on kitchen paper, while you cook the next batch. Lift them on to a warm serving dish, sprinkle lightly with sugar and serve hot with lemon quarters and extra sugar.

ELDERFLOWER FRITTERS, ALCOHOLIC

EARLY SUMMER

This is another of John Nott's recipes. The Duke of Bolton must have been a rare gourmet and a lucky man to have had such a cook. Whenever I have tried out one of his recipes I have been filled with admiration for his imagination and subtlety. He gives good advice for picking the blossom: 'Gather your Bunches of Elder Flowers just as they are beginning to open, for that is the time of their Perfection, they have just then a very fine Smell and Spirited Taste, but afterwards they grow dead and faint'.

These deliciously alcoholic fritters are first steeped in a mixture of cinnamon, brandy and sherry, before being delicately browned in a thin, winey batter.

SERVES 6
1 colander full elderflowers, the largest heads you can find
1 teaspoon ground cinnamon, or piece of cinnamon stick
1-2 tablespoons brandy
150 ml/^{3}/$_4$ cup/^{1}/$_4$ pint sweet sherry, or Madeira
BATTER
6 tablespoons plain flour
pinch salt
2 eggs
250 ml/1 cup/scant^1/$_2$ pint white wine
butter for frying

Snip each flower head into four parts—they have a natural division into four, actually five, but the fifth is usually so tiny

that it should be discarded. Put the cinnamon and brandy into a shallow dish, lay the flowers in neatly and pour over the sherry or Madeira. Cover the dish with a clean cloth and leave the flowers to soak for an hour, occasionally stirring and gently pressing them into the liquid to keep them moist.

Sift the flour and salt into a mixing bowl. Separate the eggs and stir the yolks into the centre of the flour. Add a little wine and beat with a wooden spoon until small bubbles break the surface, then beat in the rest of the wine to make a thinnish batter. Cover, and stand in a cool place until needed. Whisk the egg whites stiffly, and fold them into the batter when you are ready to cook the fritters. Heat the fat in a frying pan, drain the elderflowers and dip each bunch into the batter, shake off any surplus, and fry the fritters on each side until golden brown. Lift them on to kitchen paper to drain, while you are frying the next batch.

The old recipe tells one to 'heat the dish they are to be sent up in, and rub a lemon upon it, not cut'—this is a nice idea, as some of the oil from the lemon rind leaves a slight fragrance. John Nott strewd 'a little of the finest Orange-Flower Water over them', if you want to be strictly authentic this is a change from lemon, but either way is good.

ELDERFLOWER WATER ICE EARLY SUMMER

This water ice really is outstandingly good and unusual. Pale green, frothily granular, with the most delightful fragrance of elder blossom. When the first hot days of summer hit you, no other sweet is as cooling and refreshing.

SERVES 6
1 heaped colander full of elderflowers
pared rind and juice of 3 large lemons
175 g/scant 1 cup/7 oz sugar
^{3}/$_4$ litre/3^3/$_4$ cups/1^1/$_2$ pints water
2 drops green colouring, optional
1 egg white—see recipe

Snip the elderflowers from their stalks. Put the lemon rind into a large saucepan with the sugar and water. Heat slowly, stirring all the while, then boil rapidly for 5 minutes. Add the elderflowers, cover the pan and draw off the heat. Allow the liquid to stand until quite cold. Strain into a bowl, pressing the liquid out of the flowers with a wooden spoon to extract all the flavour. Stir in the strained lemon juice and the colouring, if using. Pour into cartons, cover and freeze. When the mixture has turned slushy after 2 or 3 hours, scrape into a chilled bowl and beat thoroughly. Whip the egg white stiffly and fold 3 heaped tablespoons of whisked egg white into the water ice. Pour back into the containers, cover and freeze until hard. Half an hour before you are ready to serve the ice transfer the containers to the fridge.

ELDERFLOWER AND GOOSEBERRY ICE CREAM EARLY SUMMER

Elderflowers and gooseberries are always a harmonious combination, the flowers impart a fresh, grapey taste to the ice cream which is simply delicious.

SERVES 6

500 ml/2 cups/1 pint measure elderflowers when
   snipped from their stalks and gently pressed down—
   about 6-8 umbels
500 g/1lb gooseberries
500 g/2 cups/1 lb granulated sugar
250 ml/1 cup/1⁄2 pint water
juice of 1⁄2 lemon
250 ml/1 cup/1⁄2 pint thick cream

Shake the flowers free of insects and snip away the stalks. Top and tail the gooseberries and wash them under the tap. Heat the sugar and water in a saucepan, stirring continuously, then boil fast for 3 minutes. Add the gooseberries and lemon juice to the hot syrup, bring again to the boil and cook for 5 minutes. Draw the pan off the heat and add the elderflowers, stir, cover the pan, and leave until quite cold. Scoop out the elderflowers and put the gooseberry mixture through a fine sieve or food mill. Pour into cartons or tubs, cover and freeze until slushy.

Scrape the mixture into a bowl beat until smooth. Whip the cream lightly and stir into the gooseberry slush. Return to the containers, cover, and freeze until firm. Transfer to the refrigerator half an hour before serving.

ELDERFLOWER SYRUP EARLY SUMMER

Fruit cooked in the syrup, without any extra sugar or water, acquires the lovely muscat grape flavour of elderflowers. Gooseberries, rhubarb, plums, fresh apricots, and redcurrants are all improved by it. About 1 1⁄2 tea-cups syrup to 1 kilo/2 lbs fruit is generally right. Serve the syrup with ice creams, fruit salads and flans; or use as a flower-flavoured cordial, diluted with sparkling water. It keeps well in the refrigerator for several months.

You can make a good supply of syrup while the blossoms are fresh in the early summer. Once they look white, instead of creamy, and have any brown flowerets, their refreshing fragrance has turned sickly sweet and they should not be used.

MAKES ABOUT 1 LITRE (5 CUPS, 2 PINTS) SYRUP

1 colander prepared elderflowers
water to cover
sugar or honey—see method

Snip the stems from the flowers, and put them in a large saucepan with enough water to completely cover them. Bring to the boil and simmer for 15 minutes. Strain and measure the liquid, then return to the pan and for each 3⁄4 litre/ 3 3⁄4 cups/1 1⁄2 pints liquid, add 400 g/2 cups/1 lb sugar. Heat slowly, stirring to dissolve the sugar, then bring to the boil and boil rapidly for 5 minutes. Pour into jugs, and allow to cool. When cold, bottle and cork, or screw on caps.

ICE CREAM WITH ELDERFLOWER SYRUP

This is the easiest ice cream to make and requires no further beating once you have put it to freeze. It is delicious served with a little extra elderflower syrup to pour over each helping.

SERVES 4

250 ml/1 cup/1⁄2 pint thick cream
250 ml/1 cup/1⁄2 pint elderflower syrup
juice of 1⁄2 lemon

Whip the cream in a bowl, and when thick pour the syrup and strained lemon juice into a jug and add gradually to the bowl of cream, whisking between each pouring. Spoon into cartons, cover and freeze.

ELDERFLOWER AND RHUBARB JAM

EARLY SUMMER

The muscat grape flavour of elderflowers is at its freshest and most fragrant in this recipe for rhubarb jam. The long steeping without cooking and the short, rapid boiling ensure a wonderful flavour and fresh pink colour.

MAKES ABOUT 2 KILOS (4 LBS) JAM

6 large umbels elderflowers
1.5 kilos/3 lbs rhubarb
1.5 kilos/6 cups/3 lbs sugar
1 lemon

Cut the thickest stalks from the elderflowers and tie them in a square of muslin, put the bag in the bottom of a large mixing bowl. String and cut the rhubarb into short lengths and pile them on top of the elderflowers. Strew the sugar over the rhubarb and cover the bowl tightly with foil or a weighted plate. Leave for 12 hours, then stir thoroughly with a wooden spoon, cover as before and leave for a further 12 hours. Put the contents of the bowl into a large saucepan, heat gently and stir to dissolve the sugar, but do not allow to boil. Cool a little, then return to the mixing bowl, cover closely and leave for 12 more hours. Take out the bag of elderflowers and tip the rhubarb into the saucepan, add the strained juice of the lemon, bring slowly to the boil and stir, then boil rapidly in the open pan for 7-10 minutes until the jam wrinkles and shows signs of setting when dripped on to a cold saucer. Pour into warm, dry jars, cover with waxed circles while hot and seal with cellophane covers when cold.

ELDERFLOWER DRINK EARLY SUMMER

This is the best wild flower drink ever. Of all the recipes in this book, it is one to which I return unfailingly, year after year.

12 large elderflower heads
2 large lemons
450g/2 cups/1lb sugar
4 litres/20 cups/8 pints water
3 tablespoons white wine vinegar

Shake any insects from the elderflowers and snip off the stems. Put the flowers into a clean plastic bucket, or a large basin, or divide the ingredients between two big bowls. Pare the rind from the lemons, squeeze out the juice and add to the elderflowers. Then add the sugar, water and wine vinegar. Stir until the sugar has dissolved, cover the bucket and leave to steep for 24 hours. Strain the liquid, and fill up bottles with corks or screw-on lids.

This delicious nectar is ready to drink immediately, but it will keep for weeks. Mine never gets the chance!

ELDERFLOWER FIZZ EARLY SUMMER

Elderflowers make a glorious flowery, grapey summer drink as sparkling as champagne. No yeast is needed to promote fermentation, and the brew is ready to drink in 3 weeks.

Store the bottles in a cool dark place.

1 litre/5 cups/1 quart measure elderflowers,
  picked from their stems
1½ lemons
500 g/2 cups/1lb sugar

5 litres/18 U.S. pints/1 gallon water

Shake off any insects from the elderflowers, and snip away the stalks. Slice the lemons and put them with the flowers and sugar in a clean plastic bucket or large bowl. Pour over the cold water, stir thoroughly with a wooden spoon, and cover the bucket or bowl with a lid or weighted plate, to exclude the air. Leave for 24 hours.

Strain into jugs and pour the liquid into clean dry bottles with strong screw-on caps. Fill the bottles to within 5 cm/2 ins of the top and screw the caps on tightly.

Drink within 3-4 weeks, it will not keep indefinitely.

TO DRY ELDERFLOWERS EARLY SUMMER

Pick batches of fully open elderflowers, shake off any insects and snip away the stalks; spread the flowers on a wire rack and stand at the back of a stove or boiler, or in an airing cupboard. When the flowers are quite dry and brittle, crumble them between your fingers over a clean cloth or sheet of paper. Spoon the dried flowers into a screw-topped jar to store.

ELDERFLOWER TEA

One cannot claim a cure for colds, but elderflower tea will reduce stuffiness, especially when taken at bed-time as a hot drink. When you feel the first symptoms of a cold it will sometimes fail to develop, or else be very slight, if you drink hot elderflower tea 3 or 4 times during the day.

2 heaped teaspoons dried elderflowers
250 ml/1 cup/½ pint boiling water

Put the elderflowers into a small jug, pour on the boiling water, stir and leave to infuse for 5 minutes, strain into a cup and drink hot. A good squeeze of lemon juice improves the flavour.

ELDER VINEGAR EARLY SUMMER

This is another recipe from *The Receipt Book* of John Nott, 1723 and should be used as you would use tarragon or any flavoured vinegar.

250 ml/1 cup/½ pint measure dried elderflowers
white wine vinegar—see recipe

Half fill small bottles with the dried flowers and top up with vinegar. Stand the bottles in the sun, or any warm place for two or three weeks to extract the elderflower flavour. Strain and pour into clean bottles to store.

ELDER – *SAMBUCUS NIGRA*

ELDERFLOWER LIQUEUR

Fragrant elderflowers lend a honeyed sweetness to this after-dinner treat.

Elderflowers, to loosely fill an empty vodka bottle
1 bottle vodka

Snip the elderflowers from their stalks, then pack them loosely into an empty bottle, or glass jars. Pour on some of the vodka and shake gently until the flowers are well soaked. Add any remaining flowers up to 2 cm/1 in of the top of the bottle, or jars, then fill up with vodka.

Cork, or screw on the lids, and leave in a dark cupboard for 3 weeks. Strain the liquid into a large jug through a fine strainer, and press out any liquid left in the flowers.

To finish the liqueur, and add to the flowery fragrance, make a syrup with any pale honey, such as white clover, but it must not be one with a strong intensity, like heather honey.

5 tablespoons honey
Boiling water—see below

Measure the honey into a jug and pour on enough boiling water to dissolve the honey. Stir briskly, then set aside to cool. Add the honey syrup to the jug of flavoured vodka, stir to mix well, then pour into bottles, shake gently, and cork or screw on the lids.

ELDERFLOWER WINE EARLY SUMMER

This sweet white wine has a gloriously grapey flavour, and is ideal to drink with dessert, at the end of a meal.

activated yeast (p. 255)
500 ml/2 cups/1 pint freshly picked elderflowers
5 litres/9 U.S. quarts/1 gallon water
strained juice 3 lemons
100 g/3/4 cup/1/4 lb chopped raisins
1.5 kilos/6 cups/3 lbs sugar
2-3 tablespoons tea or 1 teaspoon grape tannin
 (sold for wine-making)

Pick the flowers on a dry day, snip off their stalks and lightly pack them into a 500 ml/2 cup/1 pint measure. Tip the flowers into the plastic bin or bucket, pour over the boiling water, add the lemon juice, the chopped raisins and the sugar and stir until the sugar dissolves. Cover the bucket with a clean cloth and leave until cool, (about 70°F, 20°C) then stir in the cold tea, or grape tannin, and the activated yeast. Cover the bucket with its lid and leave for four or five days in a warm place, stirring daily.

Strain the liquid into the fermentation jar and follow the method given on page 254.

ELDERFLOWER WATER EARLY SUMMER

Elderflower water is used in making cosmetic creams and lotions, but the homemade version does not keep longer than two or three weeks, and is best stored in the refrigerator. Commercial elderflower water is distilled and made up into skin and eye lotions, it used to have a great reputation for clearing the skin of freckles and sunburn, and preserving a coveted fair, white complexion. The hand lotions on page 89, if used regularly, do have a softening and whitening effect.

A muslin bag filled with fresh or dried elderflowers is soothing and fragrant to use in the bath or hand basin.

1 litre/5 cups/2 pints measure prepared elderflowers
250 ml/1 cup/1/2 pint boiling water

Pick the blossom when fully open, but still fresh. Snip away all the little stalks. Measure the flowers into a bowl, pour on the boiling water, cover and leave to infuse for two or three hours. Strain into a jug and pour into small bottles.

ELDERFLOWER FACE CREAM EARLY SUMMER

Gently massage the cream into the face and neck after removing make-up and at night, it helps to fade freckles and keeps the skin soft. White wax, which is bees wax, is sold in flat cakes and can be bought from old-fashioned hardware shops. Some chemists stock almond oil and borax.

125 ml/generous 1/2 cup/41/2 fl. oz almond oil
20 g/3/4 oz white wax
75 ml/scant 1/4 cup/3 fl. oz elderflower water
1/2 teaspoon borax

Put the almond oil and white wax in a small bowl and stand in a saucepan of hot water to melt slowly over a low heat. Put the elderflower water and borax in a cup and stand this in another small pan of hot water, heat gently while you stir with a small bone or wooden spoon until the borax has completely dissolved, pour this solution into the bowl of oil and wax, then remove the bowl from the hot water and beat as it cools, until the mixture becomes thick and creamy.

Spoon into small pots or jars and cover tightly. A drop of edible green colouring stirred into the cream makes it look more attractive.

ELDERFLOWER HAND LOTION I EARLY SUMMER

Use this lotion morning and evening to soften and whiten the hands.

50 g/3 cups/2 oz elderflowers, snipped from their stems
500 ml/2 cups/1 pint water
glycerine—see recipe
2-3 drops lavender oil
1/2 teaspoon borax

Cut away the stems from the elderflowers and put 50 g/3 cups/2 oz into a jug. Pour on the boiling water, cover and leave to infuse for several hours, or overnight. Strain the liquid through muslin into a measuring jug, and to every three parts elderflower water, add one part glycerine. Stir in the lavender oil and the borax, and mix very thoroughly. Pour into clean bottles and cork or screw on the caps.

ELDERFLOWER HAND LOTION II EARLY SUMMER

A soothing lotion for the hands, and for softening a dry skin.

175 ml/3/4 cup/6 fl. oz glycerine
50 ml/1/4 cup/2 fl. oz elderflower water
pinch of borax

Stir all the ingredients together in a jug until thoroughly mixed, then pour into a small bottle. Massage the lotion into the hands night and morning and after washing.

ELDERFLOWER FACE LOTION EARLY SUMMER

A moisturising and refreshing lotion to use after removing make-up. Apply to the skin on a pad of cotton wool. Orange flower water can usually be found in Asian or Middle Eastern grocers.

4-5 tablespoons elderflower water
1 tablespoon orange flower water
4-5 tablespoons glycerine
1/2 tablespoon strained lemon juice

Mix all the ingredients together in a jug and pour into a small bottle.

ELDERFLOWER LOTION FOR SUNBURN AND CHAPPED HANDS EARLY SUMMER

This is an effective lotion for chapped hands, and for the face if you have been out in too much strong sun, or in cold winds. It has a nice smell.

4-5 tablespoons elderflower water
4-5 tablespoons glycerine
2-3 tablespoons witch hazel
1 tablespoon almond oil
2 drops lavender oil
1/2 teaspoon borax

Put all the ingredients into a jug and stir well. Pour into a small bottle and shake vigorously. Keep corked or with the cap screwed on.

ELDERFLOWER JELLY FOR HANDS

EARLY SUMMER

This hand jelly is non-greasy and rubs completely into the skin. Keep a jar in the kitchen and use it after washing-up to keep your hands smooth. Wild rose water, or rosemary water may be used instead of elderflower.

125 ml/1/2 cup/4 fl. oz elderflower water
1 tablespoon glycerine
2 level teaspoons cornflour

Measure the elderflower water into a bowl and stand over a saucepan of hot water. Warm the glycerine in another bowl and stir in the cornflour to make a thick, smooth cream. Gradually stir the warmed elderflower water into the glycerine mixture and continue to stir over the heat until the cornflour clears into a thickish jelly. Remove from the heat and allow to cool. Pour into small pots or jars and screw on the lids when quite cold.

ELDERFLOWER LOTION FOR THE EYES

EARLY SUMMER

A mildly astringent, refreshing and soothing lotion for tired and puffy eyes. Soak two pads of cotton wool in the lotion and place on closed eyelids for 10 minutes while you rest.

4-5 tablespoons elderflower water
1 tablespoon witch hazel

Mix together in a cup or jug before using.

ELDERBERRY SOUP LATE SUMMER, EARLY AUTUMN

Fruit soups are popular in some parts of Europe. This Danish elderberry soup should be served hot, with gently poached whole quarters of apple and little walnut-sized, cooked dumplings, or with small cubes of white bread fried in butter and sugar.

SERVES 6

500 g/1 lb ripe elderberries

1¹/2 litres/7¹/2 cups/3 pints water

1 lemon

small piece cinnamon stick

1 level tablespoon cornflour

4-5 tablespoons sugar

Wash the elderberries and strip them from their stems. Put the berries in a saucepan with the water, pared lemon rind and cinnamon, bring to the boil and cook gently for 10-15 minutes until the elderberries are soft, strain into a clean saucepan, remove the lemon rind and cinnamon and press out all the juice from the berries. Slake the cornflour with the strained lemon juice and add to the pan of elderberry juice, bring to the boil, stirring briskly to blend, remove from the heat when the soup thickens and stir in the sugar to taste.

ELDERBERRY SORBET LATE SUMMER, EARLY AUTUMN

Ripe elderberries make a delicious dark sorbet, absolutely good enough for a dinner party. Pick enough berries to give 500 ml/ 2 cups/1 pint juice when sieved.

SERVES 6

500 ml/2 cups/1 pint elderberry juice

strained juice of 1 lemon

200 g/1 cup/¹/2 lb sugar

3–4 tablespoons water

250 ml/1 cup/¹/2 pint thick cream

Follow the method for Blackberry Sorbet on page 39.

WILD SUMMER PUDDING

LATE SUMMER—EARLY AUTUMN

Nothing could be nicer than this pudding, which uses wild fruit and stale bread. The sweet berries and astringent crab apples make a marvellous mingling of flavours. You will find the family is more than willing to pick the fruit, as long as you produce the pudding.

250 g/¹/2 lb elderberries, stripped from their stalks

250 g/¹/2 lb blackberries

750 g/1¹/2 lbs crab apples

375 ml/scant 2 cups/³/4 pint water

300 g/1¹/2 cups/³/4 lb sugar

slices of stale bread

Put the elderberries and blackberries in a pan with the water and sugar. Bring slowly to the boil stirring all the while, then cook gently for 5 minutes. Meanwhile cut the crab apples in half and nick out any bad bits. Drop the pieces into cold water as you cut them up. Drain the elder and blackberries through a strainer and allow the juice to run into a clean saucepan. Add the crab apples to this juice and cook them gently for about 15 minutes, until they are soft. Put the crab apples through a food mill, or sieve. Mix this purée with the elder and blackberries.

Grease a bowl of suitable size and line it with slices of stale bread. Pour in the mixed fruit and juice; if there is any over, reserve it. Cover the top of the basin with bread slices, cover with a fitting plate or saucer, and put a weight on top. Leave overnight. Either turn out the pudding on to a dish, or serve it in the bowl, with the reserved juice poured over the top.

ELDERBERRY AND BLACKBERRY JELLY

LATE SUMMER, EARLY AUTUMN

When the elderberries are ripe the blackberries should be sound and rather under-ripe, which is the best time for making them into a jelly that will set well, and have a good sharp flavour.

1 kilo/2 lbs elderberries, stripped from their stalks

1 kilo/2 lbs blackberries

water—see method

sugar—see method

Wash the berries and put them in a large pan with just enough water to cover. Bring slowly to the boil and cook until the fruit is soft and well pulped, about 15 minutes, mashing occasionally with a wooden spoon. Drip through double muslin or a jelly bag overnight.

Measure the juice into a large pan and add 300 g/1¹/2 cups/³/4 lb sugar to every 500 ml/2¹/2 cups/1 pint of juice. Bring slowly to the boil, stirring continuously until the sugar has dissolved, then boil rapidly for about 10 minutes until the juice gels when dripped on to a cold saucer. Skim and pour at once into warm, dry jars, cover with waxed circles while hot, seal with cellophane covers when cold.

ELDERBERRY AND CRAB APPLE JELLY

LATE SUMMER, EARLY AUTUMN

You can use cooking apples instead of crab apples, but they must be green and hard to give acidity to the sweet elderberries.

750 g/1¹/₂ lbs elderberries, stripped from their stalks
1.5 kilos/3 lbs crab apples
water—see method
1 lemon
sugar—see method

Wash the fruit after removing the elderberry stalks, and cut the apples into pieces, but don't remove the skins or cores. Put all the fruit in a large saucepan with just enough water to cover, bring to the boil and cook for 10 minutes in a covered pan until soft, mashing occasionally with a wooden spoon. Drip through a jelly bag or double thickness of muslin overnight. Measure the juice into a pan, and to every 500 ml/2¹/₂ cups/1 pint add 300 g/1¹/₂ cups/³/₄ lb sugar. Bring slowly to the boil, stirring until the sugar has dissolved, then boil fast in an uncovered pan for 12–15 minutes until the liquid gels when dripped onto a cold saucer. Skim thoroughly and pour into warm dry jars. Cover with waxed circles while hot, and seal with cellophane covers when cold.

ELDER ROB LATE SUMMER, EARLY AUTUMN

Many old books give a recipe for Elder Rob as a remedy for coughs, colds and sore throats, and it makes a very soothing bed-time drink if you add a tumbler of boiling water to 2 tablespoons of the syrup. It is also a refreshing summer drink with ice, sparkling water and a good squeeze of lemon juice. Perhaps the most delicious way of using this claret-coloured syrup is to heat some in a small saucepan and serve it hot with vanilla ice cream. The sweet authentic flavour of the wild berries transforms a good quality commercial ice cream into a very good dish, and if served with homemade vanilla ice cream it is worthy of a dinner party. For more homely meals it is lovely poured cold over hot rice pudding.

1 litre/5 cups/2 pints measure ripe elderberries,
  stripped from their stalks
4–5 tablespoons water
sugar—see recipe

Wash the elderberries and drain in a colander. Strip the berries from their stalks through the prongs of a fork, measure and put them with the water in a saucepan. Cover the pan and simmer slowly over a very low heat. Crush the berries with a wooden spoon from time to time to extract the juice, then strain through a sieve or strainer and press all the juice from the berries with the back of the spoon.

Measure the juice back into the pan, and for every

500 ml/2¹/₂ cups/1 pint juice, add 400 g/2 cups/1 lb sugar. Bring slowly to the boil, stirring continuously until the sugar has dissolved, then continue to boil steadily, in the uncovered pan for 5–10 minutes, until the liquid is thick and syrupy.

Remove from the heat and skim. Allow to cool, then pour into clean bottles and cork or screw on the caps.

FRESH ELDERBERRY DRINK

LATE SUMMER, EARLY AUTUMN

This is a cooling, sweet drink that children love for its flavour and pretty pink colour.

500 ml/2 cups/1 pint measure elderberries
4 tablespoons sugar, or 2 tablespoons honey
strained juice 1 lemon
water—see method

Pick the elderberries when ripe. Wash the berries and strip them from their stalks through the prongs of a fork. Tip the berries into a large jug and add sugar or honey to taste, then add the lemon juice, and fill up the jug with boiling water, stir and leave until cold.

Pour the elderberry liquid through a strainer into a clean jug, crushing the berries with a wooden spoon to extract the juice.

To serve, put some ice cubes into tall glasses and top up with the fresh elderberry juice.

ELDERBERRY CHUTNEY LATE SUMMER, EARLY AUTUMN

This is an unusual addition to the store cupboard which can be a boon when you are faced with the remains of a cold joint.

500 g/1 lb elderberries, stripped from their stalks
1 small onion
¹/₂ teaspoon salt
¹/₂ teaspoon cinnamon
¹/₂ teaspoon ground ginger
a good grating nutmeg
¹/₂ teaspoon mustard seed, tied in a scrap of muslin
250 ml/1 cup/¹/₂ pint distilled malt vinegar
1 medium cooking apple
50 g/4 tablespoons/2 oz seedless raisins
75 g/6 tablespoons/3 oz soft brown sugar

Wash the elderberries and peel and slice the onion, put them in a large saucepan together with the salt, spices and mustard seed, add the vinegar and cook slowly for 1 hour.

Remove the muslin with the mustard seed and rub the

elderberry mixture through a sieve or food mill. Return to the pan with the peeled and chopped apple, and the raisins and sugar.

Bring slowly to the boil, stirring until the sugar has dissolved, then cook in the open pan for 15 minutes. Pour into warm dry jars, cover with waxed circles while hot, seal with cellophane covers when cold.

SPICED ELDERBERRY SAUCE

LATE SUMMER, EARLY AUTUMN

This spicy fruit sauce enhances all sorts of cold meat: chicken, turkey, cold roast pork or ham. It stores well and is a good way of using plentiful elderberries.

250 ml/1 cup/1/2 pint measure elderberries,
    stripped from their stalks
1 medium cooking apple
1 medium onion
250 ml/1 cup/1/2 pint malt vinegar
1/2 teaspoon salt
1/2 teaspoon cinnamon
1/2 teaspoon ground ginger
1/4 teaspoon ground mace
4 cloves
150 g/3/4 cup/6 oz brown sugar

Wash the elderberries, peel, core, and slice the apple, and peel and finely chop the onion, put them all together in a large pan with the vinegar, salt and spices, cover and simmer slowly for 1 hour. Rub the mixture through a fine sieve or food mill or liquidise.

Return to the pan, add the sugar, bring again to the boil and stir until the sugar has dissolved.

Cook in the uncovered pan for 15 minutes until the sauce has thickened. Pour into a jug, and bottle when cold.

ELDERBERRY WINE LATE SUMMER, EARLY AUTUMN

Elderberries make a delicious red wine. This recipe gives a medium sweet flavour, but you can make it sweeter or drier, by using more or less sugar.

activated yeast (p. 255)
1.5 kilos/3 lbs elderberries, when stripped from their stalks
5 litres/18 U.S. pints/1 gallon water
1.5 kilos/6 cups/3 lbs sugar
2 tablespoons grated root ginger

Pick the elderberries on a dry day and strip them from their stalks through the prongs of a fork, put the berries into the plastic bucket and crush them with a wooden spoon.

Pour on the boiling water, cover the bucket with a clean cloth and leave until cool, (about 70°F, 20°C) then stir in the activated yeast. Cover the bucket with its plastic lid and leave in a warm place for three days, stirring daily.

Strain the liquid on to the sugar and ginger and stir thoroughly until the sugar has dissolved, then strain into the fermentation jar (dark glass for a red wine) and follow the method given on page 254.

ELDER PITH FISHING FLOAT SPRING AND SUMMER

Country children used to make their fishing floats from elder pith, which function just as well as any you can buy.

The pith may be taken from any green shoots of suitable thickness.

MATERIALS
1 green elder shoot, any length
piece of bamboo cane, 20–25 cm/8–10 in long
fine emery paper/sandpaper
glue, such as Durofix
small piece of thin stiff wire
whipping silk, or thread
paints, varnish

Cut a young green shoot roughly the thickness of a finger and cut it into 15 cm/6 ins lengths. Put the pieces to dry at the back of a stove, or in the sun, for two or three days. Peel away the thin bark with a knife and leave the pith to dry for two or three hours.

With a sharp knife cut the pith into lengths of about 1 1/2-2 1/2 cm/3/4-1 in, two lengths will make a small float, three or four a larger one. Push a hole through the middle of each length of pith with a large needle.

Make the stick for the float from a thin sliver of bamboo cane about 17-20 cm/7-8 ins long. Smooth and taper the cane with emery paper.

Thread two lengths of pith on to the cane to enlarge the hole, and mark the position for the body with ballpoint pen. Slide off the pith and coat the stick with glue where the position for the body is marked. Glue the two inside edges of the pith that will fit together.

Thread the two lengths of pith on to the stick again and gently press the glued edges together. Leave to dry overnight.

Shape the float body with emery paper, tapering towards each end, and fill in any holes with scraps of pith mixed with glue.

Leave to dry, then smooth with emery paper (sandpaper U.S.) and trim the top and bottom of the float neatly with a sharp knife.

Make an eye with wire, and whip it on the bottom of the stick with thread or silk.

Paint the whole float with a thin undercoat and, when dry, paint the bottom half with brown or drab green paint and the top part with any bright, easily visible colour, paint over the whipping, but be careful not to fill in the wire eye.

When quite dry, paint the whole float with a thin coat of varnish.

FENNEL
Foeniculum vulgare

Fennel is a true native of the Mediterranean and, in Britain, grows wild only in the southern half of England, usually near the sea, and particularly in the mild maritime climate of the south west. It is also found throughout the USA both as a garden herb and as an escape from cultivation. Fennel is perennial, 90 cm-1.5 metres/3-5 ft tall, with shiny, bright green, cylindrical stems. The thread-like leaves grow in dark green, feathery plumes which give the whole plant an elegant and fine cut appearance. The umbels of bright yellow flowers appear throughout the summer and early autumn, and all parts of the plant have a strong aromatic scent and taste of aniseed.

A number of countries have developed different types of fennel: Italy, France, Saxony, Romania and Iran; even India and Japan have different varieties, mostly cultivated for the seeds which are a popular flavouring in food and liqueurs. Florentine fennel is grown for its root, which forms a large bulb, and makes a delicious and unusual vegetable, with the distinctive aniseed taste.

Modern herbalists recommend an infusion of fennel, used cold, to tighten a wrinkled skin and to bathe tired eyes; and a belief that fennel would improve bad eyesight survived for many centuries. Pliny wrote that, when casting their skins, snakes 'sharpened their sight' by rubbing against the plant, and William Coles warned 'them that live in those Countryes where there be any Serpents or Snakes, have a care they wash their Fennel before they use it: because they delight much to be amongst it; it is thought that they make use of it to preserve their Eyesight'.

Another virtue attributed to fennel that crops up in the early herbals is that it would make people thin. Coles advised fennel leaves and seeds 'in drinks and broths, for those that are grown fat, to abate their unwieldiness and make them more gaunt and lank', Culpeper wrote that the leaves, seeds and roots of fennel 'are much used as a drink, or broth, to make people more lean that are too fat'. Perhaps the slimming idea was linked with another that fennel could still the pangs of hunger; Dawson gave a recipe in *The Good Housewife's Journal*, 1585, for a decoction of fennel which taken first thing in the morning and last thing at night 'shall swage (assuage) him or her', and I have read that in medieval times the peasants chewed fennel to ease their hunger.

FENNEL – *FOENICULUM VULGARE*

In France, in the 18th century, fennel leaves and stalks were fed to cows and sheep to increase their milk yield, and it was supposed to impart a wonderful flavour to the flesh of rabbits if they were given fennel to eat.

Fennel seeds were used in the old medicines *Aqua Foeniculi, Oleum Foeniculi* and *Tinctura Foeniculi Composita*, and the Bavarian nature healer, Dr. Kneipp, said fennel seeds should be in every family medicine cupboard. The dried seeds contain a volatile oil which is aromatic and carminative and used in pharmacy today: it is given to babies for flatulence, in Fennel Water.

Andrew Borde, who was 'phisicke doctor' to Henry VIII, described a herbal brew which included fennel water for another ailment, 'horsness of Voyce'. Take of the water of scabious, of the water of fennell, of the water of lyceryce, of the water of buglose, of eche of them a pynt, of sugar candy a pounde. Sethe this togyther, and mornynge and evenynge drynke IX spone-full'. The amount chosen for the dose is intriguing, three was considered a powerful number, three times three even more, so nine spoonfuls would have added greatly to the efficacy of the brew.

FISH WITH FENNEL SAUCE

EARLY SPRING UNTIL LATE AUTUMN

Fennel is a traditional herb to serve with fish, it gives this sauce a lovely flavour, making quite ordinary fish rather special.

SERVES 2

500 g/1 lb filleted cod or fresh haddock
250 ml/1 cup/½ pint milk
salt and freshly milled black pepper
25 g/2 tablespoons/1 oz butter
1 rounded tablespoon flour
1 rounded tablespoon chopped fresh fennel leaves

Rinse the pieces of fish, drain and put them in a saucepan with the milk and a seasoning of salt and pepper. Bring to the boil gently, then lower the heat and simmer for 5 minutes. Lift the fish out carefully, reserving the milk in which it cooked, and remove any skin and bones. Arrange the fish in a well-buttered, shallow, fireproof dish and keep warm while you make the sauce.

Melt the butter in a saucepan, stir in the flour, gradually add the milk in which the fish was cooked, stirring continuously until the sauce thickens smoothly, then stir in the fennel. Check the seasoning, pour the sauce over the fish and slip the dish under a warm grill, or into a hot oven for a few minutes.

FENNEL AND GOOSEBERRY SAUCE WITH MACKEREL EARLY SUMMER

Choose green, rather under-ripe gooseberries for this sauce, their sharpness and the aromatic tang of fennel are good with an oily fish like mackerel. Serve the sauce in a sauceboat and garnish the mackerel with wedges of lemon.

SERVES 4

250 g/8 oz green gooseberries
1 tablespoon sugar, or ½ tablespoon honey
50 g/4 tablespoons/2 oz butter
1 level tablespoon flour
250 ml/1 cup/½ pint hot water
2 teaspoons finely chopped fennel leaves
salt and white pepper
nutmeg

Wash and top and tail the gooseberries and put them in a saucepan with 2 tablespoons water taken from the 250 ml/1 cup/½ pint, simmer gently until the gooseberries start to soften and turn yellow, then liquidize and stir in the sugar, or honey while the purée is still hot. Melt 15 g/1 U.S. tablespoon/½ oz of the butter in a small pan over a low heat, shake in the flour and stir to blend, add the hot water and stir until the mixture thickens; then draw off the heat and add the rest of the butter in small pieces until all are melted, return to the heat and add the gooseberry purée. Stir in the fennel and salt and pepper and add a light grating of nutmeg. Cover and keep warm while you grill the fish.

4 medium-sized mackerel
oil for grilling
salt and freshly milled black pepper
1/2 lemon

Gut the mackerel and remove the heads and tails, split them down the middle and press each fish open flat, remove the backbone and as many large bones as possible. Brush the cut sides with oil, sprinkle with salt and pepper, and a squeeze of lemon juice to each fish. Line the grill pan with foil and grill the fish cut side up for about 5-7 minutes, turn over carefully and grill on the skin side for about a further 3-4 minutes. Lift the mackerel on to a hot dish and garnish with an extra lemon cut into thin wedges.

CREAMY FENNEL SAUCE EARLY SPRING UNTIL LATE AUTUMN

This easily-made sauce is so luxurious that it is worthy of a piece of cold salmon, or a couple of large trout poached, or wrapped in foil and baked in the oven, then allowed to cool. Serve the fish with brown bread and butter and lemon wedges, and hand the sauce separately.

225 ml/1 cup/8 fl. oz thick cream
2 or 3 tablespoons lemon juice
4 or 5 tablespoons finely chopped fennel leaves
salt and freshly milled black pepper

Whip the cream lightly, stir in the strained lemon juice and the chopped fennel. Season with salt and plenty of black pepper.

The same sauce is wonderful with pork chops roasted in the oven. Smear a small nut of butter over the roasting tin before you cook the chops in a moderately hot oven (375°F, 190°C or Gas 5) for 30 minutes, when the chops are well browned, drop a tablespoonful of the sauce on to each and return to the oven for a minute, so that the creamy sauce and meat juices mingle together, scrape the juices out of the pan on to the chops to serve.

GARLIC MUSTARD
Alliaria petiolata

HEDGE GARLIC, SAUCE-ALL-ALONE, JACK-BY-THE-HEDGE, POOR MAN'S MUSTARD

Garlic Mustard grows throughout the British Isles and in most of Europe and Scandinavia. In America it is locally abundant in the mid-western and north-eastern states, but can also be found as far south as Kentucky and North Carolina. In early spring, the vivid light green leaves show up against the darker growth of hedgerows and the margins of woods. The plants vary from spindly specimens of 12-20 cm/5-8 ins to flourishing clumps as tall as 1 metre/3 ft. The broad, heart-shaped leaves are toothed, and at the base of the plant grow on fairly long stalks. Near the top, the leaf stalks are shorter, and the leaves have prominent veins, especially on the undersides. The flowers have four tiny snow-white petals that look like white cross stitch, and grow at the top of the plant in a cluster of tight green buds and white flowers. Much smaller, unopened flower heads spring from the angle of the leaf stalks and the main stem.

The plant has many common names: Hedge Garlic, Sauce-all-Alone, Jack-by-the-Hedge and Poor Man's Mustard, indicating that it has been used as a flavouring from early times. When bruised, the whole plant has a smell of

GARLIC MUSTARD – *ALLIARIA PETIOLATA*

onion rather than garlic, in spite of its names. In 1657 William Coles wrote that it was eaten by 'many country people as sauce to their Salt-fish, and helpeth well to digest the crudities, and other crude humours that are engendered by the eating thereof'.

The leaves were used medicinally by the early herbalists for dropsy and to induce sweating. In *The Family Herbal*, Sir John Hill recommended that they should be boiled with honey to make a syrup as a remedy for coughs and hoarseness. The leaves were also believed to have antiseptic properties, and were applied as dressings to open sores and ulcers.

AS A VEGETABLE

SPRING AND EARLY SUMMER

When cooked as a vegetable, the faint onion flavour of the plant is lost, and the taste and texture is more like strong turnip tops. It is still worth cooking, as it is free for the picking.

SERVES 4

1 heaped colander garlic mustard leaves and tops
  (after picking over)
butter
salt and pepper
nutmeg

Pick off and use all the leaves, large and small, and the whole tip of the plant including the small white flowers; soak in lightly salted water, then wash in fresh water and drain. Drop the leaves into a pan of boiling water and cook for 5 minutes, drain, and throw away the water. Cook again in a fresh lot of boiling, lightly salted water for 5 minutes. This reduces the strong, rather bitter flavour of the plant.

Drain the leaves thoroughly, then return to the pan with a good knob of butter, a grinding of black pepper and plenty of grated nutmeg.

GARLIC MUSTARD SAUCE, FOR FISH

SPRING AND EARLY SUMMER

A good alternative to parsley sauce can be made by stirring a handful of well washed and finely chopped garlic mustard leaves into about 250 ml/1 cup/½ pint of smooth, buttery white sauce. The onion-flavoured leaves will enliven poached or steamed fish and you can make several variations of the sauce with a mixture of chopped green herbs such as sorrel, lady's smock, fennel and balm, with perhaps a few chopped capers or gherkins added. The sauce can also be added to cooked, flaked fish and baked in the oven as a fish pie.

GLASSWORT

Salicornia europaea

he succulent, salt-loving samphires are fascinating examples of a plant's ability to adapt to its surroundings; growing on saltmarshes and tidal mud which is wetted by spray and covered by the tides, the bright green leaves and stems have fused into fleshy, cylindrical, jointed branches, making the plant look like a small juicy cactus. Under the onslaught of salt water the petalless flowers have been reduced to just one or two tiny male or female parts which are sunk in twos and threes in the junctions of the stems, they are only just visible and appear in late summer. The seeds are hairy and minute, yet they fulfil their function, for the samphires are annuals, except for one, the perennial glasswort, (*S. perennis*) which is found in firmer mud and gravel and is often orange or red, making bold patches of colour where it grows abundantly. The plants vary from 5 cm/2 ins to 30 cm/1 ft in height, and as they frequently hybridise, the various forms are not always distinct. Samphires are found in salt marshes and coastal flats throughout Europe, America and the British Isles, where they are more common in East Anglia and the south of England.

Picking samphire is usually full of fun and adventure, their habitat of estuary or marsh tends to be wild and unfrequented, and the varieties that grow in the softer mud are a challenge to one's agility and judgement of the tide. The salt scents and clean breezes seem to be distilled into the taste of the plants' funny little pointed stubs and fleshy stems, and one can eat the cleaner specimens on the spot, reserving the muddier ones to take home to wash and be made into pickle.

Samphires contain soda and have been used since biblical days for making soap and glass, hence their name. Our British samphires were used in early glassmaking, and glasswort ashes were imported for this purpose from the Mediterranean under the name of *barilla*. John Josselyn's account of his travels in North America in the 17th century mentions glasswort as growing abundantly in salt marshes, 'here called *berrelia*', obviously an anglicised version of the Spanish word *barilla*, showing that the Spaniards had already discovered the plant in America.

Coles describes the glassmaking process, 'The Salt, which extracted out the Ashes, which being mixed with a certaine kind of sand, and boiled in a furnace there ariseth a Scum called *Axungia virtri* in Latine, and in English Sandiver'; he also mentions soap, saying 'it was used to be put into castle, or rather Castile Sope, for it came first out of Spaine, the Castilians being the inventors thereof'. Coles has a long list of complaints for which glasswort was a remedy: as a purge, for dropsy, to provoke urine, to expel the dead birth, to open obstructions of the liver and spleen, to consume proud-flesh, to clear the skin of spots and freckles and to squirt into a horse's eyes 'to take away the skin that beginneth to grow there and dimm the sight . . . to dry up running sores and scabs, tetters and ring-worms . . . and to help the itch'.

Both Coles and Parkinson give the same remedy for a person 'casually taken speechless', or struck dumb. Soap, made from the ashes of glasswort, was spread on a piece of thick brown paper cut to the shape of that person's 'shooe-sole' and bound to the soles of the feet, after which, if the patient had any hope of recovery, his speech would return within a little time 'as hath been proved'.

SAMPHIRE IN SALAD AND AS A VEGETABLE SUMMER

The fleshy, green finger-like leaves are best eaten in summer when the plant is only 7-15 cm/3-6 ins high. Later, the taste becomes insipid, and the leaves and stems are tougher. Chewed raw and straight from the beach, it has the taste and texture of fresh lettuce heart with its own seasoning of slight saltiness, and can be useful to enliven sandwiches, if you find yourself in its vicinity with an uninteresting packed lunch. To prepare the samphire for salad or as a vegetable, discard the lower main stems, soak the fleshy leaves in a bowl of fresh water, then wash them thoroughly. Either use the leaves raw, or cook in lightly salted boiling water for not more than 2-3 minutes. Drain and cool.

Serve in any mixed salad with a vinaigrette dressing or serve warm as a vegetable, seasoned with pepper and a nut of butter.

GLASSWORT – *SALICORNIA EUROPAEA*

SAMPHIRE PICKLE SUMMER

One can eat samphire pickle straight from the jar, or with cold meat or poultry; it is succulent and delicious.

1 litre/5 cups/2 pints measure prepared samphire
500 ml/2 cups/1 pint white wine vinegar
2 teaspoons pickling spice

Wash the samphire in several changes of water, drain in a colander and prepare as in previous recipe. Throw the leaves into lightly salted, boiling water and blanch for 2 minutes. Drain. Boil up the vinegar and pickling spice together for 3 minutes, strain into a jug and leave to cool. Pack the samphire into jars to within 2¹/₂ cm/1 in of the top, pour over the cool, spiced vinegar ensuring the samphire is well covered and screw on plastic-lined lids, or if you are using metal lids, line them with vinegar-proof paper or two thicknesses of greaseproof paper. Store for three or four months to allow the pickle to mellow.

SWEET PICKLE FOR SAMPHIRE SUMMER

This sweet pickle is a tasy alternative to the preceding recipe.

1 litre/5 cups/2 pints measure prepared samphire
450 ml/scant 2 cups/³/₄ pint cider vinegar
100 g/¹/₂ cup/4 oz soft brown sugar, or 4 tablespoons honey
¹/₂ level teaspoon turmeric
¹/₄ level teaspoon ground cloves
1 rounded teaspoon mustard seed
¹/₄ level teaspoon celery seed

Put the vinegar, sugar or honey and spices into a saucepan, stir over a low heat while the sugar or honey melts, then bring to the boil. Draw the pan off the heat, pour the liquid into a jug and set aside to cool.

Prepare the samphire and fill the jars in exactly the same way as in the preceding recipe.

GOOSEFOOT
Chenopodium

FAT HEN *C. album* RED GOOSEFOOT *C. rubrum* MAPLE-LEAVED GOOSEFOOT *C. hybridum*
GOOD KING HENRY *C. bonus-henricus*

This is a complicated family of plants because there are several species and they all look rather alike. Each plant may vary enormously in size, from tiny specimens a few centimetres high that must have been stunted by poor soil, to great bushy plants up to 1.25 metres/ 4 ft tall where they have lighted upon a manure heap, which is their favourite habitat. Plants of the same species can vary in shape and colouring too and, to make the whole thing more baffling, the goosefoots *Chenopodium*, and oraches, *Atriplex*, are often hard to tell apart! The members of both families may be described as mealy, annual weeds with thick, roughly toothed and usually stalked leaves, and green spikes of tiny, inconspicuous, petalless flowers. The rather technical botanical distinctions between the flowers and seeds of the goosefoots and the oraches are only distinguishable with a magnifying glass. I have eaten Fat Hen, and Sowbane or Maple-leaved goosefoot, *C. hybridum* and found that they all have the same spinach-like flavour when cooked.

Goosefoots are found throughout Europe and the United States, they grow in waste places and on cultivated ground, particularly near buildings and on old manure heaps where the best and biggest specimens flourish. Among the many local country names for the plants are Dirty Dick and Midden Myles. In the British Isles, they are most common in south and south-east England and in the Midlands, but Fat Hen is common throughout Britain, except in mountainous areas. The stems are tough, stiff and well-branched and may be streaked with, or entirely, red. The leaves are usually thick, stalked and alternate, and roughly diamond-shaped or, as their name suggests, rather the shape of a goose's foot, of varying degrees of narrowness and breadth and with teeth, or lobes, of varying depth and irregularity. The green flowering spikes look granular, each flower is minute and consists of styles and stamens. Fat Hen, Nettle-leaved, Oak-leaved and Red Goosefoot have leafy flowering spikes, but Sowbane has its flowers in leafless, branching clusters.

Finally, there is our only perennial goosefoot, with the delightful name of Good King Henry, *Chenopodium bonus-henricus*, it is not a true native though it now grows wild throughout Britain on waste ground, rich pasture, arable land, roadsides and near old buildings. The plant may have been introduced by the Romans and was still being cultivated as a vegetable as recently as this century in the eastern half of England, particularly Lincolnshire and Suffolk. I have a clump in my garden given to me by a friend who remembers it as a delectable dish when she was a girl, in Dorset, in the 1930s. As well as recommending the plant as a cure for several diseases, Culpeper said, 'It is preferred to spinach, and is much superior in firmness and flavour. The young shoots, the succeeding leaves, and at last the flowery tops, are fit for kitchen purposes'.

Fat Hen is a very ancient plant, remains of it have been found in neolithic sites in various parts of Europe. It was one of the sixty-six different plants found in the stomach of the Grauballe Man dating from about 300 A.D. which was discovered in the peat bogs of Denmark in 1952. It was cultivated as a vegetable all over eastern Europe and in Russia, and an Austro-Hungarian scientific expedition that went to Asia in 1868-71 discovered that *Chenopodium* was cultivated in Japan, and mostly in the districts that had the earliest links with Europe. The plant also grows in Mexico where the Indians eat the leaves raw and cooked, and grind the dried seeds into a kind of flour. In Canada it was grown as fodder, particularly for pigs, and is known as Pigweed. In America, the tumbleweed which is blown along the ground in high winds, is a species of goosefoot.

Fat Hen was eaten in the Scottish Islands until recent times, and in Europe, in the last war, when the food shortage was acute. Goosefoots contain valuable amounts of iron, protein and calcium, and when cooked like spinach, are a healthy addition to our diet. The flowering spikes of Good King Henry are particularly delicious, and the leaves can be used in exactly the same ways as goosefoot.

GOOSEFOOT SOUP SUMMER

Goosefoot has a flavour similar to spinach, and makes an excellent green soup.

SERVES 4

500 ml/2 cups/1pint measure goosefoot leaves,
  gently pressed down
1 medium onion
25 g/2 tablespoons/1 oz butter
3/4 litre/3³/4 cups/1¹/2 pints chicken stock
salt and pepper

Soak the leaves for a few minutes and wash them very thoroughly. Peel and chop the onion and sweat in the butter in a covered pan for 5 minutes. Add the goosefoot leaves, stir round to mix with the onion, then stir in the stock. Season with salt and pepper, bring to the boil and cover the pan, simmer for 20 minutes then liquidize the soup, return to the pan to re-heat, and adjust the seasoning.

GOOSEFOOT FLAN SUMMER

Goosefoot makes a perfect filling for a savoury flan, and the recipe for sea beet flan on p. 212 may be followed exactly; just cook the goosefoot for 5-7 minutes instead of 10-12 minutes, which sea beet leaves require.

AS A VEGETABLE SUMMER

Like spinach, goosefoot goes to nothing when cooked, but the leaves are quite large and easy to pick, and the weed is prolific.

SERVES 2

1 colander goosefoot leaves, gently pressed down
1 tablespoon butter
salt
freshly milled black pepper

Soak the leaves for a few minutes and wash them thoroughly, put them damp in a large saucepan and cook for 5-8 minutes. Drain well and return to the pan with the butter, a pinch of salt and a good grinding of black pepper.
Stir while the butter melts, and serve hot.

GOOSEFOOT – *CHENOPODIUM*

GORSE
Ulex europaeus

This spiny evergreen shrub grows up to 2 metres/6 ft tall in rough grassy places, on heaths and downland and particularly near the sea. It is found all over Britain and most of Europe, but less commonly in exposed northern areas because, in spite of its tough appearance, it is not able to withstand an exceptionally hard winter. It blooms almost the entire year in California and is naturalised in many of the states of America. The rigid furrowed spines are in fact, the leaves, but the new sprouting leaf buds at the tips of the stems are soft. The bright yellow flowers consist of the keel, wings and standard petals common to the pea flower family. On hot summer days when the seeds are ripe, the hairy pods burst explosively and audibly and the seeds are scattered far and wide.

The main flowering season is in the spring, although gorse flowers may be found throughout the year, and this gave rise to the old saying 'kissing's out of season when gorse is out of bloom'. The flowers have a marvellous smell, usually described as almond-scented in the field guides, but I can only think of it as coconut, since one blazingly sunny April morning, on a cliff slope in Cornwall, when the air was vibrant with the smell of coconut from the waves of golden-yellow gorse washing over the cliffs, and thrumming with bees.

Gorse enriches the soil when it is burnt, and up to the last century was used as fuel for bakers' ovens, and for brick and lime kilns in the south of England. There are a few references to gorse as medicine in the early herbals. Gerard mentions that the seeds were used against 'the stone' and for looseness of the bowels. Parkinson said the flowers were used to treat jaundice, no doubt arising from the association of ideas between the yellow flowers and yellow jaundice. Another example of the 'Doctrine of Signatures', 'whereby', according to William Coles, 'a man may read even in legible Characters the Use of them'. He gave many examples of the plants which God had 'not only stemped upon them (as upon every man) a distinct forme, but also given them particular signatures', one of the more amusing examples being the use of hounds tongue, which had 'a forme not much different from its name which will tye the Tongues of Hounds so that they shall not barke at you: if it be laid under the bottomes of ones feet'.

Horses will eat gorse gingerly, and it provides extra food in winter for wild ponies on heath and moorland when grazing is scarce. Sometimes one may find the Common Dodder, *cuscuta epythymum* which is, in fact, an uncommon little parasitic plant that preys on gorse and heather. It has red stems that twine through and cling to the host plant and through which it draws its sustenance. The scarcely discernible leaves are reduced to mere scales, but the star-like, pale pink flowers which grow in tight heads, are beautiful, with 5 pointed petals, prominent styles and stamens, and a sweet scent. It is worth looking for.

GORSE – *ULEX EUROPAEUS*

PICKLED GORSE BUDS SPRING

John Evelyn gave a recipe for pickling gorse buds in his *Acetaria* (1622). His instructions were to 'make a strong pickle of white wine vinegar and salt, able to bear an egg'. I found that four measures of vinegar to one measure of salt made a brine which passed this test. Evelyn recommended shaking the pickle glass frequently until the buds sink under, but in spite of frequent and vigorous shakings, the buds obstinately rise to the top of the jars. It doesn't seem to affect their keeping qualities, and after three months, when the pickle will have mellowed, the little flower buds taste nutty and, drained from their brine, are an unusual addition to salads. They look pretty, and taste good scattered over a salad of skinned and sliced tomatoes.

Picking the buds is a slow and prickly business, but the April sunshine, the strange coconut smell of gorse blossom, and all the scents and sounds of spring are excuse enough for the hour you may while away.

1/2 colander unopened gorse flower buds
1 measure salt to 4 measures white wine vinegar

Remove any spines from the buds, and pack them firmly into a glass jar. Put the salt and vinegar into a bowl and stir with a wooden spoon. Leave to stand for an hour. Heat the brine pickle in a small pan, stirring continuously to dissolve the salt. As soon as it starts to boil, snatch the pan off the heat and pour the liquid into a jug and set aside to cool. Pour the cooled brine over the gorse buds, cover with a circle of vinegar proof or waxed paper cut larger than the top of the jar, and screw on the lid. Shake the jar frequently to help the buds to settle.

GORSE FLOWER SYRUP SPRING

Gorse flower syrup has a delicate almond fragrance and makes a lovely quenching drink poured over ice cubes and diluted with a little sparkling water.

Fresh apricots poached in the syrup, are particularly delicious.

500 ml/2 cups/1 pint measure gorse flowers,
    pressed down
Water, see recipe
Sugar, see recipe
60 ml/5 U.S. tablespoons/4 tablespoons strained lemon juice

Remove any spines from the flowers. Put them into a saucepan with enough water to cover. Bring to the boil, cover the pan and simmer for 8-10 minutes, pressing the flowers down with a wooden spoon occasionally. Drain through a fine strainer,

pressing out all the liquid and return to a clean pan.

For a scant litre/3 3/4 cups/1 1/2 pints liquid add 450 g/ 2 cups/1 lb sugar to the pan, heat slowly, stirring until the sugar has dissolved, then boil for 5 minutes. Skim, and allow to cool.

Pour into a large jug and fill up bottles with screw-on caps, or corks. Store in the refrigerator.

GORSE BUDS TEA SPRING

The Modern Herbal says the leaf buds have been used as a substitute for tea, although many earlier recipes for pickles and preserves just mention 'Gorse Buds', leaving one to puzzle whether flower or leaf buds are intended.

In spring the gorse bushes have a mass of tender soft green sprouts among the prickles, which must be picked carefully, and can be made into a fresh-tasting beverage the colour of pale straw.

1 heaped tablespoon gorse leaf sprouts
250 ml/1 cup/1/2 pint boiling water
squeeze of lemon juice—optional

Put the sprouts into a small jug and pour over the boiling water. Cover, and leave to infuse for 8 minutes. Strain into cups and add a squeeze of lemon.

GORSE FLOWER LIQUEUR

Gorse flowers make a pale straw-coloured liqueur with the same faint taste of almonds as their scent. To enhance the almond flavour, you can add 2 tablespoons of almonds blanched for 2 minutes in boiling water, then skinned and chopped, to soak with the flowers and vodka.

Gorse flowers, to loosely fill a vodka bottle
2 tablespoons chopped almonds—optional
1 bottle vodka

Remove any spines, and pack the flowers loosely into an empty bottle, or glass jars. If using the almonds, add them with the flowers. Pour on some of the vodka and shake gently until the flowers are well soaked. Add any remaining flowers to come within 2 cm / 1 inch of the top of the bottle or jars, then fill up with vodka.

Cork, or screw on the lids, and leave in a dark cupboard for 2–3 weeks. Strain the liquid into a large jug through a fine strainer, and press out any liquid left in the flowers.

Make a syrup to finish the liqueur.

100 g/¹/₂ cup/4 oz granulated sugar
150 ml/²/₃ cup/¹/₄ pint water

Measure the sugar and water into a small pan, bring to the boil slowly and stir until the sugar dissolves, then boil fast for 3 minutes, and set aside to cool.

Add the syrup to the jug of flavoured vodka, stir to mix, and pour into bottles. Shake gently, then cork, or screw on the lids.

GORSE WINE SPRING—SUMMER

Gorse wine tastes both nutty and flowery. It goes particularly well with fish.

activated yeast (p. 255)
2¹/₂ litres/4¹/₂ U.S. quarts/¹/₂ gallon gorse flowers
5 litres/9 U.S. quarts/1 gallon water
1.5 kilos/6 cups/3 lbs sugar
2 oranges

2 lemons
2-3 tablespoons cold tea or 1 teaspoon grape tannin
(sold for wine-making)

Pick the gorse flowers when dry and put them in a large saucepan with 2³/₄ litres/11³/₄ cups/5 pints water, bring to the boil and simmer for 10 minutes. Put the sugar and thinly pared rind (no pith) of the oranges and lemons into the plastic bucket, pour the boiling liquid from the pan into the bucket through a strainer, pressing the flowers with a wooden spoon to extract the flavour, and stir until the sugar dissolves, then make up to 5 litres/9 U.S. quarts/1 gallon with cold water, and add the strained juice of the oranges and lemons. When cool, (about 70°F, 20°C), stir in the cold tea, or grape tannin, and the activated yeast, cover the bucket with its lid, and leave in a warm place for three days, stirring daily. Strain the liquid into the fermentation jar and follow the method given on page 254.

GROUND ELDER
Aegopodium podagraria

BISHOPS-WEED, GOUTWEED

Ground elder is widespread and common throughout Britain, Europe and Scandinavia and is found throughout the western and mid-western states of North America. It grows in damp, shady places, usually in the vicinity of buildings, and is a pernicious weed in gardens. The leaves appear early in the spring, they consist of three irregularly-toothed, lanceolate leaflets which, when young, are shiny and bright green and folded together like a partly closed book; as they grow older the leaves open flat. From early summer the plant produces dense umbels of white flowers on hollow, grooved stems, 30-60 cm/1-2 ft high. Ground elder is not related to the elder tree, but the flowers and leaves superficially resemble each other. The plant spreads by its tough, creeping roots which grow between the roots of other plants, and into the crevices of walls, and quickly form large patches which smother other plants.

Most gardeners will agree with Gerard who, writing in his 17th century 'herball', noted that ground elder 'is so fruitful in his increase that where it hath once taken roote, it will hardly be gotten out again, spoiling and getting every year more ground, to the annoying of better herbes'.

The botanical name comes from the Greek word for gout, *podagra.* One often reads that the Romans introduced ground elder into this country as a vegetable, but it was most probably introduced from France after the Norman conquest, and was widely grown in the monastery gardens as a medicinal herb to treat gout. Nicholas Culpeper wrote of ground elder's curative powers with glowing confidence. 'Saturn rules it. Neither is it to be supposed that Goutwort hath its name for nothing, but upon experiment it heals the gout and sciatica; as also joint-aches and other cold pains'. And a century later, in *The Family Herbal,* Sir John Hill recommended the root and young leaves to be used as a poultice for the pains of gout, and said 'its use should not be confined to this pain alone: it will succeed in others'.

Ground elder was still being eaten as a vegetable and in salads in Russia and Lithuania in the 20th century, and in 18th century Sweden, Linnaeus described it as a good spring vegetable. Those of us who suffer from the weed in our gardens, should rejoice in the knowledge that we can eat the pest.

GROUND ELDER SOUP SPRING AND EARLY SUMMER

You could not wish for a better green soup; ground elder holds its own with spinach, watercress, lettuce or sorrel.

SERVES 4

1 heaped colander ground elder leaves
25 g/2 tablespoons/1 oz butter
1 small onion
20 g/1½ tablespoons/¾ oz flour
500 ml/2 cups/1 pint stock
250 ml/1 cup/½ pint milk
salt and pepper

Pick away the main stalks, wash the leaves well, then cook in a little boiling, salted water for 5 minutes. Drain.

Melt the butter in a saucepan, chop the onion and sauté gently, stir in the flour, add the stock, and bring slowly to the boil, stirring continuously to thicken smoothly. Season, then add the ground elder leaves, cover and simmer for 15 minutes. Liquidize the soup. Return the soup to the pan and re-heat.

GROUND ELDER SALAD

Ground elder makes an unusual and delicious cooked salad to be eaten either cold, or just warm. The generous amount of lemon juice really complements the flavour of the ground elder.

Pick the leaves when they are young and shiny, either in the spring, or when they have regrown after strimming.

1 colander ground elder leaves
Water—see recipe
2 tablespoons olive oil
1 tablespoon lemon juice
Nutmeg, grated
Salt and freshly milled black pepper

Wash the ground elder leaves and pick off any tough little stalks. Bring a small amount of lightly salted water to the boil in a large pan, tip in the ground elder leaves and cook until tender, about 5 minutes. Drain very thoroughly, chopping and pressing the cooked leaves with a wooden spoon to extract all the water.

Measure the olive oil and lemon juice into a bowl, add a good grating of nutmeg and whisk together lightly. Tip in the ground elder leaves while still hot, so they will better absorb the flavours of the dressing. Taste to adjust the seasoning.

GROUND ELDER RICE CAKES

SPRING AND EARLY SUMMER

Ground elder leaves make good fritters when mixed with rice and flavoured with a little chopped bacon and onion.

SERVES 4

½ colander ground elder leaves
75 g/½ cup/3 oz uncooked long grain rice
3 slices (U.S.)/3 rashers bacon
1 medium onion, chopped
50 g/4 tablespoons/2 oz plain flour
½ teaspoon baking powder
freshly milled black pepper
1 egg

Pick any stalks from the leaves and wash them thoroughly. Cook the rice for 12 minutes or until tender, then leave to drain. Chop the bacon into small pieces and fry in a little fat until brown. Tip into a bowl and fry the onion in the bacon fat until

GROUND ELDER – *AEGOPODIUM PODAGRARIA*

soft. Shred the raw ground elder leaves and add to the bowl of bacon, with the cooked rice and onion. Shake in the flour and plenty of black pepper and mix together with a fork. Add the egg, and mix again, then shape the mixture into 8 small cakes. Roll them in a little flour and fry in butter on both sides until well browned.

GROUND ELDER AS A VEGETABLE

SPRING AND EARLY SUMMER

It is impossible to describe the entirely original flavour of ground elder when cooked. Don't be deterred by the horrible pungent smell when you pick the leaves which, if you have the plant growing as a weed in your garden, will be all too familiar. This entirely disappears in the cooking, and you are left with one of the most delicious wild vegetables.

SERVES 4

1 heaped colander young ground elder leaves
25 g/2 tablespoons/1 oz butter
salt and freshly milled black pepper

Pick off the stalks and wash the leaves thoroughly. Put damp in a saucepan with the butter and seasoning. Cover and cook gently for 5-7 minutes. Remove the lid and stir with a wooden spoon until most of the liquid has evaporated. Drain well and serve hot.

GROUND IVY
Glechoma hederacea

ALEHOOF, GILL-GO-BY-THE-GROUND

Ground ivy is common in woods and hedgerows throughout Europe and the British Isles. In the spring, and from a distance, the plants may look deceptively like a patch of violets, but on closer inspection the flowers consist of two lips, the lower one split into three lobes with tiny purple spots leading into the centre. The flowers grow from the base of the leaves in whorls of three or four, and throughout the spring their soft violet blue makes lovely flecks of colour in the woods. The leaves, which remain green all the year, are kidney-shaped, with rounded teeth and a prominent network of veins; they have long stalks and grow opposite each other on alternate sides of the square stems. The leaves vary greatly in colour from bright to dark green, some plants being so much darker than others that the leaves are bronzed. John Josselyn noted that ground ivy was planted among garden herbs by the early settlers in America; and it has now become naturalised and is very common by roadsides and in woods from Newfoundland to Minnesota and southward to Georgia, Alabama, Missouri and Kansas. It also grows on the Pacific coast.

The whole plant is strongly aromatic and was used medicinally for all sorts of ailments, the dried leaves were included in snuff and herbal tobacco, and the plant was used to flavour ale before hops were introduced into England. One of ground ivy's country names is Alehoof, and another, Gill-go-by-the-Ground, suggests a connection with Gill House, the old name for an ale house. Gill Tea is the country name for a syrup made from an infusion of ground ivy with honey or liquorice, which was used as a cough cure.

In the first century A.D., Galen wrote that ground ivy would not only soothe inflamed eyes, but would cure failing eyesight, even in one almost blind. The early herbalists regarded the plant as something of a panacea. John Gerard wrote 'it is recommended against the humming noise and ringing sound of the ears . . . good against fistulas and hollow ulcers . . . a remedy against sciatica or ache in the huckle-bone'. William Coles asserted that '. . . this Age forsaketh all old things, though never so good, and embraceth all kinds of novelties whatsoever; but the time will come, that the fopperies of the present times shall be slighted, and the true and honest prescriptions of the Ancients come in request again'. How amusing that the attitude of the older to a younger generation has not changed much in three hundred years!

Culpeper was enthusiastic about ground ivy and said it was 'a singular herb for all inward wounds, ulcerated lungs or other parts'. Sir John Hill mentioned ground ivy as a wound herb and 'in all disorders of the breast and lungs, and in those of the kidneys', and Robert Thornton quoted the case of a Mr. Oldaire who was cured of 'an inveterate head-ach by snuffing the juice of ground ivy up his nose'. A little book with the wonderful title *A Collection of above Three Hundred Receipts in Cookery, Physick and Surgery for the use of all Good Wives, Tender Mothers and Careful Nurses*, 1746, gives 'Dr. Wadenfield's Remedy for Lunacy, with which a Person of Quality cured Threescore'. 'Take three handfulls of ground ivy, boil it in white wine and mix it with the best Sallad Oil, boil it up to an Ointment, let the Patient's Head be shaved, then rub and chafe it with the Ointment made warm.'

GROUND IVY – *GLECHOMA HEDERACEA*

GROUND IVY TISANE SPRING, EARLY SUMMER

The strongly aromatic little plant makes one of the best tisanes, gather it in the spring when the plant is in flower, but still fresh. The colour of the infusion is a delicate pale green, and the flavour is faintly reminiscent of blackcurrant.

1 handful of ground ivy
500 ml/2 cups/1 pint boiling water

Pick away the coarse lower stems, and break the plant into short lengths. Wash, if necessary, and bruise the plants with a rolling pin, put them in a jug, and pour on the boiling water. Cover the jug and infuse for 7-8 minutes, then strain into cups, and drink warm.

GROUND IVY TEA, DRIED

15 g/1 tablespoon/1/2 oz dried ground ivy
250 ml/1 cup/1/2 pint boiling water

Infuse the dried leaves in a covered jug for 7 minutes. Strain into cups, and drink hot.

TO DRY GROUND IVY SPRING

Gather the plants on a dry day and tie them in small bunches. Suspend the bunches head downwards from the slats or pipes in an airing cupboard or in a boiler room. After about three days the plants should be dry and crisp. Strip off the leaves and flowers and put them through a parsley mill, or sieve.

HAWTHORN
Crataegus monogyna

Hawthorn is widespread and common throughout Britain and most of Europe, but absent from the far north of Scotland. There are several related species of hawthorn in the United States. It grows as a tree in woods, thickets, downs and parkland, or as a quick-set hedge which becomes bushy with trimming, and makes a good barrier with its thorns and fast-growing habit. Many old hedges were planted with hawthorn for these reasons, and to provide a supply of stock on which fruit trees were grafted.

As single specimens hawthorns vary enormously in size, from wonderful little wizened miniatures on exposed hills and moors, where the shallow soil and the wind have combined to stunt and twist them into the most contorted shapes, to fine spreading trees, 6-9 metres/20-30 ft high, in the shelter of farmland and parks, or in open woods. Hawthorn leaves are deeply cleft into three or five lobes, and the flowers, known as May blossom, grow in clusters of round white buds and starry open flowers, each with five petals and a ring of stamens tipped with pink or purple anthers. The blossom has an almost overpoweringly sweet scent, sometimes even sickly, but when the flowers are fresh there is a heady fragrance about May blossom that has a romantic quality.

The berries, or haws, ripen in early autumn and remain on the trees until winter. They have a single stone inside the mealy yellow pulp, all encased in a shiny red skin, rather like a tiny apple. The Midland hawthorn, *Crataegus laevigata* (= *C. oxycanthoides*) has two stones in each berry, and the leaves are rounder and less deeply lobed.

In ancient Greece and Rome, the hawthorn was a symbol of marriage and fertility. Many of the old May Day festivities in France and England were bound up with pagan rites, using May blossom as a symbol of love and betrothal.

There are some fine wood carvings of hawthorn leaves and flowers in churches, and sometimes the carved heads on the capitals of pillars are crowned with hawthorn. In medieval times the tree was regarded with a superstitious mixture of reverence and dread, because it was believed that Christ's crown of thorns was made from hawthorn.

The legend of the Glastonbury Thorn, a miraculous tree that was said to have leaves and flowers in the spring, and again on Christmas Day, arose from the belief that Joseph of Arimathea stuck his hawthorn staff into the hill, and it at once put forth leaves and blossom. William Coles, in *Adam in Eden*, or the *Paradise of Plants*, describes three sorts of hawthorn: 'the ordinary', 'the low', and 'England's Haw-thorne, which is in all parts like the common sort, but that it flowereth twice in a yeare, to the great admiration of some wise and judicious men'. He makes no mention of the Glastonbury legend, but says the tree grows 'at Glastonbury Abby and in Whey Street, or rather High-Street in Rumney Marsh, and neere unto Nantwich in Cheshire'. Coles describes the double flowering of the hawthorn as 'in May and about Christmas, sooner or later as the temperature of the weather will permit, having at the same time both greene and ripe berries'. No mention of miracles there, yet Glastonbury has claimed centuries of prestigious sanctity from the double flowering hawthorn.

Hawthorn is recognised in modern medicine as having cardiotonic properties, and has been used with digitalis in the treatment of heart conditions. Martindale's *Pharmacopaeia* lists the countries which use the extract or tincture of the dried flowers in this treatment. Russia uses the dried flowers and fruit, and Switzerland the dried leaves.

HAWTHORN LEAF TEA SPRING

Use hawthorn leaves to mix with ordinary tea. Measure equal quantities of dried hawthorn leaves and Indian or China tea into the pot and allow to infuse for a few minutes as usual. Use a fine strainer when pouring out, the brew is delicious.

TO DRY HAWTHORN LEAVES SPRING

Gather the hawthorn leaves when young, throughout the spring, choosing a dry day. Lay the leaves out in a single layer on trays or cardboard lids in an airing cupboard or the top of a boiler. It is possible to dry the leaves in a very slow oven, but this destroys some of the flavour. After about three days the leaves should be dry and crisp. Put them through a parsley mill or sieve and store in screw-top jars away from the light.

FLOWRYS OF HAWTHORN SPRING

If you would like to try a medieval pudding, this version comes from a cookery book of the 15th century. The original recipe reads 'take flowrys of Hawthorn, boyle hem, presse hem, bray hem smal, temper hem uppe with Almaunde mylke, or gode Cowe Mylke, allay it with Flowre of Rys, take Sugre y-naw, and putte there-to, or hony in defaute; colour it with the same that the flowry be on y-peyntid a-above'. For the final instruction to colour the dish, sanders was probably used. This was a culinary dye made from sandalwood and was very popular in medieval cookery. The flavour is pleasant, if unexciting, but one should remember that by the time May came round, the people of the Middle Ages must have been longing for something fresh with which to make puddings. All their winter stores of apples and pears would have been used up, and their dried fruit, dates, currants and raisins had a limited range. May blossom, with its sweet scent, would have suggested a certain fruitiness and the flowers supplied a juicy crunch that had been lacking in their diet for weeks.

SERVES 4

500 ml/2 cups/1 pint hawthorn blossom, loosely packed
water—see recipe
500 ml/2 cups/1 pint milk
2-3 tablespoons (level) ground rice
2-3 tablespoons (level) honey
2 or 3 drops red food colouring (optional)

Snip the flowers from their stems with pointed scissors. Put them in a saucepan with just enough water to cover, bring to the boil, simmer for 3 minutes then drain through a fine strainer. Chop the flowers with a sharp knife and put them in a pan with the

HAWTHORN – *CRATAEGUS MONOGYNA*

milk. Bring to the boil, add the ground rice (or put it in a blender until it resembles finely ground coffee), add the honey and stir briskly to mix the ingredients, then cover and simmer for half an hour until the pudding is the consistency of porridge. If you would like to colour the dish according to the old recipe, stir in the colouring to make it pale pink. Serve hot, with thin cream.

HAWTHORN FLOWER SYRUP SPRING

An 18th century recipe in E. Smith's *The Compleat Housewife* used hawthorn flowers to make a syrup. The instruction was 'set the gallypot in a kettle of water for four or five hours, till the strength is out of the flowers', but there is no need to infuse the flowers for so long. The apricot-coloured syrup has a true flowery fragrance, and makes a subtle sauce to pour over flans, milk puddings and ice cream. It is also a delicious summer drink poured on to crushed ice with a splash of soda water added. Small children would love it served with drinking straws and a few hawthorn flowers scattered on the top of each glass.

MAKES ABOUT 1 LITRE/5 CUPS/2 PINTS OF SYRUP
1 litre/5 cups/2 pints measure of hawthorn flowers
granulated U.S./caster sugar—see recipe
800 g/4 cups/2 lbs granulated sugar
1.25 litres/5 cups/2 pints water
6-7 tablespoons lemon juice
6-7 tablespoons rosewater (optional, but nice)

Pick the flower sprays gently from the trees. At home snip most of the stalks from the flowers and pack them loosely into jars in layers 2.5 cms/1 in deep, sprinkling a teaspoon of caster sugar between each layer of flowers or, as the old recipe tells one, 'Put a row of flowers and a strewing of sugar, till the pot is full'.

Heat the granulated sugar, water and strained lemon juice in a pan and stir until the sugar has dissolved, then boil up for 3 minutes, set aside to cool and stir in the rosewater.

Pour the cooled syrup into the jars of hawthorn flowers, screw the lids on loosely and stand the jars in a saucepan on a sheet of folded newspaper, with some folded newspaper between to prevent them touching. Fill up with cold water as high as the pan allows, bring slowly to the boil then turn the heat low and keep the jars in the barely simmering water for one hour. Lift the jars from the pan and tighten the screw caps. When quite cold strain the flower syrup into a jug and pour into small bottles, screw on the caps or use new corks previously soaked in boiling water for 15 minutes. Store the syrup in a cool larder or in the refrigerator. It keeps for months.

HAWTHORN FLOWER ICE CREAM SPRING

This is a most unusual, smooth-textured ice cream which requires no extra beating after you have put it to freeze. As the delicate flowery flavour is so slight, hand round a little extra hawthorn flower syrup to pour over each helping. It is outstandingly good.

SERVES 4-6
250 ml/1 cup/¹/2 pint thick cream
6 tablespoons/8 tablespoons U.S/6 tablespoons hawthorn
    flower syrup—see preceding recipe
2 drops red colouring (optional)

Turn the cream into a bowl, and if very thick rinse out the carton with a little milk. Whip the cream lightly, then add the syrup gradually, whisking between each spoonful, mix in the colouring, if used. Spoon into tubs or cartons, cover with the lids or foil, and freeze until firm. Serve with extra hawthorn flower syrup to pour over the ice cream.

HAWTHORN FLOWER WINE CUP SPRING

Florence White wrote a little book called *Flowers as Food*, first published in 1934, which is full of early recipes and her own experiments, she was a scholarly and practical woman imbued with a love of rural life. From 1915-1921 she worked as a cook 'in cap and apron' in other people's houses. In one house she says, 'I had the run of an old-world flower, herb and vegetable garden. There I tried out some flower recipes in small quantities, the results of which were much appreciated. Later on my own experimental kitchen gave me special opportunities for further practical work.'

Among her recipes is this one from a pre-war cookery article in the *Evening News*, headed 'Nectar from the Hedge-row'. I have tried it out and it is rather ambrosial. Without being sweet, it tastes of the scent of May blossom with a hint of almonds and honey; the *Evening News* correspondent wrote that it had 'all the fragrance of a scented spring dawn'!

1 handful prepared hawthorn flowers
1 orange
1 bottle white wine
¹/2 bottle red wine
1 sprig lemon thyme, or lemon balm
2 sprigs borage

Snip most of the stems from the hawthorn flowers. Slice the orange into a large bowl, pour over the two wines and add the lemon thyme and borage. Scatter the hawthorn flowers to float on top of the liquid, cover the bowl with muslin or a clean tea towel, and leave to stand for 24 hours.

To serve, put plenty of ice cubes into a tall glass jug, strain the flower-flavoured wine on to the ice and stir vigorously. The original drink was served from an ice-cold cocktail shaker, and you could do the same if you have one.

HAWTHORN FLOWERS IN ICE CUBES SPRING

Freshly picked hawthorn flowers, snipped from the stem, and frozen in ice cubes look pretty floating in this wine cup, and are a spring-like addition to any cool drink.

HAWTHORN FLOWER LIQUEUR

Hawthorn flowers lend a faint, sweet flowery flavour to this peachy-pink liqueur, which looks deceptively innocent. Pick enough hawthorn blossom to roughly fill a colander. Choose a dry day, and pick the flowers while they are still fresh and newly-opened, once the flowers are past their prime they develop a sickly scent.

Enough hawthorn flowers to loosely fill an empty vodka bottle
Bottle of vodka

Remove any stems or leaves from the flowers and pack them gently into an empty bottle, or divide between glass jars. Carefully add the vodka, and shake gently until the flowers have submerged, then top up with the remaining vodka. Cork, or screw on the lids, and store in a dark cupboard for 2 weeks.

Strain the liquid through a nylon strainer into a measuring jug and press out any liquid from the flowers with a wooden spoon.

TO FINISH THE LIQUEUR
100 g /1/2 cup/4 oz granulated sugar
150 ml/2/3 cup/1/4 pint water

Measure the sugar and water into a small pan, and bring to the boil slowly, stirring until the sugar has dissolved, then boil fast for 3 minutes. Set aside to cool, then add to the flower-flavoured vodka and stir to mix. Pour into bottles, shake gently, then cork, or screw on the lids.

HAWTHORN FLOWER WINE SPRING

This is a medium sweet white wine with a delicious flowery flavour. Chill the bottle well, before opening.

activated yeast (p. 255)
2 litres/4 1/2 U.S. quarts/1/2 gallon freshly picked
    hawthorn flowers
5 litres/9 U.S. quarts/1 gallon water
1.5 kilos/6 cups/3 lbs sugar
2 lemons
2 tablespoons cold tea, or 1 teaspoon grape tannin
    (sold for wine making)

Put the sugar, thinly pared rind (no pith) and strained juice of the lemons into the plastic bucket, pour on the boiling water, stir to dissolve the sugar, cover with a clean cloth and leave until cool, stir in the cold tea or grape tannin, and the activated yeast. Cover the bucket with its lid. Stand in a warm place for 24 hours, then add the hawthorn flowers, snipped from their stems, stir well and replace the lid. Stand in a warm place for one week, stirring daily, then strain the liquid into the fermentation jar and follow the method given on page 254.

HAWTHORN BERRY JELLY AUTUMN

Haws make a deep russet-coloured jelly which is insipid without the tang of lemon juice to enhance it. It makes a good spread for bread and butter, and may be eaten with turkey or game. Hawthorn trees seem to vary greatly, some producing tiny hard berries, others big meaty ones. Go for the big ones, they can be picked from the end of summer until the end of autumn.

1.5 kilos/3 lbs haws
750 ml/3 3/4 cups/1 1/2 pints water
strained juice of 2 lemons
500 g/2 cups/1 lb sugar to 500 ml/2 cups/1 pint juice

Snip the berries from their stalks with scissors, it doesn't matter if some little stalks are left. Wash the berries thoroughly and put them in a large saucepan with the water. Bring to the boil, cover, and cook gently for 1 hour, occasionally mashing the berries with the back of a wooden spoon. Drip through a double thickness of muslin, or a jelly bag, overnight.

Measure the juice into a large saucepan, add the lemon juice and sugar and bring to the boil, stirring continuously until the sugar has dissolved, then boil rapidly for 10 minutes, or until the jelly sets when dripped onto a cold saucer. Skim, pour into warm dry jars, cover with waxed circles while hot and seal with cellophane covers when cold.

HAWTHORN BERRY CHUTNEY AUTUMN

Haws make a delicious chutney. It is good with all cold meats and poultry and makes a lovely ploughman's lunch with bread and cheese. The little berries are so plentiful that it is worth making several batches of chutney to store through the winter. You can vary the recipe by omitting the dried fruit and cooking the mixture for only 10 minutes, which results in a sweet-spicy sauce which can be bottled and stored.

1 kilo/2 lbs haws
500 ml/2 cups/1 pint cider vinegar
1 teaspoon salt
125 g/1 cup/4 oz mixed dried fruit, or seedless raisins
300 g/1½ cups/¾ lb brown sugar
1 teaspoon ground ginger
1 teaspoon ground nutmeg
¼ teaspoon ground cloves
¼ teaspoon ground allspice
freshly milled black pepper

Snip the haws from their stalks with scissors and wash them thoroughly. Put the berries in a large saucepan with the vinegar and salt, bring to the boil, cover and simmer steadily for 1 hour. Rub the contents of the pan through a sieve into a clean saucepan. You should have rather less than 250 ml (1 pint, or 2 cups) pulp. Add the rest of the ingredients with a good grinding of black pepper, and bring to the boil, stirring all the time. Then cook in the uncovered pan for 15-20 minutes until the mixture is fairly thick. Pour into warm dry jars and cover with circles of waxed paper while hot, seal with cellophane covers when cold.

HAWTHORN BERRY WINE AUTUMN

Hawthorn berries make a light red wine with a pleasant crispness.

activated yeast (p. 255)
1.5 kilos/3 lbs hawthorn berries
5 litres/9 U.S. quarts/1 gallon water
1.5 kilos/6 cups/3 lbs sugar
3 lemons

Wash the haws and snip away the stalks, put the berries in a plastic bucket and crush with a wooden spoon. Pour on the boiling water, cover the bucket with its lid and stand for 3 days, stirring daily. Add the sugar, the thinly pared rind (no pith) and strained juice of the lemons, and stir until the sugar has dissolved, then stir in the activated yeast. Cover the bucket with its lid and stand in a warm place for 2 days. Strain the liquid into the fermentation jar (dark glass for a red wine) and follow the method given on page 254.

HAZEL
Corylus avellana

Hazel is a small tree usually growing no taller than about 3½ metres/12 ft. It is common in woods and hedges throughout Britain, Scandinavia and most of Europe. In America filberts are planted in the warmer parts and a related species, *corylus cornuta*, grows wild throughout the eastern States. Hazels were often coppiced as cover for pheasants and other game, and to give a supply of young wood for hurdles. The bark is shiny, smooth and a bright reddish brown. The toothed leaves are pointed oval, and asymmetrical, one side being wider than the other; they have silky flat hairs on both sides, and deep, wide-spaced veins. Towards the end of winter, the male flowers dangle from the bare twigs in masses of yellow catkins, which are nick-named lamb's tails; they shed a shower of pollen on to the little female flowers which are very inconspicuous, and far less numerous, and look like small buds with a tuft of tiny red bristles, which are the styles. In autumn the nuts ripen in clusters of twos and threes, each oval green nut held in a green,

HAZEL – *CORYLUS AVELLANA*

jaggedly-toothed husk, which turns brown and papery as the nuts ripen.

In the Middle Ages hazel was one of the woods burned for charcoal which, with sulphur and saltpetre, Roger Bacon made into an explosive powder, an early form of gunpowder. In this country, and in Europe, the hazel was invested with magic powers that could protect one from venomous serpents, mischievous elves and evil spirits of all kinds; branches were taken into houses to ward off lightning and other dangers, and the nuts were carried to relieve toothache and lumbago. In Scotland, 'burning the nuts' was a ritual performed by lovers to reveal if they were well-matched. Two hazel nuts, named by each of the pair were placed on the embers, and if the nuts burned steadily side by side, the couple were true lovers; but, if they spluttered and one nut jumped away, they were ill-matched, and one of them was faithless.

However much we may smile at the pagan superstitions connected with the hazel, there is one very mysterious property that it undoubtedly possesses. A wide-forked twig cut from a living hazel is the rod most used by water diviners, and if you have ever seen one in action and been amazed by the way the twig completely dominates the dowser, and appears to have a life and will of its own, then you will agree that are some things for which there is no logical explanation.

The Bible (Hosea IV. 12) refers to hazel rods being used to find concealed objects, and Agricola, a 16th century writer, described their use for finding mineral veins, a belief also held by the Cornish, who attributed this power to the influence of pixies. Vallemont, a 17th century writer, called the hazel wand *Baguette divinitoire*, and said it was used in the pursuit of criminals. All these beliefs may well have been suggested by the strange water divining power of hazel—the power to find something hidden—when used by someone with the necessary empathy.

BROWN RICE WITH HAZELNUTS AUTUMN

Hazelnuts should be picked as soon as the husks start to dry early in the autumn, squirrels know when they are ripe, too, so the ideal timing is to beat them to it by a whisker! Lay the hazelnuts out in a thin layer in a cool, airy room or shed, and turn them over occasionally to prevent mildew. They won't keep much beyond Christmas.

Brown rice is the whole, unpolished grain and is much more nutritious than bleached white rice, it has a nutty flavour which goes well with the hazelnuts. Served hot, the dish makes a wholesome and sustaining meal, or cold, with two or three other dishes and salads, it is good for a buffet supper. The same mixture makes a super stuffing for poultry.

SERVES 4
50 g/4 tablespoons/2 oz toasted hazelnuts
200 g/1 cup/½ lb brown rice
100 g/1 cup/4 oz mushrooms, sliced and fried in
    15 g/1 tablespoon/½ oz butter
1 tablespoon finely chopped parsley—optional

To toast the hazelnuts put them, shelled, under a hot grill, shake the grill pan to brown the nuts evenly, and when they are brown all over allow to cool for a minute, then roll them in a clean cloth and rub between your hands to remove the skins. Chop the nuts roughly.

Bring to the boil plenty of lightly salted water in a large saucepan, sprinkle in the rice, cover the pan and keep at a fast simmer for 30-40 minutes, stir with a wooden spoon occasionally to stop the rice clinging together. Test by biting a grain, there should be no hard centre when it is properly cooked.

Tip the rice into a large strainer and rinse under the hot tap, leave to drain, then return to the pan over a low heat and stir in the hazelnuts and mushrooms which you have sliced and gently fried while the rice was cooking. Add a good grinding of black pepper and sprinkle with chopped parsley.

WILD PESTO AUTUMN

Hazelnuts and wild sorrel in place of basil and pine nuts, make a good pesto substitute to serve with pasta, or a piping hot risotto. A spoonful stirred into vegetable soup lifts the flavour from good to sublime. The pesto will keep in the refrigerator in a covered jar for several days. Cover the surface with olive oil to stop it oxidising and going brown. Freeze any excess in ice cube trays and add to soups and pasta when needed.

2-3 handfuls sorrel leaves
1 clove garlic, peeled and crushed
Maldon sea salt—see recipe
About 12 hazelnuts, shelled
2 tablespoons freshly grated Parmigiano Reggiano
3 tablespoons freshly grated Pecorino Romano
6 tablespoons best quality extra virgin olive oil

Pick the sorrel leaves from the stalks. Put the garlic and some of the sorrel leaves, roughly torn, into a mortar with a good pinch of sea salt. Pesto really tastes best when made with a pestle and mortar, it takes a bit more elbow grease, but is worth the effort. 'Pesto' means to crush or pound, and the rough sea salt helps the process. Gradually add more leaves to the mortar until all are used. Then add the hazelnuts and two cheeses—the pesto is best if fairly rough textured—and lastly blend in the oil, enough to make a fairly thick consistency. Check the flavour and add more salt if necessary.

CHOCOLATE HAZELNUT GATEAU AUTUMN

This is a cheating way to make a cake because it requires no cooking, and is so quick and easy to achieve, but it is rich and luscious, and looks very effective for a party dessert.

1 box trifle sponges, or a small sponge cake
150 g/¾ cup/6 oz softened butter
4 tablespoons sugar
2-3 tablespoons chocolate powder
1 egg yolk
50 g/4 tablespoons/2 oz toasted hazelnuts—
    see previous recipe
whipped cream—see recipe

Butter a small cake tin, preferably one with a push-up base. Break the sponge cakes into small pieces. Beat the butter, sugar and chocolate powder together in a bowl, then beat in the egg yolk—the mixture should be rather wet. Chop the toasted nuts roughly and fold half the quantity into the chocolate mixture.

Put a layer of broken up sponge cake in the bottom of the tin, spread over a layer of chocolate mixture, add another layer of sponge cake, then a second layer of chocolate mixture; top with a third layer of cake. Fit a small plate over the top, cover with a weight and leave in the refrigerator overnight. Reserve the remaining chocolate mixture.

Before serving, turn the cake out carefully, coat the sides with the reserved chocolate mixture; spread a thick layer of whipped cream on top of the gateau and sprinkle generously with the remaining hazelnuts.

GREEK NUT CAKE <small>AUTUMN</small>

Sweet cakes made with nuts and honey have been eaten in Greece for centuries. It is best to keep the cake for a day or two to allow the mixture to firm up, before cutting into fudge-sized cubes; you will find that a square or two to nibble with elevenses or at tea-time is delicious and also quite filling, or you can do as the Ancient Greeks, and eat them at the end of a meal, with wine.

100 g/1 cup/4 oz shelled hazelnuts
50 g/1/2 cup/2 oz shelled walnuts
50 g/1/2 cup/2 oz blanched almonds
3-4 tablespoons (heaped) thick honey
poppy seeds—see recipe

Put all the nuts in a shallow roasting tin and toast in a hot oven until evenly brown, grind the nuts through an electric grinder into a bowl. Heat the honey in a small saucepan until nearly boiling, draw off the heat and allow to cool a little. Stir enough honey into the grated nuts to make a soft ball then, with floured hand, shape into a flattish round cake. Sprinkle all over with poppy seeds and gently press them in with the flat of your hand.

HAZELNUT AND FRUIT LOAF <small>AUTUMN</small>

Serve the loaf fresh, in thick slices, with plenty of butter; it tends to disappear fast!

50 g1/2 cup/2 oz freshly shelled hazelnuts
50 g/1/2 cup/2 oz seedless raisins
100 g/1/2 cup/4 oz sugar, or 3 tablespoons honey
200 g/2 cups/8 oz plain flour
pinch salt
2 level teaspoons baking powder
1 egg
125 ml/2/3 cup/scant 1/4 pint milk

Roast the nuts in a moderately hot oven for 15 minutes then rub off the brown skins in a clean cloth. Leave the oven set to 325°F, 170°C or Gas 3. Chop the nuts roughly and put them in a bowl with the raisins and sugar. If using honey, gently melt it and add to the mixture last of all. Add the sifted flour, salt and baking powder and stir in the lightly mixed egg. Add enough milk to make a fairly firm dough, place in a well greased 500 g/1 lb loaf tin, spread the top level and bake in the pre-heated oven for 45 minutes, until well risen and golden brown. Cool for a minute, then turn the loaf out on to a wire rack.

HAZEL WALKING STICK <small>WINTER</small>

You can cut hazel saplings for walking sticks whenever the trees are bare. Search for a straight stick of the thickness you require and cut about 1 metre/3ft 6ins for a walking stick and 1 1/2 metres/4 ft 6ins for a thumb stick, plus 2 1/2 cms/1in or two extra on each. Find a branch which has a knob for a handle, or divides like a Y for a thumb stick.

When you have cut your stick, trim off the side shoots, but don't cut them too close to the main stem, leave about 5 cms/ 2 ins, likewise leave more than you will eventually need on the handle, or thumb stick branches. Do not peel the stick, but leave it to season for six months in a shed or garage.

After seasoning, trim off the side shoots close to the main stem and trim the handle or thumb rest to the length you require. Shape the handle with a file, and finally sandpaper until it is smooth. Smooth down all the trimmed surfaces with sandpaper. Polish the whole stick with furniture polish several times, until it acquires a nice coppery sheen.

HEATHER

Calluna vulgaris

LING

Heather is native to Britain and grows extensively on moors and hillsides in Scotland and the north of England, and is found on heaths and in boggy places wherever the soil is acid in Europe and Scandinavia. It is a rare wild plant in eastern North America, although cultivated in gardens. The shrubby plant grows 1-2 ft/30-60 cm high on stiff, wiry, branching stems. The narrow, spiky, evergreen leaves are minute; they grow in two opposite rows and crowd along the stems so closely that they overlap. The tiny, pinkish-purple flowers are bell-shaped and grow in crowded spikes; they bloom in late summer, often in such profusion that large areas of hillside and moorland are suffused in a soft, purple glow. Occasionally a white-flowered variety of ling occurs, the 'lucky' heather that gypsies peddle.

Britain has several other native heathers, the Cross-leaved Heather, Dorset, Irish and Cornish Heaths, all rather uncommon and local, and the well-known Bell Heather, which is widespread, and has flowers that are egg-shaped and much larger than the true heather, or ling.

Heather is the food plant of our native red grouse, found mostly on the moors of Scotland and northern England, and nowhere else in the world except the British Isles. Heather tops are also a source of winter grazing for mountain sheep, when there is not much else on the northern hillsides.

Country people made sweeping brooms by tightly binding heather stems on to a handle, the scientific name *calluna* comes from the Greek *kalluna*, to brush. The longer stems were used for making baskets, and the Highlanders built their sheilings of heather stems bound together with a mortar composed of grasses, straw and peaty mud; the roofs, too, were thatched with heather. Their beds were made from springy bunches of heather, and the Highlanders who emigrated to America are believed to have introduced the seeds to the New World in the heather-filled beds that they took with them. In Ireland and the Western Isles heather shoots were used in tanning leather and as a yellow and orange dye for cloth.

Heather flowers yield so much honey that bee-keepers often take their hives miles into the hills to stand them in the heather in late summer.

There is the legend of a kind of mead brewed by the Picts from heather flowers, and in the old days, young heather shoots were used instead of hops to flavour beer.

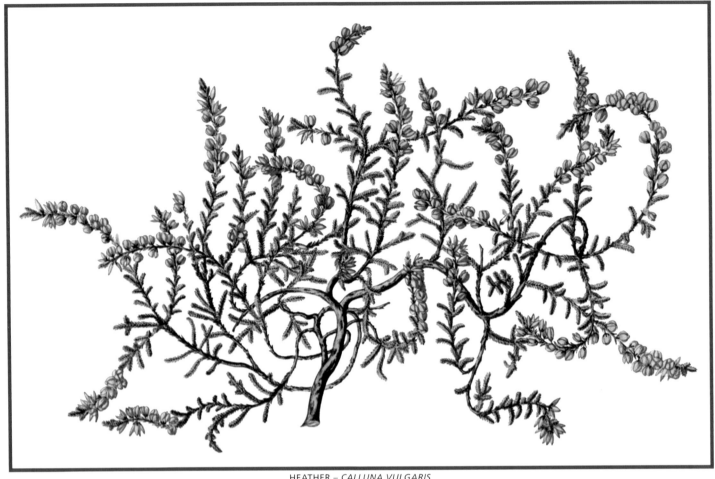

HEATHER – *CALLUNA VULGARIS*

TO DRY HEATHER FLOWERS

LATE SUMMER, EARLY AUTUMN

Hang some bunches of heather in an airing cupboard or airy room to dry. When quite dry and crisp, strip the little flowers and some leaves from the stems, and store in screw-topped jars.

DRIED HEATHER FLOWER TEA

LATE SUMMER, EARLY AUTUMN

The mauve and green speckles of dry heather flowers look most decorative in a glass storage jar but it should be kept away from the light so do not keep it on show. The drink is the colour of weak tea and has a similar taste, with a hint of honey.

2 rounded teaspoons dried heather flowers
250 ml/1 cup/½ pint boiling water

Put the flowers in a jug. Pour on boiling water, cover and infuse for 7 minutes. Strain into a cup and drink hot.

HEATHER PILLOWS SUMMER, AUTUMN

Heather beds were well known for their comfort when the Jacobites 'took to the heather' in the 18th century, and nowadays many campers have discovered that a layer of heather is a warm, springy mattress. You can stuff garden pillows with heather which makes a light, resilient and damp-proof filling, comfortable to pull under one's head when lazing on the grass.

METHOD

Cut some bundles of heather, tie them into small bunches and hang them up in a well ventilated room to dry. Cut away all the really hard, woody stems, and lightly stuff the heather into covers made of strong cotton, or canvas, cut to whatever size you wish.

HERB BENNET

Geum urbanum

WOOD AVENS

Herb bennet is quite common in woods and on damp shady banks throughout Great Britain, Europe, and most of Scandinavia, but it is rarely found in the United States. The plant is perennial, 30-60 cm/1-2 ft high, and looks rather sparsely furnished with leaves. The stems are wiry, slightly branched, and covered with small hairs. The toothed leaves are pinnate and differ according to their position on the stem: the lower leaves grow on long stalks and are interruptedly pinnate, having irregular spaces between the leaflets, the terminal leaflet is large and club-shaped, while the intermediate pairs of leaflets are small, and not uniform in size. Higher up the stem the leaves are three-fingered, and the lower ones have rounder leaflets than the narrower upper leaves: these stem leaves are placed alternately and have a leaf-like stipule at the base of each. The flowers look too small for the height of the plant, they are superficially like small buttercups, with five bright yellow petals and green sepals filling the spaces between. The fruits are more distinctive and conspicuous than the flowers, they ripen into small, round, bristly heads, like little dark red burrs; flowers and fruit appear together throughout the summer. Herb bennet, like the acanthus leaf, was used as a decorative motif on stone capitals and columns in 14th century architecture.

The plant grows from a rhizome with many small wiry rootlets, and these are herb bennet's surprise and bonus, for their delicious clove flavour and scent has been used for centuries to flavour wine, ale and broth, and they are excellent as a substitute for cloves in any dish. In the old days, the roots were put among clothes for their scent, to keep away moths, and to repel the devil, who found the odour obnoxious; the root was carried to keep off venomous beasts and evil spirits, and was used medicinally against the plague, for stomach disorders, bad breath, diarrhoea, sore throat, catarrh, fever, haemorrhage, headache, chills, ague, spots and pimples—you name it, herb bennet cured it. Culpeper said 'it is governed by Jupiter . . . it is good for the diseases of the chest or breath, for pains and stitches in the sides, it dissolveth inward congealed blood occasioned by falls and bruises and the spitting of blood . . . It is very safe and is fit to be kept in everybody's house'.

The early herbalists were very insistent that the roots should be used in the spring, even the 25th March was given as a specific date when the roots were at their peak of fragrance, but I have used them well into the summer, and they still smell and taste of cloves, also the plant is easier to find when the flowers are out.

HERB BENNET WITH APPLE PIE

SPRING AND SUMMER

For apple pie, herb bennet roots are much nicer than cloves, for the whole dish is evenly permeated with the spicy fragrance, instead of tasting strongly wherever a clove is placed, and horrible if you mistakenly bite into one. The root system consists of a small tuber $2^1/2$-5 cm/1-2 ins long, one end of which looks as if it had been cut off abruptly. From the tuber grow a number of thin, wiry roots, these are the ones to use fresh, the little tubers can be dried for use in the winter.

SERVES 4

100 g/4 oz shortcrust pastry
a bundle of 10-12 little roots of herb bennet
1 kilo/2 lbs cooking apples
2-3 tablespoons sugar, or honey
3 tablespoons water

Prepare the pastry dough and put in the fridge to rest. Soak the herb bennet roots in cold water for 10 minutes, then wash them thoroughly, rubbing them in your fingers to clean them, and finally drying them off with a paper towel. Put the roots on a board and scrape them gently with a knife, it is not necessary to remove every bit of their brown skin, and interesting at this stage to taste a bit to see how truly clove-like they are. Tie the roots in a bundle with thread.

Peel, core and quarter the apples and put them in a saucepan with the sugar, or honey, water and herb bennet roots. Bring to the boil, stir, and cook gently for 5-6 minutes, turn into a buttered pie dish and cover with a lid of pastry.

Brush the top with milk and cut a few slits in the pastry to let out the steam. Bake in a moderately hot oven for 35-40 minutes until the pastry is golden brown, sprinkle with sugar, and serve with whipped cream. As you cut the pie you can remove the little bundle of roots when you come to them.

BREAD SAUCE FLAVOURED WITH HERB BENNET SPRING AND SUMMER

Any dish that is improved by the flavour of cloves can be made with the little wiry roots of herb bennet. Bread sauce is one example. Serve it with roast chicken, turkey, pheasant, or partridge.

about 10 herb bennet roots
250 ml/1 cup/$^1/2$ pint milk
1 tablespoon grated onion
salt and pepper
50 g/1 cup/2 oz fresh white breadcrumbs
25 g/2 tablespoons/1 oz butter

Prepare the herb bennet roots as before and tie them in a bundle with thread. Put the roots in a saucepan with the milk, grated onion, and seasoning, cover the pan and simmer slowly for 15 minutes. Stir in the breadcrumbs and add the butter, cover and continue to cook slowly for a further 15 minutes, adding a little more milk if the sauce is too thick. Before serving, remove the bundle of roots.

HERB BENNET – *GEUM URBANUM*

HOP – *HUMULUS LUPULUS*

HOP

Humulus lupulus

Wild hops are found in damp hedges and thickets throughout the lowland districts of Britain and Europe, although they are rare in the north and in Ireland. In America they are found from Nova Scotia to Montana and California, South to North Carolina, Arkansas, Oklahoma and Arizona. The drooping, pale green, bell-like flowers with papery, overlapping scales are the female flowers, which develop during the summer and are used in making beer. The male and female flowers grow on separate plants, and cultivated hops grown in the hop 'gardens' of Kent and East Sussex are always female, the inconspicuous sprays of tiny, yellow-green male flowers being useless for flavouring beer. Hop leaves are palmate and deeply divided into three large lobes; these toothed leaves, and the whole plant, feel rough and hairy, even prickly. The square stems grow to a great length, with many side shoots which twine and clamber through the hedgerows.

The shoots should be cut in April and May for eating as a vegetable, which is when commercially grown hops are pruned; you can ask a farmer for some of his prunings, if you live within reach of a hop garden. If you should notice wild hops in the late summer when they are in flower, mark the place and return in the spring to cut the shoots, leaving three or four of the longest to grow, for the plant is perennial. The Romans only grew hops to eat the tender shoots, the Swedes made cloth from the tough fibres of hop stems, but during the 14th century the Dutch started using hop flowers for flavouring beer. At first the idea was regarded with suspicion, even resentment, in England and not long after the introduction of hops, the city of London petitioned Parliament against two nuisances, Newcastle coals, and hops! In Queen Elizabeth's reign an edict was issued against the use of 'that pernicious weed, the hop'.

Soon after the introduction of hops into this country the plant had one enthusiast, Reginald Scott, author of *The Perfite Platforme of a Hoppe Garden*, who complained that 'the Flemmings envy our practise herein, who altogither tende their own profite, seeking to impounde us in ignorance, to cramme us with wares and fruits of their countrie, and doe anything that myght put impediment to our cultivating the hoppe, discommending our soyle and climate, sending us to Flaunders for that which we can finde better at home'. It all sounds vaguely familiar, like the EU wrangle about Cox's apples and British ice cream!

Culpeper believed in hops as a remedy for a multitude of diseases, both internal and external, even claiming that they would cure venereal disease and jaundice. In his *Family Herbal* Thornton quotes Dr. Latham, a Fellow of the Royal College of Physicians, and physician to the Prince of Wales, who advised hops for stomach and bowel complaints, and as a substitute for laudanum. And Dr. John Mayo, who was the Princess of Wales' physician, and also a fellow of the Royal College, prescribed an infusion of hops for teething troubles in babies. At the same time, in France, Dr. Losch was using the sticky gum from hop glands to make medicines for a number of ailments, for stomach cramp, insomnia, nervous agitation, migraine, indigestion, gout and jaundice; and nowadays a tincture or concentrated infusion of the dried strobiles of the plant are used in modern pharmacy as a mild sedative.

Small pillows filled with dried hop flowers are accepted as being helpful in cases of insomnia and are sold commercially. It is not often realised that hops belong to the cannabis family and are related to the hemp plant from which marijuana is obtained.

HOP SHOOTS SPRING

Hop shoots are an unusual treat if you can find them in the hedgerows, or beg them from a hop farmer. The plant is easy to grow in one's own garden; both leaves and flowers are very decorative, and you will find the plants produce many side shoots throughout the growing season, which should be cut back and will provide hop-tops to add to soup.

There is a recipe for Hop-Top Soup in Martha Bradley's *The British Housewife*, 1750, which is unnecessarily elaborate, but the top 10 cm/3-4 ins of hop shoots dropped into any good broth or vegetable soup and simmered for 5 minutes before serving, make a delicious garnish.

hop shoots
butter
salt and pepper

Take the top 20 or 25 cm/8 or 10 ins from each shoot, and cut each length in half, leaving on the small leaves. Discard the rest, which would be tough.

Have ready a large pan of boiling salted water, gather the shoots into a bundle, drop them in the pan and boil for 5 minutes. Drain through a colander.

Melt a good knob of butter in the pan, stir the shoots gently in the butter and add a little pepper. Turn on to a warm dish with all the butter from the pan.

The top 12 or 15 cm/5 or 6 ins can be eaten whole, the lower part has a tender covering over a tougher core which you can bite off, like asparagus.

HOP PILLOW LATE SUMMER

The old herbalists recommended small pillows filled with hops to help people to sleep, and modern herbalists sell them for this purpose today. They are usually quite expensive and it is easy to make your own. I like to add a mixture of sweetly-scented dried herbs to the hops which have a faintly bitter smell. You can, of course, vary the proportions of the herbs and substitute others; dried lavender heads, cardamom seeds scraped from their nut-like case, thyme, some shavings of dried orange or lemon peel,

a little crushed cinnamon stick, anything spicy or aromatic is good. The pillow should be flat and loosely filled to slip under one's ordinary pillow, otherwise the hops rustle about and sound enormously loud under one's ear! One of these pillows would make a nice present for a traveller, the delicious herbal scent is refreshing in smelly trains and sleep-defying aircraft, and for the car passenger, the aromatic pillow can be a defence against traffic fumes. If you can't find wild hops, and don't grow them in your garden, you can use dried hops as sold for home brewing.

FILLING FOR A PILLOW ABOUT 30 X 20 CM/12 X 8 INS
approximately 2 handfuls dried hop flowers
1 rounded tablespoon dried, crumbled southernwood
1 rounded tablespoon dried, crumbled sage leaves
6 rounded tablespoons dried crumbled lemon balm leaves
6 rounded tablespoons dried, crumbled eau de Cologne mint leaves
1 rounded tablespoon dried, chopped rosemary leaves

Choose a piece of fairly strong cotton material for the cover. Cut two pieces that make the best of the design, 30 x 20 cm/12 x 8 ins is just a rough guide. With right sides together, tack and machine one short and two long seams of the cotton cover, trim the seam allowance to 5 mm/1/4 in. Turn right side out, and press.

Make a bag of two layers of muslin the same size as the cotton cover, tack and machine one short and two long seams twice, leaving 2 1/2 mm/1/8 in between each row of stitching. This stops the herbs leaking out. Trim away the seam allowance fairly close to the stitching.

Fill the muslin bag with dried hops and herbs, then turn in and oversew the open edges together. Slip the muslin bag inside the cover. Attach the edges of the muslin bag to the inside seam allowance of the cover with a few stitches on all three sides which prevents the muslin bag of herbs falling into one corner of the pillow. Catch one raw edge of the cover's open end to the corresponding edge of the muslin bag with a few stitches. Turn in the seam allowance of the cover and slipstitch together along fold line. Store the pillow in a plastic bag until ready to use.

HORSE-RADISH

Armoracia rusticana = Cochlearia armoracia

I t is not known exactly when horse-radish was introduced into Britain, but it is now a common wild plant in the south-east of England, though rare in Scotland and Ireland. It is cultivated and has become naturalised throughout southern and eastern Europe, and is also cultivated and occurs as a common weed throughout the United States. Horse-radish is often found growing on damp waste ground and by the sides of roads and on banks where the large, glossy green leaves look somewhat like dock leaves. They are wavy-edged, slightly toothed and larger, less pointed and much more shiny than dock leaves. Throughout the summer horse-radish may produce long, leafy spikes of small, four-petalled white flowers, but it does not flower regularly in Britain, and the little round seed pods hardly ever ripen.

The plant is perennial and is cultivated for its hot, peppery-tasting root in most parts of the world. It can be propagated from root cuttings in early spring ('for it shooteth up divers heads, which may be parted for increase', as one early gardener tells us); the cuttings should be planted in deeply dug and well manured soil, and as long as the roots are planted firmly in holes about 30 cm/1 ft deep and in rich ground, they need no further attention except for weeding. After several years the roots deteriorate and fresh cuttings should be planted.

Horse-radish is one of the bitter herbs eaten by the Jews during Passover, but the Germans and Slavs were probably the first people in Europe to use grated horse-radish in sauces and pickles, for its earliest uses were medicinal. The Greeks had a medicinal plant, *Raphnos agrios*, wild radish, which is thought to have been horse-radish, and by the Middle Ages the fresh root was being used in England for plaster and poultices in treating rheumatism, sciatica and gout, for the mustard oil contained in horse-radish acts like a mustard plaster, and irritates and blisters the skin; the grated root was used in the same way for neuralgia and chilblains. It was thought that if horse-radish was eaten daily it would cure a persistent cough, and even modern herbalists recommend horse-radish either grated, or in a syrup, for bronchial catarrh as well as an aid to digestion.

The root was one of the countless early remedies for worms in children, and William Coles wrote in 1657: 'Of all things that are given to Children for the Wormes, Horse Reddish is not the least effectuall, for it killeth and expelleth them, whether the juice of the green root, or the powder of the dry root . . . or an Oyntment be made thereof, and the Belly of the Child be anointed therewith.' The children of those days must have dreaded some of the violent remedies that were used on them, and the effects of blistering horse-radish ointment on a child's delicate skin must have been extremely unpleasant. To illustrate how much more medicinal than culinary horse-radish was considered to be in those days, Coles says, 'The Root is commonly used amongst the Germans, and sometimes by Gentlemen with us also, for sauce to eat Fish with, or other meats, as Mustard is, and so it heateth and Stomach more, and causeth better digestion than Mustard'.

Rheumatism and dropsy were also treated with horse-radish by Thornton, who lectured in botany at Guy's Hospital, London, early in the 19th century.

HORSE-RADISH – *ARMORACIA RUSTICANA = COCHLEARIA ARMORACIA*

HORSE-RADISH SAUCE <small>SUMMER AND EARLY AUTUMN</small>

When you have identified the plant, dig up the fattest root you can find, trim off the fine rootlets and the leaves, and scrub thoroughly in tepid water. Remove the skin with a sharp knife, as if sharpening a pencil–the pungent fumes from the root will probably make you cry, like peeling onions! Leave the root to dry, then grate it on a medium coarse grater, which will leave you with a bundle of fibres looking like an old shaving brush, which you can throw away. Reserve the grated root for the following sauce to serve with traditional roast beef and Yorkshire pudding.

3 tablespoons grated horse-radish
1/4 teaspoon mustard powder
3 tablespoons thick cream

Put the horse-radish in a small bowl, add the dry mustard, stir in the cream and mix well together.

HANS ANDERSEN SANDWICH

<small>SUMMER AND EARLY AUTUMN</small>

Of all Denmark's famous open sandwiches perhaps this is the best known. It is made with bacon and liver pâté set on rye bread and garnished with tomato and horse-radish. The rye bread is close textured and firm, so that the slices can be thin and all the interest is in what goes on top.

dark or light rye bread
butter
bacon slices
liver pâté
tomatoes, previously skinned
grated horse-radish

Butter thin slices of rye bread, allowing two slices per person for a good snack. Cut the rind from the bacon and fry until crisp and brown, drain on kitchen paper. When cool, arrange two rashers side by side on the buttered bread, on one rasher lay a narrow strip of liver pâté, on the other thin slices of deseeded tomato.

Top with grated horse-radish.

TARTAR SANDWICH

For the brave, you can make a Tartar sandwich. This consists of a slice of buttered rye bread spread with a layer of scraped raw beef. In the centre nestles the yolk of a raw egg surrounded by a circle of finely chopped onion. The whole is topped with grated horse-radish and a few capers.

HYSSOP
Hyssopus officinalis

Hyssop is cultivated in Britain, but grows wild in southern Europe where it is found on old walls and dry banks. In America, hyssop is also cultivated and has become naturalised by roadsides and in dry grassy places from Quebec to Montana and southwards to North Carolina. The rather shrubby little plant is perennial and grows 30-60 cm /1-2 ft high. The small, dark, evergreen leaves are narrow and crowd thickly along the branching woody stems. The long, narrow flower spikes appear in late summer, with flowers of a deep, intense blue growing in whorls among the upper leaves. The whole plant is deliciously aromatic and was used as a strewing herb in the old days, 'fit to be strewd in windows' according to William Coles who listed fifteen varieties of hyssop in his 17th century herbal; besides the ordinary garden hyssop, he mentions the white, golden, russet, double, broad-leaved, jagged, musked, red-flowered, dwarf Spanish, tufted, curled, mountain wild, narrow-leaved and round-leaved. Only the blue

HYSSOP – *HYSSOPUS OFFICINALIS*

flowered *H. officinalis* is now commonly grown in gardens in this country, with occasionally a pink and a white variety. Bees love the flowers, which give a wonderful flavour to their honey.

Distilled oil of hyssop is used in perfumery and also in the manufacture of Chartreuse and other liqueurs. The flowering tops were used to make a tea which has been valued medicinally for centuries. It was best known as an expectorant and to give relief in bronchitis, catarrh and all 'chesty' conditions, but rheumatism was also treated with frequent drinks of hyssop tea, and also hyssop baths. William Coles wrote 'it taketh away black and blew spots, and marks that come by stroaks, bruises, or falls', and 'it amendeth the native colour of the Body spoiled by the yellow Jaundise'. He listed quinsies, toothache, snake-bite, head lice, worms, the falling sickness, diseases of the chest and lungs, dropsy, ague 'and all cold griefs' among the many afflictions this wonder herb was said to cure, and recommended 'the hot vapours of the Decoction taken by a Funnel in the Ears'. The 19th century French physician, Dr. Losch, also suggested hyssop should be used 'in fumigations to relieve humming and buzzing in the ears'.

An infusion of fresh green hyssop tops was used by country folk in America to soothe painful bruises and contusions, and in the external treatment of muscular rheumatism; the same complaints that the early herbalists treated with hyssop in just the same way. Modern herbalists recommend hyssop tea for people who suffer from asthma and other chest ailments.

To grow hyssop—and its blue flowers are decorative enough for the flower border—seeds should be sown in the spring and, when large enough to handle, thinned out or transplanted to about 30 cm/12 ins apart. Older plants can be divided in the spring, or cuttings taken and rooted in a jam jar of water. Hyssop demands a sunny position and prefers a light soil, though I find it grows successfully in clay. The seedlings and cuttings should be kept weeded and watered, but once established, hyssop will thrive for years, and requires nothing but an occasional trim in the autumn, and the removal of any dead wood.

MEATBALLS WITH HYSSOP SUMMER, EARLY AUTUMN

Hyssop gives an exotic flavour to these meatballs, which are meltingly tender inside a crisp coating of sesame seeds. You can make them very small and neat to serve on cocktail sticks with pre-dinner drinks, or a little larger to eat with some crisp lettuce leaves and sliced tomato as a starter. As a main dish the meatballs can be flat and hamburger-shaped, and are good with rice and a fresh tomato sauce.

The quantities given will serve six people for a starter, or four as a main dish.

150 g/3/4 cup/6 oz lean beef
150 g/3/4 cup/6 oz sausage meat
1 large onion
2 large cloves garlic
1 1/2 tablespoons chopped parsley
1 1/2 tablespoons chopped hyssop
1 teaspoon chopped marjoram
1 large egg
salt and pepper
75 g/1/3 cup/3 oz sesame seeds
oil for frying

Put the beef through a mincer; to achieve a really fine texture it is best to put it and the sausage meat through twice (or pulse in a food processor); peel and quarter the onion and mince it with the meats. Mix together in a bowl and add the crushed garlic, the finely chopped herbs, a seasoning of salt, and plenty of freshly milled black pepper. Mash all together with a wooden spoon until the mixture is really pasty. Then add the egg and again mix thoroughly. The mixture should be rather soft and wet.

Form the meat mixture into walnut-sized balls and roll in sesame seeds until they are evenly coated.

Pour the cooking oil into a deep frying pan, so that it is about 1 cm/1/2 in deep and heat until very hot. Quickly fry the meatballs for about 5 minutes—turning them to brown on all sides. You will need to fry them in at least two batches, so keep the first lot warm.

HYSSOP SYRUP SUMMER, EARLY AUTUMN

Hyssop has a heady, aromatic scent, evocative of a Mediterranean hillside. Fruit gently poached in the syrup acquires a wonderful flavour, and it is delicious poured over fruit salad or any sliced fresh fruit.

1 large handful flowering stems and leaves of hyssop, about 30 sprigs
1/4 litre/1 1/4 cups/1/2 pint water
200 g/1 cup/8 oz sugar

Put the sprigs of hyssop in a small pan with the water, cover with a lid, bring to the boil and simmer gently for 10 minutes. Strain the liquid into a jug, pressing the herb with a wooden spoon to extract all the flavour, and make up to 250 ml/1 1/4 cups/1/2 pint with water, if necessary. Return to the pan, and add the sugar, heat gently and stir until the sugar has dissolved, then boil hard for 5 minutes. Skim, and when quite cold, pour into a bottle with a screw cap and store in the refrigerator.

FRESH APRICOT FLAN, WITH HYSSOP

SUMMER, EARLY AUTUMN

Fresh plums could be used instead of apricots and, to be really extravagant, fresh peaches make the most delicious flan of all. Hyssop combines beautifully with these fruits.

SERVES 4
RICH SHORTCRUST PASTRY
100 g/1 cup/4 oz plain flour
50 g/4 tablespoons/2 oz butter
1 egg yolk
25 g/2 tablespoons/1 oz icing sugar/confectioners' sugar (U.S.)
1 tablespoon water
FOR THE FILLING
400 g/1 lb fresh apricots
3 tablespoons hyssop syrup

Sift the flour into a mixing bowl, and rub in the butter with your fingertips until the mixture is crumbly. Stir in the sifted icing sugar with a fork and tip the lightly mixed egg yolk and water into the centre, continue to stir until a rough dough has formed, then turn the dough on to a floured surface and knead lightly until smooth. Chill in the refrigerator for half an hour in a polythene bag.

Roll out the dough thinly on a lightly floured surface and line a greased 20 cm/8 ins flan or pie tin. Prick the base with a fork and fill the centre with a piece of crumpled kitchen foil. Bake in a hot oven (400°F, 200°C or Gas 6) for 10 minutes, remove foil and bake for 2 or 3 minutes longer.

Halve and stone the apricots and arrange cut side down in the pastry case. Spoon over the hyssop syrup and replace the flan in the centre of the oven, cook for a further 15 minutes. Serve hot.

If you want to eat the flan cold, you should spoon a little

apricot glaze over the fruit, otherwise it will discolour as it cools. About 2 tablespoons of apricot jam boiled up with 2 tablespoons water and spooned hot over the apricots will keep them a good colour.

HYSSOP DESSERT SUMMER, EARLY AUTUMN

This hyssop-flavoured custard is delicious on its own or with sliced fresh fruit. Make it the day you want to use it, as the syrup tends to separate from the custard.

SERVES 2, OR WITH FRUIT 4
2 egg yolks
1 egg white
250 ml/1 cup/1/2 pint milk
3 tablespoons hyssop syrup
1 tablespoon sugar

Separate the eggs and put the yolks in a basin with 2 tablespoons cold milk taken from the 1/4 litre/11/4 cups/1/2 pint. Mix together with a fork. Heat the remainder of the milk in a pan, and, when hot but not boiling, pour on to the egg yolks and whisk lightly. Rinse out the pan and pour into it the egg and milk mixture, add the hyssop syrup. Cook gently and keep stirring until the mixture coats the back of the spoon, then pour into a bowl and allow to cool. Whisk the egg white until stiff, and whisk in the sugar, fold into the custard with a metal spoon and leave to cool before serving.

HYSSOP TEA SPRING, SUMMER

Hyssop tea can be made with the fresh green tops, or with dried hyssop flowers. Pick the green tops in the spring and early summer, and dry the flowers to store later on.

1 tablespoon fresh green tops hyssop, or dried flowers
250 ml/1 cup/1/2 pint boiling water

Put the hyssop in a jug, pour on the boiling water, cover and infuse for 5 minutes. The brew is improved if sweetened with a little honey.

TO DRY HYSSOP LATE SUMMER

When the vivid blue flowers are in their prime, pick them on a dry day and spread them thinly on trays or cardboard lids, and stand them at the back of a boiler or kitchen stove for 2 or 3 days, until quite dry and crisp. When cool, store the flowers in screw-topped jars, and use them whole for making hyssop tea.

JUNIPER
Juniperus communis

Juniper grows wild in Britain, Europe and Scandinavia, and is found in most of the northern states of North America. It occurs in fact throughout the northern hemisphere, but in Britain it is now found mainly in Scotland on the moors and hillsides, and in pine and birch woods. Juniper is one of the three conifers native to Britain, the other two being the yew and the Scots Pine. It used to be widespread on our heaths, chalk downs and limestone hills and still occurs in a few places on the North and South Downs, but it is thought that the decline in the rabbit population, since myxomatosis, has allowed hardier scrub to grow unchecked, and this has tended to crowd out the juniper. It is a graceful, evergreen shrub which can be spreading and prostrate, or narrowly conical when it may reach about 3 metres/10 ft high. The short, spine-tipped, needle-like leaves grow in whorls, with small yellow flowers at the base of the leaves in early summer; male and female flowers occur on separate plants, and turn into green, berry-like cones which ripen and become blue-black in their second year.

JUNIPER – *JUNIPERUS COMMUNIS*

Coles described juniper's 'small, green Berries not ripening fully till the second yeare which then will be somewhat like a peppercorn', and compiled a tremendous list of ailments for which they were 'an effectual remedy'. 'Windiness' and 'the iliack passion'; plague, pestilence, poison, strangury, stopping of urine and dropsy, cough, shortness of breath, consumption, rupture, convulsions and cramps, for the 'safe and speedy delivery to Women with Child'. No list of afflictions would be complete without the bite of adders, flies and wasps, fluxes, piles, worms, itches, scabs and pustules 'yea, the Lepry (leprosy) also, if the places be bathed therewith'. How did anyone live without it?

Henry VIII's physician, Andrew Borde, had a quaint use for juniper amongst his remedies, 'for the infirmities of the ars or fundement'. First he instructs 'to kepe the ars and buttockes warme. And syt not on the cold erth, nor upon stone or stones', then 'tak of myrtylles III onces (3 oz) of Juneper cut in small peces IIII onces (4 oz) seth it in water and wasshe the place. And after that make a perfume of juneper and syt over it'.

A little recipe book of 1746 gives a particularly revolting remedy for Convulsions, or Vertigo: 'Take one ounce of Juniper-berries, two ounces of fresh Seville Orange-peel; Male piony Roots, three ounces; Peacock's Dung, six ounces; Sugar Candy, half a pound; infuse these in two Quarts of Rhenish (wine) for twenty-four hours, in hot Ashes, then let it settle; and take two spoonfulls of this in a glass of Angelica-water. It has done great cures.' Modern herbalists agree that infusions of the twigs and berries are diuretic and will help to disperse kidney stones and gravel, and within the last thirty years, Oil of Juniper has been sold as a carminative, for flatulence.

The French physician, Dr. Losch, advised small quantities of juniper berries to promote appetite and to aid digestion, and used the berries in cases of dropsy, rheumatism and gout. He prescribed six or ten berries to be eaten daily by those exposed to contagion, and ordered the berries to be burned to fumigate the sick room and to 'destroy miasmas and contagious poisonous particles in the air'.

Linnaeus described a juniper-flavoured beer that was valued in Sweden for its diuretic and anti-scorbutic properties, and said the Lapps drank infusions of juniper berries as we do tea.

Juniper oil, obtained from the ripe berries, is a prime ingredient of gin which gives it the characteristic smell and flavour. In the 16th century gin was used as a medicine in Holland, and to make the drink more palatable, juniper berries were added as flavouring; from that early beginning the internationally famous drink never looked back. The distillers used to import juniper berries from Germany, nowadays they come mostly from Morocco. Other natural flavourings used in the manufacture of gin are angelica stem, coriander seeds and orris root.

PORK SPARE RIB WITH JUNIPER BERRY STUFFING AUTUMN

A way to improve the flavour and make a boned joint go further is to fill the cavity with a good tasty stuffing, but it should be more adventurous and individual than the stereotyped mixtures turned out in packets. Juniper berries go particularly well with pork, and this stuffing has the advantage of exciting flavours and originality.

SERVES 6

1½ kilos/3½ lbs boned and rolled spare rib pork
75 g/2½ cups/3 oz fresh white breadcrumbs
grated rind and juice of 1 orange
50 g/4 tablespoons/2 oz grated suet or butter
generous grating nutmeg
15 juniper berries, crushed
2 tablespoons chopped parsley
2 teaspoons chopped fresh sage
½ teaspoon salt
generous grinding black pepper
1 egg

Unroll the piece of pork and lay it flat on a board. Put all the ingredients for the stuffing into a basin and mix together thoroughly with a fork. Spread the mixture over the pork, then roll up and tie with string. Set the meat in a roasting tin with some hot fat, and roast in a hot oven (400°F, 200°C, or Gas 6) for 1½ hours. Serve the pork in thick slices with vegetables and a good gravy.

BRAISED PHEASANT WITH JUNIPER AUTUMN

Juniper berries are more flavourful when used fresh, than after they have been stored. They add lots of zing to an older bird.

1 large pheasant—can be an old bird
2 carrots
1 medium onion
1 bay leaf
10 juniper berries
salt and freshly milled black pepper
4 tablespoons/5 U.S. tablespoons cider vinegar
4 tablespoons/5 U.S. tablespoons water
6 thin rashers/U.S. slices fat bacon
1 rounded teaspoon plain flour
150ml/⅔ cup/¼ pint double cream

Peel the carrots and onion and slice thinly into a bowl. Add the bay leaf and lightly crushed juniper berries and the seasoning. Boil up the vinegar and water in a small pan and pour over the vegetables. Allow to cool.

Put the pheasant on its side in a large, deep dish and pour over the marinade of vegetables. Allow to stand for several hours, turning occasionally.

Pre-heat the oven to 400°F/200°C/Gas 6.

Lift the pheasant from the marinade and transfer to an ovenproof casserole, or roasting tin. Cover the breast with bacon rashers and pour the marinade over and around the bird. Roast the pheasant for 1¼ hours for an old bird, 40 minutes for a young one. Baste with the marinade 3 or 4 times.

When tender, take the pheasant from the oven, lift onto a

warm serving dish and remove the bacon. Carve into 4 helpings and keep warm while you prepare the sauce.

Remove the bay leaf and juniper berries from the pan juices. Rub the vegetables and juices through a food mill, or coarse strainer, into a small saucepan. Mix the flour and cream together in a cup, and add to the pan. Cook gently together for a few minutes, stirring constantly until the sauce thickens, then pour over the pheasant portions.

A creamy mixture of mashed potatoes with mashed celeriac goes well with this dish.

BEEF CASSEROLE WITH PRUNES AND JUNIPER AUTUMN AND WINTER

Juniper and prunes give this dish a rich flavour. Soak the prunes overnight before you start the recipe—ready-to-eat prunes do not need soaking.

1 kilo/2 lbs chuck steak
55 g/4 tablespoons/2 oz butter
2 tablespoons olive oil

2 medium onions, peeled and sliced
1 tablespoon flour
600 ml/2½ cups/1 pint light ale
salt and freshly milled black pepper
10 juniper berries—lightly crushed
8 prunes—soaked overnight

Cut the steak into neat chunks. Heat the butter and oil in a large pan and fry the steak in small batches until browned on all sides. Lift the meat out onto a plate. Lower the heat and add the onions to the pan—add a little more oil if needed, and fry gently until the onions start to colour. Add the flour and stir while it cooks for a minute or two, then add the ale and keep stirring while the sauce thickens smoothly. Return the pan to the heat with a seasoning of salt and pepper and the juniper berries.

Transfer to a casserole dish with a tight fitting lid, cover and cook in a low oven, (300°F/150°C/Gas 2) for 1½ hours. Remove the casserole from the oven and add the drained prunes. Cover the dish again and return to the oven for another hour, until the meat and prunes are tender. Serve in the casserole.

LADY'S SMOCK

Cardamine pratensis

CUCKOO FLOWER

Lady's smock occurs in most damp places in Britain, Europe and Scandinavia, and in meadows, swamps and shallow water throughout Canada and the northern states of North America. It is one of the prettiest flowers of spring, and is known as the Cuckoo Flower because it blooms in Britain when the cuckoo arrives. The plant grows from 23-46 cm/9-18 ins tall, and is very slender and graceful. The flowers catch your eye, as their mauve heads stand above the surrounding grasses, sometimes so pale, they are nearly white. Each flower has four petals, delicately streaked and veined with dark lilac, and six stamens with yellow anthers. The narrow, pinnate leaves grow at wide intervals up the smooth stem: the topmost leaves usually have three little leaflets, the middle ones five, and the lower nine. At the base the leaves grow in a rosette, where the leaflets are much rounder than those on the stem.

William Coles listed lady's smock among the plants that would cure scurvy, and Robert Thornton quoted Galen, the

LADY'S SMOCK – *CARDAMINE PRATENSIS*

ancient medical herbalist, saying the plant had the same virtues as watercress, being a gentle stimulant and diuretic. Thornton himself advised lady's smock for such serious illnesses as nervous hysteria, St. Vitus's Dance and spasmodic asthma, and said the flowering tops should be used to treat epilepsy. While Sir John Hill prescribed the plant for 'the gravel and all suppressions of urine . . . in the jaundice and green sickness . . . and against scurvy'.

One often sees lady's smock growing abundantly by roadsides, though it prefers damp places, and is found in marshy meadows and near streams. The leaves of the plants from wet meadows taste very much nicer than those from roadside verges, where they really do seem to acquire a slight taste of oil, whereas the clean meadow leaves have a lovely tangy taste, hot and peppery, rather like watercress. Use them to pep up any green salad.

See also Lady's Smock under Mixed Herbs in Wild Herb Sauce, p. 160 and Wild Sandwiches, p. 160.

LAVER
Porphyra umbilicalis

L aver grows at the middle- and low-tide levels on the Atlantic and North Sea coasts of Britain, and in the Mediterranean. North America has two related species of *porphyra* which are eaten as a delicacy by the Chinese and Japanese. It is usually found on sandy beaches attached to the stones or rocks which lie in the sand. *Porphyra umbilicalis* is classed as a red seaweed, which I find misleading, as I have never seen truly red specimens; laver is usually dark purplish brown and, when the tide is out and the seaweed lies in filmy sheets on the sand, it turns almost black as it dries. The fronds are like wide, thin leaves of semi-transparent rubber, each 'leaf' varying from 5-7 1/2 cm/2-3 ins to 60 cm/2 ft long, several layers of fronds may be attached to the rock at one point. When picking laver, one should cut it, or tear it off gently, so that you do not pull up the hold-fast which attaches it to the rocks.

LAVERBREAD SPRING AND SUMMER

Technically, laverbread is a gelatinous preparation of the seaweed *Porphyra umbilicalis*, or red laver, after it has been picked, cleaned and cooked. It will keep in this state for over a week and is the basis of several traditional Welsh recipes. Laverbread is sold in shops in south-west Wales and in the market in Swansea, and is even served as a delicacy in restaurants. A traditional way of eating laverbread is cold, spread on toast; with a seasoning of salt and pepper, its jellified sea-tang is intriguing, but, to my taste, even nicer if spread on fried bread. When picking laver, a plastic carrier bag is a handy receptacle.

METHOD

Soak the laver in fresh water for a couple of hours. Drain and wash in several changes of water to remove the sand and grit, and be careful to pick out any shells or pebbles. Put the seaweed in a large saucepan with a little water, bring to the boil, cover, then simmer very gently for about 2 hours. If the laver dries out, add a little fresh water, but although most recipes say it tends to stick to the pan, I found it didn't. Towards the end of the cooking time, pound and pulp the laver with a potato masher, or wooden spoon. By this time the weed will have turned dark green and look like rather gelatinous, stringy spinach. Allow to cool a little, then spoon the pulp into jars with screw-on tops. When quite cold, cover the jars with pieces of greaseproof paper and screw on the lids. Stored in a cool place, the laverbread will keep fresh for about 10 days.

WELSH BREAKFAST CAKES SPRING AND SUMMER

A Welsh farmer's wife gave me this recipe saying it made her hungry to talk about it! The pulped laverbread is thickly coated in oatmeal and fried in bacon fat until crisp and brown. Eaten piping hot, the breakfast cakes are delicious at any time of the day, the crisp oatmeal covering contrasting beautifully with the soft, dark filling of laverbread.

500 ml/2 cups/1 pint laverbread pulp
salt and pepper
200 g/1/2 lb fat bacon rashers/(U.S. bacon slices)
oatmeal, seasoned with salt and pepper—see recipe

Put the laverbread in a saucepan, season with salt and pepper and beat together over a moderate heat until most of the surplus liquid has evaporated. Chop the bacon into small pieces and fry them slowly until beginning to brown, lift out the bacon bits with a slice and keep hot, reserve the fat for frying the laver cakes. Take up tablespoons of the laverbread and drop them into a bowl containing the seasoned oatmeal, roll lightly until thickly and evenly coated with oatmeal, then slide each cake into the frying pan of bacon fat and flatten a little. Fry gently on both sides until the oatmeal is very well browned and makes a crisp covering. Add extra fat if needed, as the cakes absorb quite a lot. Serve with the pieces of fried bacon.

LAVER SAUCE WITH LAMB SPRING AND SUMMER

A recipe from Wales and the west coast of Scotland crops up in many books, and they all include the juice of a Seville orange in the ingredients. As the pools and beaches where laver grows are bare of almost all seaweed in the winter when Seville oranges are in season, I have never understood how the two can be combined. Nevertheless, the grated rind and juice of a sweet orange plus the juice of a lemon give the sauce a good flavour.

SERVES 4
2 tea-cups laverbread (pulp)
2 tablespoons butter
grated rind and juice of 1 orange
juice 1 lemon
salt and white pepper

Melt the butter in a heavy pan, add the laver pulp, the grated rind and juice of the orange and the lemon juice, stir well with a wooden spoon then beat over a low heat until the pulp is smooth and jellified. Season with salt and pepper, being generous with the latter, and serve hot with a tender joint of well-browned roast lamb.

SLOKEEN SPRING AND SUMMER

In the Isle of Barra off the west coast of Scotland, laverbread was eaten with potatoes, which were a large part of the islanders' diet. The healthy seaweed added vitamins and minerals, as well as flavour to the rather monotonous and bland potatoes, and if you add some crisply fried onion rings to the dish, it makes it even more tasty.

SERVES 4
1 kilo/2 lbs potatoes
4 tea-cups laverbread (pulp)
1/2 tea-cup milk
4 tablespoons butter
2 onions
salt and freshly milled black pepper

Peel, halve and cook the potatoes in boiling salted water for 20-30 minutes. Drain well and mash with a little hot milk, pile the mashed potatoes onto a serving dish and keep warm. While cooking the potatoes, gently heat the laver pulp with 2 tablespoons of butter and plenty of seasoning. Peel and finely slice the onions into rings and fry until crisp and brown in the remaining butter. Lift out the onion, and tip any brown butter from the pan over the mashed potato. Surround the potato with the hot laver pulp and scatter the onion rings over the top.

SLOKE JELLY SUMMER

Although described as jelly, the dish is more a vegetable, and is good for seaside holiday suppers with sausages and chips.

4 tea-cups raw laver
scant pinch salt
freshly milled black pepper
butter—see recipe

Soak and thoroughly wash the seaweed in fresh water to remove any debris. Put the raw weed into a pan with a little water and boil for about 11/2 hours, pounding occasionally with a wooden spoon. When tender add seasoning and plenty of butter.

LAVER – *PORPHYRA UMBILICALIS*

COMMON LIME

Tilia vulgaris

The common lime is a cross between *Tilia cordata*, our truly native tree, and *T. platyphyllos* and, being a hardy and fertile hybrid, it is the most commonly grown lime throughout the northern temperate zone of Europe. *T. vulgaris* is planted in America, where there are also several native species, one of them, *T. americana*, is found throughout the eastern United States.

Lime trees are common in Britain and are usually planted in towns, parks and large gardens and sometimes, grow wild in hedgerows, but no limes are native to Ireland. The common lime is a beautiful, lofty tree, the trunk is bossed and covered in smooth, dark brown bark. The sharply-toothed leaves are heart-shaped and asymmetrical, one side being larger than the other; they are smooth and dark green above, paler and with some silky hairs beneath. The clusters of

COMMON LIME – *TILIA VULGARIS*

creamy yellow flowers hang downwards on slender stalks, they have five petals, five sepals and numerous prominent stamens, each cluster is half-joined to a pale, papery, leaf-like bract. The flowers are so heavily scented that in midsummer, when the trees are in bloom, the air all round them is filled with a wonderful honeyed fragrance, and is usually humming with hectically industrious bees. Lime flower honey is popular for its distinctive flavour.

The flowers should be picked while they are fresh for lime flower tea, which in France is known as *tilleul* and in Germany as *Lindenblüentee*; it is famous for its delicious flavour and soothing effect on the digestive and nervous systems. As recently as World War II, lime flowers were collected on a large scale for their sedative properties.

In *Les Plantes Medicinales*, Dr. Losch recommended a tisane of lime flowers for epilepsy, and said that nervous people were soothed just by walking beneath lime trees in flower. He suggested an infusion of lime bark for burns, and the leaves as a diuretic. Culpeper seems to be the only early herbalist to recognise lime flowers as 'a good cephalic and nervine, excellent for apoplexy, epilepsy, virtigo and palpitations of the heart'. The old writers usually had confidence in the medical virtues of such a wide range of plants and though they referred to lime wood being used for carving, the fibres of the inner bark for ropes and halters, and the training of the trees for arbours and lime walks, yet apart from Culpeper, I have found no early mention of lime flowers as a herbal remedy.

Pliny refers to the timber and the fibrous inner bark, or bast, from which baskets, ropes and matting have been made over the centuries, and in Sweden these fibres were made into a kind of thread for fishing nets. Theophrastus said the leaves were used for feeding cattle, and in Switzerland and parts of northern Europe their use as cattle fodder continued for a long time. The leaves are slightly sweet, (the sap, too, yields a sugary juice) which would make them palatable to cattle. This sweetness also attracts enormous numbers of aphids which secrete a sugary fluid that makes the leaves sticky. Towards the end of summer, lime trees in towns and by roadsides look dark and begrimed because of the dust and dirt that has stuck to the leaves.

Lime timber is very smooth, white and close-grained and lends itself to carving in sharp detail. Three centuries ago Grinling Gibbons used it for many of his exquisitely detailed carvings which, largely due to the fact that lime wood is seldom worm-eaten, are in such a perfect state of preservation today.

The keys and sounding boards of musical instruments are often made of lime wood and, in stark contrast, it was used in building the Mosquito fighter planes of World War II.

LIME FLOWER TEA (fresh) MID-SUMMER

Pick enough blossom to dry for the winter, and to make this delicious tea from fresh flowers. It is pale yellow, tastes mildly of honey, and can be drunk hot, but it is best of all iced, with a dash of lemon juice. An infusion of lime flowers has mildly tranquillising properties, and is soothing taken as a daily drink when one is anxious or nervy.

  Snip the blossom heads, consisting of little flowers and buds, from the main stalk and bract before measuring.

50 g/1 cup/2 oz fresh flowers, when picked over
500 ml/2 cups/1 pint boiling water
juice of 1/2 lemon

Put the flowers in a jug, pour on the boiling water, cover and leave to infuse for 5 minutes. Drink a cup while hot, and add the lemon juice to the rest and chill in the refrigerator.

TO DRY LIME FLOWERS MID-SUMMER

Snip the blossom heads, consisting of open flowers and buds, from the main stalk and bract. Spread out in a thin single layer on trays or cardboard lids, in a well-ventilated boiler room, or any warm, dry room, for seven to ten days, until the flowers are dry and brittle. When thoroughly dry, store the whole flowers in screw-topped jars away from the light.

DRIED LIME FLOWER TEA

The tea is pale yellow and has a faint taste of honey, to intensify the flavour it can be sweetened with a little extra honey, or sharpened with lemon juice.

1 heaped tablespoon dried flowers
250 ml/1 cup/1/2 pint boiling water

Crumble the flowers into a jug, pour on the boiling water, cover and leave to infuse for 5 minutes. Strain, and drink hot or cold.

LIME FLOWER WINE MID-SUMMER

This delicious white wine has a true flowery fragrance, and is best when well chilled.

activated yeast (p. 255)
1 1/2 litres/8 cups/3 pints measures lime flowers
  snipped from their stalks
2 lemons
5 litres/18 U.S. pints/1 gallon water
1 1/4 kilos/6 cups/3 lbs sugar

Pick the lime flowers when dry and snip off the stalks and the papery bract. Put the flowers in a large bowl with the thinly pared rind (no pith) of the lemons and pour on 2 1/2 litres/9 U.S. pints/2 quarts boiling water taken from the 5 litres/18 U.S. pints/1 gallon.

  Cover the bowl with a clean cloth and stand for 30 minutes. Put the sugar and the strained juice of the lemons into the plastic bucket, pour the infusion of flowers into the bucket through a double thickness of muslin, squeeze to extract all the flavour and stir thoroughly until the sugar has dissolved, then add the rest of the water, cold, and stir in the activated yeast. Cover the bucket with its lid, and leave in a warm place for three days, stirring daily. Pour the liquid into the fermentation jar and follow the method given on page 254.

LIME LEAF SANDWICHES SPRING–MID-SUMMER

The leaves of the common lime are fresh and green when the tree is in flower, so pick a few when you are gathering the flowers, to add to a salad, or to make sandwiches. They taste pleasantly of unspecified greenery and have the texture of watercress.

lime leaves
wholemeal bread
butter
salt and white pepper

Wash the leaves thoroughly, discarding any insect-nibbled areas, pat the leaves dry in a clean cloth and shred them finely with a sharp knife.

Make the sandwiches of thin slices of buttered wholemeal bread, with a scant sprinkling of salt and white pepper, and a thin layer of lime leaves as filling.

COMMON MALLOW

Malva sylvestris

DWARF MALLOW *Malva neglecta* MARSH MALLOW *Althaea officinalis*

There are seven different wild mallows in the British Isles. Three of them, the Cornish, rough and tree mallow, are uncommon. The musk mallow, though common and harmless, is not as good to eat as the common and dwarf mallows because of the musky odour from which it gets it name. They are easy to distinguish from each other, as musk mallow leaves are very jagged and finely cut, rather like the leaves of some garden cranesbill-geraniums, whereas the leaves of the dwarf and common mallow have five broad lobes and are similar in shape to ivy leaves.

The common mallow, *M. sylvestris* is found throughout Britain and Europe, and in the northern states of North America where it is sometimes known as high mallow. It grows in waste places, near houses and by roadsides, and particularly near the sea where it often forms large patches. The crinkly, almost pleated, ivy-shaped leaves are green all the year. From early summer onwards the plant has attractive pinkish purple flowers, with five petals heavily streaked with darker veins.

The little dwarf mallow, *M. neglecta*, is widespread and frequent in waste places, farmyards and beside walls, and is also found throughout Britain, Europe and the United States, where it is known as low mallow. Although smaller, its leaves are very similar to the common mallows, they grow on longer, slender stalks, and the plant is lower and more spreading, almost prostrate. The flowers are rather small, a pale rosy mauve streaked with darker veins, with a small prominent column of stamens in the centre. The fruits of all the mallows are disc-shaped, round and flattened like buttons, or little cheeses, which is why so many of the plant's local country names are connected with cheese and cheeses.

Marsh mallow, *Althaea officinalis*, grows in clumps 60-90 cm/2-3 ft high and is found beside river banks and dykes near the sea, and in the drier parts of salt marshes in Britain, France and Germany, and in the low countries. In North America, *A. officinalis* grows in marshy places from Quebec to Virginia and is scattered as far as Michigan and Arkansas. The plant is velvety and grey and soft to touch, with broad, slightly lobed and irregularly toothed leaves and beautiful, large, pale pink flowers. The stamens are united in a tube which stands prominently as a darker column in the flower's centre. The small flowers are rather like small hollyhocks, to which the mallows are related.

Pliny is reputed to have said that 'whoever shall take a spoonful of the juice of any of the mallows, shall that day be free from all diseases that may come to him', like an ancient version of 'an apple a day keeps the doctor away'. Dioscorides suggested that to avoid bee stings one should anoint the skin with oil of mallows, and recommended the powdered leaves to relieve the pain of scorpion bite.

In France and England, country people steeped fresh mallow leaves in hot water and used them as a poultice for sprains, bruises and wasp and bee stings. Coles suggested mallows, boiled and buttered, for 'the Breasts or Paps of women: for it not only procureth great store of milk . . . but aswageth the hardnesse of them . . . as also all other hard Tumours, inflammations and Impostumes'. He added an enormous list of afflictions that mallow would cure: hot agues, wasp and bee stings, burnings and scaldings and 'wild-fire' (a name given to any fast-spreading, eruptive skin disease) to mention just a few. For cleaning and whitening the teeth, Coles recommended mallow root 'being made clean . . . and a little scotched with a knife', but his strangest advice was 'if the feet be bathed with the Decoction of the Leaves, Roots and Flowers it helpeth the flowing down of Rhume from the head, which rose out of the stomach', suggesting an anatomical peregrination of some complexity.

Sir John Hill said that dried or fresh mallow leaves should be used in 'Clysters' (enemas), and because the plant is so rich in mucilage it was used in ointments and cough medicines. In France *Pâté de Guimauve* was made with marsh mallow roots and given for a tight chest, coughs, and hoarseness. In France, too, colic and diarrhoea were treated with mallow leaves. Pastor Kneipp, known in the last century for his nature cures, suggested mallows should be planted for medicinal uses: he treated chest disorders with an infusion of the flowers, and urinary troubles with a conserve of flowers and leaves, and advised a decoction of mallow for nursing mothers to encourage milk; all of which are similar to Coles' earlier remedies.

The Romans are said to have eaten mallow leaves as a vegetable, as did the ancient Egyptians and Chinese. In Poland, the peasants used both the common and marsh mallow for coughs and as a healing herb for wounds.

There is a legend that country people made garlands of mallow flowers for May Day and scattered them on their doorsteps. I always envy our ancestors for a world in which wild flowers were so plentiful whenever I read of these lavish customs which, wasteful though they were, still did not do so much harm as modern industries, road building and the relentless spread of towns and cities. Marsh mallows are beautiful and nowadays rather rare, so it would be wrong to experiment with their flowers and roots to make the old confection which was the origin of the pink and white marshmallows sweets sold today. But if you are lucky enough to find the plant flowering, pick one of the exquisite shell pink flowers to eat raw, they are slightly sweet and coolly jellified. Four of us came across some clumps of marsh mallow flowering palely in the dusk beside the River Arun, we rounded off our supper picnic with one delicate flower apiece. A far cry from after-dinner mints!

We can encourage the lovely marsh mallow to spread by planting it in damp places in our gardens. It can be raised from seed sown in the spring, or from a piece of root taken from specimens already growing in a garden.

MARSH MALLOW – *ALTHAEA OFFICINALIS* (L); COMMON MALLOW – *MALVA SYLVESTRIS* (R)

MALLOW SOUP LEAVES THROUGHOUT MOST OF THE YEAR, FLOWERS THROUGHOUT THE SUMMER

The leaves of the common mallow are mucilaginous which gives a good, smooth body to soup. Pick the leaves when the plant is in flower, mallow remains green for most of the year, but the leaves are at their best in the summer. Collect half a dozen flowers and a few seeds when picking the leaves, the seeds are nutty and the flowers a little gelatinous, and scatter them over the soup as a garnish.

SERVES 4

1 litre/5 cups/2 pints measure fresh mallow leaves,
  without stalks
2 cloves garlic
25 g/2 tablespoons/1 oz butter
1 litre/5 cups/2 pints chicken stock
salt and white pepper

Soak the leaves for a short while and wash thoroughly, then drain and shred them finely.

Peel and crush the garlic and fry it lightly in the butter. Add the mallow leaves, stir, and pour in the stock. Bring to a slow simmer, season with salt and pepper, cover the pan and simmer for 20 minutes. Scatter the seeds and flowers over the soup, before serving.

MALLOW, AS A VEGETABLE LEAVES THROUGHOUT MOST OF THE YEAR, FLOWERS THROUGHOUT THE SUMMER

Mallow leaves make one of the best green vegetables of any wild plant. They become tender very quickly, so be careful not to overcook them. Pick the leaves when the plant is in flower.

SERVES 4

2 litres/10 cups/4 pints measure fresh mallow leaves,
  without stalks
pinch salt
25 g/2 tablespoons/1 oz butter

Wash the mallow leaves thoroughly. Drop them into a pan with 1 cm/1/2 in lightly salted, boiling water. Cook for 5 minutes. Drain thoroughly, then melt the butter in the pan and toss the mallow leaves in the butter until glistening.

WILD MARJORAM
Origanum vulgare

Wild marjoram grows on dry grassland and in waste places and is common on chalk and limestone soils throughout England and Wales, but it thins out towards the north and is rare in Scotland and Ireland. It occurs throughout Europe and Scandinavia on dry, limey soils, and is found on roadside banks, and in old fields and open woods in America from Quebec and Southern Ontario to North Carolina. Wild marjoram in flower is a feature of the roadsides in New York and Connecticut, and was cultivated by the early settlers in New England for use in medicinal herbal teas. The plant is perennial, and grows 30-60 cm/1-2 ft high with slender stems branching near the top. The oval, slightly toothed, and sometimes untoothed leaves have short stalks and grow in opposite pairs. The lilac-coloured flowers appear throughout the summer, they grow in loose heads and are dark purple in bud and have purplish bracts; the whole plant is downy and aromatic.

The volatile oil of *O. vulgare* has been used in herbal medicines as a carminative in cough syrups and, in conjunction with other herbs, and as a healing lotion for wounds. The medicinal use of the wild herb goes back to ancient times.

WILD MARJORAM – *ORIGANUM VULGARE*

The Greeks used it for healing wounds, and the early herbalists recommended wild marjoram tea for coughs, disorders of the stomach and bladder and many other ailments, including earache. Sir John Hill said an infusion of the fresh tops was 'good against habitual colics . . . head-achs, and in all nervous complaints', advice which Thornton repeated in the 19th century, in his *Family Herbal*.

The old 16th century *Lustgarten der Gesundheit* gives a recipe for wild marjoram sugar, the chopped buds and flowers to be added to a jar of sugar which was left to stand in the sun for 24 hours. A small quantity taken for two days was claimed to cure diseases of the kidneys and eyes. The aromatic sugar would be a delicious addition to cakes and desserts without worrying about the medicinal virtues.

Wild marjoram was used as a strewing herb, as a flavouring for ale, and as a red and purple dye, and it was valued for its magical as well as its practical properties. It was supposed to signify happiness, the Greeks and Romans weaving garlands of wild marjoram for betrothed couples to wear, and planting it on graves to ensure happiness in the life to come. The herb was believed to prevent milk from turning sour in thundery weather, and was hung up in dairies.

William Coles wrote of the different varieties of marjoram and said 'it is used in all odiferous Waters, Powders, etc.: and is a chief Ingredient in most of those Powders that Barbers use, in whose Shops I have seen great store of this Herb hanged up'. What a lovely glimpse this allows of the barbers' shops of those days.

Wild marjoram may be used in cooking and, in the Mediterranean, is a popular flavouring in many country dishes. Like the garden varieties of sweet and pot marjoram, the wild variety gives a delicious flavour to meat dishes and meat-based soups and, like the garden varieties, wild marjoram retains its fragrance when dried, and can be stored for use in the winter.

DUMPLINGS WITH WILD MARJORAM

SUMMER

Dumplings, made with lamb's or pig's liver, and flavoured with marjoram, are an old-fashioned dish from Germany and Northern Europe. Eaten with crisp bacon, or sausages, the dumplings make a change from potatoes.

225 g/8 oz lamb's or pig's liver, sliced
butter and oil for frying
100 g/1 cup/4 oz plain flour
55 g/1 cup/2 oz shredded suet
1 clove garlic, crushed
1 tablespoon fresh wild marjoram, chopped
½ teaspoon salt
water, see recipe

meat stock, for cooking dumplings

Remove any skin or membrane from the liver. Heat a little oil and butter in a pan and lightly fry the slices of liver for 2 minutes on each side. Lift onto a plate to cool while you make the dumpling mixture.

Sift the flour into a bowl, stir in the suet, garlic and marjoram. Mince the liver finely and stir into the dumpling mixture. Season with salt, and stir in enough cold water to make a firm dough. With floured hands form the mixture into walnut-sized balls. Have ready a pan of boiling stock and drop in the little dumplings in batches. When they rise to the surface cook for about 15 minutes, then lift out and drain with a slotted spoon. Serve hot.

Onion gravy, richly caramelised, is a lovely accompaniment.

MEADOWSWEET
Filipendula ulmaria

Meadowsweet grows throughout Britain, Europe and Scandinavia, and is widespread and common in wet meadows, by ditches, in damp woods and fens, and is often seen growing in large patches along wet roadside verges. In America, the plant is an immigrant from Europe which has escaped from cultivation, and now grows wild from Newfoundland and Quebec to New Jersey, West Virginia and Ohio. Meadowsweet is an elegant and beautiful plant related to the Spiraeas, it stands 60 cm-1.25 metres/2-4 ft high with slender, stiff, reddish stems and long-stalked pinnate leaves which are made up of several large, deeply-veined, toothed leaflets, with very small leaflets in the spaces between; the leaves are dark green above and silvery grey beneath. In the summer, the flowers make a creamy, foaming display and have a heady, honey-sweet fragrance that are to me the essence of summer; they grow in dense, upright clusters of tiny, cream-coloured flowers, with prominent stamens that release a shower of cream pollen if picked when fully open. Among the old country names for this plant are Bridewort and Queen of the Meadow; one can imagine a country bride's bouquet made of these delicious flowers, prettier and more romantic than arum lilies.

The flower smell is sweet and drowsy, but the leaves are sharply aromatic. It is believed that Meadwort, another country name for meadowsweet, does not refer to mead as an alternative word for meadow, but to the use of the plant in medieval days, and earlier, for flavouring mead. The flowers are imbued with an undeniable taste of honey which, if honey was scarce, would augment or perhaps even replace it. *Mjödört* is the Swedish name for meadowsweet, *mjöd* meaning mead, the drink, in Swedish.

STEWED APPLES WITH MEADOWSWEET

SUMMER

Apples cooked with meadowsweet flowers taste just as if they were sweetened with honey, and need very little sugar.

SERVES 4
3/4 kilo/2 lbs cooking apples
8 flowering heads of meadowsweet
1 tablespoon sugar
120 ml/2/3 cup/scant 1/4 pint water

Peel and quarter the apples. Tie the meadowsweet flowers in muslin and put them into the middle of the saucepan with the apples round them. Add the sugar and water and cook gently for about 10 minutes, until the apples are tender; and leave to cool in the pan to extract the full flavour of the meadowsweet. Remove the bag of flowers and squeeze out well.

Serve the apples with single cream. A slightly thicker mixture, using half the quantity of water can be used as a filling for an apple tart or pie.

MEADOWSWEET WITH RHUBARB SUMMER

A few meadowsweet flowers reduce the acidity of rhubarb and give a distinct taste of honey to the dish.

6 flowering heads meadowsweet
3/4 kilo/1 1/2 lbs rhubarb
3 tablespoons water
3-4 tablespoons sugar

Tie the meadowsweet flowers in a piece of muslin. Trim and wash the rhubarb and cut into 2 1/2 cm/1 in pieces. Tip the rhubarb into a saucepan and push the meadowsweet into its midst. Add the water and sugar, cook gently, stirring occasionally until the sugar has melted, then cover the pan and simmer for 5 minutes. Draw off the heat and leave the pan covered until cold; the rhubarb tenderises as it cools. Remove the meadowsweet flowers before serving.

MEADOWSWEET SYRUP SUMMER

This is a golden, honey-flavoured syrup that is delicious as a summer drink diluted with water or soda water, it can provide the juice for a fresh fruit salad, or a compôte of fresh fruit, and is lovely with ice cream.

a large bunch meadowsweet, 12-15 flowering heads
water to cover
4 tablespoons lemon juice
sugar—see recipe

Remove the stems from the meadowsweet, but use a few of the small top leaves as well as the whole flower heads. Put the meadowsweet in a saucepan with enough water to barely cover. Bring to the boil and simmer for 10 minutes. Drain and measure the liquid into a clean saucepan and add the strained lemon juice. For 750 ml/3 3/4 cups/1 1/2 pints liquid, add 400 g/ 2 cups/1 lb sugar to the pan, heat slowly, stirring until the sugar has melted, then boil for 5 minutes, skim and allow to cool. Pour into a large jug and then into bottles with corks or screw-on caps.

The syrup will keep for several months in the refrigerator.

FRESH MEADOWSWEET TEA SUMMER

Of all the herbal teas I have tried, meadowsweet makes quite the best. Better than the famous chamomile, better than—though similar to—the *tilleul* of lime blossom. The flowers are so full of sweetness and nectar that the honey flavour is very pronounced. For a delicious quenching cold drink, add 1 teaspoon lemon juice to each cup of cold meadowsweet tea, and chill in the refrigerator.

The tea is the colour of lime juice.

4 flowering heads, with about 4 leaves from
  the top of the plant
250 ml/1 cup/1/2 pint boiling water

Put the meadowsweet in a jug, bruise lightly with a wooden spoon, pour on the boiling water, cover the jug and leave to infuse for 7 minutes. Strain into cups and drink hot, without any extra sweetening, or, best of all, chill and drink iced, with lemon juice.

DRIED MEADOWSWEET FLOWER TEA

Dried meadowsweet flowers make a pale yellow tea with a faint honey flavour.

2 teaspoons dried meadowsweet flowers
250 ml/1 cup/1/2 pint boiling water

Put the dried flowers in a small jug, pour on boiling water, cover and infuse for 7 minutes. Strain into a cup and drink hot with a squeeze of lemon juice.

MEADOWSWEET – *FILIPENDULA ULMARIA*

DRIED MEADOWSWEET LEAF TEA

Dried meadowsweet leaves have more astringency than the flowers and make a refreshing, quenching drink.

2 teaspoons dried meadowsweet leaves
250 ml/1¼ cups/½ pint boiling water

Put the dried leaves in a small jug, pour on the boiling water, cover and infuse for 5 minutes. Strain into a cup and drink hot.

HOW TO DRY MEADOWSWEET SUMMER

Cut the meadowsweet before the flowers are overblown and hang up whole stems of the plant from the slats and pipes in an airing cupboard. Or, cut off the flowering heads and lay them on trays or cardboard lids in the airing cupboard or boiler room to dry, pick off the leaves and spread them to dry likewise. When quite crisp and dry, crumble the leaves and flowers separately, or put them through a parsley mill. Store in screw-top jars away from the light.

MEADOWSWEET WINE CUP SUMMER

Meadowsweet flowers give a mellowness and a mingled taste of honey and almonds to any cheap white wine.

1 bottle dry white wine
1 orange
3 sprigs thyme
8 flowering heads meadowsweet

Slice the orange into a glass jug, pour over the wine and float the thyme and meadowsweet flowers on top. Cover the jug, and chill in the refrigerator for 24 hours. Strain, and serve very cold.

MEADOWSWEET LIQUEUR SUMMER

Meadowsweet gives a mellow taste of honey to brandy, but don't forget, as I once did, to strain off the flowers after two months or the flavour will be ruined. After bottling, the liqueur keeps indefinitely.

500 ml/2½ cups/1 pint measure prepared
    meadowsweet flowers
250 ml/1¼ cups/½ pint (small bottle) brandy
2-3 tablespoons sugar

Snip the meadowsweet flowers from their stems and loosely fill two 450 g/1 lb jam jars. Put a cup of brandy in a small saucepan with the sugar, and heat gently without boiling until the sugar dissolves, pour half the warm liquid into each of the jars and fill to the brim with brandy from the bottle. Screw on the lids and store in a dark cupboard for 2 months. Strain the liquid into a jug and pour into a bottle, preferably the empty brandy bottle.

MEADOWSWEET WINE SUMMER

Meadowsweet makes a medium sweet white wine with a slight honey fragrance.

activated yeast (p. 255)
5 litres/9 U.S. quarts/1 gallon meadowsweet flowers
1¼ kilos/6 cups/3 lbs sugar
200 g/1½ cups/½ lb raisins
2 lemons
5 litres/9 U.S. quarts/1 gallon water
2 tablespoons cold tea, or 1 teaspoon grape tannin
    (sold for wine-making)

Pick the meadowsweet flowers before they are overblown, snip the flower heads from their stalks and put them in the bucket with the sugar, raisins and thinly pared rind (no pith) of the lemons, pour on the boiling water and stir until the sugar dissolves, then cover the bucket with a clean cloth and leave until cool, (about 70°F, 20°C). Stir in the strained juice of the lemons, the cold tea, or grape tannin and the activated yeast. Cover the bucket with its lid and leave in a warm place for ten days, stirring daily. Strain the liquid into the fermentation jar and follow the method given on page 254.

MINTS
Mentha

SPEARMINT *Mentha spicata* APPLE MINT *M. rotundifolia* PEPPERMINT *M. piperita*
EAU DE COLOGNE MINT *M. citrata* PENNYROYAL *M. pulegium*

There are many different sorts of mint, both cultivated and wild, and several hybrid variations. *Mentha spicata*, or spearmint, is the most common garden mint which has narrow, slightly toothed, shiny green leaves and long terminal spikes of lilac flowers; this is the variety most often used for mint sauce, and as a flavouring agent in food. It is still used as a carminative in medicines.

Apple mint, *Mentha rotundifolia*, has rounder, more deeply wrinkled downy leaves and rounder spikes of pinkish, sometimes nearly white flowers, the typical mint smell is enhanced by delicious overtones of fresh apple; it has an even better flavour than spearmint, and is worth growing in the garden.

Peppermint, *Mentha piperita*, as its name suggests, has a decided smell and taste of peppermint which makes a marvellous herbal tea, very good for indigestion and queasy stomachs; peppermint is more slender than the two previous varieties, and the whole plant looks darker, the leaves are dark, even purplish, as are the stems, and the interrupted flower spikes are a deep, reddish violet. Any of these mints may be found growing wild in Britain, but they will be garden escapes, as they were originally natives of southern Europe. Peppermint and spearmint are found growing wild in wet places and by streams throughout the United States. All the mints have long been cultivated in America, although *Mentha arvensis* is their only true native.

Among our British wild mints, *Mentha aquatica*, water mint, is widespread and common and grows abundantly in ditches, by streams and ponds and in all wet places. The plant is hairy, often purplish, with stiff branching stems and pointed oval leaves of a light green, paler beneath; the round flower spikes are pinkish with long, hairy points on the calyx. Water mint has a watery, muddy smell and though I have heard of it being used for mint sauce, I cannot recommend it, as the muddy wateriness invades the flavour.

Eau de Cologne mint, *Mentha citrata*, can be invasive when planted in the garden, but in Britain it is a very rare wild plant and found only in the south of England. It grows on smooth, stout, reddish stems and the toothed, oval leaves are usually reddish beneath; the rounded flower heads are deep lilac. Although *M. citrata* suggests a lemon scent, the common English name is much more descriptive for, when crushed, the whole plant smells strongly of eau de Cologne. It makes good bath bags, and a scented water to add to the bath. The Ancient Greeks used mint to scent the water they bathed in, and Parkinson's *Garden of Pleasure* mentions that 'mintes are sometimes used in Baths with Balm and other herbes as a help to comfort and strengthen the nerves and sinews'. Eau de Cologne mint will discourage flies if you stand a large, fragrant bunch on the kitchen window sill, but obviously one must only pick this mint from a garden, because of its rarity in the wild.

Pennyroyal, *Mentha pulegium*, is grown in gardens and is occasionally found growing wild particularly in the south and west of England. It is also found in old fields and woods in many places in America, from Quebec to Minnesota and South Dakota, and southwards to Florida, Tennessee, Arkansas and Kansas. The plant is downy and shorter than the other varieties of mint, with the lower part of the stem prostrate along the ground; the leaves sometimes droop downwards and are bluntly toothed and oval, and the flowers are lilac coloured with a hairy calyx, and grow in whorls all the way up the stem, with the leaves between.

Corn mint, *Mentha arvensis*, the only truly native mint in North America, is found on arable land, in clearings in woods and many damp waste places. It is widespread and common in Britain, and has weak, downy stems with whorls of lilac flowers growing all the way up the stem above the opposite pairs of pointed, oval leaves. Richard Mabey recommends corn mint for mint sauce, but I think its rather stale smell and taste lack the right piquancy; however he gives an intriguing recipe for an Indian Mint Chutney in *Food for Free* which is made with corn mint.

Horsemint, *Mentha longifolia*, is a tall, hairy, rather coarse plant with toothed, oval grey green leaves, very downy beneath, and thick cylindrical spikes of lilac flowers, with silky corollas; it is locally widespread by streams and ditches in Britain, and has a similar taste and smell to spearmint and may be used as a substitute, but it lacks some of the sharp freshness.

Mint is mentioned in all the early herbals and in medieval manuscripts relating to food and medicine. It was grown in England in the gardens of monasteries and convents as early as the 9th century and was probably brought to this country by the Romans. Mint was popular in Rome as a culinary herb and for flavouring wine, and the Greeks and Romans decorated their banqueting tables with it and wore garlands made from peppermint. Culpeper lists many uses for mint as a herbal remedy, including a gargle and mouth wash for 'an ill-favoured breath', and the rather nice suggestion that 'being smelled unto it is comfortable to the head'. The medieval use of spearmint for whitening the teeth is carried on today in spearmint flavoured toothpastes and chewing gum. Oil of peppermint is still used to relieve flatulence and colic, and is included in modern laxatives to prevent griping, and modern herbalists recommend a hot or cold infusion of peppermint for toning and freshening the skin.

However, Andrew Borde suggested a novel way of using mint, in 'a remedy for sighynge and sobbynge. This impedimente doth come either by thought or pencifulnesse, or else by feare, or wepynge, or by replecion, or by some evyl corrupcion in the stomach . . . First after every sighe makes an hem, or coughe after it, and use myrth and mery company, and muse not upon unkindness. . . Then use to eat a race of grene gynger and drynke a draughte or two of wine, and use to eate in sauces the pouder of mintes'. What eminently sensible advice to use mirth and merry company and not to muse upon unkindness! Even the studied little cough to hide the sigh is not a bad idea, and the wine, if not the mint sauce, would surely be better than the drugs we dole out for depression.

For over a hundred years, until the middle of the last century, acres of peppermint were under cultivation in Surrey, Hertfordshire and Lincolnshire; it was grown for the oil which was extracted in large commercial stills. France, Germany, Italy, China and Japan and, of course, America, all produce oil of peppermint, but in the last century English oil of peppermint was the best and the most expensive—in those long gone days, most things British were considered the best.

A final use for peppermint which must rank as the most unusual I have come across, was the practice of blocking rat holes with rags soaked in peppermint oil, the smell of which was supposed to be so obnoxious to rats that they could be 'driven by ferrets through the remaining holes into bags'. I suspect that the use of ferrets and the stopping of holes with rags, either peppermint-flavoured or not, was the real key to success.

MINTS – *MENTHA*

MINT JELLY SUMMER

Mint jelly is just as good as redcurrant jelly with lamb, and is very useful in the winter when there is no fresh mint. The jelly can be made with crab apples, but they come late in the year when mint is usually past its best. The small green apples that fall off the trees before the crop is ready to pick are ideal, being sour and full of pectin. It is also nice not to have to waste them.

a big handful-sized bunch of mint
250 g/2 lbs green apples
1 litre/5 cups/2 pints water
juice of 1/2 lemon
3 or 4 tablespoons finely chopped mint leaves
sugar—see recipe
green colouring, optional

Thoroughly wash the bunch of mint. Wash the apples and cut them into quarters, but do not peel or core. Put the apples, mint, water and lemon juice in a large saucepan, bring to the boil, cover and cook gently until the apples are soft. Drip through a jelly bag, or double thickness of muslin for 2 or 3 hours, or overnight if more convenient. Measure the liquid into the pan and to each 500 ml/2 1/2 cups/1 pint liquid add 400 g/2 cups/1 lb sugar. Bring slowly to the boil, stirring until the sugar has dissolved, then stir in the finely chopped mint leaves. Boil fast for about 10-15 minutes, until the liquid gels when dripped on to a cold saucer. Skim, and add two drops of green colouring if you wish. Pour into warm, dry jars, cover with waxed circles while hot, seal with cellophane covers when cold.

PEPPERMINT TEA LATE SPRING TO EARLY AUTUMN

This is one of my favourite herbal teas, it has a marvellous fresh minty taste, and is equally delicious taken hot, or iced with a sprig or two of mint floating on top. It is a great tummy settler, and good for indigestion.

2 rounded teaspoons chopped peppermint leaves
250 ml/1 1/4 cups/1/2 pint boiling water

Put the chopped mint in a small jug. Pour on boiling water, cover and infuse for 7 minutes. Strain into a cup. The tea is different but equally delicious made with apple mint.

SPARKLING PEPPERMINT TEA

LATE SPRING TO EARLY AUTUMN

As a refresher after taking exercise on a hot day, this drink is second to none for restoring energy and cooling you down. The chilled infusion will keep fresh for three or four days in the refrigerator, only needing the addition of lemon juice and soda water to complete the drink. It is just the thing to have on hand in a heatwave.

50 g/1 cup/2 oz fresh peppermint leaves
750 ml/3 3/4 cups/1 1/2 pints boiling water
4-5 tablespoons sugar, or 2 tablespoons honey
strained juice of 2 large lemons
500 ml/2 1/2 cups/1 pint soda water

After washing and stripping from their stalks, put the peppermint leaves in a bowl, pour on the boiling water and infuse for 5 minutes. Add the sugar, or honey, and stir until dissolved, then leave to cool. Strain the infusion into a large jug and chill in the refrigerator. Just before serving, add the lemon juice and soda water.

MINT LEAVES IN ICE CUBES SUMMER

Well washed leaves of peppermint, or apple mint, frozen in ice cubes, one leaf per cube, are coolly attractive in long drinks, particularly in the sparkling tea above.

DRIED PEPPERMINT TEA

This is good for indigestion and useful to keep in the store cupboard.

2 heaped teaspoons dried peppermint
250 ml/1 1/4 cups/1/2 pint water

Put the peppermint in a small jug, pour on the boiling water, cover and infuse for 7 minutes. Strain into a cup and sip slowly.

TO DRY PEPPERMINT SUMMER

Cut stems of the mint and tie into small bundles, hang them upside down from the slats in an airing cupboard, or in a warm airy room. When quite dry and crisp, strip the leaves and any flowers from the stalks and crumble finely, or put them through a parsley mill. Store in screw-top jars away from the light.

CRYSTALLISED PEPPERMINT LEAVES SUMMER

The leaves of peppermint, or any of the mints, may be crystallised, or sugared by the methods given for borage flowers on page 36.

Sugared mint leaves are particularly nice to decorate a chocolate cake that has been iced with peppermint icing, add 2 drops oil of peppermint and 1 drop edible green colouring to the icing sugar mixture.

EAU DE COLOGNE MINT BATH ESSENCE

SUMMER

Eau de Cologne mint grows like a weed in the garden and makes a refreshing infusion to add to your bath. To really scent the water, you need to use about 250 ml/1¹/2 cups/¹/2 pint bath essence in each bath, but the mint is so prolific and the infusion so easy and quick to make, that you can make a new batch every few days.

a big handful—about 10 stalks—eau de Cologne mint
1 litre/5 cups/2 pints boiling water
1 or 2 drops green colouring (optional)

Trim away the coarse end of the stems. Wash the mint thoroughly, cut each stem in half and put them in a large bowl or jug. Pour on boiling water, cover, and leave to get cold. Strain, squeezing out the leaves to extract all the scent. If you wish, add a drop of green colouring to improve the appearance and achieve a pretty pale green bath. Bottle and use within a week.

MIXED HERBS AND OTHER WILD PLANTS

Here are a few recipes which require a mixture of herbs and wild plants in their ingredients, and at the risk of destroying the reader's appetite for any of the dishes that follow, I cannot resist including this recipe from the 18th century *Collections of Receipts in Cookery, Physick and Surgery* because it contains several of the plants included in this book. A most excellent *Drink for the King's Evil in the Eyes*.

Take Sage, Celandine, Yarrow, Betony, three-leav'd Grass, Cinque-foile, Daisyroots and Leaves, of each a handful; Honeysuckles, and Ground-Ivy, the same Quantity; Pick, wash, dry and bruise them, and put to them a Quart of good White-wine, or Beer; steep them two Nights and Days; press he Herbs out, and drink four Spoonfuls, Morning and Night; just as you drink it, squeeze in the juice of fifty Millipedes, fresh bruis'd.

SPRING TART SPRING

By adding some wild plants to a small quantity of spinach leaves you can make an unusual tart that is wholesome and satisfying. The greens are set in cheesy-egg custard and baked in pastry.

SERVES 4

1 large well-packed cup young hawthorn leaves
1 large cup young nettle tops, without stalks
1 large cup dandelion leaves, stripped from mid-rib
1 large cup wild sorrel leaves, without stalks
1 colander spinach leaves

FOR THE CUSTARD

150 ml/²/₃ cup/¹/₄ pint milk
2 eggs
50 g/4 tablespoons/2 oz grated cheddar cheese
salt and freshly milled black pepper
nutmeg

FOR THE PASTRY

200 g/2 cups/8 oz plain flour
salt
100 g/1 cup/4 oz butter, or butter and lard mixed
4-5 tablespoons water

Prepare all the leaves and wash them thoroughly, cook them together in boiling salted water for 5 minutes. Drain and set aside.

Whisk the milk and eggs together in a bowl. Stir in the grated cheese and salt and pepper, and add a grating of nutmeg.

Sift the flour and salt into a mixing bowl. Soften the butter, or butter and lard, on a plate with a knife, then rub the fat into the flour until the mixture is evenly crumbly. Add the water and mix together with a fork until the dough forms a soft ball. Turn the dough on to a floured surface and knead lightly. Put inside a polythene bag and keep in the refrigerator for 30 minutes.

Divide the dough into two pieces and roll out each into a circle. Grease a 20 cm/8 ins pie plate and line with one circle of the dough. Roughly chop the cooked greens and fill the bottom of the tart, pour over the seasoned custard and keep back a spoonful of liquid in the bowl. Damp the pastry rim and cover with the second circle of pastry. Make a hole in the centre and brush the surface over with the egg and milk mixture which you reserved. Bake in the centre of a moderately hot oven (375°F, 190°C or Gas 5) for 40-45 minutes until the pastry is golden brown.

Serve hot.

GARDENER'S REVENGE OR NETTLE AND GROUND ELDER PIZZA SPRING

Gardeners will take a certain sadistic pleasure in the preparation of this dish. It uses two of the most pernicious weeds in the garden, which are remarkably good to eat.

First make the dough.

FOR THE DOUGH

2 level teaspoons dried yeast
1 tablespoon warm water
1 teaspoon sugar
225 g/2 cups/8 oz strong white bread flour
¹/₂ teaspoon salt
1 egg
3 tablespoons olive oil

Put the yeast, warm water and sugar into a jug, and stand in a warm place until frothy.

Sift the flour and salt into a large bowl, make a well in the centre and stir in the yeast mixture, the egg and the oil.

Work together with your hand to form a soft dough, then turn out onto a floured surface, and knead for 5–10 minutes, until the dough is smooth and elastic. Put the ball of dough into the bowl, cover with a clean cloth, and leave to rise in a warm place.

If you have a food processor with a dough blade, it will do all the mixing and kneading for you. Leave the dough in the food processor bowl with the lid on, until it has doubled in bulk.

While the dough rises, go and do a little weeding,

PICK FROM THE GARDEN

¹/₂ colander young nettle tops
¹/₂ colander ground elder leaves
A handful garlic mustard leaves, or ramsons leaves

Wash the weeds, and cook in a little lightly salted water until tender—about 4–5 minutes. Drain well, and when cool enough to handle, chop the leaves coarsely.

FOR THE FILLING

2 eggs
200 ml/scant cup/7 fl oz milk
100 g/1 cup/4 oz grated cheddar cheese
100 g/1 cup/4 oz grated Parmesan
Freshly milled black pepper

Lightly whisk the eggs in a bowl. Stir in the milk and the two cheeses, and season with pepper.

Grease a 30 cm/12 ins flan tin. Knock back the dough and knead again briefly. Put the ball of dough into the tin, and using your knuckles, press and push the dough flat to fill the tin and make a rim round the edge. Being a yeast dough, splits and holes are easy to mend.

Scatter the chopped weeds over the dough, and pour on the filling.

Put the tin on a hot baking sheet into a moderately hot oven (375°F/190°C/Gas 5) and bake for 30–35 minutes, until the filling is barely set and the dough puffy and golden. Serve hot, or warm, but not cold.

RICE, WITH A WILD FLAVOUR

You can add the prepared weed leaves to a pot of hot rice for a risotto-like dish, or add them—lighly cooked and roughly chopped—to a dish of cold rice with a lemony, garlicky dressing, to make a rice salad.

A colander full of mixed dandelion, ground elder and wild
   sorrel leaves—washed
1 medium onion
2 cloves garlic
Olive oil—see recipe
2 tablespoons tomato paste
Salt and freshly milled black pepper

Drain the washed leaves, then roughly chop them. Peel and slice the onion, and peel and crush the garlic. Heat some olive oil in a pan and add the onion and garlic, sauté gently until soft and yellow, then add the mixed leaves and cook together for 3–4 minutes. Stir in the tomato paste and add plenty of black pepper and a little salt, to taste.

Add to a dish of freshly cooked rice and serve hot. Or cool, and add to cold cooked rice, with a dressing made with good quality olive oil, lemon juice, and a roughly chopped clove of garlic to make a rice salad.

WILD SALSA SPRING

You can use all sorts of spring-time weeds and leaves for this peppery green sauce to serve with fish, pork or lamb chops or, as a wonderfully rustic barbecue sauce.

1 clove garlic, peeled
large handful brooklime leaves
10 dandelion leaves, stripped from their stalks
1 tablespoon Lady's Smock leaves, or wavy or hairy bittercress
   leaves, with the soft green pods
1 teaspoon Dijon mustard

1 teaspoon caster sugar
squeeze of lemon juice
freshly milled black pepper

Only wash the leaves if necessary—the brooklime leaves may be muddy—but dry them thoroughly, or the salsa will be watery.

Finely chop the garlic, and leaves in batches, and put them into a bowl. Add the mustard, sugar and lemon juice. Stir in the oil, adding more if needed to make a spoonable consistency. Add a good grinding of black pepper and stir thoroughly.

For ease and speed, put the garlic and all the leaves with 1 tablespoon of oil, into a food processor, and whiz for a few seconds. Then add the pepper and remaining 2 tablespoons oil, and whiz for 10 seconds, until the leaves are finely chopped, but not mushy.

SAUCE AU VERT WITH FISH SPRING AND SUMMER

A country medley of herbs and wild plants goes into this sauce from France. Any firm white fish such as sole, cod, turbot or small eels may be poached in the sauce, which is then served cold or cool.

SERVES 4
500 g/1 lb filleted sole, cod or turbot or
   750 g/1½ lbs small eels
10 salad burnet leaves
10 white dead nettle leaves
6 sorrel leaves
4 sage leaves
25 g/2 tablespoons/1 oz parsley
25 g/2 tablespoons/1 oz tarragon
25 g/2 tablespoons/1 oz chervil
1 tablespoon savory leaves
½ teaspoon thyme leaves
50 g/4 tablespoons/2 oz butter
250 ml/1¼ cups/½ pint dry white wine
salt and freshly milled black pepper
3 egg yolks
juice of ½ lemon

Trim the fish neatly and cut into pieces about 5 cm/2ins wide. Wash and shake dry all the leaves and herbs and strip away any stalks, then chop them all coarsely. Melt the butter in a large saucepan and tip in the mixed greenery, stir together over a gentle heat, then lay the pieces of fish on top of the herbs, and cook for few minutes until the fish is firm, add the wine and a seasoning of salt and plenty of pepper, cover the pan and cook briskly for few minutes longer, sole will only require a minute or two, cod or turbot will need a little longer, and, if using eels allow a good ten minutes. Remove the pan from the heat and carefully lift the fish on to a serving dish. Put the egg yolk into a cup and stir in the strained lemon juice, then stir this liaison into the contents of the pan, without re-heating, until the sauce thickens. Cool a little, and then spoon the sauce over the fish to cover all the pieces.

SPRING SAUCE WITH LAMB SPRING

This sauce is useful in early spring when the mint has only just started showing up in the garden and you want something piquant with young lamb. The leaves of garlic mustard and hawthorn eke out a few sprigs of mint, and make a sauce that is full of zest.

Chopped chives may be used instead of the garlic mustard.

1 rounded tablespoon young hawthorn leaves
1 tablespoon mint
1/2 tablespoon young leaves of garlic mustard
2 level tablespoons sugar, or 1 tablespoon honey
1 tablespoon white wine vinegar

Wash the leaves carefully and squeeze dry. Chop the leaves finely and put them together in a bowl with the sugar, or honey and enough vinegar to make a thickish sauce. Avoid making it runny. Serve as mint sauce with lamb.

WILD HERB SAUCE SPRING

You could use only three or four varieties of leaves, and vary them with others depending on what you can pick. Keep the proportion of mild leaves to those which are bitter or peppery balanced. The sauce is good with cold meat, or fish. As a change, you can stir the same mixture of leaves into mayonnaise, which makes a delicious sauce.

1 cup hawthorn leaves
1/4 cup lady's smock leaves
1/4 cup hairy bittercress leaves
8 sorrel leaves
8 stalks chives
3 young fennel leaves
pinch salt
1 teaspoon sugar or honey
vinaigrette dressing

Trim off any stalks. Put the hawthorn leaves in a large strainer and wash under the cold tap. Soak the other leaves in lightly salted water, then rinse in fresh water, and drain. Put all the leaves on a wooden board, sprinkle with the salt and chop finely with a sharp knife. Turn into a small bowl and add the sugar, or melted honey and enough vinaigrette dressing to make a thickish sauce.

WILD SPRING SALAD SPRING

If you have no lettuce in the garden you can make this very subtle green salad from wild plants alone. Gather enough leaves so that when picked over they yield roughly the quantities given below.

SERVES 2
1 large cup dandelion leaves
1/2 large cup young hawthorn leaves
1/2 large cup young wild strawberry leaves
VINAIGRETTE DRESING
1 small teaspoon French mustard
1 tablespoon white wine vinegar
3 tablespoons olive oil
2 rounded tablespoons sugar, or 1 tablespoon honey
salt and freshly milled black pepper

Strip the dandelion leaves from the bitter mid-rib, and pick any woody stems from the hawthorns, discard the strawberry leaf stems. Wash all the leaves, and pat dry or leave to drain until dry. Shake the leaves into a bowl and turn over and over in the vinaigrette dressing, which is made with extra sweetening to give a good flavour to the wild salad.

WILD SANDWICHES *using dandelion and hawthorn leaves, chives and sorrel* SPRING

The leaves of many wild plants make good sandwiches, and you can vary the quantities and varieties depending on your preference and what you can find in your district. All leaves should be undamaged and as young as possible, and as you will be eating them raw, will probably need a good wash. Lady's Smock has hot, peppery leaves, stronger than watercress, so use them sparingly. Hairy bittercress tastes like mustard and cress, and can be used as such. Wall pennywort, which grows in the West Country on stone walls and banks, is a juicy cross between lettuce and cucumber. Three or four different flavours make a good mixture. Below, I suggest combining dandelion leaves and young hawthorn leaves with half a dozen sorrel leaves and a few chives.

Strip the dandelion leaves from the mid-rib and pick away any stalks or damaged leaves from the others. Soak all together in a bowl of lightly salted water, and then wash thoroughly in fresh water. Drain the leaves and pat dry with a clean cloth. Chop all the leaves on a wooden board with a sharp knife until you have a fairly fine mixture. Butter thin slices of wholemeal bread and spread each half with the chopped leaves. Sprinkle each with a tiny amount of salt and pepper before closing as a sandwich.

HERBY SCONES WITH CHEESE

SPRING, SUMMER AND AUTUMN

These savoury scones are lovely eaten hot with a bowl of homemade soup, or with bacon, or sausages. Use a mixture of fresh herbs—about 6 sprigs parsley, 2 sage leaves, 2 sprigs marjoram, 2 sprigs thyme or rosemary—or a mixture of your own choosing. The scones can also be made with 2 teaspoons of mixed dried herbs, instead of 2 tablespoons of fresh.

MAKES 12 SCONES
2-3 tablespoons chopped fresh herbs
250 g/2 cups/8 oz self-raising flour (cake flour U.S.)
pinch salt
40 g/3 tablespoons/1½ oz butter
100 g/8 tablespoons/4 oz grated Cheddar cheese
1/8 litre/²/3 cup/scant1/4 pint milk

Wash the herbs and strip them from their stalks, squeeze dry and chop finely.

Sift the flour and salt into a bowl. Stir in the finely chopped herbs with a fork, rub the butter into the flour and herbs until the mixture is crumbly, then stir in 75 g/6 tablespoons/3 oz of the grated cheese (reserving the rest for the topping). Add the milk gradually to make a soft dough—you may not need quite the full amount—and mix with a fork. Knead the dough lightly on a floured surface, then roll out to 1½ cm/3/4 in thick and cut into 12 squares. Put the scones on a floured baking tray, brush the tops with a little milk and sprinkle each with a pinch of the remaining cheese. Bake on the top shelf of a hot oven (425°F, 220°C or Gas 7) for 15 minutes until the cheese is toast brown and bubbly and the scones sound hollow when tapped.

WILD FRUIT CRUMBLE EARLY AUTUMN

A family forage along the hedgerows can produce a wild version of an old favourite. You can vary the proportions of fruit—the quantities need not be exact. Choose the biggest crab apples you can find.

140 g/1 cup/5 oz blackberries
140 g/1 cup/5 oz elderberries
140 g/1 cup/5 oz crab apples—prepared weight
Water—see recipe
For the crumble
100 g/1 cup/4 oz plain flour
85 g/1/3 cup/3 oz butter
85 g/1/3 cup/3 oz demerara sugar

Pick over the blackberries, strip the elderberries from their stalks, and peel and core the crab apples. Put the fruit in a saucepan with the sugar, and add about 3 tablespoons water. Bring slowly to the boil, then turn off the heat and allow to cool a little while you prepare the crumble.

Sift the flour into a bowl. Cut the butter into small pieces and rub it into the flour with your fingertips. Stir in the demerara sugar with a fork. Transfer the fruit from the pan into a pie dish and spoon over the crumble topping. Spread level with a fork and bake in the centre of a moderate oven (350°F/180°C/Gas 4) for 45 minutes. Serve hot with a good ice cream.

BATH BAGS *using Eau de Cologne Mint, Lavender, Lemon Balm, Hyssop, Marjoram, Thyme, Rosemary or Winter Savory* SUMMER

Make a bag 23 x 15 cm/9 x 6 ins out of muslin or thin linen. Stuff it full of any freshly picked aromatic herb, or a mixture of two or three, tie with tape and use it as a bath mitt, or soak it in the bath to give the water an invigorating scent.

The bag will develop stains, but can be used again and again, just throw away the contents and fill up with fresh herbs. Pine and juniper sprouts can also be used in the same way, and fresh elderflowers are both refreshing and good for the skin.

HERBAL SURGICAL SPIRIT

SUMMER AND EARLY AUTUMN

Bed-sores are a menace to anyone who has to stay in bed for long periods, and, to prevent them, nurses will rub the patient's back and legs with surgical spirit (rubbing alcohol U.S.) which has a slightly unpleasant clinical smell. This can be turned into a welcome fragrance by steeping any aromatic herb such as thyme, rosemary, lavender or mint in the spirit, and an assortment of herbal scents would make a good present for an invalid who loved his or her garden.

1 litre/5 cups/2 pints surgical spirit (rubbing alcohol U.S.)
SMALL BUNCH OF EACH OF THE FOLLOWING:
thyme, flowers and leaves
rosemary, flowers and leaves
lavender, flowers and leaves
mint, leaves

Cut the herbs into short lengths and put one of each variety into small bottles, fill up with surgical spirit (rubbing alcohol U.S.), shake well and keep for two weeks, shaking daily. Strain each bottle through a double thickness of muslin and fill clean bottles with each fragrance. Label 'Inflammable' and store; the spirit will keep indefinitely.

FIELD MUSHROOM

Agaricus campestris

The well known field mushroom is found throughout Britain, Europe and North America. It grows in many grassy places, particularly in old pastures and sometimes on lawns. In Europe it appears in the late summer and early autumn, particularly during warm, damp weather, when it may be found in great numbers. In the States it occurs in the spring as well as autumn.

Although we are so conservative about eating other types of fungus in Britain it is, ironically, the common or field mushroom which has more often been confused with the lethal Death Cap, *Amanita phalloides*, than any other. I must assure you that this confusion is totally unnecessary if you make certain that the mushroom you pick never has white gills. The gills of the Death Cap remain white throughout all its stages, whereas the gills of the field mushroom are at first pale beige, or pink, deepening to chocolate and finally black. For this reason it is safest to avoid picking very tiny mushrooms at the tight 'button' stage, when the gills may be very pale, although if on breaking them open the gills show pink or beige, you are quite safe. Also, the Death Cap has a 'bag' at the base of the stem, which the mushroom does not.

Mushrooms grow on fairly thick, short stems up to 5 cm/2 ins high. The caps vary from 21/2-10 cm/1-4 ins across and are at first white and nearly spherical, with the gills entirely enclosed, becoming gently domed when the gills show pink, anything from shell pink to salmon, and finally the cap flattens and becomes silky-looking and grayish, with chocolate brown or nearly black gills. While avoiding the tight button stage, one should pick mushrooms before the gills are black and limp.

Nicholas Culpeper held 'garden mushrooms' (*agaricus campestris*) in esteem medically, saying 'roasted and applied in a poultice, or boiled with white lily roots, and linseed, in milk, they ripen boils and abscesses better than any preparation that can be made'. But he had no use for them in the kitchen and asserted that 'inwardly, they are unwholesome and unfit for the strongest constitution'. Happily, we now know better!

FIELD MUSHROOM – *AGARICUS CAMPESTRIS*

TO PREPARE FIELD MUSHROOMS

LATE SUMMER, EARLY AUTUMN

Only the larger, older specimens need to be peeled, otherwise wipe the caps with a damp cloth and slice the stems for cooking with the caps.

Nothing is more meltingly delicious than field mushrooms fried for two or three minutes in a very small amount of hot butter, and piled on to thick slices of hot toast. Also they are delicious in garlic butter on a baked potato, on pizza or in a quiche. No cultivated mushroom ever produces a flow of black juice like the wild field mushroom that reduces the toast to a state of exquisite grey 'sog'.

PICKLED MUSHROOMS LATE SUMMER, EARLY AUTUMN

Use small field mushrooms for this pickle when they are just opening from the tight button stage. This is when it is most important to note that the gills are pale beige or pale pink, so that there is no chance of mistaking the field mushroom for the poisonous Death Cap in which the gills are at all stages white. The pickle is extremely good, and can be made with cultivated button mushrooms in a year when wild mushrooms are scarce.

500 g/1 lb small button mushrooms
1 shallot
1 level teaspoon salt
1/2 teaspoon sugar, or honey
1/2 teaspoon white pepper
1/2 teaspoon ground ginger
1/2 teaspoon grated nutmeg
250 ml/1 cup/1/2 pint cider vinegar
250 ml/1 cup/1/2 pint malt vinegar

Wipe the mushrooms and cut away all the stalks (these can be used for flavouring soups or stews) and peel and slice the shallot. Put the mushrooms whole in an enamel saucepan, add the shallot, the sugar, or honey and the salt and spices, pour on the two vinegars, bring to the boil and cook slowly in the covered pan for about 20 minutes; the mushrooms will shrink noticeably in size. Spoon the mushrooms into a warm dry jar to within 2½ cm/1 in of the rim, then top up with the hot vinegar pickle to cover. Put a piece of vinegar-proof paper, or a double thickness of greaseproof over the top of the jar, and screw on the lid at once while still hot.

MUSHROOM KETCHUP LATE SUMMER, EARLY AUTUMN

When there is a glut of mushrooms, as happens every few years, a good way of preserving them for future use is to make ketchup.

1½ kilos/3 lbs mushrooms
2 tablespoons salt
1 litre/5 cups/2 pints cider vinegar
10 peppercorns
3 blades mace
1/4 teaspoon ground ginger
1/4 teaspoon ground cinnamon
1/4 teaspoon grated nutmeg

Wipe the mushrooms, but only peel the very large ones, cut them into small pieces with a stainless knife and put them in a large bowl, sprinkle the salt over the mushrooms, cover with a cloth, and leave overnight. Next day crush the mushrooms with a wooden spoon and stir in the vinegar and spices, pour the mixture into a saucepan, bring to the boil, stir and cover the pan, and cook gently for 30 minutes. Liquidize the mixture and pour the ketchup into a jug. Fill warm, dry bottles with the hot ketchup and screw on the caps. To sterilize the ketchup, stand the bottles on folded newspaper in a large saucepan, fill with hot water as high as possible and put pieces of newspaper between the bottles to stop them touching. Bring the water to the boil and simmer for 30 minutes, lift out the bottles with a cloth, stand them on newspaper to prevent cracking, and tighten the screw cap

See also recipe for Broad Bean and Mushroom Salad with Savory (page 208).

OAK
Quercus robur

DURMAST OAK *Q. petraea*

The English oak grows throughout Britain, Europe and Scandinavia. It is also widely planted in North America, and prefers a heavy clay soil. The sessile oak is more common in the north and west of Britain and in southern Europe, and is usually found where the soil is lighter. Old trees are massive, with a broad crown, thick trunk, and rugged, grey brown bark, heavily cracked and fissured, and like an elephant's trunk to touch. The oblong leaves have broad, rounded lobes and are paler beneath, greeny gold in early spring and golden brown in the autumn. The flowers hang in long, sparse, yellowish catkins, the male flowers longer than the females; the flowering season varies from year to year and may be as early as late March, or as late as late May. The old saying 'oak before ash, in for a splash, ash before oak, in for a soak' refers to the trees' flowers and is not to be laughed off altogether, for, like many old wives' tales, it originated from observation and experience; I, too, have noticed that when the ash flowers before the oak we usually have a very wet spring. The fruits are the familiar smooth, oval, green acorns held in a scaly cup. The acorns of the English oak have long stalks, but its leaves have almost none; whereas on the sessile oak the acorns are unstalked, and the leaves taper into a noticeable stalk.

Oak trees live to a great age, possibly a thousand years or more, and were revered as sacred trees by the ancient Greeks, the Romans, the Celts and the Druids. Pliny described how mistletoe growing from an oak should be cut by a priest with a golden sickle, and centuries later, when oaks formed part of the parish boundaries, a priest would read passages from the Gospel to his attendant congregation as they paused for a breather under 'the Gospel Oak', when beating the bounds of the parish.

Due to its slow growth, oak timber is hard and heavy, and has been the most valuable building material for houses, ships, churches and cathedrals, throughout our history. Oak logs have been dug out of peat bogs and found to be sound after hundreds of years, and oak coffins that were unearthed in Denmark have survived since the Bronze Age.

The North American Indians ground the acorns of *Quercus pubescens*, the White Oak, to make meal for bread and gruel. To remove the tannic acid and bitterness, the Indians soaked the acorns in a lye of ashes and water until they swelled up, they were then put in a bag, or basket, and thoroughly washed in running water, and afterwards dried in the sun. After this process, the acorns had a sweet, pleasant flavour. The Domo Indians of California owned certain prolific oaks, and ownership of the trees was passed from father to son. The Wintoon Indians of California used to bury their acorns in wet, boggy ground and often left them for a number of years until they were needed; although black, they were well preserved, and could be roasted, and ground into meal. The Algonquins of the eastern States ate boiled acorns with their meat and fish, and also extracted oil from the nuts. John Josselyn said that with the ashes of maple 'the Indians make a lye with which they force out oyl from oak-akorns, that is highly esteemed by the Indian'. There are many North America oaks which are planted in Europe: *Quercus rubra*, the Red Oak, is a native of the eastern States, it has dark red twigs and very large leaves which turn a rich red in autumn, and for this decorative characteristic it is widely planted.

Oak bark is important in tanning leather, and an infusion of the bark yields a purple dye which is durable and which the Highlanders used to dye their woollen yarn and cloth. In his *Family Herbal*, Thornton describes how every shade of brown can be obtained from oak sawdust and from oak apples which are the hard, round growths often seen on oak twigs, caused by a gall wasp which bores a hole in the young twigs and lays its eggs inside. When the larva hatches it feeds on the plant tissue, and produces a secretion which stimulates the plant cells to develop abnormally and form the oak galls. Another interesting pest is the oak processional moth which lays its eggs on the oak trunk in late summer, they remain dormant through the winter and the caterpillars hatch in May or June. Together they spin a web at the foot of the tree, or the fork of a branch, in which they sleep communally. The caterpillars follow a leader up the tree to feed on the leaves, each caterpillar following a thread of silk spun by the one in front. When the caterpillars pupate, they spin a communal nest in which the individual cocoons are grouped together.

Oak galls were once widely used in medicine, and the best came from a small variety of oak found growing in Asia Minor. They were known as Aleppo galls, and were collected before the fully mature wasp had emerged from the pupa and gnawed its way out of the gall. The galls are astringent and contain various acids, resin, mucilage and sugar, they were used in the manufacture of ink, as well as in medicine, and tanning and dyeing.

Gall ointment was prescribed for piles and bleeding gums in this century. It was strongly astringent. Thornton prescribed a decoction of oak bark as a gargle for enlarged tonsils and used it to treat agues, haemorrhages and 'immoderate evacuations'. Modern herbalists also recommend an infusion of oak bark as a gargle for relaxed throat and enlarged tonsils, the dried bark from the smaller branches and young stems contains quercitannic acid and was used in an astringent decoction in herbal medicine.

Coles saw the 'signature' in the acorns which 'separated from the Cups do much resemble the stone in the Bladder and therefore they not only provoke Urine and break the stone, but are an especiall remedy for the exulceration of the Bladder and pissing of blood'. He has a more than usually disgusting and disquieting list of disorders that could be treated with acorns, and follows it with a touch of pure witchcraft, 'the water that is found in hollow places of old Oakes, is very effectuall against any foule or spreading scab'. Though not above treating a skin complaint with stagnant water from an old hollow tree, Coles ends with a very superior remark, 'though the Acornes were formerly used for food, yet our Age being able to subsist without them, I shall leave them for the Hoggs to feed upon'.

ACORN COFFEE AUTUMN

Acorn coffee is probably the best known but least pleasant of the wild substitutes for coffee. It is not very coffee-like when taken black, but if you add milk, and preferably hot milk as the French serve 'café au lait', it makes a perfectly drinkable beverage. You can also infuse half acorn coffee and half real coffee together, and this tastes hardly different from the real thing. Acorns are usually abundant and the brew is easy to prepare, pick up the fallen acorns when they are greeny-yellow and sound, any nuts with brown marks, or little holes are likely to be worm-eaten.

2-3 tablespoons (heaped) roasted acorn grounds
250 ml/1¼ cups/½ pint boiling water

Remove the acorn cups and roughly chop each nut into about three pieces, drop them into salted water, otherwise they discolour quickly, like apples. Rinse in fresh water, pat dry and spread the acorns on shallow roasting tins. Roast in a moderately hot oven (350°F/180°C/Gas 4) for 30 minutes. Cool and grind. Roast the grounds again for 7 minutes in a hot oven (400°F/200°C/Gas 6). Keep an eye on the grounds at this stage, they should turn very dark brown, but not black, and a minute or so too long will scorch them.

Put the heaped tablespoons of grounds into a warmed jug, pour on the boiling water and stand for 1 hour. Strain and re-heat.

OAK LEAF WINE LATE SPRING AND SUMMER

Oak leaves make a medium-dry white wine of good flavour.

activated yeast (p. 255)
5 litres/9 U.S. quarts/1 gallon oak leaves
5 litres/9 U.S. quarts/1 gallon water
1¼ kilos/6 cups/3 lbs sugar
2 lemons

Pick fresh looking oak leaves that have not been nibbled by insects, wash the leaves and put them in a large basin, pour over 2½ litres/9 U.S. pints/4 pints boiling water, cover the bowl with a clean cloth and leave for 12 hours. Put the sugar in a large saucepan with the remaining 2½ litres/9 U.S. pints/4 pints water, bring to the boil, stirring until the sugar dissolves, then draw off the heat and add the strained lemon juice.

Strain the oak leaf infusion into the fermentation jar, add the activated yeast and shake well. See that the fermentation jar is filled to the bottom of the neck, top up with cold water if necessary and follow the method given on page 254.

Oak leaves may be preserved for winter decorations by the glycerine method described for Beech leaves on page 21. Or they may be pressed between sheets of blotting paper to preserve their golden colours in the autumn.

OAK – *QUERCUS ROBUR*

PARASOL MUSHROOM

Lepiota procera

Parasol mushrooms are found singly and in groups on the fringe of woods and in clearings, by roadsides and the edges of fields. They occur throughout Britain, Europe and Scandinavia, and in America are found in the central, southern, south-east and north-east states, as well as in Canada. The mushrooms appear during the summer and autumn and are egg-shaped at first, with a double white ring between the cap and stem. As the fungus grows, the ring becomes detached and loose on the stem, the cap opens and becomes bell-shaped and later like a shallow parasol, or even completely flat except for the darker nub in the centre. The caps are dirty white in colour and covered with large, shaggy brown scales, the broad white gills are free from the stem which is long and slender, fibrous, hollow, and bulbous at the base.

PARASOL MUSHROOM – *LEPIOTA PROCERA*

When mature, the parasol may be as much as 5-18 cm/6-7 ins across and 18-20 cm/7-8 ins tall, so it is conspicuous for its size alone. It is a very safe fungus, as the only other that resembles it is *Lepiota rhacodes*, the Shaggy Parasol, which is also very good to eat. It is found in the same sort of places as the parasol mushroom, but it is shorter and more sturdy, the cap is more grey-brown than dirty white, and the flesh stains deep yellow when broken, whereas the flesh of the parasol remains white.

TO PREPARE PARASOL MUSHROOMS SUMMER AND AUTUMN

The mushrooms are at their best when young, before the caps are fully open. The skin cannot be peeled without tearing the flesh, and each cap should be well wiped with a damp cloth and stem discarded. Cut the caps into thick slices and fry in hot butter for a few minutes, exactly like field mushrooms.

The whole, undamaged caps of older, tougher parasols may be dipped in egg and breadcrumbs and fried slowly on each side for a good 10 minutes until tender. Or they may be baked in the oven for 20 minutes in a thin, buttery white sauce, spiced with plenty of freshly milled black pepper. They are also good with pasta or in a risotto.

PIGNUT

Conopodium majus

Of the hundred and more plants I have eaten experimentally, pignut is the only one that sent me flying to my books in a panic in case I was on to the wrong thing! I wasn't, but when I had unearthed, scraped and eaten the first little tuber, which tasted like a cross between raw chestnuts and fresh hazelnuts, a sudden, hot after-taste of radish got me in the back of the throat. When you realise that this is what a pignut tastes like, it adds zest to the eating.

The plant is a very slender, delicate looking member of the umbellifer family, it is widespread and common throughout Britain, France and Scandinavia, and grows in woods, hedgerows and shady grassland, preferring a light, dry soil to a heavy one. Pignut grows 22-45 cm/9-18 ins tall on a hollow, hairless, little-branched stem, the rather sparse leaves are pinnate and thread-like, the root leaves soon withering and scarcely visible in the surrounding grass. The small delicate umbels of white flowers appear in late spring and early summer.

In the 17th century, John Pechey in *The Compleat Herball of Physical Plants*, suggested that pignuts boiled in fresh broth were both nourishing and an aphrodisiac, but a hundred years later the idea was losing ground, for Sir John Hill wrote 'the Earth Nut, or Earth Chestnut is said to have great virtues as a provocative to venery, but this is not well confirmed'. He recommended the root to be roasted 'in the manner of a chestnut'. On the other hand a Scottish legend issues a terrible warning that if you eat too many pignuts you will get lice in your hair! One of the local Scottish names for the pignut is Lousy Arnuts. Country children used to fill in the gaps between meals with pignuts on their way to and from school, much as schoolchildren today fly to the sweet shop. The clean, nutty crispness of the old earthnut was surely better for their teeth.

The tuber of the pignut lies only 2 1/2 cm/1 in or so beneath the surface of the soil, so be careful when you dig for it, because the stem breaks easily, and you may lose the place where the tuber lies, especially as it is earth-coloured and not easy to see.

VEGETABLE BROTH WITH PIGNUTS

EARLY SUMMER

Without endorsing the 17th century claim that this broth has aphrodisiac properties, I can recommend it as both nourishing and satisfying. The little pignuts taste nutty and crisp in the smooth, thick soup which, with wholemeal bread, makes a meal in itself.

SERVES 4

1 tablespoon butter
1 large onion
2 carrots
2 medium potatoes
750 ml/3 cups/1 1/4 pints chicken stock
a handful of pignuts

Melt the butter in a large pan, then add the peeled and sliced vegetables. Cover the pan with its lid and sweat the vegetables

over a low heat for 10 minutes. Stir in the stock, bring to a simmer and season with salt and freshly milled black pepper. Cook gently for 20 minutes, or until the vegetables are tender, then liquidize and return to the pan to re-heat. Scrape the pignuts and cut them in quarters, drop them into the pan of hot broth just before serving.

PIGNUTS WITH SALAD

A choice of crudités, or raw young vegetables, neatly trimmed and nicely arranged, always make an appetising first course. A few pignuts will add new zest to the usual selection.

ALLOW PER PERSON

2 or 3 pignuts, washed and scraped

2 or 3 radishes, scrubbed and trimmed with a little stalk left on

a sprig or two of cauliflower, washed and broken into small flowerets

a few sticks of cucumber, peeled and cut into batons

a sprig or two of watercress

2 or 3 tiny spring onions, washed, trimmed and left whole

a few pieces of new young carrot, trimmed, scrubbed, and cut into match sticks.

Arrange the raw vegetables in groups on a large flat dish. Reserve the pignuts for the centre. The vegetables can be eaten with or without a vinaigrette dressing and, if you are being informal, dipped into a communal bowl of dressing and eaten with the fingers.

PIGNUT – *CONOPODIUM MAJUS*

PRIMROSE

Primula vulgaris

The darling of spring, the first primrose is surely everybody's thrill. Primroses are found throughout Britain, Europe and Scandinavia and in America are cultivated in gardens. In the wild they grow under hedges, on banks—particularly railway embankments, in woods, on cliffs and even mountain-sides; but, sadly, they are less abundant nowadays because of over-picking and, worse, the indiscriminate digging up of roots. The crinkly, broadly lanceolate leaves taper into a winged stalk and are downy beneath; they appear in the middle of winter amongst the litter in sheltered woods, and in early spring the first flowers appear. The flowers at first grow on very short stalks, but as the spring progresses, the flower stalks may be to up 15 cm/6 ins long. Occasionally one finds a loose umbel of several flowers which grow from a fat, short stalk only just above ground level, but normally the flowers grow on separate stems. They are the palest, most delicate of yellows with a deeper yellow centre, and a fresh, slight scent; very rarely one may find pale pink and pure white varieties. The five petals join into a narrow tube that is held in the green calyx.

Two kinds of flowers, pin-eyed and thrum-eyed, occur on different plants, and the interesting reason for this is to ensure cross-fertilisation by insects. In the pin-eyed flowers the style, or female part, terminates in a pale green, pinhead-sized knob just above the petal tube; out of sight in the tube below are the five pollen-bearing anthers, or male parts. In thrum-eyed flowers this arrangement is reversed, the five yellow anther heads are visible in the mouth of the tube, the style is out of sight below. When the flowers are visited by long-tongued insects, the pollen from all the pin-eyed flowers adheres to the insect's tongue when it reaches down to the nectar at the base of the tube; but when visiting thrum-eyed flowers the insect's head comes in contact with the pollen-bearing anthers, and its tongue deposits the pollen from any pin-eyed flowers on to the style set lower down the tube. Thus a flower cannot be self-fertilised, and even the structure of the pollen ensures this in a very fascinating way: the pollen from thrum-eyed flowers has to reach the ovaries set below the pin-headed style, so it has larger pollen grains and puts out longer tubes for this purpose; whereas the pollen of pin-eyed flowers rubs on to the low-set thrum-eyed style and has only a short journey to the ovaries, so efficient Nature designs that pollen with smaller grains, which put out shorter tubes.

It is not only modern motorists who are responsible for the decline of primroses. In the days of early medicine, terrible ravages must have been made on the primrose population by the used of dried roots as an emetic, a remedy for headaches, and a cure for worms. Rheumatism, gout, insomnia, restlessness, nervous hysteria, all were treated with the whole plant. Culpeper said the juice from the bruised roots 'being snuffed up the nose, occasions violent sneezing . . . but without being productive of any bad effect', and Gerard recommended Primrose Tea as 'famous for curing the phrensie'.

In the Middle Ages primroses were made into puddings and used in salads, and there are fascinating old recipes for Primrose Pottage and Primerolle using pounds of the precious flowers. In the 17th and 18th centuries primroses were candied, and pickled, and made into vinegars and wines which took gallons of the flowers. It is impossible to contemplate such recipes now, but I have given a recipe for a pickle, and a medieval pudding with reduced quantities, which requires very few flowers. This early recipe cleverly reproduces the slight, fresh primrose fragrance with other ingredients. Primrose can be sugared and crystallised, and it only takes half a dozen flowers to make a lovely decoration for a cake. See list of suppliers of wild flower seeds and plants on p.9.

PRIMEROLLE, OR PRIMROSE POTTAGE

SPRING

I always think a bunch of primroses smells faintly of almonds, white wine and fresh air, so was intrigued to find a 15th century recipe using white wine and almonds which enhances the primrose fragrance, and saffron 'that it have colour like primerolle'. It also used primrose flowers pounded to a paste, but this is not necessary as they have no taste. The original ingredients included blanched almonds, 'flour of primerolle' (primrose flowers), sweet wine, sugar, salt, saffron and flour of rice, and was baked in a hard pastry case which would not be eaten, but just used as a container. It will make the dish go further if you serve it in a case of nice shortcrust pastry that you do eat.

SERVES 4
2 tablespoons flaked almonds
2 tablespoons ground rice
150 ml/2/3 cup/1/4 pint white wine
about 12 primrose flowers
large pinch saffron
pinch salt
2 tablespoons sugar, or 1 tablespoon honey
1 previously-baked pastry case (see Balmoral Flan p. 183)

Put the almonds and ground rice into a saucepan, add the wine, stir together and heat gently. Stir in the saffron, salt and sugar or honey. Bring to the simmer, stirring as the mixture thickens, then cover and cook gently for 20 minutes. It may be necessary to add a little more wine if the mixture is too thick; it should be the consistency of semolina pudding. Remove from the heat and pour the mixture into the pastry case. Pick the primrose flowers from the green calyx and arrange them on the pudding as the old recipe says: 'straw thereon flour (flower) of primerolle above'. Serve warm or cool with thin cream.

PICKLED PRIMROSES SPRING

A recipe from *The English Housewife*, 1615, gives instructions for preserving primroses to make a sharp, sweet pickle to eat with salads. The colour of the flowers is almost intensified, and they look beautiful in a small glass dish from which a teaspoonful is enough with each helping of salad.

As primrose flowers are a precious ingredient of spring, and becoming increasingly rare, only pick the flowers where they grow abundantly or from the garden.

HERE IS THE OLD RECIPE:

'After they have been pickt clean from their stalks and the white ends clean cut away, and washed and dried, And taking a glass pot like a gally-pot, or for want thereof a gally-pot itself And first strew a little crushed white sugar in the bottom

Lay a layer of the flower,

Then cover that layer over with sugar.

Then another layer of flowers and another of sugar. And this do one above the other until the pot do be filed.

And ever and anon pressing them hard down with your hand: 'This done you shall take the best and sharpest vinegar you can get (and if the vinegar be distilled vinegar the flowers will keep their colour the better) And with it fill up your pot till the vinegar swim aloft. Then stop up the pot close, and set in a dry and temperature place.'

The instructions are explicit for such an early recipe. Use distilled, white vinegar, and caster sugar, just a light sprinkling of sugar between each layer of flowers is enough. Store in a dark cupboard to preserve the colour.

CRYSTALLISED PRIMROSES SPRING

Primrose flowers may be crystallised or sugared to preserve them by the same methods given for borage flowers on page 36. Their delicate colour is perfectly preserved, and they make beautiful decorations for iced cakes or cold soufflés.

PRIMROSE – *PRIMULA VULGARIS*

PUFF BALLS

COMMON PUFF BALL *Lycoperdon perlatum* GIANT PUFF BALL *L. giganteum*

The common puff ball grows in fields and many grassy places throughout Britain, Europe and Scandinavia, and is widely distributed in America, where it is often found in the litter and humus under deciduous and conifer trees during the summer and autumn. It is round or pear-shaped, growing on a short, cylindrical stem, and covered with tiny soft spines which rub off easily; some of these are enlarged and look like little pointed warts. When young, the puff ball is white, as it matures, it turns yellowish, then brownish and bursts at the top releasing a shower of dark brown spores. Puff balls should only be picked when young, while they are still white, and roughly

COMMON PUFF BALL- *LYCOPERDON PERLATUM*

the size of half an egg, though size is immaterial as long as they are young. They cannot be confused with any other fungi, except other puff balls, which are all edible.

Bovista nigrescens is another, which is round and has no stem, when it is glossy white and as it matures the outer skin cracks into scaly flakes. The dwarf puff ball, *Bovista plumbea* is very similar and found in the same places; all should be picked young, while still white, and peeled before using.

In France, puff balls were used in country medicine to treat haemorrhages, ulcers, skin eruptions and ringworm, and in Britain the spore dust was used to quieten bees when the honey was taken.

TO PREPARE PUFF BALLS SUMMER AND AUTUMN

Puff balls should be peeled, but not washed, cut into thick slices and fried in butter. They are also good in an omelette or stirred into scrambled egg and can be used raw in salads. It is important to use puff balls soon after picking, as they continue to mature and will become brown and useless.

GIANT PUFF BALLS, STUFFED

This puff ball can grow as large as a football, it is less common than the other varieties, although quite abundant in some places. The same rules apply to it as the smaller puff balls: pick when young and still white, use as soon as possible, peel but do not wash. Giant puff balls can be sliced and fried, stewed in milk and butter, or added to soups and stews. A really large specimen is good stuffed, and baked in the oven.

1 large puff ball
1 cupful cooked rice, more if the puff ball is very big
3 tablespoons chopped parsley
1 teaspoon chopped marjoram
grated rind and juice of 1 lemon
100 g/¹⁄₂ cup/4 oz butter

Put the rice, herbs, grated rind and juice of the lemon into a bowl, melt half the butter and stir into the rice mixture. Peel the puff ball and cut a slice off the top, make a hollow inside and fill the cavity with the stuffing. Smear the remaining butter over an ovenproof dish, stand the puff ball on the dish and cover with a piece of foil. Bake in a moderately hot oven (350°F/180°C/Gas 4) for 20 minutes. Serve with melted butter.

RAMSONS

Allium ursinum

Ramsons is also known as broad-leaved garlic. It is perennial, and grows in damp woods and on shady banks, throughout Britain, Europe and Scandinavia, but is absent from the United States. There are several varieties of wild leeks and onions common to the States, which can be used as substitute flavourings. The leaves grow from the root on separate stems and are very like lily of the valley leaves, being broadly elliptical, tapering to a point and with parallel leaf veins; they are brighter green than lily of the valley leaves, and have a powerful and unmistakable smell of garlic. The flowers are beautiful, with six china white petals, held on long stalks 20-30 cm/8-12 ins tall and forming loose umbels of starry blossoms in late spring. The entire plant has the characteristic garlic smell.

Culpeper described the 'broad-leaved wild garlic' as 'a powerful opener'. He wrote 'it performs almost miracles in phlegmatic habits of body . . . and gives relief in asthmas'.

Andrew Borde, who was one of Henry VIII's physicians, mentioned ramsons amongst the vegetables to be avoided in 'the fallynge sickness. . . no salades, garlyke, ramsons, onyons, chybolles or scalyons' should be eaten, (scallions is the modern American word for spring onions, which comes direct from the early English) and the patient was sensibly warned to 'beware of clymbynge up to hygh places'. Andrew Borde cautioned against the eating of ramsons again in 'the megryme (migraine) which is a sickness that is in the head'. Following the medicines, the old physician's advice was to 'beware of too much venerious actes, and refrayne from eatynge of garlyke, of ramsons, of onyons, of chibolles, and suchlyke'. Obviously he was acutely wary of the whole onion family, but the only disaster I ever experienced with

RAMSONS – *ALLIUM URSINUM*

ramsons was on a farm where I worked during the war, when the cows got into a patch of ramsons and the whole day's milk was ruined by the pungent taint of garlic.

GREEN GARLIC BUTTER LATE SPRING

Ramsons make a delicious garlic butter to serve with steak, chops, in garlic bread and with baked potatoes. The flavour is less strong than real garlic, and has a very fresh taste.

6-8 ramsons leaves with their stalks
50 g/4 tablespoons/2 oz butter
salt and freshly milled black pepper

Wash and dry the ramsons leaves, and with a sharp knife shred as finely as possible. Cream the butter until soft and add salt and pepper to taste, then beat the shredded leaves into the butter. Leave to firm up in a cool place and serve with grilled or roast meat.

RAMSONS SAUCE, (COLD) LATE SPRING

Chopped ramsons leaves, with a little parsley, make a wonderful green mayonnaise to serve with cold fish, cold chicken or hard-boiled eggs. The flavour immeasurably improves shop mayonnaise, and with home-made mayonnaise is worthy of cold salmon.

2 rounded tablespoons chopped ramsons leaves
250 ml/1 1/4 cups/1/2 pint mayonnaise
1 rounded tablespoon chopped parsley

Wash and pat dry the ramsons and parsley. Chop them separately, then stir together into the mayonnaise.

RAMSONS SAUCE, (HOT) LATE SPRING

Use ramsons to flavour a béchamel sauce, it goes beautifully with lamb or fish.

6-8 leaves with their stalks
250 ml/1 1/4 cups/1/2 pint milk
1 level tablespoon butter
1 level tablespoon flour
salt and pepper

Melt butter and stir in the flour. Add about a third of the milk, stir briskly until starting to thicken, then gradually add the rest of the milk, stirring continuously until the sauce is smooth. If too thick, add a little more milk, season, and stir in chopped ramsons.

CASSEROLE OF BEEF WITH RAMSONS

LATE SPRING

Ramsons leaves add a mild onion/garlic flavour, and make an attractive dark green garnish to a casserole. Lay about ten ramsons leaves over meat and vegetables. Cover and cook slowly, until meat is tender.

RAMSONS BULBS IN SALAD

Dig up the bulbs in spring, when the leaves are abundant. Scrub the bulbs under a cold tap, then pat dry and slice into a bowl of mixed salad leaves. The flavour is much milder than garlic, so use plenty.

Decorate the salad with ramsons flowers.

WILD RASPBERRY
Rubus idaeus

Wild raspberries are native to Britain and many parts of Europe and Scandinavia. They are found growing in shady places in rocky woods, hedges and scrub heaths, particularly in Scotland and the north. In North America, raspberries are widespread and widely cultivated, they occur naturally from Labrador to British Columbia and southwards to New Jersey, Indiana, Iowa, Colorado and Washington. There are some species of wild bramble in America which have annual stems without thorns, and these are sometimes called raspberries.

The plant is perennial and spreads by means of its creeping suckers, it grows from 1-3 metres/3-6 ft high on woody, cane-like stems which are covered with weak prickles, and the pinnate leaves consist of three to seven broad, toothed leaflets, which are grayish and paler beneath. The flowers appear in early summer in loose, drooping clusters, with five well-spaced white petals that tend to drop off easily, they are small and rather inconspicuous. Later in the summer the berries turn red and ripen and, except for being smaller, are identical to the cultivated varieties, which have all been bred from wild raspberries. Sometimes a form with yellow berries occurs.

The scientific name *idaeus* comes from Mount Ida in Asia Minor where raspberries grow profusely. John Josselyn discovered wild raspberries growing in New England in 1663, which were similar, if not identical to *R. idaeus*. The raspberry was referred to as 'raspis' by the early herbalists. Gerard called it the Raspis Bush, and Coles, The Sweet Mountaine Bramble, or Raspis. Parkinson wrote 'the leaves of raspis may be used for want of Bramble leaves in gargles . . . The conserve or Syrupe made of the berries, is effectuall to coole an hot Stomacke, helping to refresh and quicken up those that are overcome with faintnesse . . . the iuyce and the distilled water of the berries are verie comfortable and cordiall.'

Modern herbalists recommend an infusion of raspberry leaves, 25 g/1 oz dried leaves to 500 ml/2$\frac{1}{2}$ cups/1 pint boiling water, as a gargle for sore throats and mouths, and as a lotion for cuts and ulcers. The infusion, drunk cold, will control diarrhoea, and is good for children's tummy upsets. Modern herbalists also stress the value of raspberry leaf tea during pregnancy, and say it controls morning sickness, and should be drunk warm during labour, because of the relaxing effect of one of its active ingredients, Fragrine, on the uterus. *Motherese* tablets, a proprietary medicine, contain dry aqueous extracts of raspberry leaf.

The berry contains pectic, citric and malic acids, fruit sugar and a volatile oil, and raspberry syrup is a permitted dye and flavouring for food and medicine. Both leaves and berries are astringent and a stimulant. In *A Modern Herbal*, Mrs. Grieve mentions that raspberry syrup will dissolve tartar. She also recommends raspberry vinegar as a gargle, and as a cooling drink in fevers. It is, indeed, a delicious and refreshing drink at any time.

WILD RASPBERRY SWEET OMELETTE SUMMER

A sweet omelette is rather a delightful fluffy dessert, usually made with jam, which has a slightly cloying sweetness.

Wild raspberries have a sweet sharpness that complements an omelette far better than jam.

SERVES 2
100 g/1 cup/1/4 lb wild raspberries
1/2 tablespoon caster (granulated U.S.) sugar
FOR THE OMELETTE
4 egg yolks
1 tablespoon sugar
2 egg whites
25 g/2 tablespoons/1 oz butter
a little icing (confectioner's U.S.) sugar

Lightly mash the raspberries and caster sugar together. Put the egg yolks and sugar into a bowl and beat well with a wooden spoon. Put the whites in another bowl with a pinch of salt and whisk until stiff. Fold the whites into the yolk mixture. Melt the butter in an omelette pan and when sizzling pour in the egg mixture, turn down the heat and cook for 3 minutes. Slip the pan under a pre-heated grill for a minute or two to puff up and colour the top. Slide the omelette on to a warm plate, spread one half with the crushed raspberries, fold over and dust with a little icing sugar. Eat at once while hot.

WILD RASPBERRY CRANACHAN LATE SUMMER

This is the richest, most luscious traditional Scottish dessert ever. The Drambuie is essential for purists, but for a non-alcoholic version, sprinkle a teaspoon of caster sugar over the raspberries and leave for half an hour for the juices to run.

FOR EACH PERSON ALLOW:
2 heaped tablespoons wild raspberries
generous teaspoon Drambuie
1 level tablespoon medium oatmeal (not porridge oats)
3 tablespoons whipping cream

Spoon the raspberries into individual glasses. Sprinkle a teaspoon of Drambuie over each and leave for half an hour for the flavours to mingle. Measure the quantity of oatmeal needed and spread thinly onto a baking tray. Toast in a medium oven, (180°C /350°F/Gas 4) for 4–5 minutes. Give them a shake after 3 minutes to stop the oatmeal burning at the edges. They should be lightly browned and smell richly toasted. Cool.

Measure the cream into a bowl and whip lightly, then fold in the toasted oatmeal (reserve a little for garnish). Pile spoonfuls of the mixture over each glass of raspberries, and when all is used, sprinkle a little of the reserved oatmeal on top of each.

WILD RASPBERRY JAM SUMMER

The flavour of jam made with wild raspberries is sensational; it is more intense and fruity than any made with garden fruit. Do not wash the berries, as this makes them watery, even though they may be heaving with tiny insects that feed on the raspberries, they seem to be imbued with the same flavour.

MAKES ABOUT 2.5 KILOS (5 LBS) JAM
1.5 kilos/6 cups/3 lbs wild raspberries
juice of 2 lemons
1.5 kilos/6 cups/3 lbs sugar

Put the fruit into a large pan and heat gently until the juice starts to run, then add the strained lemon juice and stir with a wooden spoon to mash the fruit a little. Cook very slowly at first, then add the sugar and boil fast—keep stirring as the jam burns easily—for about 7–10 minutes. When the mixture gels when dripped onto a cold saucer, remove from the heat and pour into warm, dry jars. Cover with waxed circles while hot, seal with cellophane covers when cold.

WILD RASPBERRY AND ORANGE JAM

SUMMER

This is a good recipe if you cannot find many wild raspberries, as the oranges, almonds and raisins add bulk to the jam, as well as giving a wonderfully subtle combination of flavours.

MAKES 1 KILO (2 1/2 LBS) JAM
500 g/1 lb wild raspberries
2 small oranges
generous 250 ml/1 1/4 cups/1/2 pint water
50 g/1/2 cup/2 oz roughly chopped almonds
50 g/1/2 scant cup/2 oz chopped raisins
300 g/1 1/2 cups/11 oz sugar

Remove any stalks from the raspberries. Peel the oranges and slice the flesh thinly. Put the raspberries, oranges and water in a saucepan and simmer together for 30 minutes.

Add the almonds, raisins and sugar, bring to the boil stirring until the sugar has dissolved, then cook fairly rapidly in an uncovered pan for about 15 minutes until the jam thickens, stir frequently to prevent sticking. Pour into warm dry jars, cover with waxed circles while hot, seal with cellophane covers when cold.

WILD RASPBERRY – *RUBUS IDAEUS*

WILD RASPBERRY LIQUEUR

Wild raspberries grow in profusion on many wooded hillsides in Scotland. Pick the raspberries in late summer, and for Hogmanay you will have a lovely warming liqueur, full of fruity flavours, to herald in the New Year.

About 1 kilo/4 cups/2 lbs raspberries
1 litre/12 fl. oz U.S./2 pints whisky
225 g/1 cup/8 oz granulated sugar

Pick the wild raspberries on a dry day. Ignore the midges in your hair and the tiny insects in the raspberries, just remove any bits of stalk.

Put the raspberries, whisky and sugar into a large bowl and stir gently to dissolve some of the sugar. Pour the mixture into a demi-john, or divide between glass jars, and fit in the cork, or screw on lids. Leave in a cool place until just before Christmas, remembering to invert the jars every other day, so the contents are well mixed. Then strain the liqueur through a double thickness of muslin until it is perfectly clear. Avoid squeezing the fruit left in the muslin.

Pour into whisky bottles, and screw on the caps.

WILD RASPBERRY WINE SUMMER

Raspberries make a delicious, fruity rosé wine, wild or cultivated berries may be used.

activated yeast (p. 255)
1¹/₂ kilos/4 lbs wild raspberries
5 litres/18 U.S. pints/1 gallon water
1¹/₄ kilos/7 cups/3¹/₂ lbs sugar

Pick the raspberries when dry and put them into the plastic bucket, pour on the boiling water and stir and mash the fruit well with a wooden spoon, cover the bucket with its lid and leave for four days, stirring daily.

Put the sugar in a large saucepan and strain on as much juice from the raspberries through a double thickness of muslin as the saucepan will hold, strain the rest into a large basin, wash out the bucket and leave it to drain.

Heat the sugar and juice together, stirring until the sugar dissolves, then pour the hot liquid into the clean bucket, adding the remaining juice from the basin, cover with a clean cloth and leave until cool, (about 70°F, 20°C). Stir in the activated yeast, cover the bucket with its lid and leave in a warm place for 24 hours. Pour the liquid into the fermentation jar and follow the method given on page 254.

ROSES

Rosa

DOG ROSE *R. canina* FIELD ROSE *R. arvensis*
SWEETBRIAR/EGLANTINE *R. rubiginosa* DOWNY ROSE *R. tomentosa*

e have at least 13 species of wild rose in Britain, among which several varieties and hybrids occur; modern botanists divide some of these into dozens of different species, but this need not concern us here. Many wild roses occur in Europe, Scandinavia and North America. All roses are edible and no part of them is poisonous.

The dog rose is widespread and common in hedgerows, thickets and open woodland throughout the south of England, but it is rare in Scotland. It is found mostly in southern districts of Europe and Scandinavia, and is naturalised in North America. Where the hedges are left uncut, or at the edge of woods, the long, arching stems armed with strong, curved thorns climb into trees and bushes and can reach 5-6 metres/16-20 ft. The pinnate leaves consist of toothed leaflets, sometimes downy beneath, and usually seven in number. The flowers, which appear throughout June, are varying shades of pale pink, with five heart-shaped petals and numerous yellow stamens, and are faintly fragrant. The plant blooms generously throughout its short season, and in early summer the swags and garlands of open, shell-pink flowers, cascading gloriously in the trees and hedges, are an exquisite sight. The fruits form hips in the autumn, which are flask-shaped and a bright, gleaming vermilion red. Within the hips are woody little seeds embedded in short, bristly, whitish hairs.

The field rose is widespread and common in hedgerows and thickets and in open woodland. The green or purplish trailing stems have short-hooked thorns and form clumps, or scramble through hedges, never reaching the height of the dog rose. The rather shiny pinnate leaves consist of hairless, toothed leaflets, and the cup-shaped, creamy white flowers appear later than the flowers of the dog rose and have a longer season. They are scentless, and grow in beautifully grouped clusters of open flowers, buds and half-open buds, at the end of the stems. The flowers have numerous yellow stamens, and only in the field rose are the styles united in a central column. The field and dog rose often hybridise, and roses occur with some of the styles detached and growing free of the central column, and with a faint flush to the petals, betraying a mixed parentage. The hips of the field rose are sealing wax red, smaller and more oval than the hips of the dog rose.

The sweetbriar grows on chalk and limestone and in open woodland. The arching stems are shorter and weaker than those of the dog rose, and covered with short, curved thorns. The pinnate leaves have slightly rough, toothed leaflets, shiny above, and sticky with minute rusty specks beneath. Although the flowers have no scent, the leaves are fragrant; and in the early morning, at dusk, and after a shower of rain, the foliage gives off a strong apple scent, which smells deliciously refreshing and sweet even from a distance. The flowers appear throughout the summer, never in great profusion, but in a succession of small, deep pink blooms lasting many weeks. The red hips are large and egg-shaped, and remain on the plant until winter. The sweetbriar makes a good garden plant, and can be grown free-standing as a single specimen or, if planted as a hedge and kept trimmed, makes a fine stock-proof boundary. It gives pleasure nearly all the year round from early spring when the young leaves give off their first luscious fragrance, in summer with the long flowering period, and through the autumn and winter when the plants are covered with cheerful scarlet hips, which provide food for birds when the hard frosts come.

The downy rose is widespread and locally common in bushy places, hedgerows and hillside scrub. The stems have nearly straight thorns and the pinnate leaves consist of toothed and downy grayish-green leaflets. The flowers appear in the summer and are varying shades of pink, but usually deep pink, and the scarlet hips are globular and bristly, with an erect tuft of dry sepals.

The huge number of cultivated roses have such a long and interesting history that it is hard to ignore them. The original rose, from which our garden roses have been developed, once grew wild in the region of the Caspian and the Persian Gulf. We know that roses were cultivated in the Middle East and ancient Greece in antiquity. From them have come all the rose oils, colourings, flavourings, scents, syrups, vinegars, medicines and folklore which, if described adequately, would fill another book.

However, our native wild roses were also put to practical use. William Coles refers to 'the fruit of the wild Bryar, which are called Heps, being thoroughly ripe and made into a conserve with Sugar, besides the pleasantness of the taste, doth gently bind the belly, and stay the defluxions from the head, upon the stomach, drying up the moysture thereof, and helping digestion.' Coles was fond of these travelling symptoms which affected different parts of the anatomy, either 'falling down', 'arising', or being 'driven' from one part to another.

One of the prescriptions of the old Tudor physician, Andrew Borde, included roses. He did not specify the variety of rose, but his list of ingredients reads like the inventory of an old-world garden. Judging by the extreme measures that were taken to treat it, the harmless-sounding complaint, 'chafynge specially under the eares', must have been considered serious, it came 'by evyll humours in the heed, or lyenge with unclene or menstrouse persons, or eatyne or drynkynge some evyll thynge'. After opening a vein, 'if strength wyll permit it', taking purges, electuaries and potions, and using 'clysters and suppositers', the physician instructed 'take of malowes, of rose leves, of camomyll, or eche an handfull, of mellylote an once and a half, sethe all this in fayre water and put into it the oyll of dyll, or the oyll of roses, of the oyll of camomyll, of eche an once, and make playsters of it and lay it to the place divers nyghtes to bedwarde'.

Losch says the name dog rose was given to the plant because the root was believed to cure the bite of a mad dog, and he quotes Pliny's story of a Roman soldier who cured himself of hydrophobia with the root of the dog rose. Professor Moszynski described the magic powers which the Polish peasants ascribed to the thorns of the dog rose. They stuck the thorns into clothing, or into the doors of houses, as a protection against witches and other evils, or a whole thorny stem might be fixed over the door of a house, or barn, as a talisman.

Strange uses were made of a by-product of the wild rose, the fuzzy, moss-like, pinkish-red growths, known as Robin's pincushions, were believed to have magic and medicinal properties. Robin's pincushions are caused by the gall wasp *Rhodites rosae*, and in the old days the growing larvae inside the galls did not detract from their medicinal value; far from it, Culpeper was quick to see the Doctrine of Signatures in this phenomenon and wrote 'in the middle of the Balls are often found white worms, which being dried and made into powder, and some of it drunk, is found by Experience of many, to kill and drive forth the Worms of the Belly'.

Some country folk believed the galls had the power to ward off whooping cough, and wore them round their necks as a protection; while Dr. Losch described how in France the peasants put the *bédégars*, or rose galls, beneath their beds to ensure sound sleep.

WILD ROSE PETAL JAM SUMMER

There are several Greek and Turkish recipes for rose petal jam using heavily scented roses, but a delicate version can be made with the pale pink petals of the English dog rose. Pick them in early summer, when the hedges are spangled with their flowers, taking a few petals here, and a few there, so that you don't spoil the sprays of roses.

The jam is very sweet without being at all sickly, and its flavour will evoke the days of high summer when you eat it for tea on a winter afternoon.

FILLS TWO OR THREE LITTLE POTS
250 ml/1¼ cups/½ pint measure dog rose petals
200 g/1 cup/½ lb sugar
2-3 tablespoons water
2 tablespoons strained lemon juice

Shake the petals on to a clean tray, or sheet of paper; they will probably be sheltering some little white spiders, and frantic, pale green bugs, which don't deserve to be squashed. I like to keep a whole flower or leaf spray on the table and guide the insects to it, and then drop them into the garden for a second chance.

Put the sugar, water and lemon juice into a saucepan, and stir over a low heat until the sugar melts, then add the rose petals and cook gently for 20-30 minutes, stirring fairly frequently to prevent the petals sticking.

Pour into little pots, the little glass jars that baby foods come in are ideal. Cover with waxed circles while hot, and seal with cellophane covers when cold.

WILD ROSE PETAL CONSERVE SUMMER

This conserve has a more runny consistency than the previous recipe, but in order to preserve the delicate wild rose fragrance it must not be boiled for long. It can be used in many delicious ways: you can make an ice cream (page 184) and a water ice; a syllabub (page 184) and a baked soufflé (page 184), and Balmoral Flan (opposite) which was supposed to be a favourite dish of Queen Victoria. A glorious way to use it is with strawberries: fold three or four tablespoons of the conserve into a large carton of lightly whipped cream, no extra sugar is needed, and the strawberries and rose-flavoured cream are an unbelievably good combination; try it this way with sliced, fresh peaches, and with sliced bananas. It is delicious stirred into plain yoghurt.

MAKES ABOUT 2 KILOS (4 LBS) CONSERVE

1 litre/5 cups/2 pints measure dog rose petals
1 litre/5 cups/2 pints water
juice of 1 lemon
1 kilo/5 cups/2½ lbs sugar

Remove any insects, then put the rose petals in a saucepan with the water and simmer gently for 15 minutes. Pour into a bowl and leave until cold. Strain the liquid back into the saucepan, reserving the petals, and add the strained lemon juice, which immediately turns the liquid a much deeper pink, then add the sugar. Stir over a low heat until the sugar has dissolved, then add the rose petals and bring to the boil. Boil fast for 10 minutes, remove from the heat and put into warm, dry jars. Cover with waxed circles while hot, and seal with cellophane covers when cold.

BALMORAL FLAN, WITH WILD ROSE PETAL CONSERVE

This is one of two rose recipes I have come across which were supposed to be favourites of Queen Victoria. I suspect that the rose petal conserve used in making this flan was probably made with the deep pink petals of the downy rose, *R. tomentosa*, which is common in Scotland, and slightly fragrant.

SERVES 4
SHORTCRUST PASTRY
200 g/2 cups/8 oz plain flour
pinch salt
125 g/1 cup/4 oz butter
4-5 tablespoons cold water
FILLING
5-6 tablespoons wild rose petal conserve
1 tablespoon strained lemon juice
¼ teaspoon ground ginger
¼ teaspoon ground cinnamon

Sift the flour and salt into a basin, cut the butter into small pieces and rub into the flour with the tips of your fingers. Add the water all at once and mix with a fork until the dough forms a soft ball, knead lightly until smooth, then put the dough inside a polythene bag, and leave in the refrigerator for 15 minutes.

Put all the ingredients for the filling into a small basin and stir with a spoon to mix evenly. Roll out the pastry to rather more than ½ cm/¼ in thick and with it line a well greased 20 cm/8 in pie plate or flan tin. Pour in the filling, and bake in the centre of a hot oven (375°F/190°C/Gas 5) for 20 minutes, then lower the heat to (325°F/170°C/Gas 3) and continue to bake for a further 15 minutes. Serve hot.

SYLLABUB, WITH WILD ROSE PETAL CONSERVE

This dessert is rich, and a heaped wine glassful is plenty for each person. It looks attractive in tall-stemmed glasses with a garnish of crystallised rose petals.

SERVES 6
250 ml/1¼ cups/½ pint whipping cream
1 tablespoon brandy
4-5 tablespoons wild rose petal conserve (p. 183)

Pour the cream into a bowl and whisk lightly, add the brandy and continue to whisk until the cream thickens to a soft peak. Fold in the rose petal conserve, and pile the syllabub into 6 wine glasses. Chill before serving.

WILD ROSE PETAL ICE CREAM

On a hot summer evening this cooling dessert embodies the very taste of June, especially if you drink with it a strawberry wine, icily chilled.

SERVES 4
2-3 tablespoons strained lemon juice
1 tablespoon sugar, or ½ tablespoon honey
250 ml/1 cup/½ pint thick cream
6-8 tablespoons wild rose petal conserve (p. 183)

Heat the lemon juice and sugar, or honey, in a small pan and stir while it comes to the boil, then boil fast for 3 minutes. Set aside to cool.

Whip the cream in a bowl, fold in the rose petal conserve and finally the cooled lemon syrup. Spoon into plastic tubs or cartons and cover with a lid or foil. Freeze until firm.

Serve the ice cream with a jug of rose petal syrup.

BAKED SOUFFLÉ, WITH WILD ROSE PETAL CONSERVE

If you have some eggs and a pot of rose petal conserve in your cupboard, this impressive soufflé is made, cooked and ready to eat in a matter of 15 minutes. It is as light as air and fool-proof. Brandy or sherry could be used instead of Maraschino.

SERVES 4
4 egg whites
4-5 tablespoons wild rose petal conserve (p. 183)
1 tablespoon Maraschino

Grease a soufflé dish. Whisk the egg whites stiffly and fold in the rose petal conserve, then the Maraschino. Pour the mixture into the soufflé dish and bake in a hot oven (375°F/190°C/Gas 5) for 10 minutes, until well risen and a glossy golden brown on top.

Serve at once.

WILD ROSE PETAL SYRUP SUMMER

Dog rose petals make a sweet, slightly scented syrup the colour of pale amber. It is best used to flavour fruit compôtes and ice creams rather than as a drink. Use rose petal syrup to supply the juice of a fresh fruit salad. Most delicious of all, pour the syrup over the ice cream made with rose petal conserve.

MAKES APPROXIMATELY 1 LITRE (2 U.S. PINTS) 1½ PINTS
500 ml/2½ cups/1 pint measure dog rose petals
375 ml/scant 2 cups/13 fl.oz water
sugar—see recipe

Remove any insects and put the petals into a saucepan, cover with cold water and simmer gently for 30 minutes. Pour into a jug or bowl, cover, and leave to infuse for several hours, or overnight.

Strain the liquid and squeeze out the petals, allow 450 g/2 cups/1 lb sugar to 500 ml/2½ cups/1 pint of liquid and heat together in a saucepan, stirring until the sugar dissolves, then boil up and keep on the boil for 10 minutes. Skim and draw off the heat. When cool pour into clean, dry bottles and screw on the caps.

WILD ROSE PETAL SANDWICHES SUMMER

Wild rose petals make a marvellous sandwich filling with a crunchy texture and sweet, scented flavour. Instead of brown bread spread with cream cheese, you could use fresh white bread with unsalted butter.

wholemeal bread
cream cheese, or cottage cheese
caster/granulated (U.S.) sugar
ground cinnamon
pink petals from the dog rose

Cut some wholemeal bread very thinly and spread each slice with cream cheese, or cottage cheese. Sprinkle one slice with sugar and one slice with cinnamon. Cover each slice with a layer of pink rose petals, close as a sandwich and trim off the crusts.

CRYSTALLISED ROSE PETALS

Rose petals may be crystallised or sugared to preserve them in the same way as borage flowers, see page 36.

WILD ROSE PETALS IN ICE CUBES

Pink dog rose petals frozen in ice cubes, one petal per cube, look delicious floating in a claret cup, or in any summer drink.

WILD WHITE ROSE PETAL WATER SUMMER

The petals of the white field rose are more astringent than those of the dog rose, and a really freshening, toning astringent lotion can be made with this rose petal water.

250 ml/1¼ cups/½ pint measure white rose petals,
   when picked over and gently pressed down
150 ml/²/3 cup/¼ pint boiling water

Gently remove any insects and put the petals into a measuring jug, pour on the boiling water, cover the jug and leave to get cold. Strain, pressing out every drop of liquid from the rose petals.

Use for the following skin lotions:

ROSE PETAL ASTRINGENT

For a skin freshener, wipe the face over with a pad of cotton wool dipped in the astringent before applying make-up.

8 teaspoons white rose petal water
1 teaspoon rose water—from chemist
1 teaspoon strained lemon juice

Mix all the ingredients together in a jug and pour into a small bottle or jar.

ROSE PETAL MOISTURISING LOTION

For a gentle overnight moisturiser, use a pad of cotton wool dipped in the lotion to smooth over the face and neck after removing make-up.

8 teaspoons white rose petal water
1 teaspoon rose water—from chemist
2 teaspoons witch hazel
1 teaspoon glycerine

Mix all the ingredients together in a jug, and pour into a small bottle or jar.

WILD ROSE PETAL MOISTURISING CREAM
SUMMER

This is nourishing cream to massage into the face and neck before you go to bed. The wild rose petal water is mildly astringent and good for soothing away wrinkles as you sleep. White wax is sold by chemists and comes in a flat cake.

75 ml/6 tablespoons/3 fl. oz almond oil
15 g/4 tablespoons/½ oz white wax
50 ml/4 tablespoons/2 fl. oz wild rose petal water
large pinch borax

Put the almond oil and white wax in a small bowl and stand in a saucepan of hot water to melt slowly over a low heat. Put the rose petal water and borax in a cup and stand this in another small pan of hot water and heat gently while stirring with a small bone or wooden spoon until the borax has completely dissolved, pour this solution into the bowl of oil and wax then remove the bowl from the hot water and beat as it cools, until the mixture becomes thick and creamy. Spoon into small pots or jars and cover tightly.

FRESH ROSE LEAF TEA SUMMER

The young leaves of wild roses gathered from the tips of the stems throughout the summer make an infused beverage which tastes very similar to tea, and is tea-coloured.

1 heaped tablespoon young green rose leaves
250 ml/1¼ cups/½ pint boiling water

Put the leaves into a small jug, bruise very thoroughly with a wooden spoon. Pour on the boiling water, cover and infuse for 10 minutes. Strain into a cup and drink hot, or warm, or iced with a sprig of mint, or a slice of lemon.

DRIED ROSE LEAF TEA

Another good tea substitute can be made with dried wild rose leaves. Put two teaspoons dried leaves in a jug, pour on 250 ml/ 1 cup/½ pint boiling water, infuse and strain as before.

TO DRY WILD ROSE LEAVES
LATE SPRING TO LATE SUMMER

Pick the young leaves from the tips of the stems of any variety of wild rose. Spread the leaves in thin layers on trays or cardboard lids, and leave in the boiler room, or airing cupboard to dry. After three or four days when the leaves are quite dry and crisp, put them through a parsley mill, and store in airtight jars away from the light.

ROSE HIP SOUP AUTUMN

When preparing rose hips for sweet recipes I have always noticed how, when raw, they are similar to tomatoes in taste, smell and colour. This gave me the idea to make a soup from rose hips, which tastes exactly like fresh tomato soup.

There are two versions, the first is lighter and, served with croutons, makes a good first course; the second soup is thicker, with more body, and makes a delicious, healthful meal with wholemeal rolls.

To make the rose hip juice needed for both recipes, simmer 1/2 kilo/1 lb rose hips, whole, but with their stalks removed, in 1/2 litre/2 1/2 cups/1 pint water for 1 hour, mash occasionally with a wooden spoon. Drip through a double thickness of muslin overnight. The juice has a strong and concentrated flavour and only 1/8 litre/2/3 cup/1/4 pint is needed for each recipe.

SERVES 4
150 ml/2/3 cup/1/4 pint rose hip juice
15 g/1 tablespoon/1/2 oz butter
1 small onion
1 teaspoon tomato purée
750 ml/3 3/4 cups/1 1/4 pints chicken stock
1 teaspoon Worcester sauce
1/2 teaspoon salt
freshly milled black pepper

Melt the butter in a saucepan, add the peeled and chopped onion and sweat in a covered pan over a low heat for 5 minutes. And the tomato purée, stir, then add the rose hip juice, chicken stock, Worcester sauce and seasoning. Cover the pan and simmer gently for 20 minutes. Liquidise the soup, check the seasoning and serve hot, with croutons.

THICK ROSE HIP SOUP AUTUMN

SERVES 2
150 ml/1/3 cup/1/4 pint rose hip juice
15 g/1 tablespoon/1/2 oz butter
1 medium onion
1 medium carrot
15 g/scant 1 tablespoon/1/2 oz flour
500 ml/2 1/2 cups/1 pint chicken stock

2 teaspoons sugar
1 blade mace, or a pinch of ground mace
salt and pepper
1 teaspoon Worcester sauce

Melt the butter in a saucepan, peel and thinly slice the onion and carrot and fry gently together for 5 minutes. Shake in the flour and stir to blend, then stir in the rose hip juice and stock and bring to a slow simmer. Add the sugar, mace, salt and pepper, and Worcester sauce. Cover the pan and simmer gently for 20 minutes. Serve hot.

A TARTE OF HIPS AUTUMN

From *The Art and Mystery of Cookery Approved by the Fifty-five years Experience and Industry of Robert May*, 1671.

The original version reads 'Take hips, cut them and take out the seeds very clean, then wash them and season them with sugar, cinnamon and ginger, close the tart, bake it, scrape on sugar and serve it in.' The warm spiciness of cinnamon and ginger is typical of many early English recipes. It gives a good flavour to the rose hips which turn a lovely cherry pink during cooking. They make a good and unusual pie filling.

200 g/8 oz short crust pastry (weight when made up)
1 large breakfast cup prepared rose hips
3/4 large breakfast cup water
2-3 tablespoons sugar, or honey
1/2 teaspoon ginger
1/2 teaspoon cinnamon
squeeze of lemon juice, optional

Cut off the stalks and calyx from the hips, cut them in half and scrape cut the seeds. Wash in a colander under a running tap very thoroughly to get rid of the little hairs, then tip the berries into a bowl of cold water and swish them about, finally rinse them in the colander under a running tap once more.

Put the hips with the water in a saucepan, bring to the boil and simmer for 15 minutes. Add the sugar, or honey, the ginger and cinnamon to the pan of hips, and lemon juice if liked, stir over the heat for a few moments then remove from the heat and set aside.

Divide the pastry into two halves. Roll out each piece into a circle. Line a small pie plate with one circle, fill with the cooked hips. Damp the pastry rim and cover the top with the second circle of pastry. Seal the edges with the back of a knife, and pierce the top in a few places to let out the steam. Bake in the centre of a hot oven (400°F, 200°C or Gas 6) for 20-25 minutes

ROSE – *ROSA*

until the pastry has coloured nicely. Remove from the oven, sprinkle generously with sugar and return the tart to the oven for a further 5 minutes. Serve—hot or cold—with cream.

A PERSIAN SWEET MADE WITH ROSE HIPS

AUTUMN

Many Middle Eastern recipes include almonds and sweet syrups. This dessert, made with rose hips, is both delicate and filling.

SERVES 4

200 g/2 cups/8 oz rose hips
water—see method
170 g/3/4 cup/6 oz sugar, or 4 tablespoons honey
strained juice 1 lemon
75 g/6 tablespoons/3 oz butter
25 g/1/4 cup/1 oz chopped, blanched almonds
50 g/1/2 cup/2 oz semolina
1 tablespoon rose water

Trim off the stalks of the rose hips and the remains of the calyx, cut them in half and scrape out the seeds and fine hairs. Wash the hips in a strainer under a running tap, then put them in a saucepan with just enough water to cover them. Bring to the boil and simmer in a covered saucepan for 30-40 minutes until tender. Strain the juice into a clean saucepan and make up to 425 ml/scant 2 cups/3/4 pint with more water if necessary. Add the sugar or honey, and lemon juice to this liquid, bring to the boil stirring all the while, then continue to boil for 3 minutes. Meanwhile rub the rose hips through a fine sieve or food mill and add the purée to the pan of juice and sugar.

Melt the butter in a pan and gently fry the chopped almonds and semolina until golden brown, then lower the heat and stir in the rose hip mixture, simmer very gently for about 5 minutes until the mixture thickens. Remove from the heat and stir in the rose water. Pour into little china pots or glass dishes and serve cool, but not refrigerated.

SAUCE EGLANTINE AUTUMN

The old books are very unhelpful about this recipe. I have read, tantalisingly, that Sauce Eglantine was another of Queen Victoria's favourite dishes; followed by a sketchy description of a sweetened purée of rose hips, with a little lemon juice added. This is easy to achieve, but I have never discovered whether the sauce was served hot or cold, with meat or with sweet dishes.

Perhaps one of my readers may have some knowledge of the menus at Balmoral, and could enlighten me. Presumably the original was made with the hips of the sweet briar, or eglantine.

I served the sauce hot with a young, French roast chicken, which was good, and cold with vanilla ice cream, which was excellent. It has a fresh, sharp taste which is adaptable.

200 g/2 cups/8 oz rose hips
water—see recipe
3-4 tablespoons sugar, or 2 tablespoons honey
3-4 tablespoons lemon juice

Halve the rose hips and scrape out the hairy seeds. Wash the hips very thoroughly in a colander, then swish them about in several bowlfuls of fresh water. Put the hips in a pan with just enough water to cover, about 125 ml/11/4 cups/1/4 pint water, bring to the boil and simmer for 10 minutes. Rub the purée through a fine sieve or nylon strainer, or squeeze through a piece of muslin. Return to the pan, and the sugar, or honey, and the lemon juice, bring to the boil and stir until the sugar or honey has dissolved. Serve hot or cold.

ROSE HIP SYRUP LATE SUMMER—AUTUMN

In the last war rose hip syrup was the most valuable source of vitamin C for children when oranges could not be imported into Britain and acres of soft fruit were ploughed up for cereal crops. In 1941 the Ministry of Health organised a collection of rose hips, and under the County Herb Committees schoolchildren and volunteers picked hundreds of tons of rose hips throughout the war. It was found that the hips needed to be transported and processed very quickly in order to preserve the vitamin C, the content of which varied with the geographical situation of the roses, those growing in the north of Scotland having ten times more vitamin C than roses in the south of England.

Pick the rose hips and prepare them as quickly as possible in order to preserve the vitamin C. The home-made syrup is delicious straight from the bottle with fruit and puddings, and when diluted with water makes a healthy drink for children.

400 g/4 cups/1 lb rose hips
200 g/1 cup/8 oz sugar
water—see method

Wash the rose hips and remove any stems or leaves. Put 750 ml/33/4 cups/11/4 pints of water on to boil in a large saucepan. Mince the rose hips through the fine blade of a mincer and immediately drop them into the boiling water, stir for a few seconds, then draw the pan off the heat and allow to stand for ten minutes. Pour the rose hips and hot liquid into a double thickness of muslin and drip the juice into a basin. Return this juice and the rose hips from the muslin to the saucepan, add 75 ml/scant 2 cups/3/4 pint cold water and bring again to the boil, stir for a few seconds, then draw the pan off the heat and allow to stand for a further ten minutes. Again drip the contents of the pan through the muslin, then pour the juice into a clean saucepan but do not squeeze the muslin, as it is essential to avoid any of the tiny hairs from the rose hips getting through.

Bring the juice to the boil and boil gently in the uncovered pan for about 5 minutes to reduce the liquid a little, then add the sugar, stir to dissolve and boil briskly for 5 minutes. Skim carefully and wipe the scum from the sides of the pan before pouring the syrup into clean, dry bottles. To sterilize the syrup, screw on the caps, then loosen them a fraction and stand the bottles on folded newspaper in a deep saucepan, fill up with warm water as high as possible and put some newspaper between the bottles to stop them toppling over. Bring the water to the boil and simmer for 10 minutes. Lift the bottles out on to a piece of newspaper to prevent them cracking, and immediately tighten the caps.

When cold, the syrup can be stored in the refrigerator or a cool larder, but once opened, it is best kept in the refrigerator and used within two weeks.

ROSE HIP JAM LATE SUMMER—AUTUMN

The original recipe came from Princess Alexandre Gazarene's *Russian Cook Book*: 1924, and the incredibly time-consuming method of preparation is so romantic and impractical, that I was moved to follow it exactly. This involved picking out the seeds with a tiny spoon or bodkin, then wiping out each hip with a piece of linen to remove the pulp and the little hairs. After rinsing in cold water, then boiling water, and boiling up over the fire, each berry had to be set up on a sieve spread with a clean cloth, with the little hole underneath so the rose hip could drain. Finally, the recipe tells one to boil 500 g/one pound of hips with 1 1/2 kilos/6 cups/three pounds of sugar and three-quarters of a cup of water until tender.

At that stage my experiment came to an end. The large amount of sugar, and small amount of water soon forms a sticky mass on the point of caramelising, long before the hips are tender.

Perhaps Princess Gazarene cashed in on the sympathy of the 1920s for the Russian émigrés, and with a girlhood memory of some exquisite rose hip jam, she wrote the recipe by guesswork. Perhaps picking the seeds out of rose hips 'with the aid of a silver bodkin or tiny spoon' was a fitting occupation for a princess in the dying days of summer; perhaps, as my husband suggested, it was performed 'by an army of little serfettes'. I like to think that time and patience is worth lavishing on such an exclusive little preserve.

Never having tasted the original, I will not have the arrogance to claim that mine is just as good, but it is good, tender and sweet with an exotic fragrance. It is not difficult to make, although de-seeding the hips takes a long time. The bowl of bright beads in one's lap, scarlet and gleaming, each one shaped like a little flask, yields, with a bit of patience, a sophisticated *bonne bouche* from the hedgerows.

I have given very small quantities for making two or three tiny pots for special occasions, but if you warm to the task you can increase the ingredients proportionately.

100 g/1 cup/4 oz rose hips
150 g/3/4 cup/6 oz sugar
250 ml/1 1/4 cups/1/2 pint water
1 tablespoon lemon juice

Pick the biggest hips you can find. Cut away the stalks and cut the tip off the other end. With a bodkin, or very fine crochet hook, pick out the seeds, being careful to keep the hips whole, and scrape out as much of the fluffy lining as you can. Put the hips into a bowl and run cold water over them, changing the water and swirling them about to wash away all the fluffy hairs. Drain on a clean cloth.

Put the hips in a saucepan with 250 ml/1 1/4 cups/1/2 pint water. Bring to the boil, cover the pan, and simmer gently for 45 minutes until the hips are tender. Drain through a strainer and save the juice in a clean saucepan, if necessary make the liquid up to 250 ml/1 1/4 cups/1/2 pint with water. Add the sugar to the liquid and bring slowly to the boil, stirring until the sugar dissolves, then add the hips and the lemon juice. Cook gently until the syrup thickens and the hips are soft, but still whole. Skim carefully, and pour the jam into two or three very small pots that are warmed and dry. Cover with circles of waxed paper while hot. Seal with cellophane circles when cold.

ROSE HIP AND CRAB APPLE JELLY AUTUMN

This is not a time-consuming recipe, the hips do not need de-seeding as they are dripped through a jelly bag, and the crab apples are easy to prepare. The resulting jelly is exactly the colour of carnelians, and is very good with game and poultry.

600 g/6 cups/1½ lbs rose hips
400 g/1 lb crab apples
1 litre/5 cups/2 pints water
sugar—see recipe

Wash the rose hips, cut the crab apples in half and cut out any worm-eaten or badly bruised bits, drop the pieces into cold water as you prepare them, then rinse them thoroughly. Put hips and apples into a large saucepan, add the water, cover and cook gently for 40 minutes until soft, mash the fruit well with a wooden spoon so that it is well pulped. Drip through a double thickness of muslin, or a jelly bag for several hours.

Measure the juice into a saucepan, and to each ½ litre/2½ cups/1 pint juice add 400 g/2 cups/1 lb sugar. Bring to the boil, stirring continuously until the sugar dissolves then boil fast for about 10 minutes, until the mixture gels when dripped on to a cold saucer. Skim, and pour into warm dry jars. Cover with circles of waxed paper while hot. Seal with cellophane covers when cold.

ROSE HIP WINE AUTUMN

Rose hips make a deep rosé wine with a clean, nutty tang.

activated yeast (p. 255)
1 kilo/8 cups/2 lbs rose hips
1 kilo/5 cups/2½ lbs sugar
5 litres/18 U.S. pints/1 gallon water
1 lemon
pectic enzyme

Rose hips need pectic enzyme, which can be bought from shops selling wine-making equipment, with instructions on the packet for using with 5 litres/18 U.S. pints/1 gallon wine.

Wash the rose hips and crush them with a rolling pin. Put the hips, sugar and thinly pared rind (no pith) of the lemon into the plastic bucket, pour on the boiling water, stir until the sugar has dissolved, then add the strained lemon juice and cover the bucket with a clean cloth. Allow to stand until cool (about 70°F, 20°C), then stir in the pectic enzyme and the activated yeast, cover the bucket with its lid and stand in a warm place for 2 weeks, stirring daily.

Pour through a strainer lined with a double thickness of muslin, to avoid any hairs from the rose hips, fill up the fermentation jar and follow the method given on page 254.

ROSEMARY
Rosmarinus officinalis

Rosemary is a native of the Mediterranean lands, and does not grow wild in Britain or America, though it is widely cultivated in both countries. We have the Romans to thank for the introduction of this lovely herb to our gardens. It likes a sheltered, sunny position and prefers a light sandy soil to a heavy one. Given a favourable spot, rosemary will spread into a shrubby bush and the trailing variety looks particularly lovely spilling on to a flagged path. The herb is evergreen, with brittle woody stems that twist and flake, and narrow, linear leaves about 2½ cm/1 inch long, dark green above, mealy grey beneath. The flowers are small and lilac blue with two lips, the lower lip divided into three lobes, the upper standing erect. Rosemary usually flowers twice in the year, during the spring and again late into the autumn. Every part of the plant is strongly aromatic, including the seeds, which grow in tight clusters where the flowers have faded.

Throughout its history the power of rosemary to strengthen the memory keeps cropping up: Greek students twined rosemary round their heads to stimulate memory for their exams; Roger Hacket, 1607, preached that 'it helpeth the brain, strengtheneth the memorie, and is very medicinal for the head'; Gerard wrote 'against weykness of the brayne and coldenesse thereof, sethe (boil) rosemaria in wyne and lete the pacyent receye the smoke at his nose and keep his heed warm . . .' and Culpeper recommended rosemary for 'cold diseases of the head and brain, as the giddiness and swimmings therein'. Sir Thomas More wrote 'I lett it runne all over my garden walls, not onelie because my bees love it, but because it is the herb sacred to remembrance and therefore to friendship.'

In Bancke's *Herball* there is a long account of rosemary's virtues: laid among books it kept moths at bay, the leaves put beneath one's bed prevented nightmares, it cured feebleness, poor appetite, gout, coughs, and shortness of breath; if properly used, rosemary could make one light and merry, fair of face, and was good for the teeth. So it goes on until the last delightful instruction, 'make thee a box of the wood of rosemary and smell to it and it shall preserve thy youth'.

The Elizabethans believed infusions of rosemary prevented baldness. Used as a rinse, it does keep the hair shiny and healthy; rosemary is included in many good commercial hair oils and lotions, in soaps and scents and pot pourris; it is an ingredient of genuine eau de Cologne and, with lavender and myrtle, was used to make Hungary Water with which Queen Elizabeth of Hungary was rubbed daily, and was supposed to be eventually cured of her paralysis.

Rosemary was used as an economy measure instead of incense, which was expensive; it was burned in sick rooms to prevent infection and, no doubt, to mask bad odours, and for the same reason it was one of the herbs used in the law courts for the protection and enjoyment of the judge, (its powers to strengthen memory may have helped him in his task!).

Rosemary became an emblem of fidelity for lovers and was twined into bridal wreaths and bridal bouquets, and gilded branches of rosemary were given as presents to wedding guests; at funerals, too, rosemary was carried, and thrown into the grave, as a symbol of remembrance. 'There's rosemary, that's for remembrance' is one of Shakespeare's immortal lines that everyone can quote without necessarily understanding the symbolism. In Italy and Spain the peasants believed rosemary would protect them from witches and the Evil Eye, and in England it was used for Christmas decorations in the old days and to decorate churches and banqueting halls. There are several old recipes from medieval times for Rosemary Snow, which was served at banquets. A large branch, or 'bush', of rosemary was decorated with whisked cream, egg white and sugar, usually set in a loaf of bread, and put in the centre of the table as an edible decoration.

There is only one discordant note in the folklore and history of rosemary; it was thought that it would only flourish in a garden where the mistress ruled the roost. In Gloucestershire one writer observed that 'so touchy are some of the lords of creation upon this point, that we have more than once had reason to suspect them of privately injuring a growing rosemary in order to destroy this evidence of their want of authority!' What a dilemma for the dutiful Tudor or Elizabethan wife, wanting her precious rosemary to flourish, yet loath to offend her lord and master.

CHICKEN WITH ROSEMARY ALL THE YEAR

A dish full of lovely Mediterranean flavours, you can use dried or fresh rosemary leaves, very finely chopped.

4 chicken joints, or 1 small chicken quartered
seasoned flour
2 tablespoons butter
125 ml/1/2 cup/1/4 pint olive oil
2 cloves garlic
1 tablespoon fresh or dried rosemary
1 teaspoon salt
2 tablespoons wine vinegar
250 ml/1 cup/1/2 pint chicken stock

Shake the chicken pieces in a plastic bag containing flour, salt and pepper, until they are lightly and evenly coated.

Heat the butter and oil in a heavy casserole and lightly sauté the chicken pieces on all sides. Add the crushed garlic, the fresh or dried rosemary and salt, stir and continue to sauté until the chicken is well browned all over. Stir in the wine vinegar and chicken stock. Cover and transfer the casserole to a moderate oven (350°F, 180°C, Gas 4) for 30-40 minutes, until the chicken is tender.

Serve in the casserole, with a green salad and plenty of hot French bread for mopping up the savoury juices.

ORANGES WITH ROSEMARY ALL THE YEAR

A few sprigs of rosemary in a light syrup give a wonderfully original flavour to a compôte of oranges, and suggest a dash of stem ginger more than any other taste.

SERVES 4
3 sprigs rosemary (each about 15 cm/6 ins long)
11/2 tea-cups water
1 tea-cup sugar, or 1/2 tea-cup honey
6 large oranges

Wash the rosemary, shake dry, and put the sprigs in a small saucepan with the water and sugar or honey. Heat slowly, stirring all the while, then boil fast for 5 minutes. Set aside to cool.

Cut away the peel and all the white pith from the oranges with a very sharp knife, slice the flesh thinly into a glass bowl. Strain the cooled syrup over the oranges and chill in the refrigerator for a few hours.

ROSEMARY CONSERVE ALL THE YEAR

Two old recipes from the 16th and 17th centuries used only the flowers of rosemary for this conserve, but as the whole plant, leaves, flowers, seeds and stems are all permeated with the matchless rosemary fragrance, the conserve can be made successfully with a decoction of whole sprigs of the plant. The result looks and tastes almost exactly like honey, and many wild flowers and herbs such as sage, thyme and borage flowers can be used in the same way, lending their individual fragrance to the conserve, which is a great deal cheaper to make than honey is to buy.

500 ml/21/2 cups/1 pint measure rosemary sprigs,
    when gently pressed down
500 ml/21/2 cups/1 pint water
juice of 1 lemon
400 g/2 cups/1 lb sugar

Wash the rosemary sprigs and put them in a saucepan with the water, bring to the boil and simmer for five minutes, draw off the heat and allow to stand until cool. Strain the liquid back into the pan, add the strained lemon juice and the sugar, heat slowly and stir while the sugar dissolves, then boil fast for 7 minutes until the syrup starts to thicken. Pour into warm dry jars, cover with waxed circles while hot, seal with cellophane covers when cold.

ROSEMARY FRUIT CUP SUMMER

This makes an exciting drink for a children's party in the summer, or a lovely and thirst-quenching one for the grown-ups just to sit around with in deck-chairs, and consume in large quantities.

1 small handful rosemary, the top sprigs
3 rounded tablespoons sugar or 1 tablespoon honey
150 ml/2/3 cup/1/4 pint water
450 ml/11/2 cups/16 fl. oz ginger ale
500 ml/21/2 cups/1 pint orange juice

Chill the ginger ale and orange juice in the refrigerator. Wash the rosemary sprigs and put them in a small saucepan with the sugar or honey and the water, bring to the boil stirring while the sugar, or honey, melts, and simmer for 5 minutes. Leave to cool.

Put lots of ice cubes in a large jug, strain over the cooled rosemary syrup and top up with ginger ale and orange juice.

ROSEMARY FLOWERS IN ICE CUBES

The tiny blue flowers of rosemary may be frozen in ice cubes and floated on top of each glass of fruit cup.

CRYSTALLISED ROSEMARY FLOWERS

SPRING, OR AUTUMN, OR WHENEVER ROSEMARY IS IN FLOWER

Rosemary flowers may be crystallised or sugared to preserve them by the same methods given for borage flowers on page 36. They are a delicate, fiddly business to paint, but extraordinarily pretty, and taste deliciously of the herb.

ROSEMARY WATER ALL THE YEAR

A fragrant infusion of fresh rosemary using the whole herb, flowers, stems and leaves, makes a herbal water for concocting lotions and creams, for adding to the bath, or as a hair rinse.

1 large handful rosemary (whole herb)
water to cover

Put the bunch of rosemary in a saucepan, add enough cold water to barely cover, bring to the boil, cover and simmer for 5 minutes. Pour into a jug and allow to get quite cold, then strain and bottle.

ROSEMARY ASTRINGENT LOTION

ALL THE YEAR

Use a pad of cotton wool dipped in the lotion for a cooling refresher after a hot bath, or to brace the skin before applying make-up.

6-7 tablespoons rosemary water
1/2 teaspoon powdered borax
1 tablespoon witch hazel
4-5 tablespoons orange flower water

Measure the rosemary water and borax into a bowl and stand it over a small pan of hot water. Heat gently and stir the mixture until the borax has completely dissolved. Remove from the heat and allow to cool. Measure the witch hazel and orange flower water into a small jug, add the cool borax solution, pour into small bottles and cork, or screw on the caps, when quite cold.

ROSEMARY – *ROSMARINUS OFFICINALIS*

ROSEMARY MOISTURISING CREAM

ALL THE YEAR

This is a pure, wholesome cream for cleansing and softening the skin. You could substitute other flower waters made with rose petals or elderflowers for the rosemary water.

15 g/¹/₂ oz white wax
75 ml/4 tablespoons/3 fl. oz almond oil
3 tablespoons rosemary water
¹/₄ teaspoon powdered borax

Put the wax and oil into a bowl over a small saucepan of hot water, heat gently until the two have melted together. Warm the rosemary water in a small pan, stir in the borax, mix together carefully and keep stirring until the borax has completely dissolved, then add gradually to the warm bowl of wax and oil beating thoroughly all the time. Remove the bowl from the heat and continue to stir and beat until the mixture is quite smooth and turns creamy, allow to cool, and spoon into small pots or jars, cover with lids and use within 2-3 weeks.

ROSEMARY HAIR TONIC ALL THE YEAR

All sorts of commercial preparations for the hair are made with rosemary, and its good effects are well known. This tonic is simple to prepare and can be used as a final rinse after washing the hair. A little rubbed into the scalp daily gives the hair a nice sheen and wholesome fragrance.

If using as a dressing, put the decoction into small bottles, as it will not keep more than a week or ten days once opened.

1 bunch rosemary
water

Cut a small bunch of rosemary and put it, twigs and all, into a small saucepan. Add enough cold water to cover the herb entirely. Bring to the boil, cover the pan and simmer for 15 minutes. Strain into a jug, and when cool, into bottles and screw on the caps.

ROWAN

Sorbus aucuparia

MOUNTAIN ASH

The rowan is common all over the British Isles and in many parts of Europe and Scandinavia. It is grown as a shade tree in America and in places has spread spontaneously. In Britain, the tree is widely planted by roadsides and in gardens, but dislikes clay and lime and is found growing wild chiefly in the north and west, and elsewhere locally in dry woods, upland heaths and rocky places. Rowans may be found at high altitudes, where they will probably be stunted and growing tenaciously in a cleft between rocks. Elsewhere, they may reach 6-9 metres/20-30 ft, but are usually small trees, with a smooth grey trunk and pinnate leaves consisting of toothed, lanceolate leaflets growing in alternate pairs, like the leaves of an ash tree. Hence the rowan's second name of Mountain Ash, although it belongs to the *Rosaceae* family, and is related to apples and pears. The small, white, five-petalled flowers appear early in summer and grow in loose, flattish heads, they are followed by the fruits which turn a bright vermilion and hang in vivid bunches in August and September.

The pliant smaller branches were used to make hoops for barrels, and the bark for tanning and dyeing. Both the bark and berries are astringent, and have been used medicinally as a decoction for treating diarrhoea, piles and vaginal discharge. Far wider than its medicinal uses were the magical powers ascribed to the rowan. The Druids planted it near their stone circles as protection against the powers of darkness, and in all the counties and countries where it grows, there is a store of superstition. The tree was frequently connected with the May Day festival, a time when fairies and witches would seem to have been particularly active; twigs of rowan were carried against sorcery, and were fixed over the hearth, and over the doors of houses, stables, barns and cow sheds, to protect the inmates against evil. Milk and butter churns were proof against theft if encircled with rowan, and walking sticks and whip stocks that were made from the wood were a strong protection for man and beast against the unseen terrors surrounding them. In Ireland the tree had a repulsive fairy guardian and, in spite of the enlightening influence of Christianity, rowans were planted in churchyards, and sometimes a bit of rowan wood might be used in a coffin, just to be safe.

These lines from a Scottish ballad seem to interpret the feelings of those days:

> *Their spells were vain. The hags returned*
> *To their queen in sorrowful mood,*
> *Crying that witches have no power*
> *Where thrives the Rowan-tree wood.*

In Scotland the old name for the rowan is bour-tree, which occurs in place names in some Scottish towns.

ROWAN JELLY LATE SUMMER

Rowanberries make a light red jelly with a sharp flavour that goes beautifully with venison or game, as well as with lamb and pork. You can make the jelly with green cooking apples, but crab apples give the best flavour.

2 kilos/4 lbs rowan berries
1.5 kilo/3 lbs crab apples
water—see method
sugar—see method

Wash the berries and strip them from their stalks, wash the crab apples, cut them in half and nick out any bad bits. Put both fruits in a large pan, add enough water to barely cover, bring to the boil and cook for about 20 minutes until the fruit is soft and pulpy. Pour into a jelly bag or double thickness of muslin and drip overnight. Measure the juice into a pan and add 400 g/2 cups/1 lb sugar for each 500 ml/2 cups/1 pint of juice, heat slowly, stirring until the sugar has dissolved, then boil rapidly for about 7-10 minutes until the liquid jells when dripped on to a cold saucer. Skim and pour into warm dry jars, cover with waxed circles while hot, seal with cellophane covers when cold.

ROWANBERRY BITTERS LATE SUMMER

Fresh rowanberry juice squeezed from the berries and added to a gin, taste exactly like Angostura bitters.

ROWANBERRY LIQUEUR

Rowanberries are usually plentiful enough to make a generous quantity of this jewel-bright liqueur. The rum gives a mellow sweetness to the rowan's sharp tang.

1 kilo/4 cups/2 lbs rowanberries—when stripped from
  their stalks
1 litre/5 cups/2 pints rum
225 g/1 cup/8 oz granulated sugar

Pick the rowanberries on a dry day and strip the berries from their stalks. Then follow the method given for sloe gin on p. 31 but without pricking the rowanberries.

ROWAN – *SORBUS AUCUPARIA*

ROWANBERRY WINE

Rowanberry wine is a light red, or deep rosé, and it needs a fair amount of sugar to prevent it tasting acid. This recipe makes a medium sweet wine, but you can reduce the sugar to 1.25 kilos/6 cups/3 lbs, if you like your wine dry.

activated yeast (p. 255)
1.5 kilos/3 lbs rowanberries
2 kilos/8 cups/4 lbs sugar
225 g/1¹/₃ cups/¹/₂ lb chopped raisins
2 lemons
5 litres/18 U.S. pints/1 gallon water

Wash the rowanberries and strip them from their stalks. Put the berries in the plastic bucket, pour on the boiling water, cover the bucket with its lid and allow to stand for four days. Strain the juice into a large basin, or divide between two basins, and wash out the bucket. Put the sugar, raisins, finely pared rind (no pith) and strained juice of the lemons into the bucket, and pour in all the rowanberry juice, stir thoroughly until the sugar dissolves, then stir in the activated yeast. Cover the bucket with its lid and stand in a warm place for two weeks. Strain into the fermentation jar and follow the method given on page 254.

SAGE

Salvia officinalis

The 'pale, ash-coloured, dry and withered deformity of the leaves of Sage, especially on the dry and burnt Hills in the hot countries, where it naturally groweth, was the Reason why it was so called, it signifying scorched, or consumed, by blasting'. Thus wrote William Coles in 1657, and though lacking the botanical terms we use, the way in which the early herbalists described their plants, often gives such a vivid picture in words that they are more descriptive than the scientific jargon of the present day.

Sage grows like a small, low shrub, and from wiry stems the 'pale, ash-coloured, dry and withered' leaves grow in opposite pairs on short stalks. The small flowers which appear in the summer are mauve, or pale lilac, with a short hood and the lower lip divided into two. The leaves have a wonderfully strong aromatic tang, spicy and clean, for which sage is grown as a garden herb in most parts of the world. It was planted in New England by the early settlers and thrived there. *Salvia officinalis* and *S. sclarea* may sometimes be found growing wild in the United States, and until recently, sage was prescribed as an official medicine in the United States *Pharmacopeia*.

Sage was introduced into China from Europe, one of the few cases of the West exporting plants to the East, and the Chinese developed such a taste for sage tea, that they traded their own world famous tea in exchange for it.

The herb was popular in early medicine, and powdered sage leaves, sprinkled over food in the same way as pepper, were used to treat the palate and throat. Andrew Borde suggested that the gums 'which may have many impedimentes, as wheles, blysters, fystles, bledynge, excoriacion, and superfluous growynge of the flesshe' should be 'fricated or rubbed with sage leaves'. He also gave a remedy for a sickness which 'doth make a mannes hed to shake or the handes or other partes to quake . . . Firrt beware of cold, of feare, and of anger . . . and then to wasshe the neck and the handes with the water that sage and balme hath ben soden in'.

William Coles was enthusiastic about sage: 'Such is the Vertue of Sage, that if it were possible, it would make a man immortall.' He recommended gargles 'made with Sage, Rosemary, Honeysuckles and Plantain' for 'Cankers, Sore Mouths and Throats, or the secret parts of Man or Woman, as need requireth'. He suggested sage should be boiled 'to serve for the bathing of the Body or Legges in summertime' and he made the astonishing claim that sage is 'good for Teeming women, such as are subject to miscarry through the too much moisture or slipperinesse of their Wombs'. This colourful account ended with the warning: 'At all times be sure to wash your Sage, for fear that the Toades, who as I conceive come to it to relieve themselves being overcharged with poyson, should leave some of their venom upon the Leaves, the danger whereof is upon record; and therefore it is good to plant Rue amongst your Sage, and then they will not come near it.'

With rue, or without, sage should be in every kitchen garden. It likes a warm dry position, but in spite of its Mediterranean origins, it will thrive almost anywhere, in any soil, and will stand up to most British winters. It is easily propagated from cuttings, and one should strike new plants every three or four years, as the old plant becomes rather woody and straggly. You simply break off young shoots from the main plant in the spring and stick them into the bed where they are wanted, or, if the weather is cold and dry, stand them in a jam jar of water until you see some little roots have formed. It is best not to plant the cuttings in full sun, and to keep them watered if the weather is dry. Sage can also be increased by layering, which it sometimes does of its own accord; the branches of the old plant can be pegged down and covered with some soil, then when they have sent up new growth, you can cut away the section of the old branch where it enters the soil, and carefully dig up the new shoots which will have a clump of rootlets attached.

BACON AND ONION TART, WITH FRESH SAGE SPRING AND SUMMER

This creamy, herb-flavoured tart is delicious hot or cold. It goes well with roast pork and apple sauce. For a light meal, serve the tart with a green salad, or tomato salad.

SERVES 4

Shortcrust pastry, see Balmoral Flan on page 184.
25 g/2 tablespoons/1 oz butter
3 medium onions
3 rashers bacon
1 tablespoon freshly chopped sage leaves
1 tablespoon finely chopped parsley
1 whole egg and 1 egg yolk
4-5 tablespoons sour cream
freshly milled black pepper

Make up the pastry and put in the fridge to rest. Melt the butter in a pan. Peel and chop the onions and sweat them in butter for 5 minutes. Remove the rind and cut the bacon into small squares, add them to the onions in the pan, turn up the heat and fry together for a few minutes more until the onions are yellow, but not brown.

Put the chopped herbs in a bowl with the eggs and sour cream. Beat all together with a fork and add a good grinding of black pepper.

Roll out the pastry to rather more than 5 mm/1/4 in thick. Line a greased 20 cm/8 ins pie plate with pastry, trim the edges neatly and fill with the onion and bacon, pour over the herb mixture and bake in the centre of a hot oven (375°F/190°C/Gas 5) for 20 minutes, then lower the heat to (325°F/170°C/Gas 3) and continue to cook for a further 20 minutes until the pastry is golden and the filling is set.

ROAST OR FRIED DUMPLINGS WITH FRESH SAGE SPRING AND SUMMER

A change from boiled dumplings made with flour and suet, these appetising sage and onion-flavoured dumplings are light in texture made with breadcrumbs and an egg, and can be roasted round the joint, or fried in shallow fat.

MAKES ABOUT 14 DUMPLINGS

1 1/2 tablespoons finely chopped fresh sage
2 large onions
250 g/4 cups/8 oz fresh white breadcrumbs
salt and white pepper
1 egg
25 g/2 tablespoons/1 oz melted butter

Wash the sage leaves, pick off the stalks and chop them finely. Peel and finely chop the onions and put them in a bowl with the sage, breadcrumbs and a seasoning of salt and pepper. Add the egg, lightly beaten, and the melted butter, mix all the ingredients with a fork and with floured hands make about 14 balls. Add the dumplings to the hot dripping round the joint about 35 minutes before the end of the cooking time, or gently fry in shallow fat for 10 minutes on each side.

FRESH SAGE TEA SPRING AND SUMMER

When you are feeling tired or in low spirits half a cup of sage tea is a stimulant and tonic. It also makes a very good mouth wash and gargle for sweetening the breath. Raw sage leaves rubbed on the teeth and gums will clean them and leave a fresh taste in your mouth, they also remove the smell of garlic and onion.

15 g/1 tablespoon/1/2 oz sage leaves—use the young tips
250 ml/1 1/4 cups/1/2 pint boiling water

Wash the leaves and put them in a jug. Bruise the leaves lightly with a wooden spoon, then pour on the boiling water.

Cover with a clean cloth and leave to infuse for 10 minutes. Strain, and drink warm or cool, half a tea-cupful at a time.

DRIED SAGE TEA

Drink half a tea-cupful warm or cold, or use warm as a mouth wash.

15 g/1 tablespoon/1/2 oz dried sage
1/4 litre/1 1/4 cups/1/2 pint boiling water

Put the sage in a small jug and pour on the boiling water. Cover with a clean cloth and leave to infuse for 10 minutes. Strain and use at once, or store in the refrigerator for two or three days.

TO DRY SAGE SPRING AND SUMMER

Dried sage leaves can be used in the winter to flavour stuffings and soft cheeses, and to make sage tea which can be drunk or used as a mouth wash.

Cut the fresh stems in early summer. Strip away the lower leaves which may be turning yellow, and tie in bundles of five or six stems. Hang the bundles tips downwards in a boiler room or from the slats and pipes in an airing cupboard. When, in about 5 days, the leaves are quite dry and crisp, crumble them and store in screw-topped jars away from the light.

SAGE TEA FOR A SORE THROAT OR COUGH SPRING AND SUMMER

Another old recipe with soothing properties, which can also be used as a gargle—two parts sage tea to one part warm water.

1 handful fresh sage leaves
500 ml/2 1/2 cups/1 pint boiling water
2-3 tablespoons cider vinegar
1 teaspoon honey

Wash the sage leaves, put them in a jug and bruise lightly with a wooden spoon. Pour on the boiling water, cover with a saucer and leave to infuse until the jug is just warm to touch. Remove the sage leaves and add the vinegar and honey. Stir until the honey has melted, and bottle when cold.

For a cough or sore throat, take a teaspoonful at a time.

SAGE – *SALVIA OFFICINALIS*

OLD-FASHIONED MEDICINAL SAGE TEA

SPRING AND SUMMER

This is an old recipe which claims to purify the blood. However, I have found it genuinely cooling and reviving in thundery weather when feeling oppressed by the sultry heat.

15 g/1 tablespoon/¹⁄₂ oz fresh sage leaves
1 tablespoon sugar, or ¹⁄₂ tablespoon honey
juice of ¹⁄₂ lemon
500 ml/2¹⁄₂ cups/1 pint boiling water

Wash the sage leaves and put them in a jug with the sugar or honey and the lemon juice. Bruise the leaves with a wooden spoon, then pour on the boiling water. Cover with a clean cloth and leave to infuse for 30 minutes. Strain, and bottle when cold.

SAGE HAIR RINSE SPRING AND SUMMER

After washing and rinsing the hair with clear water, pour a cupful of sage hair rinse over the head and rub well into the hair and scalp with your finger tips.

6 stems fresh sage, about 15 cm/6 ins long
500 ml/2¹⁄₂ cups/1 pint boiling water

Put the whole stems with their leaves in a jug and bruise with a wooden spoon. Pour on the boiling water, cover with a clean cloth and infuse for 20 minutes. Strain and bottle when cold. The lotion should be used within a week, as it does not keep.

SALAD BURNET

Sanguisorba minor

Salad burnet was once widespread in Britain, for Culpeper wrote in the 17th century 'the wild kind groweth in divers counties of this island . . . as also near London by Pancras church, and by a causeway-side in the middle of a field by Paddington'. Although sites such as these are now denied it, this attractive little plant still grows throughout Europe and the south of England and is found in dry grassy places on chalk or poor limey soils, or on rocks near the sea. It is cultivated in North America and occasionally escapes into the wild. The American burnet, *Sanguisorba canadensis* is a large relative which reaches 1³⁄4 metres/6 ft in height. The rather strange-looking bobbly flower heads appear from late spring and throughout the summer; they stand above the leaves on thin, wiry, reddish stems; these flower heads are a mixture of rusty red and creamy yellow, the upper parts contain the reddish styles, the lower parts the yellow stamens. The leaves are fern-like, consisting of many small-toothed leaflets with well-defined veins, matt green above, grayish and slightly rough beneath; they smell and taste of cucumber.

Salad burnet used to be cultivated in the early herb gardens, and it can be propagated from seed in the autumn, or by dividing some roots in the spring. It likes a poor, dry soil, and a little extra lime will help to keep it happy. The plant is perennial and green all the year, so the leaves will come again after cutting, once the plant has become established. In Italy they use the little leaves raw in salads.

SALAD BURNET WITH COTTAGE CHEESE SPRING, SUMMER, AUTUMN

Salad burnet has a pronounced cucumber taste, plus a tang of its own. A slimmer's meal with cottage cheese can be made a lot more interesting with the help of this pretty little herb.

about 8 sprays of leaves
1 small carton cottage cheese
freshly milled black pepper

Wash the leaves and shake dry, strip them from the stalk, then chop coarsely or put through a parsley mill. Turn the cottage cheese into a small bowl, add a good grinding of pepper, then mix in the chopped salad burnet with a fork.

The leaves prepared as above are delicious stirred into mayonnaise with a little chopped parsley.

SALAD BURNET WITH DRINKS

SPRING, SUMMER, AUTUMN

Many drinks are enhanced by the leaves of salad burnet. Bruise two or three sprays with a rolling pin and put them in a tumbler with some ice, pour over some fruit juice or lime juice diluted with water.

Half a dozen sprays of leaves bruised, and stirred into a jug of Pimm's is every bit as good as the traditional cucumber and borage, and any wine cup made with white wine is enlivened by steeping a few sprays of salad burnet leaves in the wine cup, while it is being chilled. Although it is recommended as a tisane, I think the cool freshness of the plant is ruined as a hot drink, but a few leaf sprays bruised and added to a cup of iced tea and lemon is simply delicious.

SALAD BURNET VINEGAR

SPRING, SUMMER, AUTUMN

The fern-like leaves of salad burnet give a fresh herbal taste to vinegar.

Wash the leaves and shake them dry. Fill a jam jar nine-tenths full of leaves, then fill the jar to the top with white wine vinegar. Cover the jar with a square of greaseproof paper, and screw on the lid. Shake the jar daily for two or three weeks, then strain and bottle.

SALAD BURNET – SANGUISORBA MINOR

ROCK SAMPHIRE

Crithmum maritimum

Rock samphire is quite common round the coasts of southern Europe and south and south-west England, Wales and southern Ireland, but it is less common in the north, and rare in Scotland. It does not occur in North America. The plant grows 30-60 cm/1-2 ft high, with smooth, fleshy, bright green leaves and stems; the leaves are cut into narrow untoothed leaflets, which are usually in groups of three. The umbels of yellow flowers appear from early until late summer, and are followed by oval seeds that are ridged and corky. Rock samphire is perennial and grows from rocks and shingle and on cliffs. It has a powerful resinous smell, reminiscent of varnish, and yet wholesome and appetising.

Pickled samphire was once so popular and saleable that men risked their necks to collect it from the cliffs. It grew abundantly on the Isle of Wight where, according to Coles, 'there is so great plenty that it is gathered, (yet not without danger) for some have ventured so far upon the craggy precipices that they have fallen down and broken their necks, so that'—making a rather sick joke—'it might be said they paid'. Coles described how the plant was pickled and sent to London and other places, 'of all the sawces (which are very many) there is none so pleasant, none so familiar and agreeable to Man's body as samphire, both for digestion of meates; breaking of the Stone, and voiding of Gravell in the Reines and Bladder'. No doubt this last property was attributed to rock samphire because it grows out of stones and rocks, and a plant that had the ability to 'pierce stone' was reckoned to be able to break up and disperse stones in the kidneys. Sir John Hill agreed that rock samphire was 'good against the gravel and stone' and warned that the pickle was often adulterated 'and other things pickled in their place'.

The German name for rock samphire is *Meer fenchel*, sea fennel, and it was locally known as sea fennel in parts of England. Coles patronisingly comments that 'it is also called *Foeniculum marinum*, which name the Italians and French follow, as neer as their dialect will permit'.

Samphire leaves are at their best and freshest in the spring, until early summer, before the plant flowers. The old, dry stems and seed-heads of the previous year often survive, in spite of winter gales, and are a help in guiding one to where the new vivid green growth is vigorously springing from the barren rock.

ROCK SAMPHIRE – *CRITHMUM MARITIMUM*

ROCK SAMPHIRE AS A VEGETABLE SPRING, EARLY SUMMER

Rock samphire is best picked in late spring and early summer when it is bright green and fresh. The raw plant's strange smell of varnish is too strong in salads, and even when cooked the first mouthful is a shock to the taste buds because, never having eaten anything like it before, one is like a child being introduced to an entirely new taste. Yet the flavour becomes increasingly enjoyable, so I can envisage acquiring a taste for it raw, and even ending up agreeing with John Evelyn that 'you cannot provide too much of this excellent ingredient in all crude sallads'.

I always think it must contain quantities of health-giving properties, growing as it does from clean rock or shingle, and bathed by the salt sea spray; a dish of rock samphire is perhaps the greenest green vegetable imaginable.

SERVES 4

1 heaped colander full of rock samphire
butter—see recipe

Wash the samphire in fresh water and pick away any hard stems. Throw the clusters of fleshy leaflets into plenty of lightly salted boiling water, cover the pan and cook briskly for 10 minutes. Drain well, and return to the pan with a generous knob of butter, turn the samphire gently with a wooden spoon until the butter has melted. Serve hot.

ROCK SAMPHIRE PICKLE I SPRING, EARLY SUMMER

The varnish smell and taste of the raw plant entirely disappears when rock samphire is pickled, and it makes a delicious crisp green relish to eat with all cold meats and to add to salads.

1 colander picked-over rock samphire leaves
250 ml/1¼ cups/½ pint water
750 ml/3¾ cups/1½ pints white wine vinegar
1 teaspoon salt
3 teaspoons pickling spice
1 teaspoon ground mace
6 peppercorns

Pick off the hard, main stems from the samphire and soak the leaflets in salted water for 1 hour. Wash in fresh water and drain through a colander.

Put the samphire in a large saucepan with just enough cold water to cover, bring to the boil and cook for 10 minutes, drain well. Boil the vinegar, water, salt and spices together for 5 minutes then pour into a bowl and allow to cool. Spoon the samphire into jars to within 1 cm/½ in of the top, strain the spiced vinegar into a jug and fill up the jars so that the samphire is well covered. Screw on plastic-lined lids or, if using metal lids, line with vinegar-proof paper or two thicknesses of greaseproof paper. Store for 4 months before using, to allow the pickle to mellow.

ROCK SAMPHIRE PICKLE II SPRING, EARLY SUMMER

This is an up-dated version of the 'Dover Receit' given in John Evelyn's *Acetaria*, 1699. He recommended gathering the samphire 'about Michaelmas or the Spring'. I have only gathered rock samphire in late spring and would have thought it would be too old by Michaelmas, but cannot say that John Evelyn is wrong. He also says 'if you be near the Sea that water will supply the Brine'. If you are fortunate enough to be near a stretch of coast far from holiday-makers, industry and buildings, I think you could soak the samphire in clean sea water, otherwise it is safer to use a brine solution of salt and fresh water.

1 colander picked-over rock samphire leaves
white wine vinegar—see recipe
water—see recipe
2 teaspoons salt

Pick away any hard stems from the samphire and put the fleshy leaflets into a large bowl of water into which you have stirred about 2 handfuls salt. Soak the samphire for 2-3 hours, then drain and put the leaflets into a large saucepan, add vinegar and water in the proportion of 3 parts vinegar to 1 part water, to cover the samphire, add 2 teaspoons salt, cover the pan with a tight layer of kitchen foil (John Evelyn pasted up the lid 'to keep the vapour from issuing out') and then cover with the saucepan lid. Bring to the boil slowly, lower the heat and simmer very gently for 30 minutes.

Remove the covers, allow to cool a little, then spoon the samphire and pickling liquid into clean jars and, if necessary, top up with fresh vinegar and water 'and thus' says the originator 'it will keep very green'.

WINTER SAVORY

Satureja montana

SUMMER SAVORY *S. hortensis*

B oth the savories are natives of the Mediterranean and south-west Asia and are cultivated as garden herbs in this country. They have been established in central Europe, India, South Africa and North America, where John Josselyn noted 'both sorts of savory' thriving in the herb gardens of the early settlers in New England. They were grown in monastery gardens in Europe from early medieval times, and in France and Germany are still the classic flavouring for beans. Savory is known as *Bohnenkraut*, bean herb, in Germany and Switzerland.

The summer variety is an annual. The seeds must be sown each spring in good, moist soil and require a sheltered position. Winter savory is perennial and is one of the easiest herbs to grow. It will thrive in any poor, stony soil, as it is a native of rocky hillsides.

Summer savory grows about 30-45 cm/12-18 ins tall, it has slender, upright stems, untoothed narrow, linear leaves and small pale lilac flowers, hooded and lipped as all the *Labiatae*, growing from the joints above a pair of leaves. The herb should be used fresh before the flowers appear in the summer, but it should be cut and dried for winter use before the flowers fade.

Winter savory grows like a small, wiry shrub about 30-45 cm/12-18 ins tall. The branching stems are dark and woody, the untoothed, pointed, narrow leaves grow thickly on the stems, they are unstalked and joined in pairs at the base, dark green and slightly leathery. The flowers may be pale mauve, pale pink, or white and appear throughout the summer, growing in sparse clusters amongst the leaves. The whole herb is strongly aromatic and because it withstands a hard winter and is evergreen, it provides fresh herb flavouring when others have been dried and put away in jars.

Both the herbs were known to and used by the ancients. The Romans used the leaves for flavouring and sauces; Virgil, who praised savory for its fragrance, advised planting it near bee hives, and as some of the old writers believed that wasps and bee stings were relieved by rubbing them with savory leaves, perhaps he was thinking of the remedy as much as the honey.

Culpeper and Coles ran neck and neck with their medicinal claims for the herb: they both recommended dropping savory juice into the eyes for bad eyesight and claimed that savory 'expels tough phlegm from the chest and lungs', adding that the juice snuffed into the nose 'quickens the dull spirits in the lethargy'. They both suggested a poultice of savory made with wheat flour for sciatica and palsy, and both gave the same formula for ear drops of savory juice heated with 'oyl of Roses' to cure deafness and singing in the ears. Probably the warm oil would have softened any wax and temporarily relieved deafness and 'singing', whether mixed with savory or any other juice.

There are occasional references by modern herbalists to the aphrodisiac properties of savory and its beneficial effect on the reproductive system, and the old herbalist, Coles, was very emphatic about this, saying the Latin name *satureia* came from *satyrus*, a satyr, 'because they used it to provoke Venery'; he recommended a drink of savory boiled in wine or water for women's disorders and also for 'women with Child to take thereof inwardly, and to smell often thereunto'. He advised savory as an aid to conception and said 'those things which incite to Venery are commonly windy, but this expelleth wind'. Coles' chapter on savory ends with a truly dramatic recipe, 'If a Woman's belly be swollen, as if she were with Child, when indeed she is not, savory stamped (pounded) and strained with Ale, and drunk with the powder of Jet and White Amber, and the said Herb with Hyssop and Leeks fryed with fresh Butter, and applyed to the back and belly, maketh her gaunt, and reduceth her to due proportion' adding defiantly, 'and it is like enough to be true'.

RICE STUFFING FOR CHICKEN WITH WINTER SAVORY ALL THE YEAR

Winter savory is rather a neglected herb, but it has such an excellent, strongly aromatic taste that quite a small quantity will flavour enough rice to stuff a chicken. As it grows fresh and green all the year round, you can use this recipe for stuffing the Christmas turkey; treble the quantities given and add a tablespoon of finely chopped turkey liver.

STUFFING FOR A 2 KILO (4 LB) CHICKEN

6-8 tablespoons cooked rice
1 tablespoon finely chopped winter savory
2-3 tablespoons finely chopped parsley
2-3 tablespoons chicken stock, made from the giblets

Put all the ingredients into a bowl and stir together with a fork to mix thoroughly. Fill the body cavity of the bird and secure the skin with cocktail sticks or a small skewer. Roast as usual.

SAVORY WITH BEANS SUMMER

Broad beans, French and runner beans or dried haricots as well as American lima beans may all be flavoured with summer or winter savory in this way.

SERVES 4

1.5 kilos/3 lbs young broad beans
25 g/2 tablespoons/1 oz butter
1 tablespoon chopped savory leaves, fresh or dried
freshly milled black pepper

Prepare the beans and cook them in a small amount of boiling salted water until tender. Drain, and keep warm. Melt the butter in a small pan, add the savory and a good grinding of pepper, and pour this over the beans.

BUTTER BEANS IN A GARLICKY SAUCE WITH SAVORY

This warming dish of butter beans is the ultimate comfort food. It can be made with any dried beans—haricot, red kidney, borlotti—or as a short cut, with tinned beans, rinsed and drained, before adding to the sauce.

About 200ml/3 cups/1 pint measure butter beans,
    soaked overnight

FOR THE SAUCE

25 g/2 tablespoons/1 oz butter
1 level tablespoon plain flour
250 ml/1¼ cups/½ pint milk
1 large or 2 small cloves garlic, crushed
1 tablespoon finely chopped savory leaves
Seasoning

If using dried beans, soak them overnight in plenty of cold water. Next day, drain and rinse the beans and put them in a saucepan with enough cold water to amply cover them, but no salt. Bring to the boil, cover and simmer gently for 1–1½ hours until the beans are tender. Time varies according to the variety, and length of time the beans have been stored. Drain well.

Make the sauce. Melt the butter in a pan, stir in the flour and cook gently for a minute or two. Slowly add the milk and stir until the sauce thickens smoothly. Stir in the garlic, the savory and seasoning. Add the drained beans to the pan—they may need more salt as they were cooked without—heat through and serve on a warm dish. Scatter over a few whole savory leaves.

WINTER SAVORY – *SATUREJA MONTANA*

BROAD BEAN AND MUSHROOM SALAD WITH SAVORY SUMMER

Because of its affinity with beans, savory mingles beautifully with a summer salad of broad beans and mushrooms.

285 g/5 cups/10 oz young broad beans, shelled weight
170 g/2 cups/6 oz mushrooms
4 spring onions
1 heaped tablespoon savory, finely chopped
Vinaigrette dressing—see recipe
Nutmeg—see recipe

Cook the beans in lightly salted water for 4–5 minutes, until just tender. Drain and cool.

Unless they are tiny, peel the mushrooms and slice thickly. Trim the spring onions and cut away the green, finely chop the white part and put the beans, mushrooms and onions into a salad bowl.

Make enough vinaigrette dressing to mix the salad—the mushrooms absorb quite a lot—stir in the chopped savory and pour the dressing over the salad. Finish with a generous grating of nutmeg.

SCURVY GRASSES

COMMON SCURVY GRASS *Cochlearia officinalis* EARLY SCURVY GRASS *C. danica*
ENGLISH SCURVY GRASS *C. anglica* NORTHERN SCURVY GRASS *C. scotica*

These four species of scurvy grass are very similar and variable, and produce hybrids which make them hard to identify, but they are all edible and none of them deserves their misleading name which conjures up a sere, bedraggled grass. They are not grasses at all, but *cruciferae*, or members of the cabbage family. All the scurvy grasses have tiny four-petalled white, or lilac-tinted flowers, which grow in loose heads at the top of the branching juicy stems, all have fleshy leaves of slightly varying shape and all are low growing, from 7-23 cm/3-9 ins high. Sometimes the central reservation of motorways is carpeted with the tiny mauve flowers of *C. danica*, which thrives on the salt used on the roads in winter.

Common scurvy grass has rounded untoothed root leaves and broadly toothed upper leaves, the topmost clasping the stem. The seed pods are like little, round, green bobbles and form while the plant is flowering, throughout the spring and summer. It is widespread and common on cliffs, estuaries and banks by the sea, and sometimes grows so abundantly that the ground is carpeted with the small white flowers which fill the air with a marvellous scent of honey. It occurs throughout Britain, Europe and Scandinavia, and in America is found growing along the North Pacific coast to central Washington.

The English, or long-leaved scurvy grass has larger flowers, the root leaves are more oval than round, the upper leaves are narrower and less toothed and usually stalked. The seed pods are double egg-shaped and the plant flowers during the spring. It can be found on muddy shores and estuaries round the coasts of Britain, Germany and Scandinavia. It is less common in Scotland, and rare in Ireland.

Early scurvy grass is smaller and more creeping, with heart-shaped root leaves and ivy-shaped upper leaves, all stalked. The flowers are usually lilac and appear very early in the spring, the seed pods are egg-shaped. The plant sometimes grows in great profusion on sand and shingle by the sea, and can be found on coastal rocks and walls and old railway tracks. It occurs throughout Europe and is common in the south-west of England.

Northern scurvy grass is very similar to the English variety, but tends to be smaller and flowers during the summer and early autumn. It grows abundantly along the shores of north Scotland and inland along some of its rivers.

Scurvy grass was greatly valued by early mariners and was taken on sea voyages as a scurvy preventive. It was cultivated in gardens, and until the last century people took infusions of scurvy grass as a medicinal drink, and ate the leaves in salads and sandwiches. Robert Thornton recommended 'the expressed juice mixed with some convenient vehicle' and gave this recipe: '2 pints juice of scurvy grass, 1 pint juice of brooklime, 1 pint juice of watercress, 20 oz by measure juice of Seville oranges. Mix them and, after the faeces have subsided, pour off the liquor, or strain it'. Culpeper told of a drink made from the juice of Seville oranges and the leaves of scurvy grass which was sold in shops 'by the name of antiscorbutic juices'. Since citrus fruit became available, people have neglected scurvy grass, which is a pity, for besides being a source of vitamin C, it is excellent in salads, and makes the best sandwiches of any wild plant I know, a cross between cucumber and mustard and cress, very cool and juicy. Scurvy grass does not make good tea, it is insipid and slightly salty when drunk as an infusion.

TO PREPARE SCURVY GRASS FOR SALADS

SPRING AND SUMMER

Pick the whole plant, soak in fresh water for at least half an hour, then wash very thoroughly to remove any tidal mud. Pick the leaves from the stems and use them whole, with a few flower-heads in a mixed salad. Omit salt from the salad dressing as the scurvy grass has just enough of its own.

SCURVY GRASS SANDWICHES

SPRING AND SUMMER

Pick and prepare as before, then slice the leaves into fine shreds and fill slices of buttered wholemeal bread, add a little black pepper, but no salt, before closing as a sandwich.

SEA BEET

Beta vulgarise ssp. maritima

It is easy to recognise this plant as the ancestor of our garden spinach, although sea beet usually makes much taller, stouter and stronger-looking plants than any cultivated variety; it has shiny, dark green, leathery leaves which are untoothed and roughly triangular in shape, the upper ones are narrower and strap-like. Throughout the summer the tiny, green flowers are inconspicuous amongst the upper leafy spikes, and turn to hard, prickly seeds later in the summer. Sea beet always looks to me as if it were bursting with health and health-giving properties: certainly it is full of valuable iron and minerals and though the flavour is nearly identical to cultivated spinach, it is, if possible, even more delicious. The plant grows close to the sea all over Britain and southern Europe, you can find it on shingle banks, at the back of beaches and salt flats, beside estuaries and along sea-side paths. Sometimes, on low cliff slopes, sea beet is very small and close to the ground, with tiny, dark, fleshy leaves which are good in salads; in favourable situations it makes glistening clumps 1 metre/3 ft high and these, with their large leaves, are easier for picking as a vegetable, which can be eaten from early spring until late autumn, or whenever the plant is fresh looking.

When you realise that the various cultivated forms of spinach, mangolds, sugar beets and beetroots were all developed from sea beet, it is a tribute to the gardener's skill. One often finds red-veined and red-stemmed plants of sea beet, the descendants of those that must have been coaxed to produce the swollen roots of our modern beetroot.

SEA BEET SOUP SPRING, SUMMER AND AUTUMN

Sea beet soup is identical to spinach soup, and for health and enjoyment is worth making whenever you can pick the wild beet.

SERVES 4

500 g/1 lb sea beet leaves
25 g/2 tablespoons/1 oz butter
1 small onion
1 level tablespoon flour
500 ml/2½ cups/1 pint stock,
    or water in which the sea beet cooked
salt and freshly milled black pepper
250 ml/1¼ cups/½ pint milk
nutmeg
1 tablespoon thick cream

SEA BEET – *BETA VULGARISE SSP. MARITIMA*

Wash the leaves and put them in a saucepan containing $2^{1}/_{2}$ cm/1 in boiling, lightly salted water, cook briskly for 12 minutes, drain the sea beet and reserve the cooking water, if using instead of stock.

Melt the butter in the pan and add the finely sliced onion, sauté gently until soft and starting to turn yellow, shake in the flour and stir to blend, then add the stock or vegetable water, stir while the soup thickens, then add the sea beet and a seasoning of salt and pepper. Cover the pan and simmer for 15-20 minutes. Liquidise the soup and return to the pan. Heat the milk until nearly boiling, and stir into the soup, add a good grating of nutmeg and check the seasoning. Stir in the cream just before serving.

SEA BEET AS A VEGETABLE

SPRING, SUMMER AND AUTUMN

Wash leaves and remove any long stalks, put damp in a large pan and cook for 10-12 mins. Drain thoroughly. Sea beet takes longer to cook than garden spinach and does not reduce so drastically.

SEA BEET FLAN SPRING, SUMMER AND AUTUMN

When mingled with spices, cheese and breadcrumbs, sea beet leaves make a delicious filling for a flan. Eaten hot or warm the flan is a good dish for supper or a light lunch.

SERVES 4

500 g/1 lb sea beet leaves
50 g/1 cup/2 oz fresh white breadcrumbs
2 tablespoons grated Cheddar cheese
1/4 teaspoon ground mace
1/4 teaspoon grated nutmeg
salt and milled black pepper
2 egg yolks
50 g/4 tablespoons/2 oz butter
175 g/6 oz shortcrust pastry

Prepare and cook the leaves as above and chop them roughly. Mix the sea beet, breadcrumbs, cheese and seasonings in a bowl and stir in the lightly beaten egg yolks. Melt the butter and add half to the mixture. Line a 20 cm/8 in flan tin with pastry, fill with the sea beet mixture and pour over the rest of the melted butter. Bake in a moderate oven (350°F/180°C/Gas 4) for about 40 minutes, until the pastry is cooked.

SEA LETTUCE

Ulva lactuca

GREEN LAVER

Sea lettuce grows on rocks and in rock pools mostly mid-way between the low- and high-tide levels on coasts all round Britain and North America. It is also found in the Mediterranean and the Baltic. The very bright green fronds are translucent and irregularly shaped, about 15 to 60 cm/6 ins-2 ft long, widening towards the top and, where they are attached to the rocks, narrowing into a short, solid stalk, though sometimes the fronds may have no stalks. The weed is often found washed up, after it has become detached.

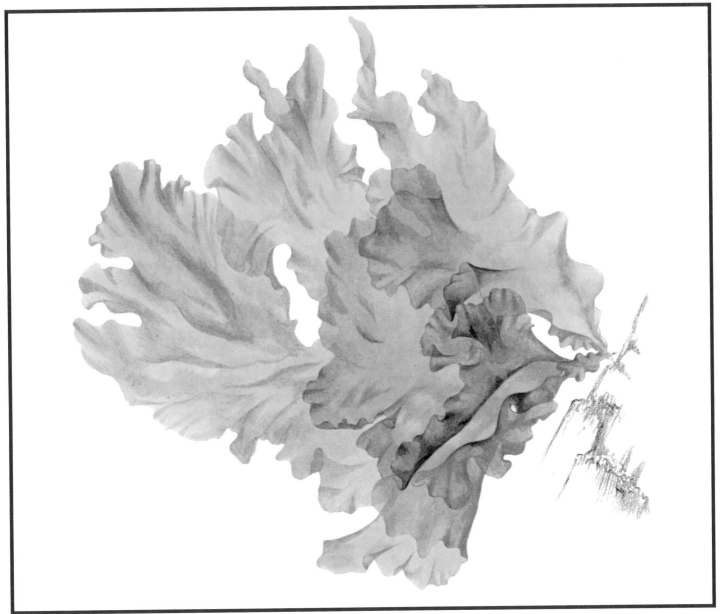

SEA LETTUCE – *ULVA LACTUCA*

SEA LETTUCE SOUP SPRING AND SUMMER

Sea lettuce, or green laver is much tougher than red laver, even after prolonged cooking, but it can picked, pulped and stored in jars exactly the same way, see page 139.

The gelatinous texture gives a good consistency to soups and stews, so one should use it as a thickening agent rather than champing on the tough weed. This garlic-flavoured soup is a good vehicle for sea lettuce.

SERVES 4

1 large cup sea lettuce pulp
3/4 litre/3³/4 cups/1¹/2 pints stock
salt and white pepper
6 cloves garlic, peeled and crushed

Put all the ingredients into a saucepan, bring to the boil, stir gently and cover the pan, then simmer slowly for 45 minutes. To achieve a smooth texture, liquidise the soup well for a few minutes as the pulp can be stringy. Check the seasoning and serve very hot with crusty rolls or wholemeal bread.

SEA PURSLANE

Halimione portulacoides

S ea purslane is found along the southern coasts of Britain, France and Germany. It is a grey-green shrubby plant with woody stems which grows in straggling clumps, 20-45 cm/8-18 ins high along the creeks and tidal pools of estuaries and salt marshes. In many places in east and south-east England, south-west England and Wales it is common and grows abundantly; but further north and in Scotland and Ireland it is rare. It does not occur in the United States. The flowers are small and grow in slender, yellowish-green spikes, some flowers have stamens (male) others styles (female); both on the same plant. The flowers appear in late summer, but the downy, oval leaves may be picked from late spring until late autumn, they are thick and fleshy and have a good crunchy texture and a natural saltiness.

SEA PURSLANE – *HALIMIONE PORTULACOIDES*

DRESSING FOR SEA PURSLANE SALAD

Pick the top 5 cm/2 ins of the plant where the leaves are new and fresh and not only more tender, but cleaner. First soak the leaves in fresh water for half an hour, then wash very thoroughly, as a certain amount of tidal mud may adhere to them, drain the leaves and pick off the stalks. Use about a tea-cupful of leaves with a plain lettuce or mixed salad. Make the dressing with sugar, or honey, but without salt as the sea purslane supplies its own.

2-3 tablespoons white wine vinegar
1 tablespoon sugar, or 1/2 tablespoon honey
1 teaspoon French mustard
6-8 tablespoons olive oil or pure vegetable oil

Put all the ingredients into a screw-topped jar, shake well to blend, then pour over the salad and mix together gently. Finish with a grinding of black pepper.

PASTA WITH SEA FOOD AND SEA PURSLANE SUMMER

The astringent salty taste of sea purslane goes well with all sorts of fish. You can vary the fish, but keep a proportion of shellfish—halved scallops with monkfish, shrimps with salmon.

340 g/3 cups/12 oz penne
225 g/2 cups/8 oz smoked haddock
Milk—see recipe

1 tablespoon vegetable oil
1 generous tablespoon butter
6 spring onions
1 clove garlic, peeled and crushed
140 g/1 cup/5 oz shelled prawns—fresh or frozen (if frozen, de-frost briefly, and drain)
a good handful sea purslane leaves, washed
5 tablespoons crème fraîche
freshly milled black pepper

Cook the pasta according to the instructions on the packet. Drain and keep warm.

Rinse the haddock and put in a pan with enough milk to barely cover the fish. Bring to the boil, cook for one minute, then draw off the heat and leave until cool enough to handle. Lift the fish onto a plate and remove all skin and bones, break the haddock into flakes.

Meanwhile melt the oil and butter in a clean pan. Trim the onions, leaving some of the green part, and slice them thinly into the pan. Add the crushed garlic and sauté gently, then add the prawns—if raw, cook for a minute until they turn pink—and the sea purslane leaves. Stir all together to heat through, then add the crème fraîche and allow to bubble briefly. Add plenty of freshly milled black pepper and pour the sauce over the dish of pasta.

Serve with a green salad to which you have added some wild coastal leaves—sea purslane, scurvy grass, marsh samphire, or shredded sea beet.

SHAGGY CAP

Coprinus comatus

LAWYER'S WIG

he shaggy cap is common throughout Britain, Europe and Scandinavia, and is widely distributed throughout the United States. It is found in many grassy places, in fields and gardens, on roadside verges, in ditches and along woodland paths. In may appear throughout the spring, summer and autumn. The fungus grows from

SHAGGY CAP – *COPRINUS COMATUS*

5-15 cm/2-6 ins high, and at first looks like the top of an egg coming from the ground: it is whitish and covered with uneven, overlapping white and brownish scales; the cap then lengthens to a candle shape, rounded and pale brown at the top, pink at the margin and lying close to the stem at the base where the gills are just visible, the gills are white at first, turning pinkish, then brown, and finally inky black when the cap opens away from the stem and dissolves into a revolting black fluid. The stem is white with a hollow fibrous core, and a narrow white ring which in the young fungus at first encloses the lower edge of the cap, but later may fall away.

The shaggy cap should be picked when it is young, at the egg-shaped or candle-shaped stage, and while the gills are still white or pale pink. However, no one is likely to want to try it at the later, black slime stage.

The shaggy cap is easy to identify safely. The only other fungus at all similar is the related *Coprinus atramentarius*, which is greyer, without scales and has no ring, but it is not poisonous or harmful, so confusion would not be dangerous.

Only one word of caution, a chemical contained in shaggy caps when mixed with alcohol can make you sick, so don't drink when eating them. But don't be put off, for the shaggy cap is a safe and delicious fungus.

BAKED SHAGGY CAPS SPRING, SUMMER, AUTUMN

Shaggy caps are delicious baked slowly in the oven, or you can simmer them in a saucepan on top of the stove for 20 minutes. The cream may be omitted, but it does improve the sauce. Shaggy caps may also be added to soups and stews 30 minutes before the end of cooking time.

about 12 shaggy caps
salt and freshly milled black pepper
250 ml/1 cup/scant 1/2 pint milk
2 tablespoons cream

Wipe the caps and remove the stems, slice each cap in half. Lay them in a thickly buttered ovenproof dish, add a seasoning of salt and pepper, pour over the milk and cream, cover the dish with foil or a lid and bake in a moderate oven (325°F/170°C/Gas 3) for 30 minutes.

SOAPWORT
Saponaria officinalis

You can grow soapwort as a medium-tall herbaceous perennial in the garden, and it may be found growing wild along roads and by streams in lowland areas throughout Britain, Europe and Scandinavia. Soapwort was cultivated in North America, and now grows wild in fields and waste places throughout the United States. In late summer, when the plant is in flower, it is strikingly beautiful, with large, soft pink flowers consisting of five petals with inrolled margins and faint, deeper pink veining; plants with double flowers can often be found. The calyx is slightly inflated, like a little green sausage, and sometimes has reddish blotches. The leaves are smooth and lanceolate, they grow in pairs from the rather sprawling, brittle stems which have a characteristic knot, or swelling, at the junctions of the leaves.

The plant owed its name to its foaming and cleansing properties and decoctions of the roots are still used to clean delicate and valuable old fabrics and needlework. An old name for soapwort was Fuller's Herb, and in the Middle Ages it was used by fullers for washing their woollen cloth; and in Switzerland sheep were dipped in a wash of soapwort to clean their fleeces before shearing. The herb was used for bathing and washing in Roman times and is sometimes found growing wild near the sites of Roman baths. The early herbalists used soapwort for many skin diseases, and a belief that it would cure venereal disease continued long after Culpeper proclaimed, 'it cures gonorrhoea, by taking the inspissated juice of it'. Dr. Losch said that country people in France used a decoction of soapwort to treat syphilis, and also for gout and rheumatism. The French names for the plant are *Herbe à foulon* (Fuller's herb) and *saponnière*. The saponin constituents in soapwort are used in modern pharmacy in expectorants and diuretics. When driving in Spain recently, a botanist friend of ours had the bad luck to get a puncture. A session of wheel-changing left him hot and dirty, but he had noticed *saponaria* growing by a stream, so scrambled down to it, picked large handfuls of the plant, and had a good soapy wash before continuing to his lunch-date as fresh as paint.

SOAPWORT – *SAPONARIA OFFICINALIS*

SOAPWORT SHAMPOO WITH HERBS

You can buy packets of dried soapwort root from herbalists. The latter is used in this shampoo. Steep the root overnight before you wash your hair, the shampoo leaves the hair shiningly clean and sweet-smelling. Soapwort is renowned as a gentle cleanser, and doesn't sting if it gets in your eyes, so is very good for babies and small children.

25 g/1 oz dried soapwort root
750 ml/3 cups/1¼ pints boiling water
6 sprigs rosemary tops
3 sprigs sage tops
8 sprigs lemon-balm tops
3 sprigs southernwood tops

Break up the dried root and crush it with a rolling pin. Put the root in a large china jug and pour on the boiling water, cover and leave it to steep for 12 hours. Put the root, and the water in which it soaked, in a stainless steel saucepan and boil for 15 minutes. Meanwhile, pick your herbs, wash and chop them into short lengths. Put the herbs in a large bowl and pour on boiled soapwort and its water, stir well and leave to stand until cool. Strain the liquid into a jug and use it all to wash your hair.

HOW TO CLEAN UPHOLSTERY WITH SOAPWORT

A solution of soapwort is wonderful for cleaning delicate old upholstery and tapestry. Wet a cloth, or sponge, with the solution and squeeze out the surplus liquid, or use a very soft brush, rub the material lightly and, if it is not sufficiently clean, allow to dry before applying the solution again for a second time.

15 g/½ oz dried soapwort root
750 ml/3 cups/1¼ pints water

Crush the root with a rolling pin, put it into a stainless steel saucepan with the cold water, bring to the boil and simmer for 20 minutes, stirring occasionally. Allow to stand until cool. Strain through muslin into a bowl.

COMMON SORREL

Rumex acetosa

Sorrel grows wild throughout Britain and most of Europe and Scandinavia. It is found in grassy places, hedge banks and woods. The long-stalked dark green, arrow-shaped leaves grow in a layered basal rosette from which rises a juicy hollow stem, 15-60 cm/6 ins-2 ft tall. The leaves mid-way up the stem have short stalks, and at the top are unstalked, with a papery sheath where they clasp the stem. In late spring and summer sorrel produces whorled spikes of inconspicuous greenish flowers, with male and female flowers on separate plants; as they ripen, the seeds turn red then rusty brown. Docks are related to sorrels, but they are stouter, and the leaves are larger and not arrow-shaped like sorrel, both plants have inconspicuous greenish flowers, followed by brown clusters of seeds, and if there is doubt in identifying sorrel, test by nibbling a leaf. Sorrel has a sharp, lemony flavour, the dock tastes sour and bitter, but it is harmless. Sheep sorrel, *R. acetosella*, is a much smaller relative of the common sorrel, it grows in dry and rather bare places, and the small leaves may also be used in salads and for flavouring. It is a common little weed in the United States, which was introduced from the Old World.

All the early physicians and herbalists were full of praise for sorrel. William Coles described a string of violent and terrifying diseases 'for which there is nothing better than Sorrel-Possett drink, which may be made by putting the juice to milk when it beginneth to seethe (boil)'. He advised the leaves to be eaten 'in the morning fasting, in the time of Pestilence', to prevent infection, and John Parkinson advised sorrel in sauces 'both for the whole and the sicke . . . procuring unto them an appetite unto meate, when their spirits are almost spent with the violence of their furious of fierie fits.'

Culpeper described how sorrel leaves 'wrapt in a colewort leaf, and roasted in the embers and applied to a large imposthume, botch, boil or plague-sore, doth ripen and break it', and even affirmed that sorrel was 'powerful to resist the poison of the Scorpion'. John Evelyn wrote that sorrel 'in the making of Sallets imparts a grateful quickness to the rest as supplying the want of oranges and lemons', with which Sir John Hill agreed, adding 'the leaves eaten as salad, or the juice taken, are excellent against the scurvy'. In his *Family Herbal* Thornton advised sorrel for scurvy and for 'phlogistic or imflammatory habits', whatever they may be!

For all the wild claims made by the early physicians, modern herbalists recommend infusions of sorrel leaves for kidney disorders, and for throat and mouth ulcers. It is a wholesome vegetable and salad plant, and may be grown from seed, or transplanted into the garden by digging up a root in the spring or autumn, if you find an abundant colony of the wild plant. There is a garden variety which has exactly the same taste but much larger, more tender, spinach-like leaves, and can easily be grown from seed sown in shallow drills from early spring onwards. The seedlings should be thinned out to 23 cm/9 ins apart, and the flowering stems cut to the ground to encourage a fresh supply of leaves. Sorrel produces leaves through most of the winter, and a short row of five or six plants will be enough for most cooks.

SORREL SOUP MOST OF THE YEAR

This soup can be made in advance and reheated without allowing it to boil. The sorrel has a delicious sharp lemony flavour quite unlike any other vegetable.

100 g/4 oz wild sorrel
½ small lettuce, or a handful of spinach leaves
1 tablespoon chopped chervil, dried or fresh
1 tablespoon butter
generous 1¼ litres/6¼ cups/2½ pints chicken stock
½ teaspoon salt
good grinding of black pepper
2 egg yolks
1 tablespoon cream

Wash all the leaves thoroughly and pick away the stalks and any damaged parts. Melt the butter in a large pan and add the sorrel, lettuce or spinach, and chervil. Cover, and simmer very slowly for 15-20 minutes. Add the stock, and simmer for a further 15 minutes. Season with salt and pepper and put the contents of the pan through a food mill, or liquidiser. At this stage the soup can be set aside until needed. Ten minutes before serving, put the egg yolks in a cup and add a little cool liquid from the pan, then heat the soup thoroughly and add two spoonfuls of hot soup to the egg yolks, mix together and stir into the pan. Immediately draw off the heat, as the soup must not boil once you have added the egg yolks. Stir in the cream and serve.

ANGUILLE AU VERT À LA FLAMANDE

SPRING AND SUMMER

This is one of Madame Prunier's famous dishes using not only sorrel, but intriguingly, white dead nettle tops, too. The astringent sorrel and herbs are a noteworthy complement to rich chunks of eel.

SERVES 4

1 kilo/2 lbs small or medium-sized eels
25 g/2 tablespoons/1 oz butter
1 small onion
3 sticks celery
white wine, see recipe
salt and pepper
150 g/2½ cups/5 oz sorrel leaves

150 g/2½ cups/5 oz watercress
50 g/1 cup/2 oz white dead nettle tops
15 g/1 tablespoon/½ oz chopped parsley
15 g/1 tablespoon/½ oz chopped chervil
small bag of muslin containing 1 teaspoon each fresh sage,
   savory and mint
4 egg yolks
2 -3 tablespoons cream

Remove the heads and skin the eels (a fishmonger will do this) and cut them into pieces about 6-7½ cm/2½-3 in long. Heat the butter in a large saucepan and lightly fry the eel pieces on each side. Peel the onion, scrape the celery sticks and slice them into small pieces, add to the pan of eel and sauté gently until beginning to soften.

Add enough white wine to cover the eel, season with salt and freshly milled black pepper, bring to the boil and cook briskly for 12-15 minutes, until a sharp knife point easily pierces the largest chunk of eel. Meanwhile wash and finely chop the sorrel and watercress leaves and the dead nettle tops, parsley and chervil, and add them to the pan five minutes before the end of cooking time. Remove from the heat. Mix the egg yolks with the cream in a cup, add a little of the hot liquid from the pan and stir to blend, and then pour into the pan of eel to bind the liquid. Serve hot or cold.

SORREL SAUCE MOST OF THE YEAR

The sharp, lemony tang of sorrel makes a perfect sauce for pork and duck, or any rich fat meat. It is made in a matter of minutes, without any of the problems associated with sauce-making.

MAKES ABOUT 250 ML/1 CUP/½ PINT SAUCE
1 litre/5 cups/2 pints measure sorrel leaves
butter
freshly milled black pepper

Wash the sorrel leaves and put them damp in a saucepan. Cook for 5 minutes, drain and return to the pan with the butter and pepper. Beat to a purée with a wooden spoon and serve hot.

COMMON SORREL – *RUMEX ACETOSA*

SOUTHERNWOOD

Artemisia abrotanum

LAD'S LOVE, OLD MAN

S outhernwood is grown as a herb throughout Europe, the Mediterranean and in the temperate regions of North America, and grows wild as a garden escape from cultivation in Texas, although John Josselyn said of southernwood, 'it is no plant for this country', when he listed the garden herbs that were introduced into New England in the 17th century. Southernwood also grows wild in the warmer countries of the Mediterranean; it is shrubby, with straight, woody stems which reach 60-90 cm/2-3 ft in height, the finely divided feathery leaves are grey-green and have a strongly sweet pungency, which keeps moths away if the dried sprays are laid among clothes. The French name for the herb is *garderobe*.

The country name, Lad's Love, comes from the old custom of putting sprigs of southernwood in the posies that young lovers gave to their sweethearts. An ointment made from the ashes of southernwood was thought to encourage the growth of a beard, which was an asset to downy-cheeked youths. Culpeper wrote 'the ashes mingled with old salad oil helps those that are bald, causing the hair to grow again on the head or beard'; and William Coles agreed that if this same mixture was used twice daily, 'it causeth the Beard to come forth speedily'.

Southernwood was believed to prevent infection and was one of the herbs used in court to protect the judge from jail fever and foul smells; ladies used to take a bunch of southernwood to church so that the sweet, aromatic scent would refresh them and keep them awake throughout the lengthy sermons; and amongst country folk in the Slav countries, southernwood was burned like incense in the belief that it kept away thunder. The Lithuanians used it for divination, three pieces of southernwood 'each the length of a finger' were thrown into the air, and whether the omen was good or bad was decided by which side of the herb landed uppermost.

Southernwood contains absinthol, a bitter essential oil, and had a wide range of medicinal uses for gastric disorders and as a tonic and antiseptic. The leaves, dried and powdered, were given in treacle to children with worms, which must have been a disgusting and dreaded mixture, in fact Sir John Hill, the 18th century herbalist, described a decoction of southernwood tops as 'good against worms, but it is a very disagreeable medicine'. More pleasantly, an infusion of southernwood was used for aromatic and tonic baths.

By far the most extravagant claim for southernwood made by Coles is, 'it is said that if a bunch of southernwood be laid under one's Bed, Pillow, or Bolster, it provoketh carnall Copulation, and resisteth all inchantments that hinder the same'. After that, should I hasten to give the method for cultivating the herb?

Southernwood may be propagated by taking cuttings which should be half-buried in a cutting compost, or a mixture of sand and loam, and kept well watered. It is not fussy about soil, but needs a sheltered, sunny position, and is best cut down to about 15 cm/6 ins each autumn, to prevent it becoming straggly.

SOUTHERNWOOD CAKE SPRING AND SUMMER

The aromatic, bitter-sweet taste of southernwood makes an exceptionally good flavouring in a plain Madeira cake mixture. Put all the ingredients in a bowl, beat with a wooden spoon for one minute, and the mixture is ready for the oven.

150 g/1½ cups/6 oz plain flour
50 g/½ cup/2 oz self-raising flour
4 teaspoons finely chopped southernwood
175 g/scant 1 cup/7 oz granulated sugar
150 g/ ¾ cup/6 oz softened butter
4 eggs

Sift the two flours into a mixing bowl, stir in the chopped southernwood and sugar. Add the butter and lightly mixed eggs, stir with a wooden spoon to draw the ingredients together, then beat well for one minute (this only takes seconds in a food processor). Pour the mixture into a lined and greased 15 cm/6 ins cake tin, and bake in a moderate oven (350°F/180°C/Gas 4) for 30 minutes. Lower the oven heat to (325°F/170°C /Gas 3) and finish baking the cake for 45 minutes to 1 hour, until a warm skewer comes out cleanly. Stand for a minute, then turn the cake out on to a wire rack to cool.

SOUTHERNWOOD TEA SPRING AND SUMMER

The great 18th century herbalist, Sir John Hill, advised southernwood made into a paste, and 'the bignesse of a nutmeg' taken as tea three times a day. He wrote 'it is pleasing, and one thing in it is particular, it is a composer and always disposes persons to sleep'. I have wondered if being disposed to sleep three times a day is a good thing or not, but southernwood tea makes a pleasant bed-time drink and, like most herbal teas, is digestible and soothing.

100 g/1¼ cups/4 oz southernwood tips
150 g/¾ cup/6 oz sugar

Pick the feathery new growth at the top of the plant, wash and shake dry. Chop finely with a sharp knife and spoon it into a bowl or mortar. Add the sugar and pound together with a wooden spoon or pestle until you have a wet paste. Store in a screw-topped jar in the fridge. To make the tea, put a good teaspoonful into a small jug, and pour over 250 ml/1 cup/½ pint boiling water, cover and infuse for 5 minutes, then strain into a cup and drink hot at bed-time.

SOUTHERNWOOD – *ARTEMISIA ABROTANUM*

SOUTHERNWOOD, TO REPEL MOTHS SPRING AND SUMMER

The strongly aromatic smell of southernwood keeps moths away from woollens. It can be picked and dried from late spring and throughout the summer.

Cut stems of the green herb 20-25 cm/8-10 ins long and tie in bundles of four or five stems, hang them upside down from the slats and pipes in an airing cupboard. After about a week the herb will be dry and you can lay the whole sprays between sheets of tissue paper with your winter woollies.

SMOOTH SOW-THISTLE
Sonchus oleraceus

PRICKLY SOW-THISTLE *Sonchus asper*

Sow-thistles are found throughout Britain, Europe, Scandinavia, and America, and are widespread and abundant weeds of waysides, waste places and cultivated ground. Where they grow among stones, or from walls, the plants may be only a few inches/centimetres high, but in deeper soil they will reach at least 1 metre/3 ft. The smooth sow-thistle is greyish green, hairless and with long, lobed, arrow-shaped leaves that have wavy edges and clasp the stem loosely; the stems are hollow and contain a milky juice. The flowers, which appear in the summer, grow in loose clusters at the top of the stem and are like small, elongated, very pale yellow dandelion flowers and, like dandelions, a fluffy clock forms as the small, dark brown seeds ripen.

The prickly sow-thistle is similar in every way, except that the leaves have small prickles, and instead of the sharp arrow-shaped points where the smooth sow-thistle leaves clasp the stem, they have rounded lobes and clasp the stem more tightly, and are crisper and more distinctly wavy-edged. In both varieties the flowers, flowering season and fluffy seed-heads are the same. Sow-thistle is also known as Hare's Thistle, or Hare's Lettuce and, in fact, hares and rabbits are very fond of it, so it is a useful source of green food for children to collect when they go foraging for their pets.

Sow-thistles were among the plants listed by John Josselyn in *New England's Rarities Discovered*, 1672, that had sprung up 'since the English planted and kept cattle in New England', and they are now common weeds throughout the United States. They have been eaten as a vegetable since ancient times and were renowned for their strengthening properties. Pliny wrote that Theseus was given sow-thistles to eat before he captured the Marathonian bull, and they have been eaten raw in salads and cooked in soup and as vegetables on the Continent for centuries. Andrew Borde, physician to Henry VIII, wrote of a remedy for 'a passion of the liver', first cautioning 'purge coler, and use easy purgaciouns, and beware of every thynge that doth hurt the liver, as hote wines and spices and aqua vite, and use colde thynges as saunders, southystel (sow-thistle), endive, dandelyon, cicory and liverwort'. William Coles also recommended for the heat and itchings of the, 'Hemorrhoides or Piles . . . By applying Cloathes or Spunges wetted

PRICKLY SOW-THISTLE – *SONCHUS ASPER*

therein, it is likewise wonderfully good for women to wash their faces, to clear the skin, and give a lustre thereunto . . . The milk that is taken from the stalks when they are broken is beneficial to those that are short winded, and have a wheesing withal . . . and faith that the eating thereof helpeth a stinking breath. The Juyce thereof to the quantity of three spoonfuls taken in Wine warmed, and some Oyl put thereunto causeth Women in Travel of Child, to have so easie and speedy delivery, that they may be easy to walk presently after . . . When Sowes have Piggs, they do most greedily desire it, because they know by a certain natural instinct, wherewith most Brutes are indued, that it doth very much increase their milk; and for that Reason, I conceive it is called by the name of Sow-Thistle.'

A weed that was held in such esteem is surely worthy of our attention.

SOW-THISTLE SOUP SUMMER

Sow-thistle makes as good a soup as any garden vegetable, and as the leaves are quite large and the plant grows abundantly, it doesn't take long to pick and prepare.

SERVES 4
1 colander sow-thistle leaves
1 small onion
25 g/2 tablespoons/1 oz butter
20 g/1½ tablespoons/¾ oz flour
500 ml/2½ cups/1 pint chicken stock
salt and pepper
1 tablespoon cream—optional

Pick out the coarse mid-rib from the leaves, wash them thoroughly, and drop them into 2.5 cm/1 inch of boiling salted water. Cook in a covered pan for 5 minutes, then drain and reserve the cooking liquid.

Peel and slice the onion, and heat the butter in a saucepan, sauté the onion lightly until just beginning to soften, and then stir in the flour. Add the chicken stock gradually and keep stirring, finally add ¼ litre/1¼ cups/½ pint of the liquid that the sow-thistle cooked in, and the sow-thistle leaves. Season with pepper, and a little salt if needed, and simmer for 10 minutes.

Liquidise the soup, re-heat gently, and just before serving stir in the cream.

SMOOTH, OR PRICKLY, SOW-THISTLE AS A VEGETABLE SUMMER

Sow-thistle leaves taste extra good in this easy recipe. Pick the leaves when young and from the tops of the plants.

1 colander full sow-thistle leaves
2 tablespoons olive oil
2 tablespoons butter
1 clove garlic, peeled and crushed
1 teaspoon ground coriander
salt and freshly milled black pepper
2 tablespoons crème fraîche

Wash the sow-thistle leaves and drain. Pick away the coarse mid-rib.

Heat the oil and butter in a saucepan, add the crushed garlic and coriander. Stir together and fry gently for a minute or two then tip in the wet sow-thistle leaves and season lightly. Cover the pan and cook over a medium heat until the leaves are tender. Chop the leaves in the pan with a wooden spoon until any excess liquid has evaporated. Stir in the crème fraîche, check the seasoning, and serve straight from the pan.

STINGING NETTLE

Urtica dioica

Stinging nettles grow abundantly in far too many places; they flourish throughout Britain, Europe and most of Asia, and in North America, Australia, South Africa and Japan. They will grow in river valleys and on mountainsides, and almost every farmyard, hedgerow, roadside, wood, churchyard, ruined building and patch of waste ground has its clumps of stinging nettles. But, with the spread of concrete and tarmac, one should be grateful for the flourishing greenery of even this spiteful weed. Nettles are normally 60 cm-1¼ metres/2-4 ft high, but in damp woods they may grow as tall as a man. The plant has square, fibrous stems and long, sharply-toothed, heart-shaped leaves; both stems and leaves are covered with coarse, stinging hairs, yet the fen district produces freak varieties that don't sting. In summer nettles have bunches of small green catkins, with male and female flowers on separate plants. Several butterflies, the Red Admiral, Peacock, Small Tortoiseshell and Comma, all choose nettles as the food plant for their caterpillars on which to lay their eggs; the Red Admiral caterpillars make a shelter for themselves by drawing the two edges of a leaf together with silk.

In Hans Andersen's story *The Wild Swans*, the princess had to weave coats of mail for the eleven swans from tough nettle fibres. Since early times the people of Eastern Europe believed in the magic power of nettles as protection against thunder and witches and demons of all kinds. In the Balkans, nettles were applied as a local anaesthetic in cottage surgery, and in various places country people still employ the masochistic remedy for rheumatism of urtication, in which a painful joint is flogged with nettles: seemingly, if worse pain is inflicted, the previous one seems trivial.

The early herbals are full of nettle remedies, and even Thornton's 19th century *Family Herbal* gives nettle prescriptions; a broth for scurvy, a daily dose of four ounces of nettle juice for cancers, the nostrils to be plugged with lint dipped in the juice for nose bleeds, and paralysed limbs to be stung with the herb 'to regain their vigor'. Thornton advanced a surprising claim for nettle seeds which 'produce a fine oil, and taken inwardly in moderate quantity excite the system, especially *les plaisirs de l' amour*, and are very forcing', so much so, apparently, that he warned they 'should be cautiously employed'. This belief in the aphrodisiac properties of nettle seeds goes back to the 16th century and maybe earlier, for Andrew Borde wrote 'yf any maried man the whych would have this matter or desyre and can not thorowe imbecyllyte use the act of matrimony . . . in the mornynge use to eat II or III new layd eggs rosted, and put into them the pouder of the sedes of nettles with sugar'. He continued 'but nowe a dayes fewe hath this impediment, but hath erection of the yerde to synne. A remedy for that is to leape into a great vessell of colde water or to put nettles in the cod pece about the yerde and stones'. A suggestion that would hardly have endeared him to Henry VIII, whose physician he was!

William Coles gave thirty or forty ailments of extreme diversity that should be treated with nettles. He advanced a bizarre suggestion that if a nettle 'be put into the Urine of a sick body, if it be fresh and green after it hath lyen four and twenty hours therein, the party shall recover of that sicknesse, but if it do not abide green, it signifieth death or danger'. What an unnerving experiment to make, with no possibility of a compromise. No compromise either in his test for 'one that is suspected to have lost her maidenhead'. The juice of nettle roots mixed with ale or beer was given to the suspect to drink, 'if it remain with her she is a maid, otherwise not'. Coles did not only confine his experiments to the sexual conduct of people, 'it is said also that if the herb be rubbed on the privities of female beasts that will not suffer the males to cover them; it will cause them the more willingly to suffer them to do it'. After such treatment, one would expect the poor beasts to be unaware of any other creature's attentions. Hens got off lightly, they were given 'some dry Nettles broken small with their meat in Winter', to make them lay eggs all the winter 'more plentifully'.

The British chemical industry still uses nettles with grass and lucerne in the manufacture of technical chlorophylls, obtained by extraction with alcohol, and used to colour fats, oils, soaps and foodstuffs. The extraction is also used externally for wounds and ulcers, and Martindale's *Pharmocopaeia* states 'although there is no clear evidence that this product accelerates healing, it has a deodorant action on foul smelling wounds, and when kept in constant contact tends to give a healthy granulating appearance'. It all sounds rather prosaic after the dramatic claims made by the early physicians.

STCHI, OR GREEN BORTSCH EARLY SPRING

This recipe is adapted from Marie Alexandre Markevitch's *The Epicure in Imperial Russia* and it must be one of the simplest and nicest possible ways of cooking nettles.

SERVES 4

1 rounded colander of young nettle tops
1 medium onion
15 g/1 tablespoon/½ oz butter
¾ litre/3¾ cups/1½ pints light stock
salt and pepper
2-3 tablespoons cream

Pick the nettles in rubber gloves, pick off any coarse stalks and wash the nettles, still in rubber gloves. Then tip them into a large saucepan containing a small amount of boiling salted water, and cook for 10 minutes. After this the nettles will no longer sting. Drain through a colander.

Meanwhile, finely slice the onion, melt the butter in a saucepan and sauté the onion in the butter until it begins to soften, then add the stock and simmer for 10 minutes. Liquidise the contents of the pan, re-heat the soup carefully, and season with salt and pepper. Stir in the cream just before serving.

CREAM OF NETTLE SOUP SPRING

You can use the tops of rather older nettles for this soup, picking them in April or May, but never use nettles for food after the beginning of June, as they are then too tough and fibrous.

SERVES 4

250 g/8 oz nettle tops
15 g/1 tablespoon/½ oz butter
1 shallot or ½ small onion
15 g/1 tablespoon/½ oz flour
450 ml/scant 2 cups/¾ pint stock, or nettle water
salt and pepper
125 ml/⅔ cup/generous ¼ pint milk
nutmeg
squeeze of lemon juice
1 tablespoon cream
1 hard-boiled egg for garnish, optional

Pick any coarse stalks from the nettles and wash them thoroughly. Cook the nettles in a pan of boiling salted water for 20 minutes.

Meanwhile, melt the butter in a pan, finely chop the shallot, or onion, and sauté gently in butter until beginning to soften. Stir in the flour, then add the stock, or nettle water, stirring all the while, boil up for a few minutes and stir until smoothly thickened. Season with salt and pepper, add the drained nettles to the pan of soup, and cook together gently for 10 minutes. Liquidise the soup, then return to the pan. Heat the milk and stir it into the soup. Finally, add a good grating of nutmeg, a squeeze of lemon juice, and the cream just before serving.

♂

♀

STINGING NETTLE – *URTICA DIOICA*

NETTLE AND OATMEAL STUFFING FOR CHICKEN EARLY SPRING

This is a rather delicious and unusual stuffing for roast chicken. The oatmeal goes particularly well with the nettles. You may vary the dried herbs, or use fresh chopped parsley instead.

SUFFICIENT STUFFING FOR A CHICKEN OF 2 KILOS (4¹/₂–5 LBS)

¹/₂ colander nettle tops
3 rashers (U.S. slices) bacon
125 g/1 cup/4 oz oatmeal
1 level teaspoon dried marjoram
1 level teaspoon dried tarragon
salt and pepper
1 large clove garlic
50 g/4 tablespoons/2 oz butter

Pick any coarse stalks from the nettles and wash them thoroughly. Drain the nettles and chop them finely with a sharp knife. Remove the rind and cut the bacon into small squares, then fry gently until starting to brown. Put the chopped nettles, fried bacon and any bacon fat from the pan into a large bowl, add the oatmeal, the dried herbs, a good pinch of salt and lots of freshly milled black pepper. Crush the garlic with a little salt and stir into the other ingredients with a fork, mix all together very thoroughly. Melt the butter in a small saucepan and stir this into the mixture.

Cram the mixture fairly tightly into the chicken, as the nettles will shrink during cooking, secure the tail skin with a skewer or cocktail stick, and roast as usual.

SPICED NETTLES WITH OATMEAL EARLY SPRING

Another recipe using nettles with bacon and oatmeal, which tends to be a harmonious combination. This time the dish is spicy with nutmeg, ginger and a dash of cayenne. Use the nutmeg generously, unless it is a flavour you actively dislike, for it greatly enhances the taste of nettles. Even if you're not fond of nutmeg, you will not taste it if grated sparingly, and the nettles will be much improved in flavour.

SERVES 4

1 colander nettle tops
butter—see recipe
1 small onion
6 rashers (U.S. slices) bacon
50 g/¹/₂ cup/2 oz oatmeal
salt

freshly milled black pepper
2 rounded teaspoons grated fresh ginger
small pinch cayenne pepper
grated nutmeg—see recipe

Pick any coarse stalks from the nettles and wash them thoroughly. Have ready a large pan with ¹/₄ litre/1¹/₄ cups/¹/₂ pint boiling salted water, cook the nettles in this for 10 minutes. Drain the nettles, but save the green cooking water.

Put the nettle water into a saucepan, bring to the boil and sprinkle in the oatmeal, add a good pinch of salt, and simmer for 15 minutes, stirring frequently, until the oatmeal is cooked.

Meanwhile melt the butter in a frying pan, peel and slice the onions into rings and fry in butter until golden brown, lift out the onion and fry the bacon in the remaining fat until crisp.

Chop the cooked nettles and stir them into the pan of oatmeal. Add a good grinding of black pepper and stir in the ginger and cayenne. Grate lots of nutmeg over the top and then add any fat from the pan of bacon. Stir over the nettle and oatmeal mixture with a wooden spoon to mingle the seasonings, then turn into a warm dish and top with fried bacon and onion rings.

NETTLE PUDDING EARLY SPRING

There are several versions of an old recipe for nettle pudding with cabbage or Brussels sprouts, which is boiled in a muslin bag. It is much nicer without cabbage or sprouts, as both these vegetables are ruined by long cooking, and it is better cooked in a bowl than in a cloth or muslin bag, which tends to make the pudding soggy. Served with chicken, meat or sausages, it is a tasty alternative to potatoes and a green vegetable.

SERVES 4

1 heaped colander young nettle tops
100 g/³/₄ cup/4 oz rice (uncooked)
3 medium leeks, or 2 large onions
butter
1 level teaspoon dried marjoram
salt and freshly milled black pepper

Pick any coarse stalks from the nettles and wash them thoroughly, drain through a colander.

Cook the rice in boiling salted water for 5 minutes, tip into a large strainer and wash under a running tap until the water runs clear, to remove surplus starch. Leave the rice to drain. Finely slice the leeks or onions. Melt a knob of butter in a large pan; tip in the nettles, leeks or onions, sprinkle in the dried herbs and season with salt and pepper. Sweat the vegetables over a low heat for 5 minutes.

Generously grease a pudding bowl with butter and put a layer of vegetables in the bottom, then a layer of rice, another layer of vegetables, a layer of the remaining rice and a top layer of the remaining vegetables. Dot with butter and cover the bowl with buttered greaseproof paper, pleated down the middle, and a pudding cloth or double thickness of muslin. Tie down securely with string, and put the pudding to boil in a large saucepan with enough water to come half way up the bowl. Boil briskly for 1 hour. Serve with melted butter.

Another version of this pudding can be made with suet and breadcrumbs instead of rice.

1 heaped colander of young nettle tops
50 g/4 tablespoons/2 oz shredded suet
100 g/2 cups/4 oz fresh breadcrumbs
water—see recipe
2 large onions
butter
1 level teaspoon dried herbs, thyme or marjoram
salt and pepper

Prepare the nettles as in the previous recipe, and likewise prepare and fry the onions. Mix the suet and breadcrumbs together in a bowl with a pinch of salt, and enough water to give a medium dropping consistency, then layer this mixture with the nettles and onions, and cover and tie down the pudding exactly the same as before. Boil for 2 hours, instead of only 1 hour.

BAKED NETTLES AND POTATOES EARLY SPRING

Spicy layers of nettle and onion are baked with sliced potatoes in the oven, to serve with any poultry, meat or fish. You could add some lightly fried, chopped bacon to make a light lunch or supper dish on its own.

SERVES 4
1 colander young nettle tops
50 g/4 tablespoons/2 oz butter
1 large onion
5 medium-sized potatoes
salt and pepper
1 teaspoon grated nutmeg
1 teaspoon grated fresh ginger
milk—see method

Pick any coarse stalks from the nettles and wash them thoroughly. Melt the butter in a saucepan, slice the onion and drain the nettles. Add the onion and nettles to the pan, cover with a lid and sweat gently in the butter for 10 minutes.

Peel the potatoes and slice them into thin rounds. Generously butter a pie dish and put in a layer of potato, season with salt and pepper. Add a layer of nettles and onion from the pan, with half the nutmeg and ginger. Add another layer of potato seasoned with salt and pepper and then a layer of the remaining nettles and onion, and the remaining nutmeg and ginger. Top with a layer of the remaining potato slices, pour in about a cupful of milk to come half way up the dish, dot with plenty of butter and bake in a moderate oven (350°F, 180°C or Gas 4) for 1 hour, until the potatoes are brown and crisp on top.

NETTLES AS A VEGETABLE

Nettles may be picked and prepared as above, and cooked in a small amount of boiling, salted water for ten minutes. Drain well, and add a little chopped onion previously sautéed in butter, or a few spoonfuls of buttery white sauce or some crème fraîche.

TO DRY NETTLES SPRING AND EARLY SUMMER

Cut whole stems of the plant, tie into bunches of four or five stems and hang them up in an airy room for about seven to ten days until dry and crisp. Strip off the leaves and put them through a parsley mill, spoon into screw-top jars and store away from the light.

DRIED NETTLE TEA

Dried nettles make a dark green beverage that tastes very tea-like.

2 teaspoons dried nettle leaves
250 ml/1 cup/1/2 pint boiling water

Put the dried nettles into a small jug, pour on boiling water, cover and infuse for 5 minutes, strain into a cup and drink hot.

NETTLE WINE SPRING

Nettle wine is much better than it sounds! This recipe makes a medium sweet white wine, which should be well chilled before serving.

activated yeast (p. 225)
2¹/₂ litres/4¹/₂ U.S. quarts/4 pints young nettle tops
5 litres/9 U.S. quarts/1 gallon water
2 lemons
1 small piece root ginger, peeled
1¹/₂ kilos/7 cups/3¹/₂ lbs sugar

Wash the nettles and put them in a large saucepan with 2¹/₂ litres/9 U.S. pints/¹/₂ gallon water, the thinly pared rind (no pith) of the lemons and root ginger, bruised with a rolling pin. Bring to the boil and simmer for 45 minutes. Put the sugar in the plastic bucket and strain over the hot liquid from the pan, stir to dissolve the sugar, then add the remaining 2¹/₂ litres/9 U.S. pints/¹/₂ gallon water, cold, and the strained juice of the lemons. Cover the bucket with a clean cloth and leave until cool (about 70°F, 20°C) then stir in the activated yeast. Cover the bucket with its lid and leave in a warm place for four days. Stir, and then pour the liquid into the fermentation jar and follow the method given on page 254.

NETTLE RINSE AND HAIR TONIC SPRING

Use as a final rinse after shampooing your hair, and reserve a small quantity to rub into the scalp and comb through the hair every other day. After a week or two, your hair will acquire an extra shine of health.

1 bunch stinging nettles
water—see recipe

Pick a big handful-sized bunch of nettles, wash thoroughly and put the whole bunch into a saucepan with enough cold water to cover. Bring to the boil, cover the pan and simmer for 15 minutes. Strain into a large jug and cool a little, then pour the infusion into bottles with corks or screw-on caps.

WILD STRAWBERRY

Fragaria vesca

The little wild strawberry grows in dry, grassy places, on banks, and in open woods, and is found throughout Britain, Europe and Scandinavia, often on limey soils. The plant spreads rapidly from its rooting runners; the leaves are toothed and trefoil-shaped, with distinct veining, the undersides silky, and paler than the shiny green upper surfaces. The white five-petalled flowers have a cluster of yellow stamens and when ripe the scarlet berries are studded with dry, brown seeds. The flowers stand erect on their stems, the berries droop, their sepals curled back. The wild strawberry is altogether a ravishingly pretty little plant, with leaves, flowers and fruit neatly arranged together; and it always reminds me of the early Florentine paintings of groups outdoors, seated or strolling in the 'flowery meads' which were the precursors of our lawns and, in medieval paintings, always studded with fruiting and flowering wild strawberries, as well as other low-growing spring and summer flowers. In fact *Fragaria vesca* and the French *F. moschata* with a slightly larger fruit, were the only strawberries known in Europe until after the 17th century, when the ancestors of our large garden strawberries were introduced from America. Gardeners in Europe had tried to develop strains with the largest possible fruit from wild plants, 'big Berries as Berries of the Bramble in the hedge' were described, but a strawberry as big as a blackberry would still fall far short of our large garden strawberries derived from *Fragaria*

WILD STRAWBERRY – *FRAGARIA VESCA*

virginiana and *F. chiloensis* of the New World. The former grows wild in fields, open woods and on slopes from Labrador to Newfoundland, and from Alberta southwards to Georgia, Alabama and Oklahoma. The little European wood strawberry, *F. vesca*, is also found in rocky woods and open places from Newfoundland to Alberta, and southwards to Virginia, Indiana, Missouri, Nebraska and New Mexico.

Strawberries have been used cosmetically for removing stains from teeth and to soothe and whiten a sunburnt skin; and the leaves and fruit were used medicinally in fevers and dysentery. Linnaeus believed that the berries were a cure for gout, while Polish peasants treated erysipelas with wild strawberries.

Sir John Hill advised an infusion of fresh wild strawberry leaves as a gargle and wash for sore throat and mouth; and in *Les Plantes Médicinales*, Dr. Losch described the leaves as mildly laxative, curing gout and gravel in some, but causing indigestion in others. He recommended a *tisane* of the leaves as a blood purifier and pick-me-up for convalescents, and gave some delicious ways in which *fraises des bois* were eaten in France; with sugar, with wine, with cream, orange juice, champagne or vinegar.

If you are looking for wild strawberry leaves to pick before the berries appear, do not be confused by the Barren Strawberry, *Potentilla sterilis*, (which has similar flowers and leaves, but quite dissimilar hard, dry fruits), especially as the two plants can be found growing together. The leaves of the Barren Strawberry are less shiny and less distinctly veined than those of the wild strawberry, and the flowers of the former have gaps between the petals which are slightly notched at the tip, making the petals heart-shaped, whereas the petals of the wild strawberry are gently, though not sharply, pointed. The fresh leaves of wild strawberry are good in salads.

WILD STRAWBERRIES WITH CREAM CHEESE SUMMER

I can still remember the thrill of my first introduction to this dish in Paris before the war. As a schoolgirl I thought nothing in the world was as good as English strawberries and cream, until I tasted wild strawberries served this way.

French *fraises des bois* are slightly larger than our British wild strawberries, but the flavour is the same—ours just take longer to pick. It is important to use full-cream cream cheese, untreated and fresh, no processed or 'cottage' cheese is any good at all.

100 g/3/4 cup/4 oz wild strawberries, per person
75 g/scant/1/2 cup/3 oz fresh cream cheese, per person
1-2 tablespoons caster sugar, per person

Put the cream cheese into a bowl, add the sugar and beat together with a fork. Serve with each helping of strawberries.

WILD STRAWBERRY LEAF TISANE
SPRING AND EARLY SUMMER

Wild strawberry leaves make a pale yellow tisane which is refreshing and thirst quenching. The taste is delicate and faintly herbal, and needs no sweetening, but is enhanced by a squeeze of lemon juice.

1 handful of young leaves
250ml/1 1/4 cups/1/2 pint boiling water
lemon juice

If you have to wash the leaves, pat them dry with a clean cloth.

Put the leaves on a wooden board and bruise them with a rolling pin. Drop the leaves into a jug and pour on the boiling water. Cover, and leave to infuse for 6 minutes. Strain into cups and serve with the lemon juice, or a slice of lemon in each cup.

Dried strawberry leaves do not make a good tea. Their flavour is too delicate to survive the process.

TANSY

Tanacetum vulgare

ansy grows throughout Britain, Europe and Scandinavia, except in the more mountainous districts, and is found on river banks, grassy verges and in many waste places. It was introduced into America by the early settlers and now grows freely throughout most of the United States.

Tansy grows 60 cm-1 metre/2-3 ft tall with stiff stems, and dark green, fern-like pinnate leaves consisting of numerous narrow, deeply-toothed leaflets. The flowers have no ray florets, and grow in terminal clusters of small, hard, flat-topped 'buttons'. Each little button-like flower has a dimple in the centre and is bright egg-yellow. The flowers appear throughout the summer, and stay fresh-looking for a long time. William Coles wrote that the Greek name signified that, 'it is immortall because the yellow Flowers gathered in due time, will continue very lively a long while'. This endearing quality makes tansy flowers ideal to stand in a jug on the kitchen table or window sill, especially as the strongly aromatic, spicy scent keeps flies away. In the old days tansy was used as a strewing herb, its pungency and fly-repelling properties making it doubly valuable.

Most of the early herbalists set great store by tansy as a medicine for getting rid of worms, and the cakes, known as 'tansies' and traditionally eaten at Easter, were bound up with this idea, since there seems to have been a widely-held belief that fish, which was eaten during Lent, somehow encouraged worms in people. The tansy, which went into the cakes, was intended more as a spring medicine than Easter flavouring, although some writers connect Easter with tansy because it was said to be one of the bitter herbs of Passover.

William Coles was quite disparaging about his contemporaries who 'are so squeamish, that they put little or none of it into them, (the cakes) having altogether forgotten the reason of their Originall, which was to purge away from the Stomach and Guts the Phlegme engendered by eating of Fish in the Lent Season, which Lent was kept stricter than it now is, whereof Wormes are soon bred in them that are thereunto disposed.' I must confess to using tansy sparingly myself, for a little is a good flavouring, but too much can make 'a nauseous dish', as one 19th century writer described a tansy pudding.

Many of the early physicians used tansy as a remedy for gout, and the Scottish highlanders until recently used the dried flowers and seeds for treating gout; they also used to cash in on tansy's pungent scent and mix it with their winter stocks of corn to keep the mice away. In Ireland tansy was used to flavour locally made sausages known as drisheens, and in Sussex there was an old superstition that tansy leaves worn inside the shoes would prevent an attack of the ague. The Finns used tansy as a green dye, the Danes as a substitute flavouring for nutmeg and cinnamon, but in Italy it was considered a deadly insult to be presented with a piece of tansy. William Coles mentioned that tansy 'applyed to the lower part of the Belly . . . is very profitable for such Women as are apt to miscarry in Child-bearing' and Culpeper also prescribed tansy for 'those Women that desire Children . . . 'tis their best Companion' adding significantly, 'their Husband excepted'.

Modern herbalists recommend an infusion of tansy as a tonic for a weak heart and to stimulate the kidneys, the infusion may also be used externally for sprains and swellings and as a lotion for varicose veins.

Tansy is easily propagated by dividing a root and planting out the bits in the autumn. It grows in almost any soil, but should be kept well watered until it has established itself. The creeping roots will soon spread and can be a nuisance if left unchecked. Parkinson, Gerard and Coles noted that 'the roote creepeth underground and shooteth up againe in divers places' and even Eleanor Sinclair Rhode, a crusader for old-fashioned plants and herbs, warns that 'tansy is a rampant grower and should not be put near any choice plants, for the roots soon fill solidly several square feet of ground'. But because it is an attractive plant, as well as an interesting one, and was once to be found in every cottage garden, although it is now seldom cultivated, I refuse to confine its natural vigour, and don't begrudge the space demanded by a flourishing patch of tansy.

TANSY OMELETTE SPRING AND SUMMER

A small amount of tansy does wonders for an omelette, and the same amount—half a tablespoon of chopped tansy leaves to 6 eggs—is equally nice with scrambled eggs.

SERVES 2
6 eggs
pinch salt
freshly milled black pepper
1/2 tablespoon chopped tansy leaves
1 tablespoon chopped parsley
butter, for frying

Break the eggs into a bowl, add the salt and pepper and mix lightly with a fork. Strip the tansy leaves from the mid-rib, remove the parsley stalks, then chop both herbs finely and stir them into the eggs. Heat a small nut of butter in an omelette pan or small frying pan, when very hot pour in the egg mixture and stir round with a fork, keeping the mixture moving so that the uncooked top runs to the hot bottom of the pan. Do not overcook—the top of the omelette should look like runny scrambled eggs. Leave on the heat for a few seconds to set the bottom, then fold the omelette in half with a palette knife and slide on to a well-heated serving dish.

SOUSED MACKEREL WITH TANSY SPRING AND SUMMER

Another way of flavouring fish with tansy is to souse them with a whole leaf inside each, which gives a subtle spicy tang.

SERVES 4
4 mackerel
4 whole tansy leaves

150 ml/2/3 cup/1/4 pint cider vinegar
150 ml/2/3 cup/1/4 pint water
8 black peppercorns
a good grinding of nutmeg
salt
a few thinly cut onion rings

Gut and split the mackerel and cut off the heads and tails. Wash the fish thoroughly and lay a tansy leaf inside each. Pack the mackerel neatly into a deep ovenproof dish, pour over the vinegar and water, add the peppercorns and nutmeg and a good pinch of salt, and arrange the onion rings over the fish.

Cook in a very moderate oven (325°F/170°C/Gas 3) for 1 hour. Leave the fish to get cold, and remove the tansy leaves before serving with plenty of fresh brown bread and butter.

MACKEREL, OR HERRING, WITH TANSY STUFFING SPRING AND SUMMER

Tansy has a very pungent taste but, used sparingly, it does give an interesting spicy flavour to several dishes, particularly to fish. There is a 16th century recipe for 'a tansy in Lent' using fish roe, and Izaak Walton described 'a minnow tansy'. Neither sounds particularly inspiring, but the trace of tansy flavour in this stuffing is unusual and pleasant.

SERVES 4
4 mackerel, or large herrings
4-5 tablespoons medium oatmeal
grated rind of 1 lemon
salt and freshly milled black pepper
2 teaspoons chopped tansy leaves
3 tablespoons boiling water
butter for frying

1 egg beaten
a little extra oatmeal

Gut the fish and remove their heads, then rinse them and dry with a paper kitchen towel. Wash the tansy leaves, pick out the mid-rib and chop the leaves finely. Put the oatmeal and lemon rind in a bowl with a pinch of salt, a good grinding of black pepper and the chopped tansy leaves. Stir to mix the ingredients, then add the boiling water, mix with a fork and form the stuffing into four sausage-shaped rolls. Press each roll into the cavity of the fish and secure the opening with a cocktail stick.

Heat the butter in a large frying pan, dip each side of each fish in the beaten egg and then in the oatmeal, and fry gently for about 5-6 minutes each side until cooked through. Lift on to a warm dish and remove the cocktail sticks before serving.

SAVOURY CHICKEN PANCAKES WITH TANSY SPRING AND SUMMER

Thyme and tansy make the filling for these pancakes very aromatic and special. They are a good supper dish and can be made in advance, then loosely wrapped in foil and reheated in a hot oven (400°F/200°C/Gas 6) for 15 minutes.

MAKES 12 PANCAKES
100 g/1 cup/4 oz plain flour
pinch salt
1 egg
250 ml/1 1/4 cups/1/2 pint milk
1 tablespoon vegetable oil
oil for frying or a piece of fat bacon

Sift the flour and salt into a bowl, tip the egg and half the milk into the centre and stir together with a wooden spoon, beat well until smooth, then gradually beat in the rest of the milk. Pour the batter into a jug and when you are ready to make the pancakes stir in the oil.

Pour a few drops of oil into the pancake pan or wipe round with the fat bacon. Heat until just smoking, turn down to a moderate heat and pour about two tablespoons of batter into the pan and swirl it evenly round to make a thin pancake, loosen all round the edges with the tip of a knife and turn over when the underside has browned—you can lift it to have a look—then cook the second side. The whole process should only take 2 or 3 minutes. Cook the rest of the pancakes the same and spread them flat on greaseproof paper to cool.

CHICKEN AND TANSY FILLING
300 g/1 1/2 cups/12 oz cooked chicken, cut into chunks
50 g/1/4 cup/2 oz butter
50 g/1/2 cup/2 oz plain flour
450 ml/2 cups/3/4 pint chicken stock
salt and pepper
1 rounded teaspoon chopped tansy leaves
1 rounded teaspoon chopped
fresh thyme

Put the chicken meat in a bowl and prepare the sauce. Melt the butter in a saucepan and shake in the flour, stir to blend then add a little stock, mix smoothly and add the rest of the stock gradually, bring to the boil, beating well all the time, season with salt and pepper and stir in the chopped tansy and thyme. Cook very gently for 2-3 minutes then pour some of the hot sauce on to chicken pieces until you have a moist mixture, reserve the rest of the sauce.

Well butter an ovenproof dish that will take 12 pancakes neatly. Fill the pancakes with the chicken mixture, roll up and arrange them in the buttered dish. If the reserved sauce is too thick to pour, thin it down with a little milk and pour it evenly over the dish of pancakes. Bake in a hot oven (400°F/200°C/Gas 6) for 10 minutes until the pancakes are nicely browned.

ROAST LAMB WITH TANSY SPRING AND SUMMER

Tansy leaves give a very excellent spicy flavour to roast lamb. Make small cuts in the meat with a sharp knife and insert the tansy leaves, as you would rosemary.

SERVES 8
1 shoulder of lamb—about 2 kilos (4-4 1/2 lbs)
6 medium-sized tansy leaves
freshly milled black pepper
2 tablespoons olive oil

Wash the tansy leaves and strip them from the mid-rib. Make small cuts in the meat and push a piece of tansy leaf in each cut until they are all used up. Grind plenty of black pepper over the lamb, and set it in a roasting tin with the olive oil. Cook for 1 1/2 hours in a hot oven (400°F/200°C/Gas 6) until the joint is brown and crisp on the outside.

COLD BELLY PORK WITH TANSY SAUCE

SPRING AND SUMMER

Choose the leanest piece of pork you can find, it varies quite a lot. The sauce has plenty of spicy green flavours which ideally suit the mild, but fat pork. It is also very good with a cold boiling fowl.

SERVES 4

750 g/1¹/₂ lbs unsalted belly pork
2 bay leaves
4 juniper berries, crushed
water
vinegar

Rinse the joint in cold water and place in a saucepan with the bay leaves and juniper berries, pour on equal quantities of water and vinegar so that the liquid just covers the pork. Bring slowly to the boil, skim, and then cover the pan and simmer for 1¹/₂ hours. Lift the pork from the pan, and when cool enough to handle, strip off the skin. Cool a little, then press between two plates with a heavy weight on top. When cold, serve the pork in thick slices with the following sauce.

TANSY SAUCE

2 egg yolks
250 ml/1 cup/¹/₂ pint chicken stock
50 g/¹/₄ cup/2 oz butter
1 teaspoon chopped tansy leaves
1 teaspoon chopped fresh tarragon
1 tablespoon chopped parsley
1 tablespoon cider vinegar
salt and pepper
1 rounded teaspoon powdered gelatine
1 tablespoon water

Lightly beat the egg yolks in a small bowl and stir in the cool chicken stock. Pour into a small pan and set over a low heat. Add the butter in small pieces—as soon as one melts, add another—and stir constantly while the mixture thickens.

Draw off the heat, stir in the chopped herbs and add the vinegar slowly. Return to the heat, season with salt and pepper and stir briskly until the sauce is nearly boiling. Soak the gelatine in a tablespoon of water for a few minutes and when spongy stir into the pan of hot sauce. Turn into a sauceboat and serve when cold, or cool. Do not refrigerate.

LAMB CHOPS WITH TANSY STUFFING

SPRING AND SUMMER

A good way of making lamb chops really filling and tasty is to fill them with a savoury stuffing of herbs, then wrap them in foil and cook them in the oven in their own juices.

SERVES 4

4 lamb chops
50 g/1 cup/2 oz fresh breadcrumbs
25 g/¹/₂ cup/1 oz shredded suet
1 teaspoon chopped tansy leaves
1 teaspoon chopped fresh thyme
2 tablespoons chopped fresh parsley
salt and freshly milled black pepper
2 tablespoons finely chopped onion
1 egg

Trim the chops and pull any skin away from the fat. Cut from the fatty side through the meat towards the bone, until each chop is almost halved horizontally. Put all the ingredients for the stuffing in a bowl, adding the egg last, stir thoroughly with a fork, then knead well to bind the mixture together. Divide the mixture into four equal portions and pack one portion into the middle of each chop.

Cut 4 pieces of foil 30 cm/12 ins square and butter lightly. Wrap each chop individually allowing plenty of space and pinch the edges of the foil together tightly. Arrange in a shallow roasting tin and cook in a moderately hot oven (375°F, 190°C or Gas 5) for 30 minutes. Unwrap the foil and serve the chops in their juices.

TANSY WITH CABBAGE SPRING AND SUMMER

The pungent flavour of tansy adds a spiciness, like caraway seeds, to cabbage. A white drum-head cabbage is best, but any firm variety will do.

750 g/1¹/₂ lbs firm cabbage
2 teaspoons finely chopped tansy leaves
2 tablespoons butter
salt and pepper

Shred the cabbage with a sharp knife and wash well. Cook the cabbage in a little lightly salted water until just tender, but still crisp. Drain thoroughly. Melt the butter in a saucepan, shake in the chopped tansy, add the cabbage and a little pepper and stir together to mix.

TANSY – *TANACETUM VULGARE*

TANSY MAYONNAISE SPRING AND SUMMER

Tansy adds zest to mayonnaise which is nice with fried or grilled fish, or spooned over halved hard-boiled eggs set on a bed of shredded lettuce.

250 ml/1¼ cups/½ pint mayonnaise
1 heaped tablespoon finely chopped parsley
1 level teaspoon finely chopped tansy leaves
1 level teaspoon sugar
2 teaspoons strained lemon juice

Put the mayonnaise in a bowl and stir in the parsley, tansy and sugar, when well mixed stir in the lemon juice. The sauce will keep in the refrigerator for several days.

TANSY PUDDING SPRING AND SUMMER

A recipe for Tansy Pudding in *The Good Housewife's Handmaid*, 1588, is simply delicious, but frankly owes little to the flavour of tansy and more to the other good ingredients! 'Jordan almonds, syrup of roses, the crumb of a French roll, some grated nutmeg, half a glass of brandy, two tablespoons of tansy juice, three ounces of fresh butter, and some slices of citron', and then to crown it, you added 'a pint and a half of boiling cream, the juice of a lemon and eight eggs beaten'. One must remember that without mechanical separators cream was thinner, and the eggs of those days were smaller eggs. Producing food for size and bulk was yet to come, with all the loss of flavour that it has brought.

Below is a substitute for the 16th century pudding, which is still very good without being wildly extravagant.

SERVES 4
50 g/½ cup/2 oz ground almonds
100 g/1 cup/4 oz self raising flour
a little grated nutmeg
1 tablespoon brandy, or sherry
½ tablespoon chopped citron peel, or mixed chopped peel
1 tablespoon rose petal syrup, see page 184 or ½ tablespoon
    rose water with ½ tablespoon sugar, or honey
1 rounded teaspoon finely chopped tansy leaves stripped from
    the mid-rib
35 g/¼ cup/1½ oz melted butter
450 ml/scant 2 cups/¾ pint milk
strained juice of ½ lemon
4 eggs

Mix together all the ingredients except the last three (milk, lemon juice and eggs) in a bowl. Boil the milk and pour onto the mixture, stirring together with a fork. When the mixture is blood-warm, add the lemon juice and the lightly whisked eggs. Pour into a well-buttered pie dish and bake for 45 minutes in a moderate oven (350°F/180°C/Gas 4) until well risen and lightly browned.

TANSY CAKE SPRING AND SUMMER

The old recipes for tansy cakes which I tried out proved to be rather nasty, but as the pungent spicy taste of tansy is not unlike caraway seed, I flavoured a Madeira mixture with chopped tansy leaves and it turned out to be delicious, rather like an old-fashioned seed cake.

150 g/1½ cups/6 oz plain flour
50 g/½ cup/2 oz self-raising flour
2 rounded teaspoons finely chopped tansy leaves
175 g/scant 1 cup/7 oz sugar, or melted honey
150 g/¾ cup/6 oz soft margarine
4 eggs

Follow exactly the method given for southernwood cake on page 223.

WILD THYME – *T. SERPYLLUM*

THYME

Thymus

GARDEN THYME *T. vulgaris* WILD THYME *T. serpyllum*

There are several sorts of cultivated thyme, with leaves of varying breadth and narrowness, some with variegated leaves, and all with deliciously subtle variations of flavour, such as lemon, orange, ginger and caraway. The common garden thyme grows wild throughout the Mediterranean, and is sometimes found growing wild in America, as a garden escape. It is a low, wiry plant, 10-20 cm/4-8 ins high, with many thin, twiggy branches and small, narrow, dark grayish-green leaves. The tiny mauve flowers grow in whorls at the tops of the stems throughout the summer and early autumn.

Wild thyme, *T. serpyllum*, has a wide distribution throughout the temperate zones of Europe and Asia, and grows as far north as Iceland, Greenland and Siberia. It was introduced into North America, where it has now become established, and grows wild in woods and fields from Quebec and Ontario to North Carolina and Indiana. In Britain, it is widespread and common in dry grass and heathland, and on dunes, but is uncommon in south-east England, except on the chalk downs where it is locally abundant. Wild thyme is a creeping, prostrate perennial. The tiny, oval leaves grow in opposite pairs on thin, wiry stems and the round terminal heads of pinkish-purple flowers are quite large and conspicuous for the size of the plant; they appear throughout the summer.

The dry, sunny hillsides of the Mediterranean are redolent with the scent of thyme, which Kipling described as, 'like the perfume of the dawn of Paradise'. The wild thyme of the Mediterranean, *T. vulgaris*, is the plant which gives the inimitable flavour to the honey of Mount Hymettus. The Romans burnt thyme to ward off 'venomous creatures'. It was carried in Judges' posies as a protection against infection, and in the Highlands, wild thyme tea was believed to prevent nightmares. Linnaeus claimed the tea would 'dispell the fumes of drunkenness' and the inevitable headache which followed, and William Coles claimed many cures for thyme. He described it as 'good for Women's diseases . . . to cure those that are in hard labour to be delivered, be the Child alive or dead' and for coughs and shortness of breath.

It is interesting to discover that thyme oil, distilled from the leaves and flowering tops, is a recognised anti-spasmodic which is used as an ingredient in medicines for whooping cough and bronchitis today. The dried leaves of thyme yield a volatile oil with a pleasant, aromatic odour and taste which is still used in cough linctuses. As recently as 1972 a successful experiment was carried out on a number of older children suffering from enuresis (incontinence). They were given a small dose of distilled thyme tea at bed-time, and 78% of the cases were cured. Thyme oil contains Thymol and Carvacrol, and is a recognised antiseptic and carminative. It is used with other oils as a rub for rheumatism, acting as a counter-irritant. The oil is used for scenting soap and other cosmetic preparations, and the dried herb in sachets and pot pourri.

Wild thyme, *T. serpyllum* may be used in cooking, but it is only mildly aromatic, and the cultivated thymes are too well known as flavourings for vegetables, stuffings, fish, game and poultry to require recipes in this book. You can hardly go wrong by adding a little thyme to any savoury dish.

WALL PENNYWORT
Umbilicus rupestris

NAVELWORT

Wall pennywort is common in south-west England, where it grows on nearly every wall and hedge bank and on rocks near the sea; but elsewhere in Europe it is rather uncommon, except in western France. The plant has circular fleshy leaves, with a dimple in the middle over the stalk, hence its Latin name and the country name of navelwort. One of the plant's names in America is also navelwort, where it is known, but not native to the United States. The small tubular flowers appear throughout the spring and summer, and are greenish, cream-coloured

WALL PENNYWORT – *UMBILICUS RUPESTRIS*

or tinged with red, they grow in spikes, sometimes with layers of tiny leaves between the rows of flowers, and the whole flowering stem looks like a little church steeple. The plants vary in size from tiny specimens 2.5-5 cm/1-2 ins high on dry walls or stony banks, to quite large plants of 30-46 cm/12-18 ins where the soil is damp and deeper.

In the 17th century Sir John Hill recommended the leaves of wall pennywort as 'cooling and good against pains', saying he had treated piles with the bruised leaves with great success, and stranguaries, gravel, and inflammations of the liver and spleen with doses of the juice.

Coles called the plant Kidney-wort, or Venus Navel-wort and said it was good for sore kidneys, dropsy, 'the wringing paines of the Bowells', for piles, gout, sciatica, 'pimples, rednesse and St. Anthonies fire', and many other disorders. He completed his chapter on wall pennywort saying: 'Those that have consecrated the Fore-head to modesty, the Eare to Memory, the Knee to mercy, have assigned the Navel to be the Seat of Luxury or Love; and therefore the Leafe hereof having the Signature of the Navel, is very prevalent in things belonging to love.'

WALL PENNYWORT IN SALADS AND SANDWICHES EARLY SPRING TO MID-SUMMER

The fleshy leaves are succulent in salads, just washed and eaten whole. They taste every bit as good as lettuce. Wall Pennywort makes good sandwiches chopped and mixed with a few snipped chives, or an equal amount of finely chopped sorrel.

WHITE DEAD-NETTLE
Lamium album

White dead-nettle is widespread and common throughout Britain, Europe and Scandinavia, and grows on banks and waste ground, beside roads and at the edge of woods. In North America it is found in similar places from Quebec to Minnesota and southwards to Virginia. The plant is a hairy, faintly aromatic perennial, 15-46 cm/6-18 ins high and is related not to nettles, but to mint. The leaves are toothed, roughly heart-shaped, and grow in pairs on opposite sides of the stout, square stem. The flowering season is unusually long, from spring until late into the autumn. The whorls of flowers grow at the base of the leaves and the buds, like round white knobs set in the five long, pointed teeth of the calyx, open into beautiful flowers with an arched hood over the lower lip, which is faintly streaked with green. The petals are delicately fringed with white hairs, and beneath the hood lie four black anthers arranged in a rectangle, which give the flower an air of chic and elegance. William Coles described them as 'open-gaping white flowers in husks . . . like to little gaping Hoods or helmets'.

The flower is designed so that only a large, long-tongued insect can reach the nectar at the bottom of the corolla tube: the stigma projects a little beyond the anthers, and when an insect such as a bumble bee alights on the lip, with pollen from the previous flower on its back, the first thing it touches is the stigma, which receives the pollen; the bee then presses further into the flower and the anthers under the hood deposit their pollen on to its back which, in turn, fertilises the next flower on which the bee alights. A small insect could crawl down the tube and take the nectar without touching the stigma or pollen bearing anthers, but the dead-nettle will have none of this plunder without its reward of fertilisation, and the flower has a barrier of hairs set above the nectar. Some insects cheat, and you may find dead-nettle flowers that have a hole bitten through the corolla tube, where a thwarted bandit has stolen the nectar.

WHITE DEAD-NETTLE AND SORREL OMELETTE SPRING, SUMMER AND AUTUMN

You can vary the proportions of dead-nettle leaves and sorrel; together or separately they make a good filling for an omelette. Young dead-nettle leaves are good in mixed salads.

Pick a large bunch of dead-nettles—they don't sting—and pull off the leaves. If you do this carefully, you will be left with leaves for your omelette and a bunch of unexpectedly rare-looking flowers. I once saw a flower arrangement of great charm in one of England's most beautiful stately homes, a porcelain bowl was massed with exotic, orchid-like flowers. I asked what they were, and was told white dead-nettles with the leaves removed! Since then I have used them as cut flowers every year, not only do the flowers look prettier without their leaves, but they last much longer in water.

SERVES 2

1 handful picked-over dead-nettle leaves
3 handfuls sorrel leaves
25 g/2 tablespoons/1 oz butter

FOR THE OMELETTE
1 nut butter
6 eggs
salt and pepper

Wash the dead-nettle and sorrel leaves thoroughly. Put them damp in a small saucepan, bring to the boil and cook for 5 minutes. Drain. Melt the butter in the saucepan, then tip in the cooked leaves and keep warm.

WHITE DEAD-NETTLE – *LAMIUM ALBUM*

Heat a small nut of butter in an omelette pan. Break the eggs into a basin, season with salt and pepper and mix lightly with a fork. When the butter in the pan is sizzling hot, tip in the eggs and keep stirring with the fork to let the uncooked mixture on the top run down to the hot bottom of the pan. Be careful not to overcook, and when the top is still like runny scrambled eggs, spread the cooked dead-nettle and sorrel leaves on one half of the omelette and, with a palette knife or fish slice, fold over the other half and slide on to a warm dish.

WHITE DEAD-NETTLE SHAMPOO FOR GREASY HAIR SPRING, SUMMER AND AUTUMN

White dead-nettle is advertised as a valuable ingredient for combating greasy hair in some commercial shampoos today. The fresh herb, boiled with soapwort root, makes a good shampoo for any type of hair, and used regularly will reduce greasiness, although obviously just one or two applications will have no effect. The shampoo leaves the hair very clean and sweet smelling.

1 large handful white dead-nettle, whole herb
25 g/1 oz soapwort root, dried—see soapwort p.219
500 ml/2½ cups/1 pint water

Prepare the soapwort root overnight before you want to wash your hair. Break up the roots and crush with a rolling pin, put them in a large jug, pour on the boiling water and leave to stand overnight. Put the root and its water into a saucepan, bring to the boil, add the bunch of dead-nettle leaves, flowers and stems, and simmer together for 20 minutes. Allow to cool, then strain the liquid into a jug and use all of it to shampoo your hair.

WILD CABBAGE
Brassica oleracea

This is one of several wild brassicas to be found growing on cliffs and waste ground near the sea, particularly in south-west England and western France, and also on the chalk cliffs of south-east England. Some plants are probably naturalised escapes from gardens, and although they are not common, they grow freely in some places. In America, *B. oleracea* is found as a weed on the Pacific coast, and in Texas. The plant is a good 60 cm/2 ft high with a stout woody stem, usually covered with old leaf-scars. The leaves are broad with wavy edges, like kale, and have the greyish undersides characteristic of many seaside plants. The yellow flowers are quite large for a brassica, and rather striking, growing in a loose spike with the buds enclosed in yellow sepals above the opened flowers. They make vivid splashes of colour along the cliffs from late spring throughout the summer.

TO COOK WILD CABBAGE LATE WINTER—SPRING

Wild cabbage is perennial and can be picked in moderation without damaging the plant. The leaf sprouts are ready for picking at the end of winter, just like a winter garden vegetable, and should be cooked like sprouting kale, or sprouting broccoli. The flavour is identical to the garden varieties.

WILD CABBAGE – *BRASSICA OLERACEA*

WOODRUFF

Galium odoratum

SWEET WOODRUFF

Woodruff is widespread and locally abundant in woods and on shady banks throughout Britain, Europe and Scandinavia. In America it is a cultivated ground cover and rock garden plant. Books on wild plants say that woodruff grows mainly in beech woods and on chalk and limestone, but although I have scoured many beech woods on the Sussex Downs, I have never found woodruff growing there. However, my daughter has it growing in acid soil beside the burn on their Scottish hillside, and my sister found large patches flourishing in mixed woodland beside a Cornish river, where the soil is damp and acid. Both situations are puzzlingly different to the calcareous soils mentioned in the field guides. Wherever you happen to find woodruff, pick it with care, the plant is perennial and spreads from a weak, creeping root stock which is easily damaged, if you pull it carelessly.

The leaves grow in whorls rather like the spokes of a wheel at spaced intervals up the weak, unbranched stem; the tiny, white, four-petalled flowers appear in spring and early summer, and grow in loose heads at the top of the stems. Like cleavers, woodruff is a member of the bed-straw family, but it is a neat little plant, 20-25 cm/8-10 ins high, and practically hairless, and never develops into the sprawling tangle that cleavers produces.

Woodruff owes its delicious scent to coumarin, a chemical ingredient whose fragrance becomes stronger when the plant is dried. Coumarin is sometimes used in the manufacture of perfumes for its peculiar ability to fix other scents, as well as for its fragrance. Dried woodruff was used in the old days to scent linen, as an ingredient of pot pourri, and even to stuff mattresses, a practice which shows how much more common woodruff was than it is now.

The leaves were used in the old days as a dressing for wounds, and decoctions of the plant were taken for stomach disorders. The old pharmacists also used woodruff to disguise unpleasant smelling medicines. Nicholas Culpeper said the plant was 'nourishing and restorative, good for weak consumptive people: it opens obstructions, of the liver and spleen, and is said to be a provocative to venery'.

Gerard describes the lovely old practice of hanging bunches of woodruff in houses; 'the flowers are of a very sweet smell as is the rest of the herb, which, being made up into garlands or bundles, and hanged up in houses in the heat of summer, doth very well attemper the air, cool and make fresh the place, to the delight and comfort of such as are therein'. He also said, 'It is reported to be put into wine, to make a man merry, and to be a good comfort to the heart and liver'.

Probably the best known use for woodruff, and one which is still in use today, is as the essential ingredient of Maibowle, the famous German winecup, which derives its unique bouquet from woodruff and for which you will find a recipe on the following page.

WOODRUFF TEA LATE SPRING, EARLY SUMMER

Woodruff transfers its lovely scent to any liquid in which it is infused. It makes a pale green herbal tea with a unique fragrance.

Put a small bunch of fresh woodruff complete with leaves, flowers and stem, into a jug and bruise lightly with a wooden spoon. Pour on 250ml/1 cup/1/2 pint of boiling water, cover and infuse for 8 minutes. Strain into warmed cups and drink without sweetening.

To make tea from dried woodruff, crumble 2 or 3 sprigs into a small jug. Pour on 250ml/1 cup/1/2 pint of boiling water, cover and infuse as before.

If you add a sprig of dried woodruff to a pot of ordinary tea, it gives it a most expensive flavour.

Another delicious tisane is made with equal quantities of young wild strawberry leaves and fresh woodruff, bruised and infused as above.

TO DRY WOODRUFF LATE SPRING, EARLY SUMMER

Hang a few stems of woodruff in the boiler room or from the slats or pipes in an airing cupboard until dry and crisp, then crumble and store in a screw-topped jar.

WOODRUFF SWEET BAGS

Only small amounts of dried woodruff are needed to fill little muslin bags, which are lovely to put with your undies or in the linen cupboard, as you would lavender bags.

MAIBOWLE, OR MAITRANK
German Punch, flavoured with woodruff LATE SPRING, EARLY SUMMER

This delectable wine cup comes from Germany where woodruff grows in woods beside the Rhine. The German name for woodruff is Waldmeister, or Master of the Woods.

The wine absorbs woodruff's marvellous scent, which is a mingling of vanilla and newly-mown hay; one could not wish for a more delicious summer drink, quite unique in flavour and appeal.

1 small bunch woodruff
1 bottle Moselle or Rhine wine
2 tablespoons sugar
125 ml/2/3 cup/1/4 pint water
1 orange

WOODRUFF – *GALIUM ODORATUM*

Pick any damaged or withered leaves from the woodruff, and put the whole bunch, including stems and flowers, into a punch bowl or tall glass jug. Pour over the wine. Gently heat the sugar and water in a small pan and stir until the sugar has dissolved, cool a little, then stir into the bowl of wine. Cover closely with a plate or sheet of foil and chill in the refrigerator for an hour, or longer. Before serving, peel the orange and slice the flesh thinly, add the orange slices to the punch, and if you wish, remove the woodruff, although your guests may like to see what gives such an intriguing flavour to the drink.

YARROW

Achillea millefolium

Yarrow is a common weed throughout Britain, Europe and Scandinavia, and grows in most grassy places, by roads and waysides, in meadows and in lawns. An almost identical species grows in fields and waste places throughout most of the United States. The whole plant is downy and aromatic, it is perennial, 15-45 cm/ 6-18 ins tall, with tough angular stems and long, dark green, feathery leaves made up of numerous tiny linear leaflets; fresh leaves spring up thickly after the plant has been cut down, and these are good to pick as a vegetable. The flowers grow in flat umbels that are sometimes lilac pink, but usually a dirty white, the flowering season is prolonged, from early summer until well on into late autumn.

The early herbalists treated wounds with yarrow, and the Latin name for the yarrow family, *Achillea*, comes from the legend that Achilles used the herb to staunch the blood of his soldiers wounded in battle. A few of yarrow's many country names suggest this: Soldier's Woundwort, Herbe Militaris, Bloodwort, Sanguinary and Staunchweed; there were strange and contradictory beliefs that yarrow could stop nose bleeds and also promote them, to relieve headaches. A decoction of yarrow was used as a remedy for piles, and the bitter astringency of the plant may have been genuinely effective. The physician, Haller, prescribed an infusion of yarrow leaves to be applied externally and taken internally for a patient who had fallen from a tree, which 'speedily succeeded in dissipating dreadful bruises arising from the fall'.

There is an amazing amount of folk lore and superstition connected with yarrow: in the 17th century a witch was tried for using it with her incantations, for yarrow was thought to be under the influence of Satan, and two more of its country names, Devil's Nettle and Devil's Plaything, suggest this. It was also made into snuff, and has Old Man's Pepper as another synonym. Among the superstitions was an attractive one that yarrow could conjure up visions of a future sweetheart: there are several old rhymes that had to be repeated for invoking its power, with one of them some yarrow must be sewn up in a bit of flannel and put under one's pillow, then the future partner would be revealed in a dream. A sad little ballad from the Hebrides tells of a poet who was still hopelessly in love with a girl, after she had married his rival. With the help of yarrow he conjured up her image so frequently and was reduced to such a shadow with longing, that his father had to carry him about in a fisherman's creel! Yet not so far away, in the Orkneys, yarrow tea was taken as a cure for melancholy, and in Sweden it was used, like hops, to flavour ale.

The dried flowering tops which contain aconitic acid, achilleine, ivain, tannin, and a volatile oil obtained as a liquid extract, are still used in alternative medicine as a stimulant, to promote perspiration, and as a haemostatic.

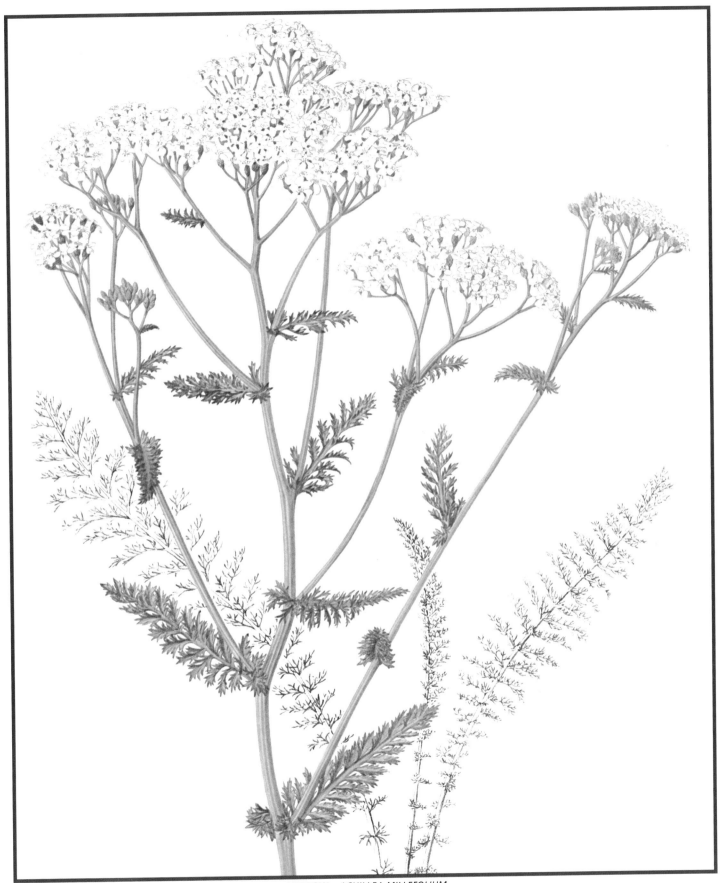

YARROW – *ACHILLEA MILLEFOLIUM*

YARROW SOUP SUMMER AND AUTUMN

A good soup can be made with yarrow leaves. They should be picked while they are fresh and young.

SERVES 4

1 colander yarrow leaves

25 g/2 tablespoons/1 oz butter

1 small onion

1 tablespoon flour

500 ml/2½ cups/1 pint stock, or water in which
    the yarrow has cooked

salt and freshly milled black pepper

250 ml/1¼ cups/½ pint milk

nutmeg

1 tablespoon thick cream

Wash the leaves and put them in a saucepan containing 3 or 4 tablespoons boiling water. Cook gently for 10 minutes, drain the leaves and reserve the cooking water, if using instead of stock. Melt the butter in the saucepan, add the finely sliced onion and sauté until soft. Shake in the flour, stir to blend, and gradually add the stock or vegetable water, keep stirring while the soup thickens, then add the yarrow leaves and a seasoning of salt and pepper. Cover the pan and simmer gently for 15 minutes. Liquidize the soup and return to the pan. Heat the milk until nearly boiling and stir into the soup, add a good grating of nutmeg, and, just before serving, stir in the cream.

YARROW AS A VEGETABLE

Yarrow was used in salads in the 17th century, but it is bitter and hairy to eat raw. However, it makes a good vegetable with a little garlic and coriander for extra interest. Pick the younger leaves from the middle and top of the plant, the leaves near the base are coarse.

1 colander yarrow leaves

2 tablespoons olive oil

2 tablespoons butter

1 clove garlic, crushed

1 teaspoon ground coriander

salt and freshly milled black pepper

2 tablespoons crème fraîche

Wash the yarrow leaves and drain. Bring a couple of inches of water to the boil in a saucepan. Add the yarrow leaves and cook briskly for 5 minutes. Drain. Heat the oil and butter in the pan, add the crushed garlic and fry gently, stir in the coriander. Add the yarrow leaves, cover the pan, and sweat gently over a low heat until the leaves have wilted and are tender. Remove the lid and chop the leaves in the pan with a wooden spoon, allow any excess liquid to evaporate, and add salt and pepper. Check the seasoning, then stir in the crème fraîche and serve straight from the pan.

YARROW LEAVES IN A WHITE SAUCE

SUMMER AND AUTUMN

Yarrow has a faintly aniseed taste, which is pleasant, but for those who dislike aniseed, blend the cooked leaves into a little buttery white sauce. It is then very similar to creamed spinach. Avoid picking the lower leaves which have a tough mid-rib.

SERVES 4

1 colander yarrow leaves

FOR THE SAUCE

25 g/2 tablespoons/1 oz butter

1 level tablespoon flour

250 ml/1¼ cups/½ pint milk

salt and pepper

Soak the yarrow leaves in water for 10 minutes, then wash them thoroughly and cook damp in a covered saucepan for 5-7 minutes. Drain well and chop the leaves thoroughly.

Melt the butter in a small pan, shake in the flour and stir to blend, add half the milk stirring all the time until the sauce thickens smoothly, then add as much milk as you need to make a medium thick sauce. Tip the cooked yarrow leaves into the sauce and re-heat. Serve hot as a vegetable.

OTHER EDIBLE PLANTS

The following plants are edible and the leaves may be added to salads and sandwiches to give variety and extra bulk, but they are not worth cooking.

HAIRY BITTERCRESS *Cardamine hirsuta*
WAVY BITTERCRESS *C. flexuosa*
BLADDER CAMPION *Silene vulgaris*
DAISY *Bellis perennis*
IVY-LEAVED TOADFLAX *Cymbalaria muralis*
NIPPLEWORT *Lapsana communis*
PLANTAIN *Plantago major*
RED-LEG *Polygonum persicaria*
SHEPHERD'S PURSE *Capsella bursa-pastoris*
COMMON WINTERCRESS *Barbarea vulgaris*

Cow parsley, *Anthriscus sylvestris*, is a wild chervil but as it could be confused with the very poisonous hemlock, *Conium maculatum*, and fool's parsley, *Aethusa cynapium*, which is also poisonous, it is better to grow chervil as a herb in your garden then to risk picking the wrong plant in the wild.

Sweet cicely, *Myrrhis odorata*, has a sweet taste and pleasant aniseed scent and can be used with fresh or stewed fruit and in drinks and salads, but I would advise anyone, unless they are really knowledgeable about plants and botany, to avoid experimenting with it. It, too, is not unlike hemlock, although sweet cicely has a pleasant scent when bruised and hemlock an unpleasant smell. Hemlock is the only white umbellifer with hollow purple-spotted stems, and sweet cicely has a whitish fleck on some of the larger leaves, which hemlock does not. Sweet cicely flowers in spring and early summer, hemlock later in the summer. The fruits, too, are different but none of the differences is very obvious to the amateur and both plants have white umbels of flowers and finely cut leaves.

Finally, there are several edible thistles. I have experimented with creeping, Scotch, and marsh thistles and at none of their stages have I been able to make them eatable. Even after peeling, pounding, chopping, snipping off prickles and prolonged boiling, they have only produced a mass of stringy fibres. So I must admit defeat and congratulate any of you who can cook them.

WINE-MAKING

Most of the plants in this book can be made into wines, but home wine-making is a big subject and, for the sake of space, I have given only the ingredients and shortest instructions with each recipe. Below are general instructions for making wines which apply to them all.

Enthusiasts tend to get carried away with technical jargon and scientific explanations, which can be boring and difficult to understand. Generations of country people have made wine without knowing exactly how or why it works, so I have described the process in very basic terms, and have included two recipes made in the old-fashioned way, for anyone tempted to try the more happy-go-lucky approach of our forebears. It is only fair to say that modern methods and equipment are more reliable; floating a bit of baker's yeast on a slice of toast and covering the crock with a blanket is a cosy idea; but well-fitting plastic lids and glass fermentation locks exclude more efficiently the variety of wild yeasts that are in the air around us and which can alter, or even spoil, the wine in the making. For finding out all you need to know about the subject there are scores of good books on home wine-making, which clearly describe the process of fermentation, and all aspects of making wines at home for the beginner.

Apart from ordinary kitchen equipment such as jugs, bowls and wooden spoons, you will need a large stainless steel, or unchipped enamel saucepan, and a 5 litres/9 U.S. quarts/1 gallon plastic bucket, or bin, with a well-fitting lid, in which to ferment the wine. It should be white, not coloured, and it is best to start with a new one, as germs and odours cling to plastic which may spoil the wine.

You will also need two 5 litre/9 U.S. quarts/1 gallon glass fermentation jars, (for red wines use jars made of brown-coloured glass), a rubber bung to fit into the neck of the jar like a cork with a hole in it, and a glass or plastic fermentation lock which fits firmly into the hole in the bung. A metre or yard of plastic tubing for syphoning off the wine so that you leave behind the sediment, and a large nylon strainer and plastic funnel. You will need sodium metabisulphate, for sterilising the equipment and, before starting the process, you should dissolve 1 teaspoon sodium metabisulphate, in 1/2 litre/21/2 cups/1 pint water, and use this to wash out all the utensils, then rinse everything twice in fresh water. A wine hydrometer is useful, as with it you can calculate the sugar and alcohol content of the wine, and it comes with clear instructions for use. All these items can be bought from any shops which sell wine-making equipment.

For bottling, used wine bottles are fine, as long as you sterilise and wash them thoroughly, but you should use new corks, and soak them in boiling water, or the sterilising solution, before using them.

The chief reason for using a fermentation lock is to keep out the vinegar fly. These tiny flies are the same that settle on over-ripe fruit, they can appear out of the blue, and if even one gets into the wine, it will turn it sour. Yeast produces more alcohol if fermented without air, and the fermentation lock excludes air, but allows the fermenting gases to escape; it also allows the wine to ferment without overflowing, and when the bubbling stops, you know the fermenting process is complete.

The flavour of flowers, fruits or leaves is extracted by steeping them in boiling water, or simmering them in water with sugar and any other ingredients. When the liquid is cool, yeast is added, and the wine 'must', as the liquid is called, is allowed to ferment. It is helpful to start the yeast working 24-28 hours before it is needed, for this way you can be sure it is frothy and active. An easy method is to make a 'starter bottle' of yeast, before you begin the wine-making process.

Put 250 ml/1 cup/1/2 pint water and the juice of 1 lemon into a small stainless steel or enamel saucepan, add 1 tablespoon sugar, bring to the boil and stir to dissolve the sugar. Allow the liquid to cool to less than 70°F/20°C (when the outside of the pan will feel cool, not warm, to the touch) then stir in the yeast. A general purpose wine yeast, from shops selling wine-making equipment, will have the amount needed to ferment 5 litres/9 U.S. quarts/1 gallon wine printed on the packet. Pour this yeast liquid into a small sterilised bottle and plug it with cotton wool. Leave in a warm place, and when the yeast is frothing, after about 24 hours, stir the contents of the bottle into the cooled wine 'must', in the plastic bin, or bucket, and cover with its lid. Yeast must be added to cool liquid as temperatures over 70°F/20°C can kill it, and very cold temperatures will inhibit it.

After three or four days, strain the liquid from the bin into a fermentation jar, fit the bung and fermentation lock, and allow the wine to ferment in a reasonably warm place (about 65°F/18°C) until a sediment has settled at the bottom of the jar and the bubbles in the fermentation lock have ceased. This takes several weeks, after which the wine should begin to clear, maybe only a clear layer at the top of the jar, but the wine is now ready to be siphoned off through a length of plastic tubing into a second fermentation jar, which you have previously sterilised. Don't let any sediment from the bottom of the jar get into the siphon tube and, to make up for the small amount of wine left behind with the sediment, top up the new jar with a little cooled, boiled water. This process is called 'racking' the wine, and it can now be left in a cool place for about three months, or until it has cleared completely. It is then siphoned into sterilised bottles and corked with new, sterilised corks. If the wine has not completely cleared, you should rack it again into a sterilised fermentation jar, top up again, if necessary, with cool, boiled water, fit the bung and fermentation lock again, and leave it for a few more weeks.

Given enough time, it is rare for wine not to clear, but should it stay cloudy, you will need to use finings, which are sold with instructions for use, or you can stir a little whisked egg-white into the wine to clear it, 2 teaspoons egg-white to 5 litres/9 U.S. quarts/1 gallon wine.

The bottled wine should be kept at least six months before you drink it, and patience will be rewarded if you wait a year. The bottles should be stored on their sides, so that the corks are covered with wine. Before opening a bottle, stand it upright for a few hours, so that any sediment will sink to the bottom.

BIBLIOGRAPHY

ANONYMOUS: *A Collection of Above Three Hundred Receipts in Cookery, Physick and Surgery; for the use of all Good Wives, Tender Mothers and Careful Nurses.* By Several Hands. London 1746.

ANONYMOUS: *The Forme of Cury.*

ARNOLD A.F.: *The Sea-Beach at Ebb Tide.* New York 1901.

BAILEY'S *Manual of Cultivated Plants.* New York 1949.

BEEDELL, SUZANNE: *Herbs for Health and Beauty.* London 1974.

BERRY, C.J.J.: *First Steps in Winemaking.* Andover n.d.

CAMPBELL, A.C. d.phil: *The Hamlyn Guide to the Seashore and Shallow Seas of Britain and Europe.* London 1976

COLES, WILLIAM: *The Art of Simpling.* London 1656.

COLES, WILLIAM: *Adam in Eden, or Nature's Paradise.* London 1657.

CULPEPER, NICHOLAS: *The English Physician etc.* London 1653.

DIGBY, SIR KENELM: *The Queen's Closet Opened.* London 1654.

FITTER, RICHARD and FITTER, ALASTAIR: *The Wild Flowers of Britain and Northern Europe.* London 1974.

GERARD, JOHN: *The Herball or Generall Historie of Plantes.* London 1633.

GRIEVE, MRS. M.: *A Modern Herbal, ed. Mrs. C.F. Leyel.* Harmondsworth 1976.

GRIGSON, GEOFFREY: *The Englishman's Flora.* London 1960.

HARRIS, BEN CHARLES: *Eat the Weeds.* New Canaan. Conn. 1973.

HILL, SIR JOHN: *The Family Herbal.* London 1755. *The British Herbal.* London 1756.

HYDE, MOLLY: *Hedgerow Plants.* Princes Risborough 1976.

GENT, JOHN JOSSELYN: *New England's Rarities Discovered in Birds, Beasts, Fishes, Serpents and Plants of that Country.* London 1672.

LOSCH, DR. FR.: *Les Plantes Mèdicinales.* Paris 1907.

MABEY, RICHARD: *Food for Free.* London 1976.

MACNICOL, MARY: *Flower Cookery.* New York 1967.

MARKHAM, GERVASE: *The Country Housewife's Garden.* London 1617.

MARTINDALE'S *Pharmacopoeia.* London 1978.

McCLINTOCK, DAVID AND FITTER, R.S.R.: *Collins Pocket Guide to Wild Flowers.* London 1971.

MELLER, CONSTANCE: *Natural Remedies for Common Ailments.* St. Albans 1975.

MOSZYNSKI, KAZIMIERZ: *Kultura Ludowa Stowian.* Warsaw 1967.

PALSBO, SUSANNE: *Danish Cookery.* Copenhagen 1968.

PARKINSON, JOHN: *Paradisi in Sole. Paradisus Terrastris.* London 1629.

PECHEY, JOHN: *The Compleat Herbal of Physical Plants.* London 1694.

PHILLIPS, ROGER: *Wild Flowers of Britain.* London 1977.

PLATT, SIR HUGH: *The Garden of Eden.* London 1594.

RANSON, FLORENCE: *British Herbs.* London 1949.

RICKETT, HAROLD WILLIAM: *Wild Flowers of the United States.* New York 1967-73.

RICKETTS, E.F. and CALVIN, J.: *Between Pacific Tides.* Stamford 1962.

ROHDE, ELEANOR SINCLAIR: *Culinary and Salad Herbs.* London 1944. *The Old English Herbals.* London 1974.

SMITH, E.: *The Compleat Housewife.* London 1736.

STARY, DR. FRANTISEK and JIRÁSEK, DR. VÁCLAV: Herbs. London 1977.

THORNTON, ROBERT JOHN: *A Family Herbal.* London 1810.

WHITE, FLORENCE: *Flowers as Food.* London 1934.

ZEITLMAYR, LINUS: *Wild Mushrooms.* London 1968.